THE CHARL[illegible]
STANDARD

MW01708500

CANADIAN GOVERNMENT PAPER MONEY

FOURTEENTH EDITION

W. K. CROSS
PUBLISHER

The Charlton Press
TORONTO, ONTARIO • PALM HARBOR, FLORIDA

Canadian Cataloguing in Publication Data

The National Library of Canada has catalogued this publication as follows:
Main entry under title:
The Charlton standard catalogue of Canadian government paper money
Annual.
1st edition May 1984
ISSN 0835-3573
ISBN 0-88968-264-X (14th ed.)
1. Paper money—Canada—Catalogs—Periodicals
I. Charlton, J. E., 1911- II.Charlton Press.
CJ1861.S83 769.5'5971'075 C87-032281-8

Printed in Canada
in the Province of Ontario

The Charlton Press

Editorial Office
P. O. BOX 94
THORNHILL, ONTARIO L3T 3N1
Tel.: (416) 488-1418 (800) 442-6042
Fax: (416) 488-4656 (800) 442-1542
www.charltonpress.com
E-mail: chpress@charltonpress.com

EDITORIAL

Editor — Robert J. Graham
Assistant Editor — Lub Wojtiw

ACKNOWLEDGEMENTS

The Charlton Press wish to thank all those who have in the past helped and assisted with The Charlton Standard Catalogue of Canadian Government Paper Money.

Contributors to the 14th Edition

Doug Adams
Claude Beaulieu
Marvin Berger
Harold Brown
Paul Berry
Arthur John Boyko
Jim Caddy
James E. Charlton
Frank Clark
Norman Cunningham
Harry M. Eisenhauer
J. Graham Esler
David Evans
Nick Gerbinski
Ian Laing
Peter McDonald
Andrew McKaig
Tom Merritt
Hugo Normandeau
Don Olmstead
Jim Richardson
Paul Wallis

Institutions

Bank of Canada, National Currency Collection
Canadian Paper Money Society Newsletter

Corrections

The Publisher welcomes information, for future editions, from interested collectors and dealers concerning any aspect of the listings in this book.

CONTENTS

PROVINCE OF CANADA ISSUES

DOMINION OF CANADA ISSUES

BANK OF CANADA ISSUES

INTRODUCTION

THE TRANSITION TO AN IRREDEEMABLE GOVERNMENT PAPER CURRENCY

For over a hundred years banks and governments engaged in a struggle for the lucrative right to issue paper currency. The banks at first succeeded in keeping the various governments pretty well shut out. This was fortunate because notes of the reputable chartered banks represented cash while government issues often represented the lack of it. Bank notes were generally redeemable in gold or silver, while governments often backed their notes only by securities based on land, of which there was an almost inexhaustible supply, or by the promise of anticipated revenues. The Province of Canada succeeded in making a major intrusion into the banks' prerogative in 1866, and thereafter the government continuously nibbled note-issuing privileges away until 1945, when it became illegal for banks to issue any more of their notes for circulation in Canada.

In the early colonial days, before Confederation, the issue of paper currency was almost exclusively a function of the chartered banks. The right to issue bank notes was a very valuable one, effectively providing the bank with an interest-free loan from the time it issued one of its notes until it redeemed it in specie (gold or silver coin). The usual lending rate was around six per cent per annum and the circulation of notes provided banks with one of their principal sources of revenue.

Provincial and municipal governments were fully aware of the benefits of a paper currency to its issuer, and sometimes plotted jealously to obtain some of those benefits for themselves. The municipal councils of urban centres including Toronto, Kingston, Hamilton, London and others issued notes over the period from the late 1830's to the early 1860's. The provincial governments of New Brunswick, Nova Scotia, Prince Edward Island and Newfoundland issued Treasury Notes. The Treasury Notes of Prince Edward Island and Nova Scotia were often poorly secured and difficult to redeem, causing them to circulate at a discount to the detriment of their reputation. In the Canadas, New Brunswick and Newfoundland, these municipal and provincial forms of paper money usually did not constitute a very substantial part of the currency, and for the most part offered the banks little serious competition.

The Province of Canada, formed in 1841 by the union of Upper and Lower Canada, was in dire need of financing with distressing regularity, sometimes for public works and sometimes just to pay the interest on previous loans. The government was so deeply in debt that its credit with the banks and European lending houses had reached its limit. In 1841 the Governor General, Lord Sydenham, proposed a government-issued paper currency, redeemable on demand, to pay for an ambitious public works programme. The banks, which stood to lose their note-issuing privileges under the plan, resisted and Sydenham's proposal was defeated. As a consolation measure, the banks were taxed one per cent of their circulation, and thus had to turn over to the government a small share of the proceeds arising from their note issues.

Various municipal and other governments then met their need for financing by issuing interest-bearing debentures, which looked like bank notes and could, and to an extent did, circulate as money. Denominations varied from a $1 note issued by the District of Wellington to a $100 note issued by the United Counties of Leeds and Grenville. The Province of Canada briefly issued $1, $2, $5, $10 and $20 debentures.

Financial woes prompted the Province of Canada Government to make another attempt in 1860 to replace bank notes over a period of time by government notes. Again the banks prevailed, and A. T. Galt, the Inspector-General, was forced to abandon his plan. In 1866 the Provincial Government was again embarrassed, its funds being locked up in the tottering Bank of Upper Canada. In league with its new banker, the Bank of Montreal, the government issued Province of Canada notes in denominations from $1 to $1000. Our present currency system has its origin in these Provincial notes.

Abetted by the Bank of Montreal, the first Dominion Government sought to introduce a system comparable to the new American model, the National Banking System. Under this scheme a uniform currency backed by government securities would be issued by the banks. The other banks as usual were opposed, since they would be forced into buying securities which would pay interest only for the first ten years, and because the circulation would lose its flexibility which was needed to allow for seasonal expansion for "moving the crops". Again the banks were able to muster enough support to defeat the proposal.

The new Finance Minister, Sir Francis Hincks, had the wisdom to realize that a piecemeal approach would be more successful. His legislation of 1870 and 1871 generally removed from the banks the right to issue $1 and $2 notes, which would be issued by the Dominion Government, (some of the eastern banks, as well as one or two others, were exempted for special reasons). The notes of $4 and up were left to the banks. Some banks then took such heroic measures as the issue of $6 and $7 notes to avoid the use of Dominion notes wherever possible and thus maximize their own circulations. The loophole was plugged in 1881 when the Dominion Government assumed the right to issue $4 notes, a denomination which was considered useful then because it corresponded to One Pound in the old Halifax currency, while restricting most banks to issues of $5 and its multiples. The banks were also required to hold a greater part of their reserves in Dominion notes. The high denomination Dominion notes were principally used for this purpose.

The Bank Act of 1890 provided some fine tuning for a system which had worked tolerably well for the previous two decades. Bank notes were made redeemable at par at all branches of the issuing institution throughout the country, and a redemption fund was established to guarantee the notes of any bank which might subsequently fail. Thereafter no note of a Canadian bank depreciated as the result of the failure of the issuing bank. In 1912 $5 Dominion notes entered circulation, in competition with chartered bank issues.

With the outbreak of World War I in 1914, drastic changes were made in anticipation of currency upheavals resulting from the war. The gold standard was suspended, bank notes were declared legal tender, and the redemption of Dominion notes was suspended. Paper money became in effect irredeemable, but little panic ensued apart from a few minor runs on banks. The gold standard was partially restored from 1926 to 1929, when the Depression brought on a growing awareness of the need for a central bank and a centrally managed economy.

When the Bank of Canada began business in 1935, the banks were given ten years to reduce their note circulation to 25 per cent of their paid-up capital. Bank of Canada notes would make up an increasing proportion of the currency and replace the Dominion notes, which were rapidly being withdrawn. The 1944 revision of the Bank Act removed the right of the banks to issue or reissue any of their notes at all after the end of that year except outside Canada, where the circulation was limited to 10 per cent of the capital. In 1950 the banks paid over to the Bank of Canada a sum corresponding to their outstanding notes, and in 1954 even the right to issue notes outside of Canada was removed. The long process of establishing an irredeemable currency issued solely by the government was complete.

THE CHARLTON CATALOGUE NUMBERING SYSTEM

The numbering system used for several years to identify notes issued by the Province of Canada, the Dominion of Canada and the Bank of Canada has been modified in this catalogue to accomodate newly discovered varieties. The renumbering should not be too great an inconvenience for collectors, and since the listing of all notes except for current issues is now believed to be complete, no further changes should be necessary in future editions.

Each identifying number begins with a letter code indicating the issuing authority, as follows:

A	-Alberta	NB	-New Brunswick
BC	-Bank of Canada	NF	-Newfoundland
BrC	-British Columbia	NS	-Nova Scotia
DC	-Dominion of Canada	PEI	-Prince Edward Island
PC	-Province of Canada	UC	-Provisional Government of Upper Canada

The number that follows refers to the type (basic design) of the note. If varieties of major significance occur within the basic type, such as changes in signatures, seals, colour of back, domicile or border pattern, these are indicated by lower case letters following the number. Minor varieties such as change in the imprint or hyphenation of a series letter are distinguished by lower case Roman numerals.

NUMBERS PRINTED, SCARCITY AND PRICES

It seems obvious that notes which were printed in small quantities should be scarce and accordingly command substantial prices. There are, however, several factors which may disturb this simple relationship. First, notes most recently printed often have a higher survival rate. For instance, the "no letter" 1870 "shinplasters" were printed in the smallest quantities of the three varieties. Yet they are the commonest because they were the latest to be issued, after most of the A series and many of the B series were worn out and destroyed. Secondly, notes which have turned up in hoards tend to be more readily available, distorting the relationship between number issued and scarcity. As an example, more 1912-$5 "Train" notes were printed in the series A than in the series B "seal over" type. The former are nevertheless scarcer because no hoards have been found. A corollary to this fact is lower denomination notes tended to be held as mementos while high denominations represented more money than many individuals were able to set aside. Finally, price is determined not only by the survival rate and consequent scarcity of a note, but also by the collector demand for it. This is determined by the appeal and popularity of a note or series. The 1935 Bank of Canada $25 note does not rank among the rare Canada notes, but its high price attests to its popularity.

Where a large number of series occurs within a given issue and variety of Dominion notes these have been recorded in detail as far as possible in this catalogue, but they have not been individually priced. The same applies to the Bank of Canada regular issues and asterisk notes. Although numerous series or prefixes may be priced together, it is certain that they are not all equally available. As the trend to collect by series or prefix develops, these are being priced separately.

SUBSIDIARY INFORMATION

DESIGNS AND COLOURS: The main vignettes appearing on each note are described in the same order as they occur on the notes, with oblique lines separating description, e.g., beaver/ship/cattle. Where there is no vignette illustrating a particular portion of the note, a dash (-) appears in place of the description.

IMPRINT: The banknote company imprint is given for each note or issue. The imprint indicates the company that engraved the plates and/or printed the notes from them. The dual imprint, e.g., "ABNCo. and BABN" indicates plates originally engraved by the American Bank Note Company that were later used by the British American Bank Note Company for printing notes.

SIGNATURE DETAILS: For each issue, all of the printed and some of the manuscript (mss.) (handwritten with pen and ink) signatures are given. There are two kinds of printed signatures, engraved (engr.) and typographed (typed).

Engraved signatures are engraved into the face plate and are printed at the same time as the face design. For notes printed from the same part of a plate, the positions of the engraved signatures relative to the frame do not vary.

Typed signatures, however, are added as overprints after the rest of the note has been printed. Consequently, the signatues may be found to be in slightly different positions when the notes are compared. Typed signatures also usually have flat, broad strokes in contrast to the thin, raised strokes of the engraved signatures.

DATING: Where the notes are fully dated by mechanical means, whether by engraving or letterpress (typography), the dates are listed in the form:

Engraved	Letterpress
Jan. 2, 1845	Jan. 2, 1845

This form is used regardless of whether the day of the month occurs before or after the month on the actual notes.

Partially engraved dates are listed with blanks where some information was left to be filled in manuscript, and the completed dates, if known, follow in the form:

Partially Engraved 18__
Jan. 2, 1845

OVERPRINTS AND STAMPS: Overprints, extra details added by a printing press after the notes have otherwise been completed, are listed for each issue. Stamps differ from overprints in being added by hand, with a rubber or wooden implement. If an overprint appears on separate lines on the note, this is indicated by an oblique (/), e.g., PROVINCIAL NOTE/LEGAL TENDER/PAYABLE IN MONTREAL/FOR THE RECEIVER GENERAL.

PROOFS, SPECIMENS AND REMAINDERS: Whenever possible, fully completed notes (those signed, numbered and dated) are listed. In cases where fully completed notes are not known or when other forms are much more common, remainders, proofs or specimens are listed: FP=Face Proof, FPNT=Face Proof without Tint, BP=Back Proof, R=Remainder, S=Specimen.

A remainder is a regular note which has not had all of the blanks filled in. Remainders are sometimes encountered with spurious signatures, dates, etc.; this does not change their status. Failing the availability of completed remainder notes either specimens or proofs are listed.

A specimen is not intended for circulation, but is used to acquaint bank employees and others with the characteristics of the genuine notes. It is usually printed on banknote paper with face and back designs same as issued issuable notes; however, it usually has serial numbers consisting of all 0's and is overprinted or stamped "SPECIMEN" usually in the signature or sheet number areas.

Proofs are trial or sample impressions taken from the printing plates on very thin paper backed with card and some are printed directly on card. They often have no serial numbers and may or may not be stamped with the word "SPECIMEN". Proofs can be distinguished from specimens insofar as proofs are usually printed only on one side and are not printed on banknote paper. Where it is known that Proofs were made only from the face of the note, "FACE PROOF" is indicated. Where notes are not known to exist the designation SENC (Surviving examples not confirmed) may be used. Term courtesy of Dr. James Haxby.

GRADING

Methodology

When grading a note it is essential to first determine if the note may be safely removed from its holder without causing any damage due to brittleness, unseen tears, glue remnants, etc. Then, carefully remove the note and holding it lightly, consider the general appearance, amount of wear, the hue and intensity of the colour of both the face and back. Determine a preliminary grade. If the note is Fine or better it should be held obliquely in line with a good light source. Move it around at various angles, such that the light will reflect off the note highlighting any ripples, counting creases, heavy creases, pressed out creases, tears, pinholes, cancellations, repairs or fading. Mastery of this technique is mandatory for successful grading of paper money. When these aspects have been carefully considered, decide if they are "normal" for the preliminary grade which was determined. If not, the grade may have to be reduced depending on the number and severity of the defects, or the defects will have to be listed in addition to the overall grade, followed by any unusual defects that would downgrade the note. Careful inspection to determine the correct grade will lead to greater trust and confidence between buyers and sellers of notes.

Grade Descriptions

UNCIRCULATED UNC: A perfect note. Crisp and clean as issued and without any folds, creases, blemishes or discoloration. Colours have original hue and brightness. Some issues may have ripples (as made). Mention must be made if the design is not perfectly centered with usual width of margins.

ABOUT UNCIRCULATED AU: Similar to Uncirculated but with the allowance of a light fold (usually a vertical centre fold) or two or three very light counting folds, but not both. Counting creases resulting in broken paper fibres, or any other creases, reduce the grade depending on their number and severity. The practice of using "almost" and "about" to designate a slightly lower grade, or a plus in the case of lower grades to designate in-between grades is common, e.g. "almost AU" or "EF plus". Notes not perfectly centered with usual width of margins must be so described.

EXTREMELY FINE EF: Similar to Almost Uncirculated but the centre fold, vertical or horizontal, may be a crease, i.e. paper fibres are broken, or there may be up to three heavy counting folds (not creases) or two light creases, but no combination of the above. There should be almost no evidence of wear, soling or blemishes. The centering and margins if not perfect must be noted.

VERY FINE VF: A fairly crisp and clean note. It may have several major and minor creases and folds, and some evidence of wear especially along the edges or at the corners. There may be some slight decrease in hue and intensity of the colours. The design in the creases should not be worn off.

FINE F: A note with considerable evidence of circulation. Numerous creases and folds, but a small degree of firmness remaining. Usually fairly soiled and the hue and intensity of the colour are slightly reduced. There may be a slight amount of the design worn off along the major creases.

VERY GOOD VG: A heavily circulated note but with all the major design still visible. Usually limp with no crispness or firmness, quite soiled, hue and intensity of the colour will be faded or altered. A moderate amount of the design may be worn off along the major creases or in the "counting crease" areas. Numerous other defects may apply (see list below).

GOOD G: Soft and very limp, often with tears and small pieces missing. Usually some of the major design is worn off. Note may be quite dark in appearance. Manuscript signatures, dates and sheet numbers may be faint or unreadable. Usually has numerous other defects.

FAIR FR: Similar to Good, but larger pieces missing. Manuscript signatures, dates and sheet numbers may be worn off or entirely faded out. Often has numerous tears and other defects.

POOR P: As a Fair note, but with a major portion of the note torn off or the design obliterated. Often numerous tape repairs. Generally collectable only because of rarity.

In addition, to accurately grade a note it is necessary to consider any additional impairments. These should include:

1. Minor counting creases or edge defects, especially for EF and AU grades.
2. Tears, pinholes or signature perforations.
3. Stains, smudges, crayon marks or writing.
4. Missing corners, cut and punch cancellations or edge defects.
5. Rubber stamp impressions.
6. Any repairs, such as with sticky tape, scotch tape, stamp hinges, etc.
7. Chemical damage, paste or glue from attachment to a page.
8. Poorly centered or badly trimmed edges.

A note with portions missing should be graded as if it were a whole note, then the amount missing should be fully described.

Proof, specimen and essay notes are commonly accepted as being in uncirculated condition. Otherwise, they should be described as impaired, with the type and degree of impairment stated.

This Grading guide has been endorsed by the Canadian Paper Money Society.

USEFUL TERMINOLOGY AND INFORMATION

Kinds Of Fraudulent Notes

Counterfeit:	A facsimile copy of a note of a legitimate bank.
Raised:	A note which has been fraudulently modified so as to appear to be of higher denomination.

Parts Of Notes

Face: The front of a note, sometimes incorrectly referred to as the obverse.

Back: The subordinate side of a note sometimes incorrectly called the reverse. Many notes were printed with blank or "plain" backs.

Vignette: An engraved picture (portrait or scene) on a bank note.

Counter: A word, letter or number indicating the denomination of a note.

Payee: The person or organization to whom a note is made payable. The payee on many modern notes is simply referred to as "the bearer".

Domicile: The specific branch or branches where the note was made payable.

Tint: The background coloured design found on notes. The tint is printed before the face or back plate, as opposed to a protector, which is an overprint. In the 19th century tints were usually printed by the engraved plate method. Gradually, beginning in the late 19th century, banknote companies switched over to printing tints by lithography.

Plate Number: In many cases, notes can be traced to the plates used in printing them by means of plate numbers. These are tiny numbers inobtrusively printed on the notes, each having a face plate number on one side and a back plate number on the other. Where plate numbers are not present on the notes, these were often printed on the salvage, or waste paper on the edges of the sheet of notes and trimmed off before the notes were issued.

Imprint

The imprint on a banknote refers to the designation used to show what individual or company printed any specific note. It is usually comprised of a name and domicile which was engraved on the original plate, i.e. British American Banknote Company, Ottawa; American Banknote Company, New York or N.Y.; Rawdon, Wright, Hatch & Edson N.Y. etc. Imprints are often found just inside or outside the borders of the notes and frequently on both the face and back of each note. Some early imprints represent the engraver and printer of the note i.e. Reed. Sometimes more than one imprint can be found. This can occur when notes were originally printed or engraved by one company and that company was later taken over or amalgamated with another company, the same note or design being still in use. Example a note with Rawdon, Wright, Hatch & Edson imprint may also have an American Banknote Co. imprint or an ABN Co. logo imprint. In another case original plates of one company were for various reasons given over to another company i.e. see early Dominion of Canada notes. In this catalogue the imprint is normally spelled out exactly as found on the note. Some checklists may have an abreviated form i.e. BABN for British American Banknote Co., CBN - for Canadian Banknote Co. and ABN for American Banknote Co.

Printing Methods

Letterpress (Typography) In this process the design is the highest part of the printing plate and is flat. When the plate is inked only the design receives the ink by virtue of its location. Letterpress results in a fairly thick and flat layer of ink on the note. Sheet numbers, protectors, some signatures and most overprints were added by this method of printing. We have used the word "typed" to describe an addition to the note by this process.

Engraved Plate: (Intaglio) The design is cut into a flat sheet of metal, and in contrast to letterpress the design is below the flat upper surface of the plate. The plate is inked and the flat surface wiped clean, leaving ink only in the recessed (engraved) areas which is transferred to the paper during printing. The resulting image has a 3-dimensional character. Most parts of the notes were printed by this means since it made possible the highest resolution of fine lines and the most life-like portraits. This method also provided the best security against the practice of counterfeiting.

Lithography: In the latter part of the 19th century lithography was used to print the coloured background (tint) on some notes. As it was practiced then, lithography involved the photography of a design and its transfer via a negative to the surface of a special stone coated with a layer of a photo-sensitive material. After treatment, only the image on the stone would pick up ink. This type of printing resulted in the transfer of a thin flat layer of ink.

The Numbering Of Dominion Notes

Sheet Number: Province of Canada and Dominion of Canada notes were usually numbered in sheets of four, each note having the same number.This is called the sheet number. Many people mistakenly refer to the sheet number as the "serial number".

Check Letter: Since more than one note in a sheet could bear the same number, each note was provided with a distinguishing letter, representing the position of the note on the plate and differentiating it from the other notes with the same sheet numbers called a check letter. Check letters A, B, C and D were used for sheets of four notes. In later years Dominion notes were printed on larger sheets, up to 24/on (i.e. sheets of 24 notes). However, these were still numbered in groups of four notes, with check letters A, B, C and D. The 25-cent fractional notes of 1923 were numbered in sheets of ten, all having the same sheet number, so check letters A, B, C, D, E, H, J, K, L and M were used.

Series Letter: For a particularly large issue of notes, where the available sheet numbers had all been used, the same numbers would be started over again, accompanied by a new series letter. A different series letter would be used for each successive cycle of sheet numbers. The first usage of a series letter on Dominion notes occurs on the 1878 $1 issue, where the first series was "plain" (i.e., no letter), followed in turn by series A, B, and C. The use of a "plain" series to initiate a new issue was discontinued by the end of the nineteenth century, and thereafter new issues began with series A. Before the 1923 Dominion note issue, series letters were variously printed preceding or following the sheet number or in other locations on the note face. The precise locations are explained in the text for each issue where necessary. From 1923 to 1935 the series letter always preceded the sheet number.

Serial Number: From the above it should be clear that the serial number, the designation that uniquely identifies a note, must include not only the sheet number but also the check letter and the series letter if they are present. The check letter is normally written last, separated from the rest of the serial number by an oblique line. Thus the serial number C6364208/D denotes sheet number 6364208, check letter D, in series C.

The Numbering Of Bank Of Canada Notes

The 1935 issue of Bank of Canada notes used the same numbering system as the Dominion notes. For later issues the system was substantially changed. Since 1937 check letters have not been used. Complete specification of the serial number requires two (or, very recently, three) prefix letters and the number on the note. For the $5 and $20 notes of the 1979 issue, the serial number consists only of an eleven-digit number.

THE DISTRIBUTION NETWORK FOR CANADIAN GOVERNMENT NOTES

The Province of Canada notes were issued by the branches of the Bank of Montreal, the only chartered bank willing to surrender the privilege of issuing its own notes. This arrangement continued for a few years after Confederation. During the period 1870-72 branches of the Receiver General's Department called A.R.G. (Assistant Receiver General) offices were established in the largest city in each province and gradually assumed the functions of issue and redemption. In this transitional period some shipments of Dominion notes were made directly from the Receiver General's Department to the chartered banks. Additional A.R.G. offices were established as new provinces were added to the Dominion.

When the Bank of Canada took over the government note issue, branches of the bank were established in each province. These branches took care of the distribution of Bank of Canada notes to financial institutions within their respective provinces. Banks and individuals have also been able to acquire notes directly from the Bank of Canada in Ottawa.

FRATERNAL ORGANIZATIONS

Listed below are a number of organizations dedicated to the preservation, study and enjoyment of paper currency. All will be delighted to hear from collectors interested in any aspect of paper money collecting.

The Canadian Paper Money Society

Established in 1964 and incorporated in 1972, the Society is a non-profit educational organization interested in Canadian bank notes, banking, and other Canadian paper money. It publishes The Canadian Paper Money Journal annual and four newsletters and has library and other facilities available. The Society is sustained by regular members' contributions of $25.00 per year or $335.00 Life Membership (U.S. and foreign members $25.00 U.S. funds). The official address of the Society is P.O. Box 562, Pickering, Ontario, Canada, L1V 2R7.

The Canadian Numismatic Association

The CNA was founded in 1950 and incorporated in 1963. It is a non-profit educational association which has members in every province in Canada, every state in the U.S. and many other countries. Its objective is to encourage and promote the science of numismatics by acquirement and study of coins, paper money, medals, tokens, and all other numismatic items with special emphasis on material pertaining to Canada. Membership includes use of the associations library material as well as a subscription to The Canadian Numismatic Journal, a monthly magazine devoted to Canadian numismatics. Annual membership fees are $25.00 for those over 21 years of age, $12.50 for those under the age of 21, $35.00 for a family membership and $25.00 for a club, society, library or other non-profit organiztion. Life membership is $400. The current executive secretary is Mr. Kenneth B. Prophet and he may be reached at P.O. Box 226, Barrie, Ontario, Canada, L4M 4T2.

The International Bank Note Society

The IBNS was founded in 1961 and now has a membership of over 1,500 with representation from over 60 countries. The current annual dues (in U.S. funds) are as follows:

Regular Membership $17.50, Family Membership $22.50 and Junior Membership $9.00. Life Memberships are also available for $300.00 U.S. The Society publishes the IBNS Journal quarterly which is distributed free of charge (by surface mail) to its members. The mailing address is P.O. Box 1642, Racine, Wisconsin, 53401, U.S.A.

Society of Paper Money Collectors

In June 1964 the Society was incorporated as a non-profit organization under the laws of the District of Columbia. Membership now numbers approximately 2,300 the majority of which reside in Canada and the U.S. but there is representation throughout the world. The SPMC publishes Paper Money bimonthly in the odd months and sends it to its members. Annual dues are $24.00 (U.S.A.), $29.00 (Canada and Mexico) and $34.00 (Foreign), in U.S. funds. Make remittance payable to SPMC and send application and cheque to: Frank Clark, SPMC Membership Director, P.O. Box 117060, Carrollton, TX 75011, U.S.A.

Latin American Paper Money Society

This Society was organized in 1973. It publishes a small journal. For information write Peter G. Burkhart, P.O. Box 3467, Sarasota, Florida. 34230, U.S.A.

FRENCH COLONIAL ISSUES

PLAYING CARD MONEY
1685-1719
QUEBEC CITY

Desperate for funds to pay the troops stationed in New France, the intendant wrote pledges on the backs of playing cards in June 1685. Because of the illiteracy of the inhabitants, the cards were cut in halves or quarters to assist in the recognition of denominations — four livres on a whole card, two livres on half a card and 15 sols on a quarter card. When specie arrived from France in September, the playing cards were all redeemed.

Despite the King's disapproval of the practice of issuing card money, the failure of the supply ships to arrive on time (or at all) forced the colonial administration to resort to its issue again and again. At first the system worked well, the playing cards being promptly redeemed. After 1700 the French Treasury was often unable to pay the amounts appropriated for New France, and the shortfall had to be made up by more playing card money, with no immediate prospect of redemption. Inflation was the predictable result. In 1714 the King of France offered to redeem the playing card money at 50 percent of its face value, in silver. By 1720 virtually all of the playing cards had been redeemed and burned, and any not turned in for redemption were proclaimed worthless. Over the next ten years no card money circulated in New France. Coin was scarce because it was hoarded by the habitants rather than lent out at interest, "usury" being offensive to their religious beliefs. The colony was once again plagued by the lack of a circulating currency.

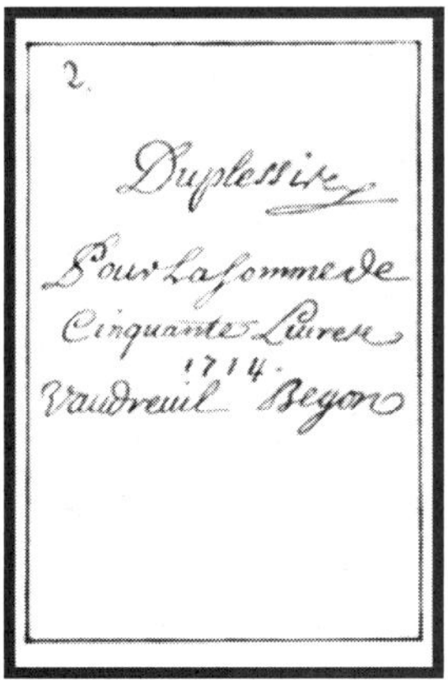

50 Livres, 1714

CARD MONEY
1729-1757
QUEBEC CITY

New card money appeared again in 1729, on plain white cardboard. This and later issues were sanctioned by the King. The card money was redeemable in bills of exchange which were in turn to be redeemed regularly in silver coin. The cards were clipped in various ways to indicate the denomination. They were signed (or in the case of smaller cards, initialled) by the governor and the intendant, who also affixed their seals to the notes. Again the system worked well at first, the cards being preferred by the habitants even to the bills of exchange on France by which they were to be redeemed. The habitants then began to hoard the cards, which necessitated that more and more be issued, with inadequate means of redemption. After the fall of New France, the card money was redeemed at one-quarter of its face value.

6 Livres, 1735

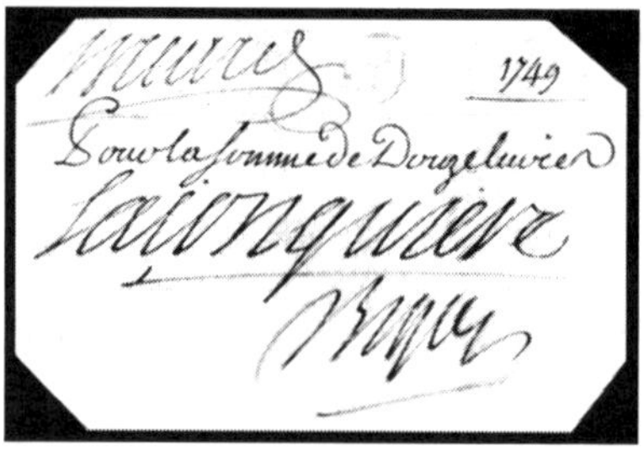

12 Livres, 1749

24 Livres, 1735

30 Sols, 1733

Denom.	Issue Date	G	VG	F	VF
7 sols 6 deniers	1749				
15 sols	1747, 1749, 1757				
20 sols	1734				
30 sols	1733, 1738, 1752, 1757				
3 livres	1742, 1747, 1749				
6 livres	1729, 1735, 1749				
12 livres	1729, 1730, 1733, 1735, 1742, 1747, 1749				
24 livres	1729, 1730, 1733, 1735, 1742, 1749				

All card money is very rare
Estimate: G-$2,250. to VF-$10,000. up*
* A 15 sols card dated 1757 sold for $15,400 in Jeffrey Hoare sale #58, February 1998

ORDONNANCES OR TREASURY NOTES
QUEBEC CITY AND MONTREAL

Orders on the local treasury, or treasury notes, began to circulate in the 1730s in increasing quantity, overshadowing the amount of card money in circulation. These notes were issued to pay for military expenditures. The amount of treasury notes expanded rapidly after 1743, while the more reputable card money was hoarded. During the last years of the French Regime, treasury notes were issued in extravagant amounts to meet the cost of war with England, despite the exhausted state of the treasury. By 1759 they totalled 30 million livres. An even greater sum in bills of exchange on France were in circulation. The amount of paper in circulation in 1760 was 15 times greater than in 1750, and once again severe inflation was the result. With the cession of New France to England, the status of all the treasury notes and bills of exchange was rendered even more dubious.

Sharp English merchants trading in Canada bought up the discredited paper at one-sixth of face value or even less. After the Treaty of Paris and subsequent negotiations, bills of exchange were redeemed in specie at half of their face value (although some were paid in full). Treasury notes were paid at one-quarter of face value, with some additional indemnification for holders who were British subjects. The harsh experiences of the habitants with a poorly secured paper circulation resulted in a deep mistrust of paper money that endured for generations.

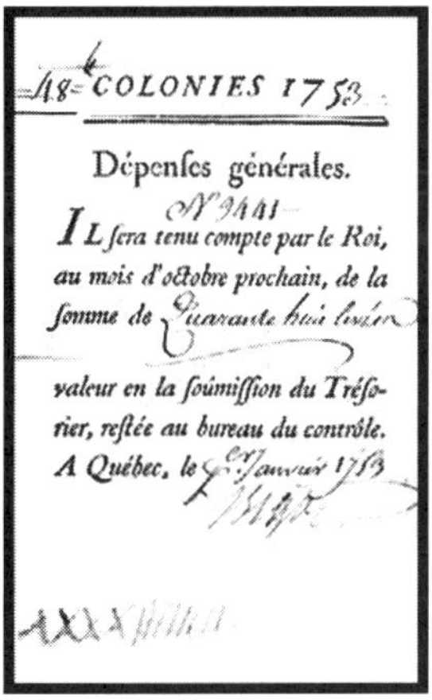

48 Livres, 1753

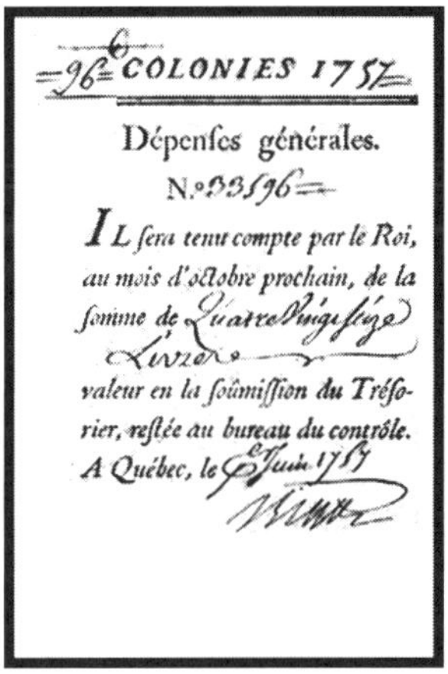

96 Livres, 1757

Signatures: mss. Quebec City; mss. Montreal (after the fall of Quebec)

Denom.	Issue Date	G	VG	F	VF
20 sols	1754, 1757, 1758, 1759				
3 livres	1756, 1758				
6 livres	1758, 1759				
12 livres	1757, 1758, 1759		All treasury notes are rare		
24 livres	1753, 1756		Estimate: G-$1,500. to VF-$6,000.		
48 livres	1753. 1758				
96 livres	1757. 1759				

ARMY BILLS

ISSUES OF 1813-1815

Army bills were issued for the purchase of supplies and the payment of troops during the War of 1812 to 1814. Normally these military expenditures were met by the sale of bills of exchange drawn on the British Treasury. However, when war broke out the greatly increased sums required could only be raised from the small amount of specie in the country, if at all, by heavily discounting the bills of exchange. To meet this situation, legal tender notes were issued from the Army Bill Office in Quebec City which had been established for that purpose.

I. First Issue 1813

The army bills were first issued in 1813 in denominations of $4, $25, $50, $100 and $400. The denominations of $25 and up were made to bear interest at the rate of 1d per £100 currency ($400) per day, or 6 1/12 percent per annum. They were redeemable in cash or bills of exchange on London, at the option of the Commander of the Forces. These notes, which were in reality investment securities, were not reissuable after redemption. The $4 notes, on the other hand, were reissuable and did not bear interest. They were redeemable in specie on demand. Notes of this issue are quite large, measuring about 5 1/4 by 7 1/2 inches.

When the notes were issued two manuscript signatures were applied over the headings "CASHIER" and "DIRECTOR". Denominations were given in Spanish-American dollars only. Each note was printed with a wide variety of sizes and styles of type as a security measure. In addition, each note was printed with a counterfoil at the left, consisting of the spelled-out denomination in alternating English and French, in graduated sizes of type. The counterfoil was bisected when the note was issued, and if the stub portion did not match the note portion upon presentation for redemption, any attempted counterfeiting would be exposed.

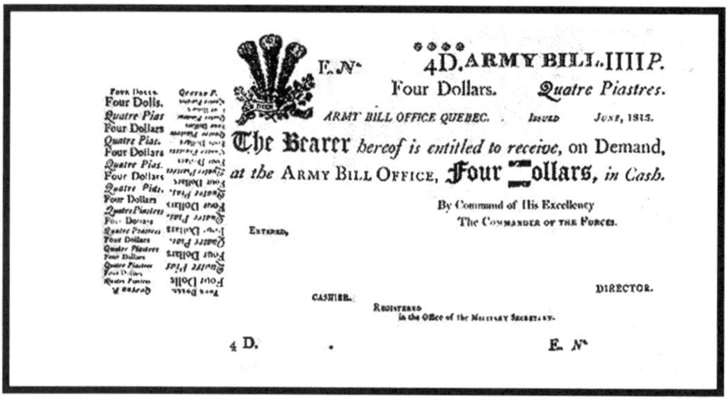

$4

Face Design: Crest of Prince of Wales
Colour: Black
Back Design: Plain
Issue Date: Partially engraved May 1813 or June 1813
Imprint: None

Signatures

Left: mss. various
Right: mss. various

Denom.	Issue Date	G	VG	F	VF	EF	Unc
$4	1813	VERY RARE — Estimate: $2,000. to $6,000.					

PHOTO NOT AVAILABLE

$25-$400

Face Design: Royal crest /—/—
Colour: Black
Back Design: Plain
Imprint: None
Issue Date: Partially engraved: ____1813; May 1 or June 15 1813

Signatures

Left: mss. various
Right: mss. various

Denom.	Issue Date	G	VG	F	VF	EF	Unc
$ 25	1813						
$ 50	1813		ALL VERY RARE				
$100	1813		Estimate: $2,000. to $6,000.				
$400	1813						

Note: Above prices are for issued bills, remainders will possibly realize 50 percent of these values.

II. Second Issue c.1813

Historical records imply that there was a second issue of army bills, probably dated late in 1813. It consisted of non-interest-bearing denominations of $1, $2, $8, $10, $12, $16 and $20. The other details of this issue are unknown, and no notes are known to have survived.

III. Third Issue 1814

The third issue of army bills is dated March 1814 and consisted of non-interest-bearing denominations of $1, $2, $3, $5 and $10, with the equivalent amounts also stated in shillings (Halifax currency). These have counterfoils at the left consisting of the word "BON" in graduated sizes, with alternating normal and italicized characters. Notes of this issue bear a single signature but are also initialled at the left. They were redeemable in government bills of exchange on London. Notes of this issue are much smaller, measuring about 2 1/2 by 4 inches. Large black capital letters appear in the upper left corners, that relate to the denomination as follows:

G/$1, H/$2, I/$3. K/$5 and L/$10

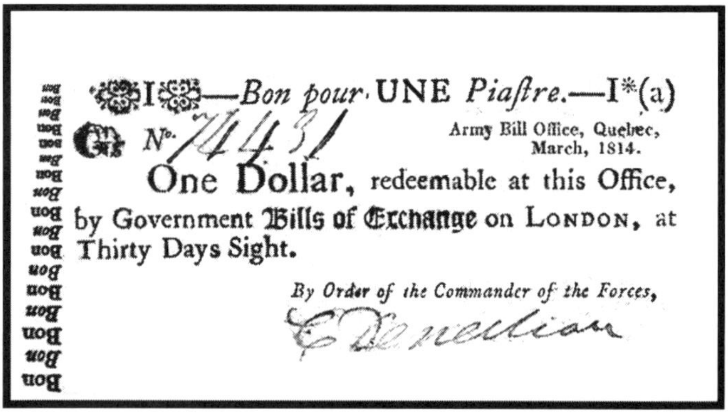

$1 (5s.)

Face Design: No vignettes
Colour: Black
Back Design: Plain

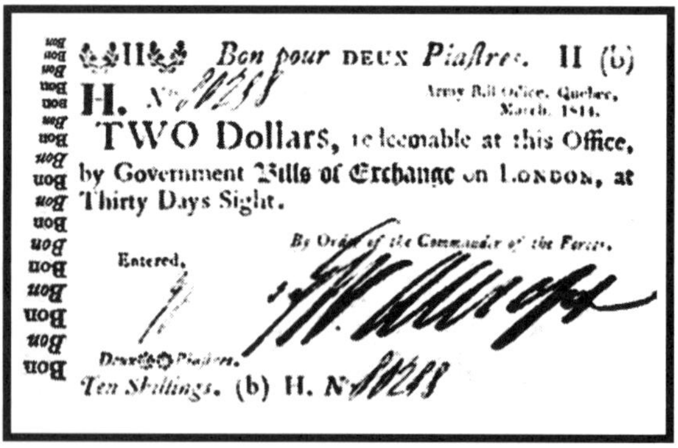

$2 (10s.)

Face Design: No vignettes
Colour: Black
Back Design: Plain

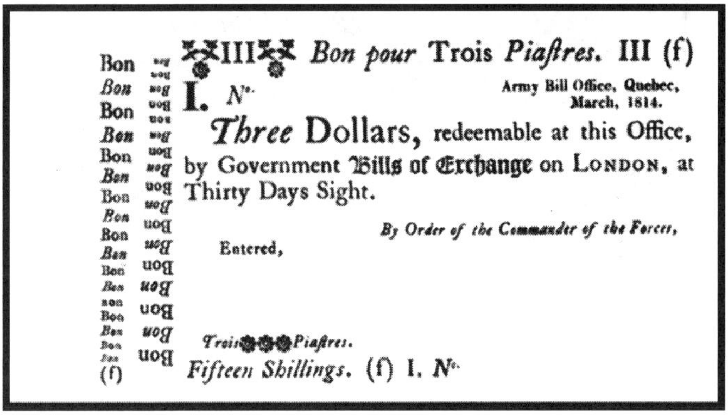
III Bon pour Trois Piaſtres. III (f)
I. No.
Army Bill Office, Quebec,
March, 1814.
Three Dollars, redeemable at this Office,
by Government Bills of Exchange on LONDON, at
Thirty Days Sight.
By Order of the Commander of the Forces,
Entered,
Trois Piaſtres.
Fifteen Shillings. (f) I. No.

$3 (15s.)

Face Design: No vignettes
Colour: Black
Back Design: Plain

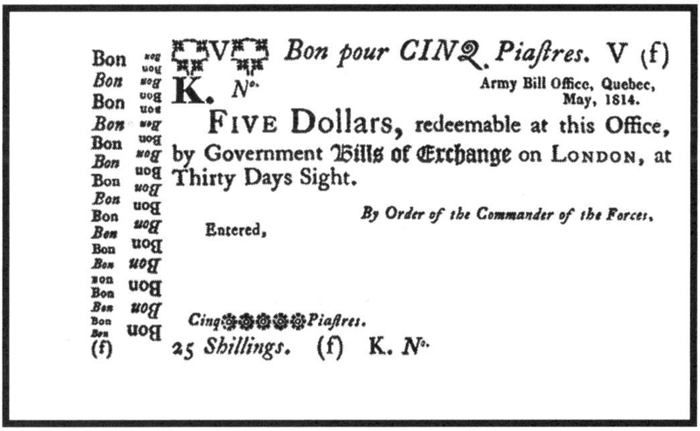
V Bon pour CINQ. Piaſtres. V (f)
K. No.
Army Bill Office, Quebec,
May, 1814.
FIVE Dollars, redeemable at this Office,
by Government Bills of Exchange on LONDON, at
Thirty Days Sight.
By Order of the Commander of the Forces,
Entered,
Cinq Piaſtres.
25 Shillings. (f) K. No.

$5 (25s.)

Face Design: No vignettes
Colour: Black
Back Design: Plain

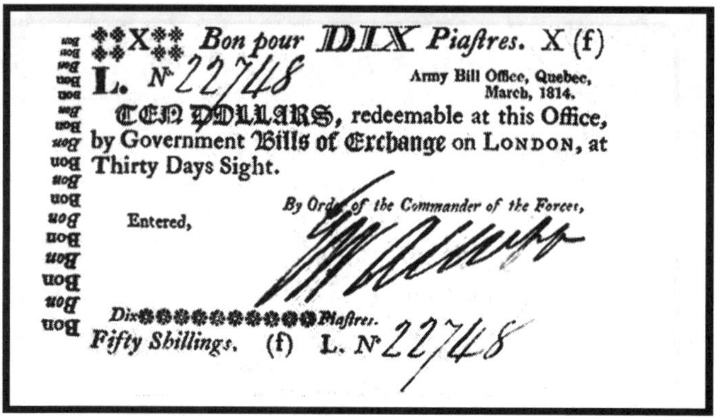

$10 (50s.)

Face Design: No vignettes
Colour: Black
Back Design: Plain
Issue Date: Engraved: March 1814, May 1814, August 1814
Imprint: None
Signatures: mss. various

Denom.	Issue Date	G	VG	F	VF	EF	Unc
$1 (5s.)	1814 Issued		VERY RARE - Estimate: $2,000. to $5,000.				
$1 (5s.)	1814 Remainder		VERY RARE - Estimate: $700. to $800.				
$2 (10s.)	1814 Issued		VERY RARE - Estimate: $2,000. to $5,000.				
$2 (10s.)	1814 Remainders		VERY RARE - Estimate: $700. to $800.				
$3 (15s)	1814 Issued		VERY RARE - Estimate: $2,000. to $5,000.				
$3 (15s.)	1814 Remainders		VERY RARE - Estimate: $700. to $800.				
$5 (25s.)	1814 Issued		VERY RARE - Estimate: $2,000. to $5,000.				
$5 (25s.)	1814 Remainders		VERY RARE - Estimate: $700. to $800.				
$10 (50s.)	1814 Issued		VERY RARE - Estimate: $2,000. to $5,000.				

Note: Remainders are unsigned and not numbered.

IV. Final Quebec Issue 1815

Only $10 notes of the January 1815 issue have been recorded, although other denominations were probably issued. Like the previous issue, a large *M* at the top seems to be associated with the denomination. The counterfoil at the left consists of the words “dix Piastres” and “Exchange” alternately in various sizes and styles of type. The notes are of the large 5 1/4 by 7 1/2 inch format.

The authorized extent of all issues totalled $6,000,000, and at the end of the war about $4,996,000 remained outstanding. Of this, about $3,000,000 was in the larger interest-bearing denominations. The notes were rapidly redeemed after the war ended, with the provinces paying the interest and the British Treasury paying the principal.

Their use coincided with a period of wartime prosperity, brought on by high prices for produce coupled with a massive influx of capital from Great Britain. The fact that the notes could always be readily converted into cash went a long way toward ending the deep distrust of paper money by the French Canadian population, who had learned from the harsh lesson of the French Regime paper that it was better to hoard coin. Since the army bills were virtually all redeemed in 1815, after which date no further interest was allowed, they are now very scarce.

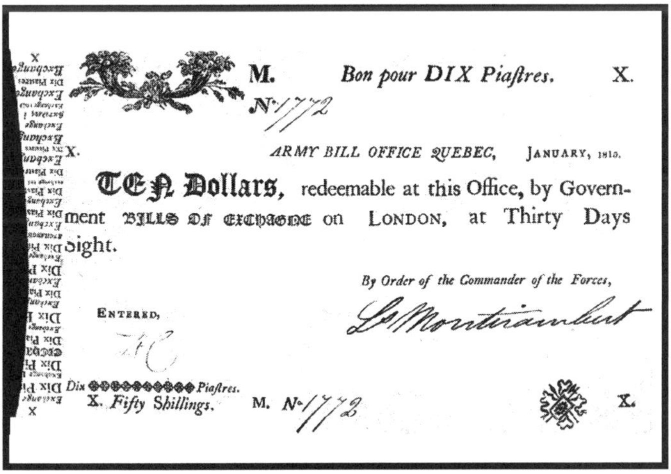

$10 (50s.)

Face Design: Cornucopia, ribbons and leaves /—/ tiny crest on bottom
Colour: Black
Back Design: Plain
Issue Date: Engraved: January 1815
Imprint: None
Signatures: mss. various

Denom.	Issue Date	G	VG	F	VF	EF	Unc
$10 (50s.)	1815	VERY RARE - Estimate: $2,000. to $6,000.					

V. Michilmackinac Type

Although only one army bill office is known to have been established, the one at Quebec City, a note having the appearance of an army bill issued at Michilmackinac has been discovered. Michilmackinac Island was captured by the British in 1812 and restored to the United States after the war ended. This $4 note, unlike the Quebec army bills, was payable in drafts on Quebec or Montreal. It bears a single signature, that of the deputy assistant commissary general. There is a counterfoil at the left consisting of a patterned design rather than words.

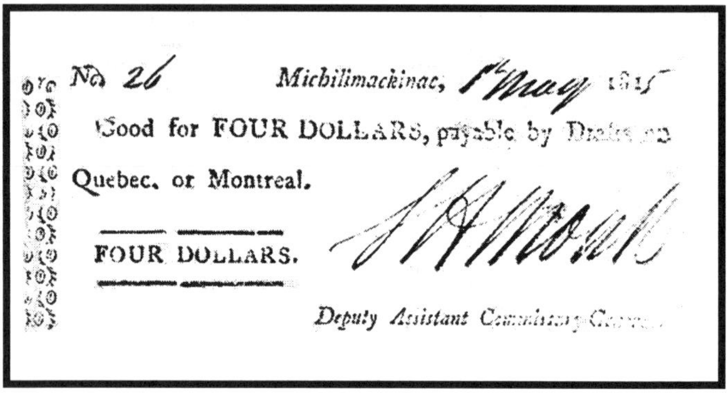

$4

Face Design: No vignettes
Colour: Black
Back Design: Plain
Issue Date: Partially engraved: ____181_, May 1 185__
Imprint: None
Signature: mss. S.H. Monk

Denom.	Issue Date	G	VG	F	VF	EF	Unc
$4	1815		VERY RARE - Estimate: $2,000. to $6,000.				

PROVINCIAL ISSUES

ALBERTA
PROSPERITY CERTIFICATE
REDEEMABLE 1936

Alberta's Social Credit government introduced "prosperity certificates" in 1936 in an attempt to alleviate the effects of the Great Depression. The Prosperity Certificate Act (1936) authorized the issue of twenty-five cents, one dollar and five dollar denominations, to a maximum of two million dollars. Only the one dollar denomination was printed and issued. Every week the holder of a note had to affix a one-cent stamp to the back to maintain its validity. The intended effect was to increase the velocity of circulation and discourage hoarding. As the end of each interval approached, the note holders spent their prosperity certificates in order to avoid having to purchase and affix the stamps. This obligation consequently often fell on the merchants. The government injected the prosperity certificates into circulation by using them to pay part of the salaries of the provincial civil servants. The original intention was that the notes would be redeemed by the provincial treasurer after two years, by which time 104 stamps would have been attached, yielding the government a small profit on the issue.

However, the prosperity certificate experiment only lasted for about one year. The necessity for affixing one-cent stamps was not popular, and to make matters worse, the stamps kept falling off. The newspapers spearheaded a campaign to boycott the notes. Of the 250,000 prosperity certificates issued, all but 19,639 were redeemed.

Numbering started with serial number A 1001, and this was bought by Hon. W.A. Fallow, Minister of Public Works, for one dollar. Surviving prosperity certificates have been observed with serial numbers from A 1027 (lowest) to A 240962 (highest).

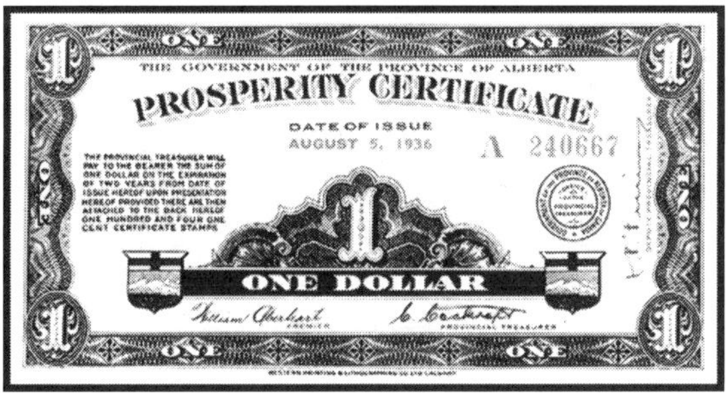

A-1

Face Design: Provincial shield/lathework/provincial shield
Colour: Black with green tint

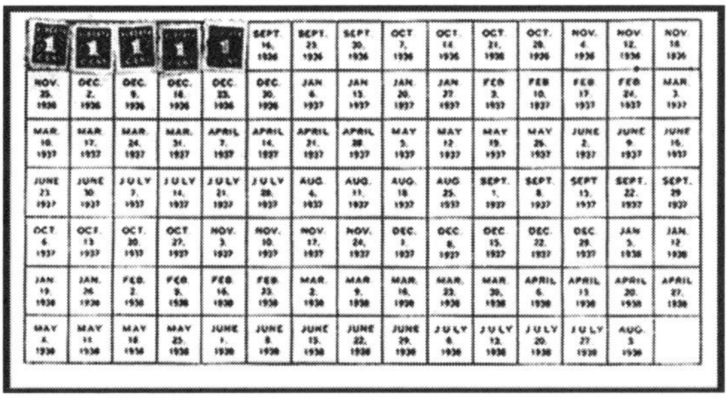

Back Design: Grid, with dated squares (varying numbers of green 1-cent stamps usually attached)
Colour: Black

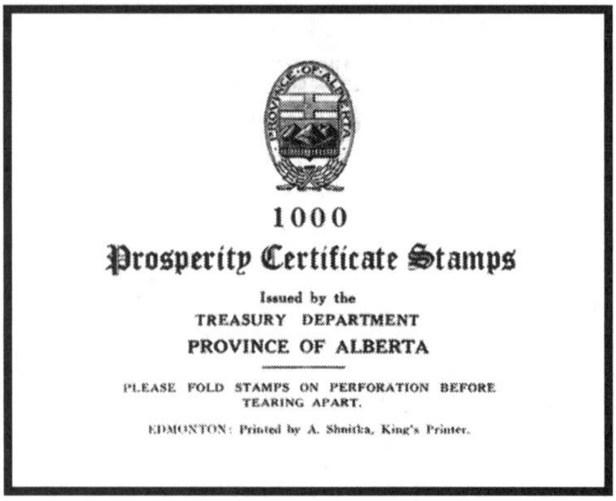

1000
Prosperity Certificate Stamps
Issued by the
TREASURY DEPARTMENT
PROVINCE OF ALBERTA
PLEASE FOLD STAMPS ON PERFORATION BEFORE TEARING APART.
EDMONTON: Printed by A. Shnitka, King's Printer.

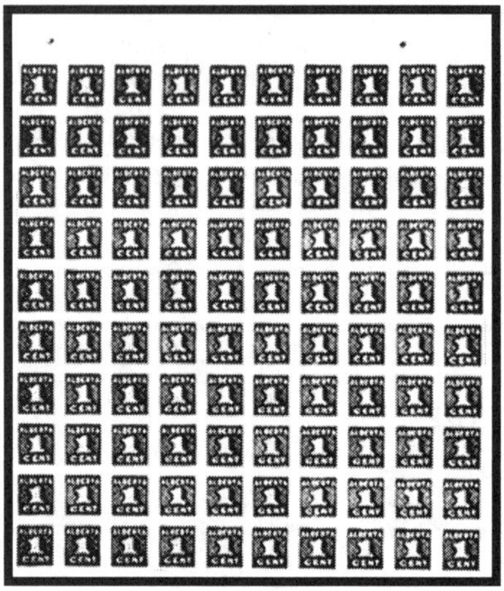

Issue Date: **August 5, 1936**
Imprint: **Western Printing & Lithographing Co. Ltd. Calgary**

Signatures

Left: Engr. William Aberhart
Right: Engr. C. Cockroft, J.F. Percival in blue vertically.

Note: Certificates with a higher quantity of stamps on the back will command a higher price. The catalogue premium is usually calculated by surcharging $5.00 per stamp attached.
Uncirculated certificates cannot have stamps attached.
Mint stamps will usually sell for $2.00 each and $400.00 for a mint sheet of 100.
The pricing table is for the Prosperity Certificate without stamps. To obtain the value of a certificate with stamps, the premium for each stamp must be added to the base value.

Cat.No.	Denom.	Issue Date	G	VG	F	VF	EF	Unc
A-1	$1	1936	50.	100.	165.	250.	325.	450.

COLONY OF BRITISH COLUMBIA TREASURY NOTES

An issue of treasury notes took place in 1862 to the amount of some $34,000 or £6,800, which consisted of 1,200 $25.00 notes, 200 $10.00 notes and 400 $5.00 notes. The attempt to circulate a government paper currency failed, and the notes were almost immediately withdrawn from circulation. The amount outstanding is only $40, apparently representing one of each denomination saved as specimens. (*From Treasury Notes of the Colony of British Columbia* by W. E. Ireland and R. A. Greene).

Cat.No.	Denom.	Issue Date	G	VG	F	VF	EF	Unc
BrC-1	$5	1862						
BrC-2	$10	1862		Surviving examples not confirmed				
BrC-3	$25	1862						

NEW BRUNSWICK TREASURY NOTES

Unlike the other Maritime colonies, New Brunswick did not indulge extensively in the issue of treasury notes. Two small issues were released in 1805 and 1807 to cover a temporary shortfall in provincial revenue. These were redeemed in gold and silver, with interest.

ISSUE OF 1805		ISSUE OF 1807	
Denomination	Number Issued	Denomination	Number Issued
$4	900	$1	1,200
$6	600	$2	800
$8	600	$4	800
$10	400		
$20	200		

Cat.No.	Denom.	Issue Date	G	VG	F	VF	EF	Unc
NB-1	$4	1805						
NB-2	$6	1805						
NB-3	$8	1805		A $1 1807 TREASURY NOTE HELD				
NB-4	$10	1805		AT THE NEW BRUNSWICK MUSEUM				
NB-5	$20	1805		IS THE ONLY NOTE KNOWN TO				
NB-6	$1	1807		HAVE SURVIVED.				
NB-7	$2	1807						
NB-8	$4	1807						

Until 1818 other provincial obligations called treasury warrants were issued to pay for the construction of roads and bridges. Since these had no specie backing, redemption was slow and difficult, and the warrants were discounted up to 10 percent when used in transactions. Treasury notes were again issued in 1818 to pay off the treasury warrants, but these too soon fell to a discount. The poor reputation of the provincial paper was cited as an argument against further issues that were proposed, in vain, from time to time until 1865.

Summary of Technical Details

Denomination	Number Authorized for Issue	Denomination	Number Authorized for Issue
5s. (currency)	2,000	£2	500
10s.	1,000	£2.10	1,000
£1	1,000	£3	400
£1.10	1,000	£5	260

Note: (Denominations and quantities from *Money and Exchange in Canada to 1900*, by A. B. McCullough)

Cat.No.	Denom.	Issue Date	G	VG	F	VF	EF	Unc
NB- 9	5s.	1818						
NB-10	10s.	1818						
NB-11	£1	1818						
NB-12	£1.10	1818			Surviving examples not confirmed			
NB-13	£2	1818						
NB-14	£2.10	1818						
NB-15	£3	1818						
NB-16	£5	1818						

NEWFOUNDLAND

GOVERNMENT TREASURY NOTES

Treasury notes were issued through the Newfoundland Savings Bank in 1834 in denominations of £25, £50 and £100 local sterling. These notes bore interest at 6 percent per annum. By 1836 all had been redeemed and destroyed.

The next issue was authorized in 1846, in denominations of £10, £25 and £50 local sterling, bearing interest at 5 percent. None are known to have survived. As these earlier notes were more like debentures (bonds), they are not given numbers.

Non-interest-bearing treasury notes in denominations more suitable for general circulation were authorized in 1850. While denominations of £1, £5 and £10 currency were provided for under the act, only £1 notes (NF-1 type) are known to exist as issued notes. The £1 notes were printed in sheets of four on paper watermarked "ISLAND OF NEWFOUNDLAND" at the centre of each note. The notes were to be signed by two treasury note commissioners as well as by the colonial treasurer. Twenty-three sheets of partially signed remainder notes, bearing the signatures of two treasury note commissioners only, have been found.

The Treasury Note Act was amended in 1851 and again in 1855 under pressure from the British government, but no notes are known with these dates.

The number of notes authorized by the Act of 1850 is as follows:

£1 currency — 16,076; £5 currency — 1,000; £10 currency — 200

NF-1a

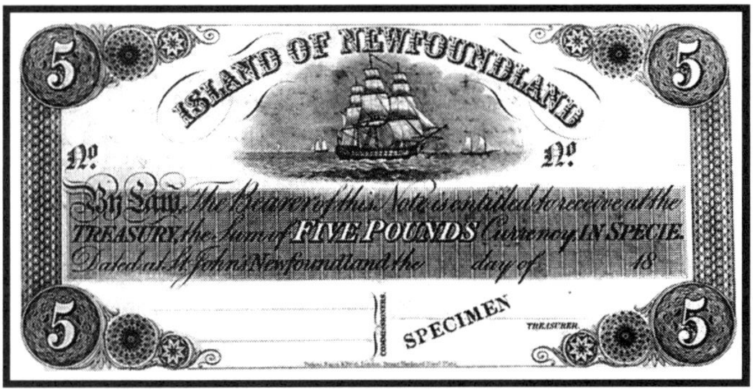

NF-1A

Face Design: —/sailing ships/—

Colour: Black

Back Design: Plain

Issue Date: £1 Partially engraved: ____18__, October 16, 1850
£5 Partially engraved: ____18__,

Imprint: Perkins, Bacon and Petch, London,

Signatures

Left: Any two: Wm. Thomas, Lawrence O'Brien, C.F. Bennett
Right: R. Carter

Cat.No.	Denom.	Variety	G	VG	F	VF	EF	Unc
NF-1	£1	Unsigned remainder	75.	150.	250.	325.	450.	800.
NF-1a	£1	Two signatures (at left), remainder	175.	350.	550.	800.	1,350.	—
NF-1b	£1	Three signatures * (Carter, r.)	500.	1,000.	2,000.	—	—	—
NF-1A	£5					Proof		2,000.

Note: Uncut pairs and sheets of four are known to exist for the £1. For the £5 only a single proof is known.

* Authenticity of the right signature on some notes has been questioned.

NEWFOUNDLAND GOVERNMENT CASH NOTES

I. Department of Public Works Type 1901-1909

The "black and white" cash notes were designed to be a secure and prompt means of paying for materials and labour for road construction and maintenance. The notes were issued by the Department of Public Works, and bore the typed signatures of the minister and secretary of the department. The notes were distributed as needed to each local road superintendent, whose manuscript signature at the lower centre was required to make the notes negotiable. The total issue in each fiscal year was limited to the amount voted by the legislature.

The fully completed cash notes were redeemable at Bank of Montreal branches and charged against a special liquidation account held by the bank for the government. Upon presentation for payment, the notes were immediately removed from circulation and cancelled.

Summary of Technical Details

Year	Denomination				
	40¢	50¢	80¢	$1	$5
1901	45,000	54,755	47,500	27,000	6,200
1902	17,500	15,000	65,000	50,000	5,000
1903	5,000	5,000	60,000	50,000	8,200
1904	5,000	5,000	59,896	57,500	8,000
1905	5,000	5,000	13,000	100,000	15,000
1906	1,990	2,000	4,994	49,992	25,000
1907	2,000	2,000	5,000	50,000	25,000
1908	2,000	2,000	5,000	50,000	25,000
1909	200	1,200	400	50,000	5,000

Total face value: $1,384,578.00

The numbers of notes issued do not necessarily reflect present-day availability. The $5 notes have virtually disappeared, while the lower values have had a slightly better rate of survival.

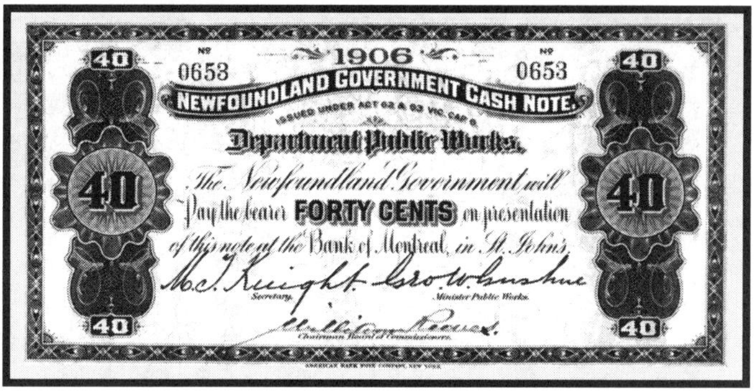

NF-2f

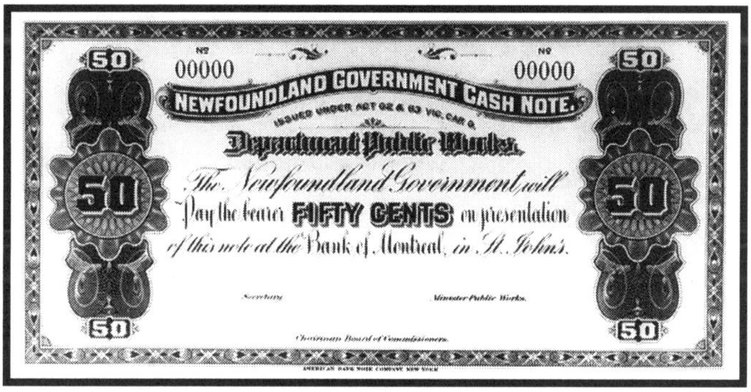

NF-3

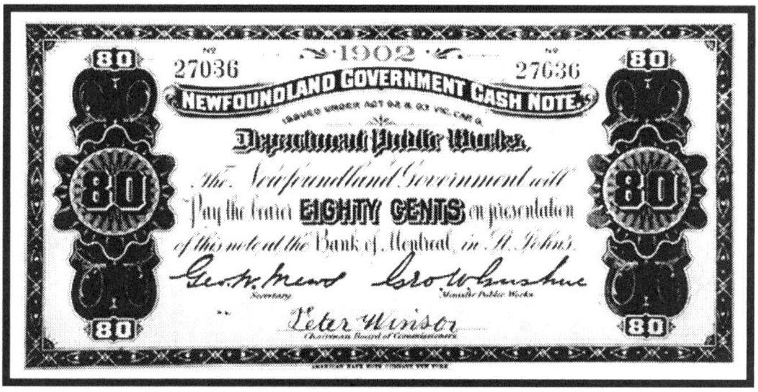

NF-4b

NF-5a

NF-6h

The following design applies to all denominations.
Only the denomination counters and issue dates change

Face Design: Lathework and counter/—/lathework & counters
Colour: Black, with year in red
Back Design: Plain
Issue Date: Letterpress Year only, 1901 to 1909
Imprint: American Bank Note Co. New York

Signatures

	Left	Lower Centre	Right
Typed:	(1901-2) Geo. W. Mews	mss. various	Typed: Geo. W. Gushue
	(1903-4) James Harris		
	(1905-9) M.T. Knight		

Cat.No.	Denom.	Issue Date	G	VG	F	VF	EF	AU
NF-2a	40¢	1901	125.	250.	400.	800.	1,400.	2,200.
NF-2b	40¢	1902	135.	275.	450.	900.	1,650.	2,500.
NF-2c	40¢	1903	150.	300.	500.	1,000.	1,800.	2,750.
NF-2d	40¢	1904	150.	300.	500.	1,000.	1,800.	2,750.
NF-2e	40¢	1905	150.	300.	500.	1,000.	1,800.	2,750.
NF-2f	40¢	1906	175.	350.	600.	1,200.	2,000.	3,000.
NF-2g	40¢	1907	175.	350.	600.	1,200.	2,000.	3,000.
NF-2h	40¢	1908	175.	350.	600.	1,200.	2,000.	3,000.
NF-2i	40¢	1909	500.	1,000.	1,650.	2,500.	4,500.	7,000.
NF-3a	50¢	1901	125.	250.	400.	800.	1,400.	2,200.
NF-3b	50¢	1902	135.	275.	450.	900.	1,650.	2,500.
NF-3c	50¢	1903	150.	300.	500.	1,000.	1,800.	2,500.
NF-3d	50¢	1904	150.	300.	500.	1,000.	1,800.	2,500.
NF-3e	50¢	1905	150.	300.	500.	1,000.	1,800.	2,500.
NF-3f	50¢	1906	175.	350.	600.	1,200.	2,000.	3,000.
NF-3g	50¢	1907	175.	350.	600.	1,200.	2,000.	3,000.
NF-3h	50¢	1908	175.	350.	600.	1,200.	2,000.	3,000.
NF-3i	50¢	1909	300.	600.	1,100.	2,000.	3,750.	5,500.
NF-4a	80¢	1901	200.	400.	675.	1,275.	2,250.	3,600.
NF-4b	80¢	1902	200.	400.	675.	1,275.	2,250.	3,600.
NF-4c	80¢	1903	200.	400.	675.	1,275.	2,250.	3,600.
NF-4d	80¢	1904	200.	400.	675.	1,275.	2,250.	3,600.
NF-4e	80¢	1905	225.	500.	825.	1,550.	2,850.	4,400.
NF-4f	80¢	1906	250.	550.	925.	1,750.	3,100.	4,600.
NF-4g	80¢	1907	250.	550.	925.	1,750.	3,100.	4,600.
NF-4h	80¢	1908	250.	550.	925.	1,750.	3,100.	4,600.
NF-4i	80¢	1909	600.	1,250.	2,000.	3,500.	6,500.	—
NF-5a	$1	1901	225.	500.	825.	1,375.	2,500.	4,000.
NF-5b	$1	1902	200.	400.	675.	1,275.	2,250.	3,600.
NF-5c	$1	1903	200.	400.	675.	1,275.	2,250.	3,600.
NF-5d	$1	1904	200.	400.	675.	1,275.	2,250.	3,600.
NF-5e	$1	1905	160.	325.	550.	1,000.	1,800.	2,750.
NF-5f	$1	1906	200.	400.	675.	1,275.	2,250.	3,600.
NF-5g	$1	1907	200.	400.	675.	1,275.	2,250.	3,600.
NF-5h	$1	1908	200.	400.	675.	1,275.	2,250.	3,600.
NF-5i	$1	1909	200.	400.	675.	1,275.	2,250.	3,600.
NF-6a	$5	1901	900.	2,000.	3,500.	6,000.	—	—
NF-6b	$5	1902	900.	2,000.	3,500.	6,000.	—	—
NF-6c	$5	1903	900.	2,000.	3,500.	6,000.	—	—
NF-6d	$5	1904	900.	2,000.	3,500.	6,000.	—	—
NF-6e	$5	1905	800.	1,750.	3,000.	5,000.	—	—
NF-6f	$5	1906	800.	1,750.	3,000.	5,000.	—	—
NF-6g	$5	1907	800.	1,750.	3,000.	5,000.	—	—
NF-6h	$5	1908	800.	1,750.	3,000.	5,000.	7,000.	—
NF-6i	$5	1909	900.	2,000.	3,500.	6,000.	—	—
NF-6b-r	$5	1902	Two sign remainder			1,500.	2,500.	3,500.

Note: Specimen and proof notes exist of each denomination.
Specimen: $750 to $1,000.
Proof: $600 to $850

II. Double Date Multicoloured Type 1910-1914

In 1910 the Newfoundland government enacted legislation extending the use of cash notes to other departments. Besides paying for the construction and maintenance of roads, the new type cash notes were used for welfare payments and marine works.

These notes bore two consecutive years, printed in red ink, corresponding to the government's fiscal year. They were signed by the colonial secretary and minister of finance. The third signature, formerly applied by hand to the earlier type of cash notes, was omitted. The notes were printed by Whitehead, Morris & Co. Ltd., of London, England, in denominations of 25¢, 50¢, $1, $2 and $5, with tints of various colours for each denomination.

As before, the notes were withdrawn from circulation and cancelled upon presentation for payment at the Bank of Montreal. The cancelled notes were destroyed in the presence of the auditor general. The issue of cash notes was not continued beyond 1914. Cheques and stocks of surplus silver coin took their place, although these forms of payment were not always as convenient as the cash notes.

Two basic varieties occur. The 1910-1911 notes have a lathework "scallop" design in the upper right corner. This was replaced on later issues by a denominational counter. Other accompanying changes were made. On the 1910-11 notes, the word form of the denomination found below the vignette is partially covered by the tint, while on later issues the tint is clear of the value.

Quantities of Notes Issued by Denomination and Fiscal Year

Fiscal Year	Denomination				
	25¢	50¢	$1	$2	$5
1910-11	10,000	7,000	56,000	10,000	37,000
1911-12	8,000	20,700	73,000	29,000	35,000
1912-13	20,750	81,250	171,700	22,000	25,800
1913-14	12,000	20,000	44,000	19,500	15,800

Total face value: $1,150,862.50

The lower denominations are now more frequently encountered, having been kept as mementoes.

1910-1911 Issues

All denominations have a "scallop" design in the upper right corner.

NF-7a

1911-1914 Issues

All denominations have a "counter" in the upper right corner.

NF-7c

Face Design: —/waterfall/—
Colour: Black with dull red and grey-brown tints.

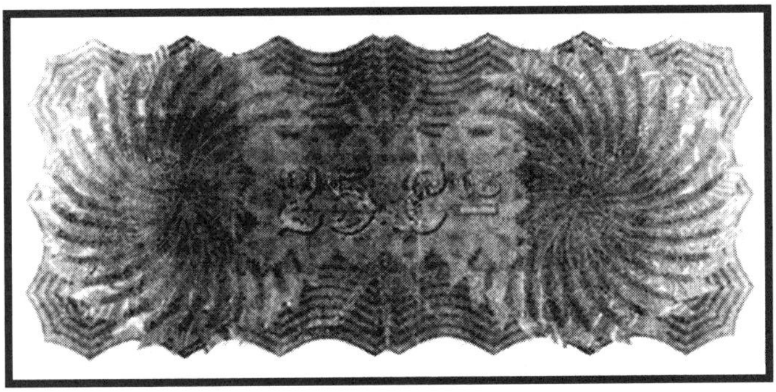

NF-7c

Back Design: Lathework and counter
Colour: Ochre ends, blue centre, grey diagonal shading.

NF-8c

Face Design: —/waterfall/—
Colour: Black with dull red and grey-brown tints.

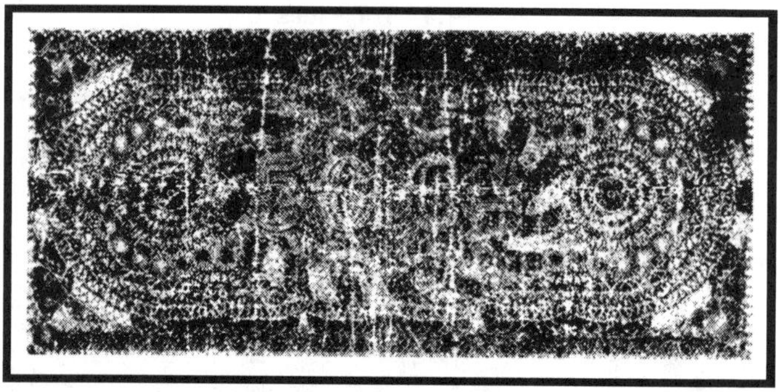

NF-8c

Back Design: Lathework and counter
Colour: Dull red, brown and grey diagonal shading.

NF-9c

Face Design: —/waterfall/—
Colour: Black with bright green, dull red and grey-brown tints.

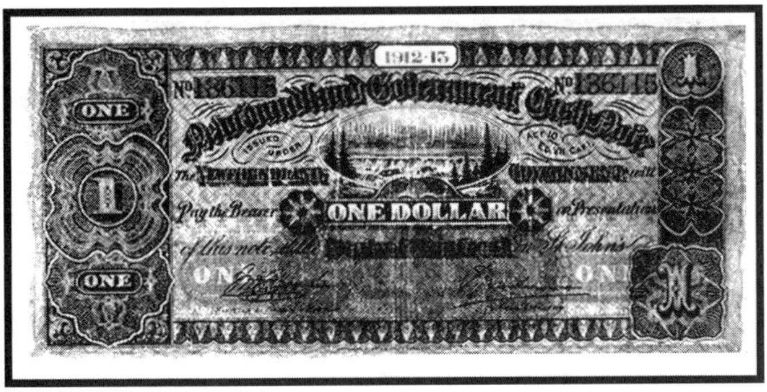

NF-9d

Face Design: —/waterfall/—
Colour: Black with bright green, dull red and grey-brown tints.

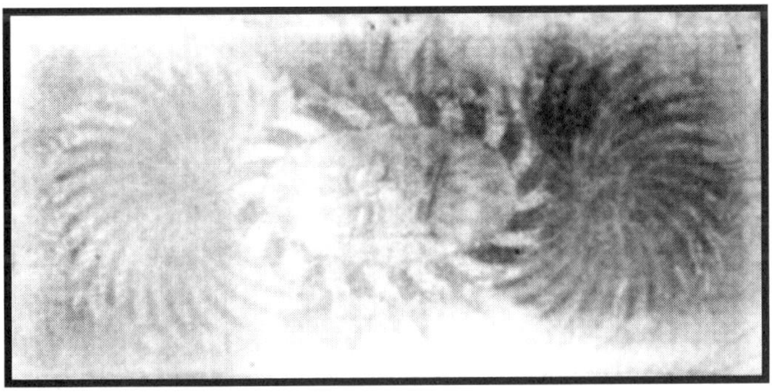

NF-9d

Back Design: Lathework and counter
Colour: Dull rose red ends, green centre, peripheral grey diagonal shading.

NF-10b

Face Design: —/waterfall/—
Colour: Black with yellow, grey-blue and grey-brown tints.

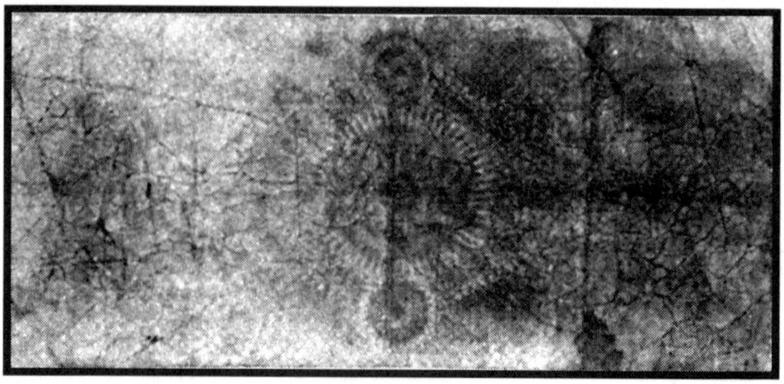

NF-10b

Back Design: Lathework and counter
Colour: Grey-blue ends, ochre centre, grey-brown diagonal shading.

NF-11a

Face Design: —/waterfall/—
Colour: Black with blue and grey tints, dull red at ends and light yellow centre.

NF-11a

Back Design: Lathework and counter
Colour: Green and blue ends, dull red centre, grey-brown diagonal shading.
Issue Date: 1910-11, 1911-12, 1912-13, 1913-14
Imprint: Whitehead, Morris & Co. Ltd. Engravers, London

Signatures

Left: Engr. M.P. Cashin **Right:** Engr. R. Watson

Cat.No.	Denom.	Issue Date	G	VG	F	VF	EF	AU
NF-7a	25¢	1910-11	60.	145.	250.	500.	1,000.	1,600.
NF-7b	25¢	1911-12	70.	160.	300.	650.	1,250.	1,900.
NF-7c	25¢	1912-13	45.	125.	225.	475.	800.	1,250.
NF-7d	25¢	1913-14	45.	125.	225.	475.	800.	1,250.
NF-8a	50¢	1910-11	85.	200.	350.	700.	1,400.	2,250.
NF-8b	50¢	1911-12	65.	135.	250.	550.	1,000.	1,600.
NF-8c	50¢	1912-13	55.	120.	240.	525.	950.	1,450.
NF-8d	50¢	1913-14	65.	135.	250.	550.	1,000.	1,600.
NF-9a	$1	1910-11	200.	400.	550.	1,000.	1,800.	2,700.
NF-9b	$1	1911-12	150.	300.	450.	800.	1,500.	2,400.
NF-9c	$1	1912-13	125.	250.	350.	600.	1,100.	1,800.
NF-9d	$1	1913-14	225.	450.	600.	1,100.	2,250.	3,400.
NF-10a	$2	1910-11	1,000.	1,800.	3,500.	5,500.	—	—
NF-10b	$2	1911-12	1,000.	1,800.	3,500.	5,500.	—	—
NF-10c	$2	1912-13	1,000.	1,800.	3,500.	5,500.	—	—
NF-10d	$2	1913-14	1,000.	1,800.	3,500.	5,500.	—	—
NF-11a	$5	1910-11	1,250.	2,500.	4,000.	7,000.	—	—
NF-11b	$5	1911-12	1,250.	2,500.	4,000.	7,000.	—	—
NF-11c	$5	1912-13	1,250.	2,500.	4,000.	7,000.	—	—
NF-11d	$5	1913-14	1,250.	2,500.	4,000.	7,000.	—	—

NEWFOUNDLAND
TREASURY NOTES OF 1920

Treasury notes in $1 and $2 denominations dated 1920 were issued to deal with a shortage of silver coin (precipitated in part by the withdrawal of the cash notes) at a time when the price of silver was very high on world markets.

Two tints, four face plates and four back plates were engraved for the $1 denomination, two tints, two face plates and two back plates for the $2 denomination. There were no check letters, the notes being numbered serially. All notes printed were in series A, which is shown by the letter A prefixing the number.

The Admiral portrait of King George V on the left of the $1 note was the same as the one used on the centre of the 1911 $1,000 Canadian Dominion notes.

Of the $1,200,000 worth of these notes printed, $1,181,704 had been destroyed by December 8, 1939. This amount includes both stocks of unissued notes and notes withdrawn from circulation. Small additional quantities were subsequently redeemed, leaving an outstanding total of about $12,000 face value.

Summary of Technical Details for 1920 Issues

Cat.No.	Denom.	Series	Serial Numbers	Quantities Printed	Quantities Issued
NF-12	$1	A	000001-600000	600,000	407,000
NF-13	$2	A	**000001-300000**	**300,000**	**261,000**

NF-12

Face Design: "Admiral" portrait of King George V/—/caribou head
Colour: Black with blue tint.

NF-12

Back Design: —/Official seal of Newfoundland, supported by ship and anchor/—
Colour: Blue.

NF-13

Face Design: —/mining scene/ caribou head
Colour: Black with light brown tint.

NF-13

Back Design: —/Official Seal of Newfoundland, supported by ship and anchor/—
Colour: Brown
Issue Date: Engr. Jany 2nd, 1920
Imprint: American Bank Note Co., Ottawa

Signatures

Left: mss. C.F. Renouf, mss. F.A. Hickey,
Geo. Bursell, mss. J.S. Keating
Right: Typed, H.J. Brownrigg, Typed, H.J. Brownrigg,
Typed, H.J. Brownrigg, Typed, H.J. Brownrigg

Cat.No.	Denom.	Signatures	G	VG	F	VF	EF	AU	Unc
NF-12a	$1	Bursell-Brownrigg	125.	225.	450.	1,000.	1,750.	2,200.	3,000.
NF-12b	$1	Hickey-Brownrigg	60.	175.	275.	800.	1,350.	1,700.	2,300.
NF-12c	$1	Keating-Brownrigg	60.	175.	300.	850.	1,450.	1,800.	2,500.
NF-12d	$1	Renouf-Brownrigg	60.	175.	275.	750.	1,250.	1,600.	2,200.
NF-13a	$2	Bursell-Brownrigg	175.	325.	600.	1,400.	2,200.	2,800.	4,000.
NF-13b	$2	Hickey-Brownrigg	140.	275.	500.	1,200.	1,300.	2,300.	3,400.
NF-13c	$2	Keating-Brownrigg	150.	300.	550.	1,300.	2,000.	2,400.	3,500.
NF-13d	$2	Renouf-Brownrigg	125.	275.	475.	1,100.	1,800.	2,200.	3,200.

PROVINCE OF NOVA SCOTIA
TREASURY NOTES

I. Treasury Receipts 1763-1782

The Nova Scotia colonial government frequently found its supply of specie inadequate for its needs. It then appealed to the wealthier citizens to bring in their silver and gold to the treasury, in return for which they would receive treasury receipts payable at a future date and bearing 6 percent annual interest in the meantime. Originally issued only for various larger sums, these debenture-like documents soon assumed a currency function, which led to their being issued for more suitable amounts, such as 10 shillings and 20 shillings currency. In 1765 legislation was enacted to provide for the exchange of large denominations for smaller ones. From 1773 they could be made payable either to the bearer or to the original recipient, at his discretion. In 1776 all old interest-bearing treasury receipts (as well as treasury warrants, a form of promissory note used by the government to pay for supplies and services) were called in and exchanged for new notes.

None of these early notes are known to have survived, and they were not specifically issued for currency purposes, so catalogue numbers are not assigned to them.

II. Provincial Treasury Notes 1812

The first treasury notes, issued specifically for circulation were authorized in 1812 to the extent of £12,000 currency. Five copper plates were engraved in denominations of £1, £2.10, £5, £12.50, and £50 (a £20 denomination was authorized but not used). The notes were printed locally, and although the treasury note commissioners thought the cost was excessive, no competing printers could be found.

These are the only treasury notes to bear interest, which was paid at 6 percent per annum. For this reason the government was unusually keen to have them withdrawn and cancelled over the next few years. Once redeemed at the treasury, notes of this issue were not reissuable, but were cancelled and destroyed.

The original plates are still in the possession of the Province of Nova Scotia, and a few reprints were made early in the twentieth century.

£2.10 Issue —1812

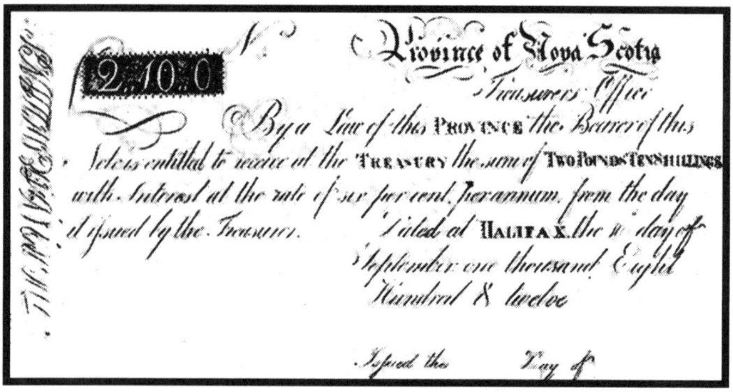

NS-2

Face Design: Wording only
Colour: Black
Back Design: Plain
Issue Date: Engr. (September 10, 1812)
Imprint: None
Signatures: **Left:** mss. John Black, mss. Law. Hartshorne, mss. James Foreman
Right: mss. Mich. Wallace

Cat.No.	Denom.	Issue Date	G	VG	F	VF	EF	Unc
NS-1	£1	1812						
NS-2	£2.10	1812	ISSUED (FULLY SIGNED AND DATED)					
NS-3	£5	1812	TREASURY NOTES OF 1812 TO 1838 ARE					
NS-4	£12.10	1812	EXTREMELY RARE. Estimate: G-$1,000. to VG-$4,000.					
NS-5	£50	1812						

III. Non-Interest Bearing Issue 1813-1817

Two copper plates were engraved for the printing of £1 and £2 non-interest-bearing treasury notes thatwere issued in 1813 and 1814. These were issued in large quantity to replace the 1812 interest-bearing notes, and a total issue of £20,000 was authorized. A further issue of £5 notes was made in 1817, but some were antedated 1813.

These notes were fundable; that is, if they were presented at the treasury and specie was unavailable, they could be exchanged in multiples of £100 for interest-bearing provincial securities. The £1 and £2 notes could be reissued when received by the treasury. Reprints exist.

Summary of Technical Details

Denomination	Quantity Printed	Amount (Halifax Currency)
£1	14,000	£14,000
£2	3,000	£ 6,000
£5	1,000	£ 5,000

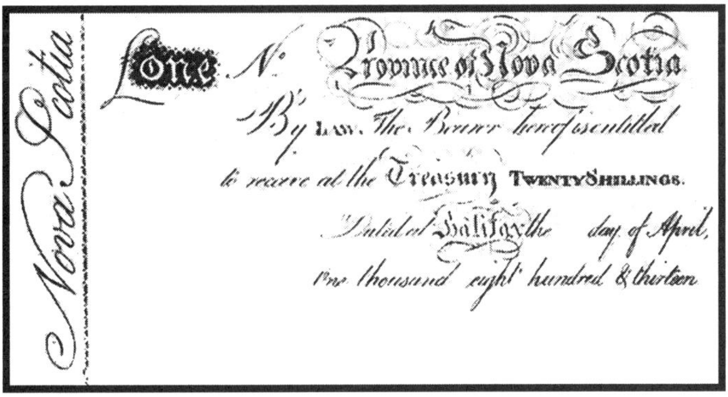

NS-6

Face Design: Wording only
Colour: Black
Back Design: Plain
Issue Date: Partially engraved: ___April 1813,
£1, £2 - April 30, 1813
£5 - April 30, 1813, April 30, 1817
Imprint: None

Signatures

Left: mss. John Black, mss. Law. Hartshorne, mss. James Foreman
Right: mss. Mich. Wallace

Cat.No.	Denom.	Issue Date	G	VG	F	VF	EF	Unc
NS-6	£1	1813	ISSUED (FULLY SIGNED AND DATED)					
NS-7	£2	1813	TREASURY NOTES OF 1812 TO 1838 ARE					
NS-8	£5	1813-17	EXTREMELY RARE: G-$1,000. to VG-$3,000.					

IV. Issues of 1817-1823

A new £15,000 issue consisting of £1, £2 and £5 notes, in unknown proportions, was authorized in 1818 but dated April 20, 1817. A further £10,000 was authorized in 1819, £20,000 more in 1820 and £5,000 in 1823. The notes were printed in Boston.

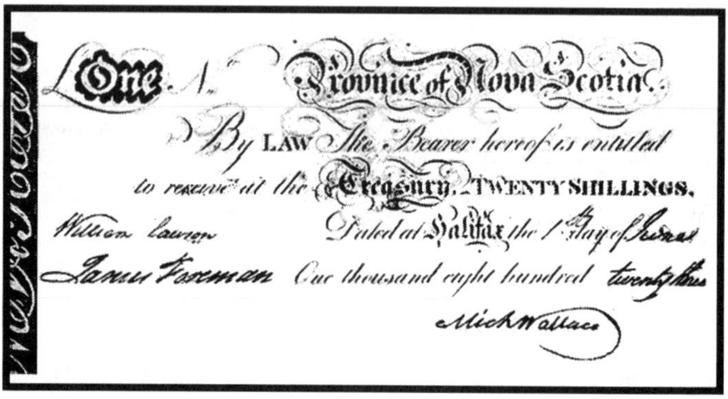

NS-9

Face Design: Wording only
Colour: Black
Back Design: Plain
Issue Date: Partially engraved: ___ 18__, April 20, 1817, June 1, 1820 January 1, 1821, July 2, 1821, June 1, 1823 and possibly others
Imprint: None

Signatures

Left: mss. Wm. Lawson, mss. J. Foreman
Right: mss. Mich. Wallace

Cat.No.	Denom.	Issue Date	G	VG	F	VF	EF	Unc
NS- 9	£1	1817-23	ISSUED (FULLY SIGNED AND DATED)					
NS-10	£2	1817-23	TREASURY NOTES OF 1812 TO 1838 ARE					
NS-11	£5	1817-21	EXTREMELY RARE: G-$1,000. to VG-$3,000.					

V. The Dollar Issue of 1820

Notes of 5 shillings and 10 shillings currency (equivalent to $1 and $2) were authorized to the extent of £8,000 by an act of 1821. However, the notes of these denominations that have turned up are dated September 5, 1820. They are hand-drawn counterfeits, bearing the (forged) signature of the provincial treasurer only. The note shown below is one such counterfeit.

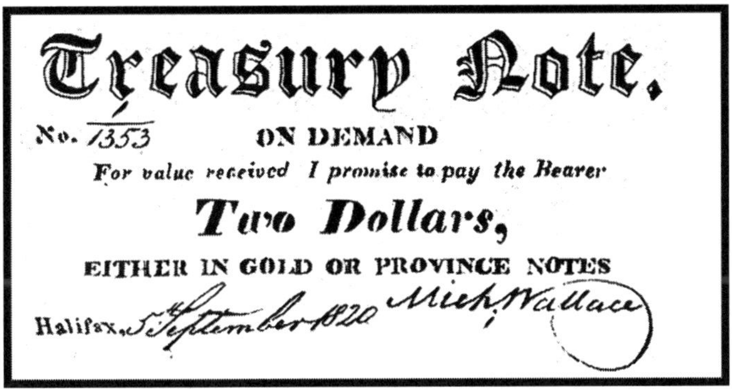

NS-13

Face Design: Wording only
Colour: Black
Back Design: Plain
Issue Date: mss. 5 September, 1820
Imprint: None
Signatures: mss. Mich. Wallace

Cat.No.	Denom.	Issue Date	G	VG	F	VF	EF	Unc
NS-12	$1	1820	ISSUED (FULLY SIGNED AND DATED)					
NS-13	$2	1820	TREASURY NOTES OF 1812 TO 1838 ARE					
			EXTREMELY RARE: G-$1,000. to VG-$3,000.					

VI. Engraved Issues 1824-c.1832

The £1 and £2 plates used for printing treasury notes in Boston until 1823 were sent to the province's agents Smith, Forsyth & Co., in Liverpool, England, in 1824. A new £5 plate had to be prepared in England, the old one having been lost. A large number of notes, consisting of £1, £2 and £5 denominations, was prepared, and these were probably issued over a number of years, with various dates. In 1829 the addition of the 10 shilling denomination was authorized and was probably printed by an English firm, dated 1830. More 10 shilling notes were provided for by an act of 1832 and 5 shilling notes also entered circulation about the same time. At least some of the plates still exist.

Summary of Technical Details

Denomination	Date	Quantity Printed	Amount(Halifax Currency)
5s ($1)	1830-ca. 1832	3,900	£ 975.
10s ($2)	1830-ca. 1832	3,000	£ 1,500.
£1	1824-	40,000	£40,000.
£2	1824-	15,000	£30,000.
£5	1824-	2,000	£10,000.

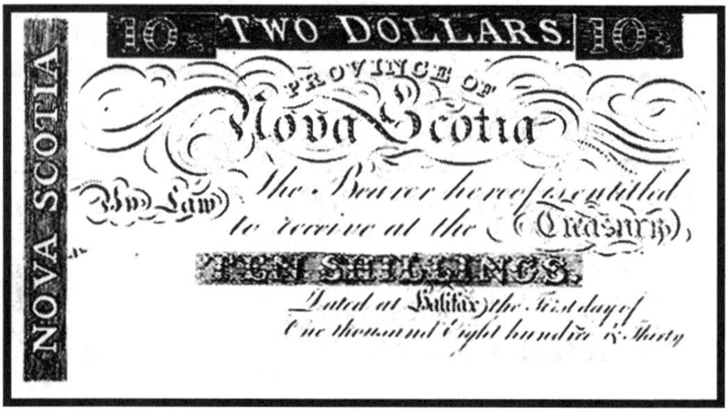

NS-15

Face Design: Wording only
Back Design: Plain
Issue Date: 10s.: Partially engraved: ___1, 1830
5s., £1, £2, £5: uncertain
Imprint: None

Signatures

Left: mss. various (two)
Right: mss. Mich. Wallace or Charles W. Wallace

Cat.No.	Denom.	Issue Date	G	VG	F	VF	EF	Unc
NS-14	5s. ($1)	1830-ca. 1832						
NS-15	10s. ($2)	1830-ca. 1832						
NS-16	£1	1824			ISSUED (FULLY SIGNED AND DATED)			
NS-17	£2	1824-			TREASURY NOTES OF 1812 TO 1838 ARE			
NS-18	£5	1824-			EXTREMELY RARE: G-$1,000. to VG-$3,000.			

VII. Lithographic Issues 1825-c.1832

These notes are characterized by large oblong shapes in blue or black ink in the centre of the notes, in which the printed details appear in white letters. They were printed by Peter Maverick of New York. At least two modifications of the design exist.

FIRST ISSUE

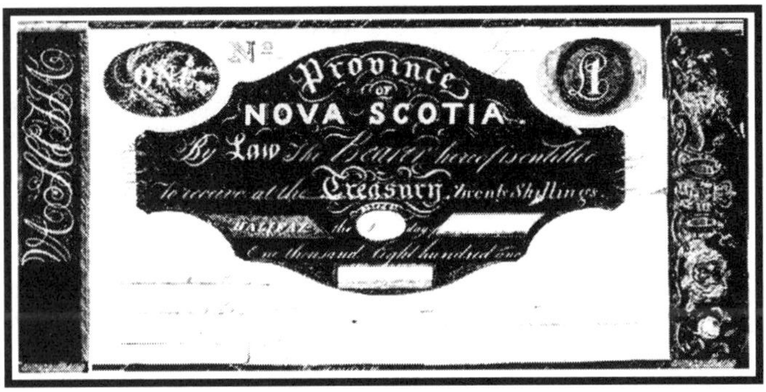

NS-19

Face Design: Thistle/“scalloped” centre block/floral panel with small crown
Colour: Black
Back Design: Plain

SECOND ISSUE

NS-20

Face Design: —/oval centre block/ floral panel with large crown
Colour: Black or blue
Back Design: Plain
Issue Date: Partially engraved: ____ 18_, August 1, 1825
June 1, 1829, January 1, 1831, March 1, 1832
Imprint: 1825: Peter Maverick, 1829-32: D. Henderson

Signatures

Left: mss. various (two or three)
Right: mss. Mich. Wallace or Charles W. Wallace

Cat.No.	Denom.	Issue Date	G	VG	F	VF	EF	Unc
NS-19	£1	1825	ISSUED (FULLY SIGNED AND DATED)					
NS-20	£1	1828-32	TREASURY NOTES OF 1812 TO 1838 ARE					
			EXTREMELY RARE. Estimate: G-$1,000. to VG-$4,000.					

VIII. Rawdon, Wright & Hatch Issue 1838

A new issue of 8,000 £1 notes, prepared from a 4/on steel plate, was prepared in 1838, replacing earlier notes as they became too worn or soiled for further use. By this time chartered banking was well established in Nova Scotia, and the banks were prohibited from issuing their own notes in denominations of less the £5 currency, to prevent bank notes from competing with the provincial notes.

PHOTO NOT AVAILABLE

NS-21

Face Design: Floral panel/Royal crest/scrollwork panel
Colour: Black
Back Design: Plain
Issue Date: Engraved: _____18__
Imprint: Rawdon, Wright & Hatch
Signatures: Unknown

Cat.No.	Denom.	Issue Date	G	VG	F	VF	EF	Unc
NS-21	£1	1838	ISSUED (FULLY SIGNED AND DATED) TREASURY NOTES OF 1812 TO 1838 ARE EXTREMELY RARE. Estimate: G-$1,000. to VG-$4,000.					

IX. Perkins, Bacon And Petch Issue 1846-1854

All old issues of treasury notes were withdrawn in the late 1840s and replaced by notes of the £1 denomination only. Sixty thousand of these were printed initially. A subsequent printing with the date engraved became the first treasury notes of the province to be numbered by machine. Those of later dates were used to pay for railroad construction.

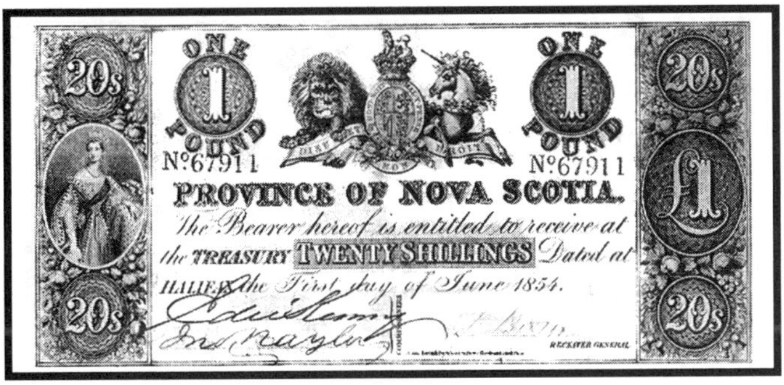

NS-22b

Face Design: 3/4 length portrait of Queen Victoria (Chalon)/Royal Crest/—
Colour: Black
Back Design: Plain
Issue Date: Partially engraved:____ 18__;
The first day of: August 1846; May 1, 1848; June 1, 1853
or Engr. The first day of June 1854
Imprint: Perkins, Bacon & Petch

Signatures

Left: mss. various, Two signatures
Right: mss. various

Cat.No.	Denom.	Issue Date	G	VG	F	VF	EF	Unc
NS-22a	£1	1846-54, MSS Serial No.		Extremely Rare. Estimate $1,000 to $4,000				
NS-22b	£1	1846-54, Printed Serial No.		Extremely Rare. Estimate $1,000 to $4,000				

Listed prices are for WHOLE NOTES. Notes which have been CANCELLED by cutting out the signatures are worth 25 percent of the price.

X. Decimal Currency Issues 1861-1866

Nova Scotia adopted decimal currency in 1860. All subsequent treasury notes were issued in the denomination of $5 (Nova Scotia currency) only. The previous £1 treasury notes were equivalent to $4. After Confederation all treasury notes were to be withdrawn and destroyed. By 1875 only $46,194 remained outstanding of a total circulation of $622,458.

NS-23

Face Design: Queen Victoria (Winterhalter portrait)/shield and Indian/ Prince of Wales
Colour: Black with green tint

NS-23

Back Design: —/St. George slaying dragon/—
Colour: Orange
Issue Date: Engraved: First day of June 1861, May 1865, May 1866, Aug 1866
Imprint: American Bank Note Company, New York

Signatures

Left: miss. various (two)
Right: mss. J.H. Anderson or James McNab

Cat.No.	Denom.	Issue Date	G	VG	F	VF	EF	Unc
NS-23	$5	1861-66	350.	700.	1,000.	1,700.	3,500.	—

Listed prices are for WHOLE NOTES. Notes which have been CANCELLED by cutting out the signatures are worth 25 percent of the price.

PRINCE EDWARD ISLAND
TREASURY NOTES

I. Island Of St. John Issue 1790

Known as Island of St. John until 1799, Prince Edward Island had become a separate colony from Nova Scotia in 1769. Trade was conducted by a primitive means of barter until 1790, when provincial treasury notes were issued to provide a circulating medium. The notes were used to pay for public works, and were receivable for taxes and duties.

The first issue consisted of a total of £500 P.E.I. Currency, to be redeemed in three years. The enabling legislation was passed by the General Assembly on November 20, 1790, and this is the date printed on the notes. The notes carry the warning "Death to Counterfeit" vertically at the right end.

Summary of Technical Details

Denomination	Dated	Quantity Printed	Amount (Currency)
1s.	1790	500	£25.
1s.3d.	1790	480	£30.
2s.6d.	1790	480	£60.
5s.	1790	500	£125.
10s.	1790	100	£50.
20s.	1790	110	£110.
40s.	1790	50	£100.

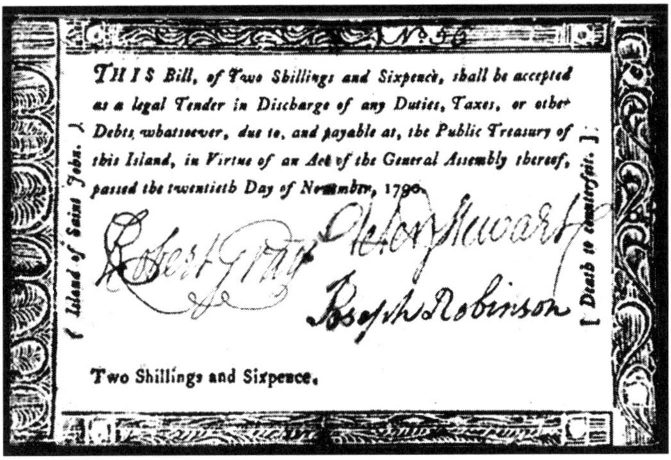

PEI-3

Face Design: Pattern of leaves and scrollwork margins
Colour: Black
Back Design: Plain
Issue Date: Engr. Nov. 20, 1790 **Imprint**: None

Signatures

Left: mss. Robert Gray
Right: mss. Peter J. Stewart and Joseph Robinson

Cat.No.	Denom.	Issue Date	G	VG	F	VF	EF	Unc
PEI-1	1s.	1790	750.	1,500.	2,500.	4,500.	6,000.	—
PEI-2	1s.3d.	1790	750.	1,500.	2,500.	4,500.	6,000.	—
PEI-3	2s.6d.	1790	750.	1,500.	2,500.	4,500.	6,000.	—
PEI-4	5s.	1790	750.	1,500.	2,500.	4,500.	6,000.	—
PEI-5	10s.	1790	750.	1,500.	2,500.	4,500.	6,000.	—
PEI-6	20s.	1790	750.	1,500.	2,500.	4,500.	6,000.	—
PEI-7	40s.	1790	750.	1,500.	2,500.	4,500.	6,000.	—

II. Issues of 1825-1834

The Legislature of Prince Edward Island authorized the second issue of provincial treasury notes in 1825. Originally consisting of an issue of £5,000 currency in £1, £2 and £5 notes, a 10 shilling denomination was subsequently added at the insistence of the merchants, to the extent of an additional £800.

Three treasury note commissioners were appointed to procure and sign the notes and to superintend their circulation. All notes of the issue were to be given the same date. The provincial treasurer countersigned the notes prior to issue. The notes could be reissued by the treasury. If they were presented for payment when no specie was available (the usual situation), they could be exchanged for interest-bearing "funding certificates." The Islanders seemed to accept the notes readily enough, for none were presented for funding over the next decade. Originally the notes were supposed to be withdrawn and redeemed after three years, but the authorizing act was repeatedly renewed for several years at a time whenever the redemption date drew near.

The notes were very plain, with the following format:

"No.____Prince Edward Island
Charlotte Town, 1825
By Law, the bearer of this note is entitled
to receive at the Treasury the
sum of ( )".

In 1830 and again in 1831 it was represented that the volume of treasury notes in circulation was inadequate, and in each case the circulation was expanded by an additional £3000 cy. In 1833 a further issue of £5,000 was enacted and put in circulation the following year, with the provision that £1,000 be withdrawn and redeemed at the end of each year after the date of issue, for five years.

The redemption process was suspended at first, but the required total redemption of £5000 was carried out at the insistance of the British Colonial Office, which took a dim view of the ever-increasing irredeemable circulation and consequent public debt. By 1839 the total circulation had been reduced from £16,800 to £11,800, only to make room for treasury warrants, irredeemable notes of small denomination thatbore interest at 6 percent. There were three unfortunate results of such a currency. In accordance with Gresham's Law, "bad money drives out good," there was no metallic currency on the island. Shopkeepers resorted to dispensing alcoholic libations in lieu of small change. The establishment of chartered banking facilities in the colony was discouraged. The currency itself became increasingly inflated, so that by 1839, 20 shillings sterling equalled 30 shillings P.E.I. currency.

Summary of Technical Details

Denomination	Date*	Quantity Printed	Amount (PEI Currency)
10s.	1825	1,600	£ 800
£1	1825	1,700 (est.)	£1,700
£2	1825	900 (est.)	£1,800
£5	1825	300 (est.)	£1,500
5s.	1830	2,000 (est.)	£ 500
10s.	1830	3,000 (est.)	£1,500
£1	1830	1,000 (est.)	£1,000
5s.	1831	2,000	£ 500
10s.	1831	3,000	£1,500
£1	1831	1,000	£1,000
5s.	1833	2,000	£ 500
10s.	1833	1,000	£ 500
£1	1833	1,000	£1,000
£2	1833	1,000	£2,000
£5	1833	200	£1,000

Note: The date listing refers to the date of passage of the authorizing legislation, and the notes may not have entered circulation until the following year. The issue authorized under the act of 1833 is believed to have been dated 1834.

PHOTO NOT AVAILABLE

Face Design: Presumed to have no vignette
Colour: Black
Back Design: Plain
Issue Date: Uncertain
Imprint: Unknown
Signatures: mss. various

Cat.No.	Denom.	Issue Date	G	VG	F	VF	EF	Unc
PEI-8	5s.	1830-34						
PEI-9	10s.	1825-34						
PEI-10	£1	1825-34		Surviving examples not confirmed				
PEI-11	£2	1825-34						
PEI-12	£5	1825-34						

III. Issues of 1848-1870

The Legislature attempted to issue a further £15,000 in treasury notes in 1845, to be redeemed in 15 years. This was to be in addition to the £11,800 still in circulation. The Colonial Office adamantly refused to permit it, and was not swayed by offers to limit the issue to £10,000 payable in ten years. A request for a loan of £12,000 sterling to back a redeemable treasury note issue was likewise rejected in 1848. In the early 1850s the prosperity of the colony and growing government revenues permitted the redemption of a large part of the old treasury notes still in circulation. With confidence restored, new issues were circulated over the period 1851 to 1870. The numbers issued have not been determined.

PEI-13

Face Design: —/sailing ship/seal on ice floe
Colour: Black
Back Design: Plain

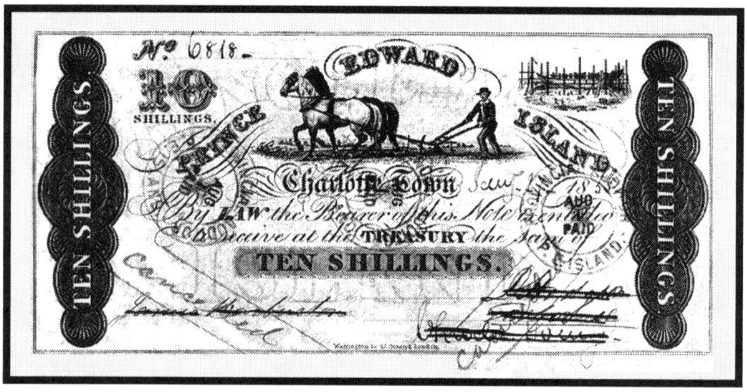

PEI-14

Face Design: —/Farmer ploughing with team of horses/shipbuilding
Colour: Black
Back Design: Plain

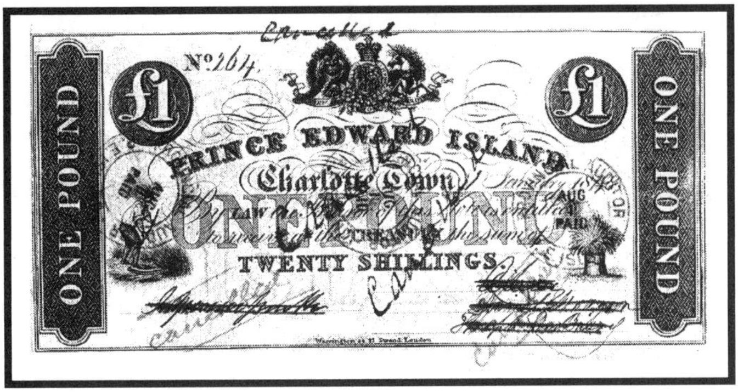

PEI-15

Face Design: Farmer mowing hay/Royal Crest/sheaf of grain
Colour: Black
Back Design: Plain

PEI-16

Face Design: —/Provincial Legislature Building/—
Colour: Black
Back Design: Plain

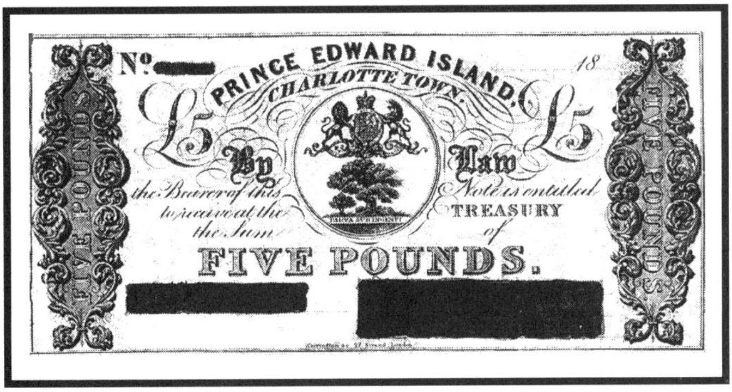

PEI-17

Face Design: —/Provincial Seal/—
Back Design: Plain

Issue Date: Partially engraved: ____18__, Jan. 1, 1848, Jan. 27, 1855, July 23, 1858, 1866, Sept. 12, 1868, Mar. 9, 1870
Imprint: Warrington (1848-58) or Warrington and American Bank Note Co. Logo (1858-70)
Signatures: mss. various

Cat.No.	Denom.	Issue Date	G	VG	F	VF	EF	Unc
PEI-13	5s.	1848-1870	600.	1,500.	2,500.	4,000.	5,500.	—
PEI-14	10s.	1848-1870	600.	1,500.	2,500.	4,000.	5,500.	—
PEI-15	£1	1848-1870	750.	1,500.	2,500.	4,000.	5,500.	—
PEI-16	£2	1848-1870	750.	1,500.	2,500.	4,000.	5,500.	—
PEI-17	£5	1848-1870	750.	1,500.	2,500.	4,000.	5,500.	—

Note: These treasury notes are usually found cancelled, with number, date and signature inked out. Prices are for cancelled notes.

IV. Dollar Issue of 1872

Prince Edward Island adopted decimal currency in 1871, the last of the colonies now comprising Canada to do so. A new issue of treasury notes in $10 and $20 denominations was released to replace the former notes expressed in pounds and shillings. An extravagantly meandering railroad had been built, greatly increasing public debt, and the colony joined Confederation in 1873 as an alternative to insolvency. Treasury notes were then called in and redeemed, after only a small quantity of notes of the 1872 issue had been put into circulation.

PEI-18

Face Design: Prince Arthur/seal, Royal Crest/Britannia seated
Colour: Black with green tint

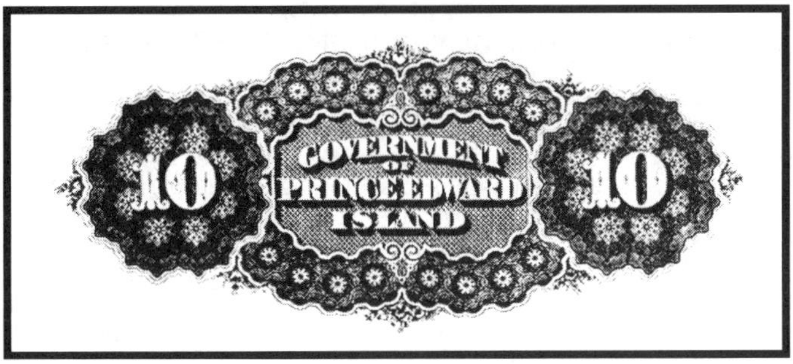

PEI-18

Back Design: Lathework and counters
Colour: Green

PEI-19

Face Design: Agricultural implements/seal, Royal Crest/ sailor on dock
Colour: Black with green tint

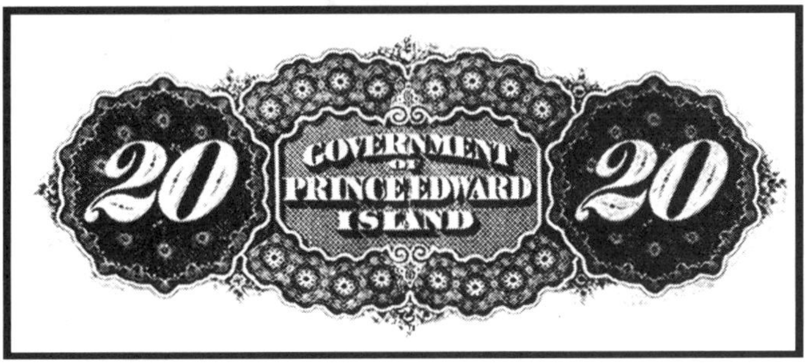

PEI-19

Back Design: Lathework and counters
Colour: Green
Issue Date: Engraved: 2nd January, 1872
Imprint: British American Bank Note Co., Montreal & Ottawa

Signatures

Left: mss. various
Right: mss. various

Cat.No.	Denom.	Issue Date	G	VG	F	VF	EF	Unc
PEI-18	$10	1872	2,000.	4,000.	6,000.	8,000.	10,000.	—
PEI-19	$20	1872	2,000.	4,000.	6,000.	8,000.	10,000.	—

UPPER CANADA
PROVISIONAL GOVERNMENT NOTES OF 1837

Following the collapse of the 1837 Rebellion in Upper Canada, its leader, William Lyon Mackenzie, fled with some of his supporters to New York State. He then set up a "provisional government" on Navy Island, a small island in the Niagara River about three miles above the falls. The island was used as a base for predatory raids against the Canadian mainland. Mackenzie issued scrip when all other means of acquiring supplies failed. The notes were allegedly payable four months after date at City Hall, Toronto, and were based on nothing more substantial than the dream of a successful invasion of Upper Canada.

In a desperate bid to make his scrip more appealing to the business community of Buffalo, Mackenzie had the signature of David Gibson forged on the notes. Gibson, a prominent and wealthy man, had been one of Mackenzie's supporters, but at the time the scrip bearing his name was issued, he was a hunted fugitive with a £500 bounty on his head, hiding under a straw-stack near Oshawa. The forgery was in vain, for the notes never circulated to a significant extent. In fact, the scrip was ridiculed on both sides of the border. Finally Mackenzie, finding no other use for his paper pledges, used the notes as wrappers for his newspapers.

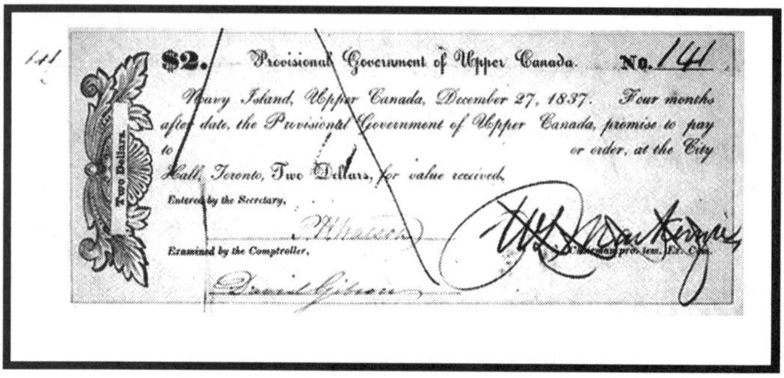

UC-2

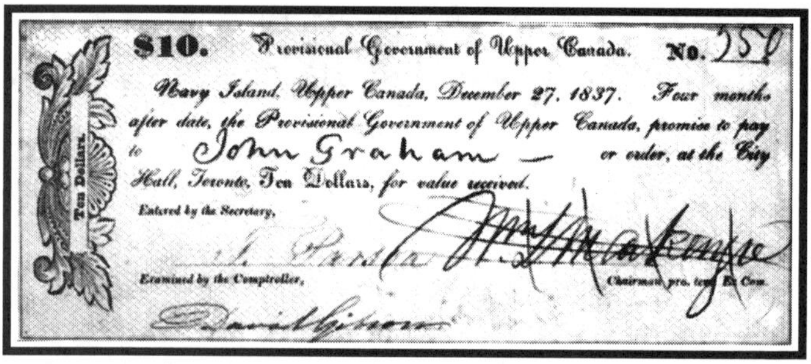

UC-3a

Face Design: Floral scroll work/—/—
Colour: Black, with light blue tint
Issue Date: Engr.: December 27, 1837

Back Design: Plain

Imprint: None

Signatures

Left: mss. T. Parson
or P.H. Watson;
David Gibson (forged)

Right: mss. Wm. L. Mackenzie

Cat.No.	Denom.	Issue Date	Variety	G	VG	F	VF	EF	Unc
UC-1	$1	1837					Extremely Rare		
UC-2	$2	1837			Estimate:		G $2,000.	F $6,000.	
UC-3a	$10	1837	Large Letter						
UC-3b	$10	1837	Small Letters						

MUNICIPAL ISSUES

Although the redeemable status of these municipal notes is questionable, the majority are scarce and have considerable value. Some are actually debentures (similar to bonds). The listings are alphabetical according to city.

BROCKVILLE

THE MUNICIPAL COUNCIL OF THE UNITED COUNTIES OF LEEDS AND GRENVILLE

The United Counties of Leeds and Grenville issued £25 (currency) debentures in the early 1850's, which bore six per cent annual interest paid twice yearly. Although these securities had the appearance and dimensions of bank notes, it is doubtful whether they circulated to any great extent because of their large denomination. Interest payments are usually found recorded on the back. The debentures were pen cancelled.

MU-1

Face Design: —/Royal Crest/—
Colour: Black
Back Design: Plain
Issue Date: Partially engraved:____18__, 12th Dec'r 1850, July 9, 1850, 3rd Jan'y, 1851, July 2nd, 1851, 4 Sept, 1851, Jan. 8, 1852, 14 Feb, 1852, 12 May, 1852
Imprint: Rawdon, Wright, Hatch & Edson, New York

Signatures

Left: mss. J.L. Schofield
Centre: mss. James Jessup
Right: mss. George Sherwood

Cat.No.	Denom.	Issue Date	VG	F	VF	EF	Unc
MU-1	£25 ($100)	1850-52	50.	100.	165.	225.	300.

COBOURG

BOARD OF POLICE

These notes were repayable one year after date, with interest. Both issues are usually found pen cancelled.

I. Coat of Arms Type
1848

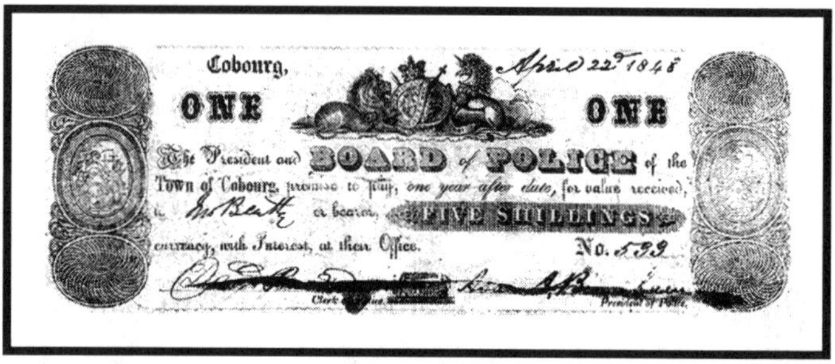

MU-2

MU-3

Face Design: Woman seated at dockside/Royal Crest; small steamboat below/ women seated at dockside
Colour: Black
Back Design: Plain
Issue Date: Partially engraved: ____184_,
1848: various, May or earlier
Imprint: None

Signatures

Left: mss. David Brodie
Right: mss. Asa A. Burnham

Cat.No.	Denom.	Issue Date	G	VG	F	VF	EF	Unc
MU-2	5s. ($1)	1848	90.	150.	210.	300.	500.	1,000.
MU-3	10s. ($2)	1848	50.	90.	150.	250.	350.	700.

II. Sailing Ships Type
1848

MU-4

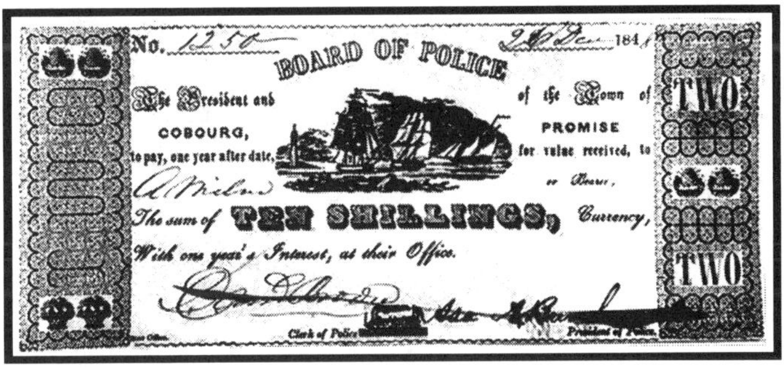

MU-5

Face Design: —/sailing ships/—
Colour: Black
Back Design: Plain
Issue Date: Partially engraved: ____184_,
1848: various, Oct. to Dec.
Imprint: Star Office

Signatures

Left: mss. David Brodie
Right: mss. Asa A. Burnham

Cat.No.	Denom.	Issue Date	G	VG	F	VF	EF	Unc
MU-4	5s. ($1)	1848	15.	30.	60.	90.	150.	300.
MU-5	10s. ($2)	1848	15.	30.	55.	90.	150.	300.

GUELPH

DISTRICT OF WELLINGTON

These crudely produced notes were repayable in varying numbers of years after date, with interest. They were issued in connection with road construction. Many of the notes were used to pay the labourers, a purpose for which the 5 shilling denomination was suitably chosen. The notes are usually pen cancelled.

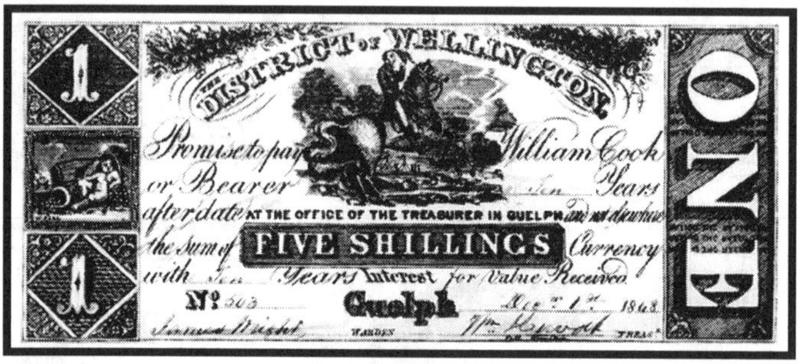

MU-6

Face Design: Cherub/Duke of Wellington on horseback/—
Colour: Black
Back Design: Plain
Issue Date: Partially engraved: ____18__, 1 Dec'r 1848
Imprint: Fell, Hamilton

Signatures

Left: mss. James Wright
Right: mss. Wm. Stewart

Cat.No.	Denom.	Issue Date	VG	F	VF	EF	Unc
MU-6	5s. ($1)	1848	20.	30.	40.	70.	90.

HAMILTON

These notes were repayable 12 months after date, with interest. They feature medallion engraving above and below the portraits. Different check letters were used for each year of issue, a peculiarity shared with the notes of the Corporation of the City of Toronto. The check letters of the surviving notes suggest that the notes may have been issued annually from 1848 until at least 1861, but only those known to exist are listed.

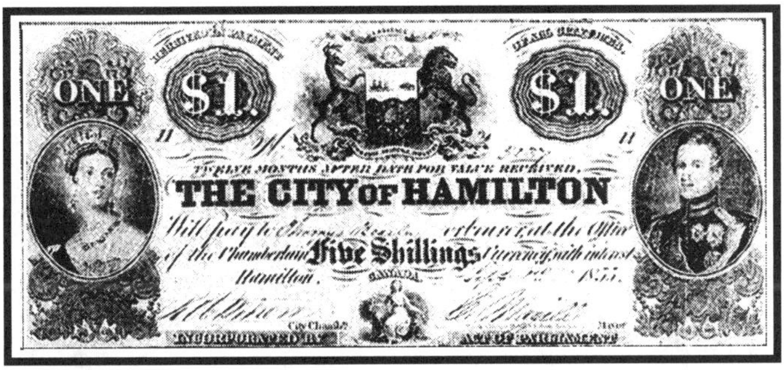

MU-7

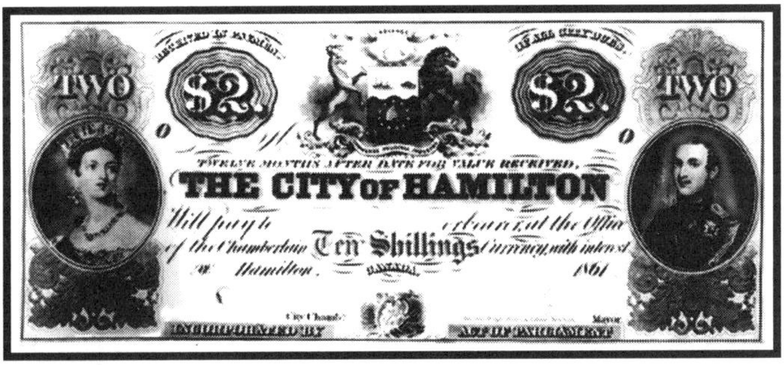

MU-8

Face Design: Queen Victoria (Chalon portrait)/crest/Prince Consort
Colour: Black
Back Design: Plain
Issue Date: May 9, 1849, Sept. 1, 1855, Apr. 1, 1856, 1859, June 1, 1860, 1861
Imprint: Rawdon, Wright, Hatch & Edson (American Bank Note Co. logo added after 1858)

Signatures

Left: mss. Robt. M. Kerr
Right: mss. various

Cat.No.	Denom.	Issue Date	G	VG	F	VF	EF	Unc
MU-7	$1 (5s.)	1849-61	750.	1,500.	2,500.	—	—	—
MU-8	$2 (10s.)	1849-61	750.	1,500.	2,500.	—	—	—

KINGSTON

I. Commonalty of Kingston Issue 1842

The Town of Kingston issued a total of £2,000 currency in 5 shilling and 10 shilling notes in 1842 to help meet the cost of an ambitious program of public works. A red "City of Kingston" seal (often found badly faded) was stamped at the lower right. The notes bore interest and were repayable after one year, but were not uniformly well received by the townsfolk. In 1846, when the town had amassed such a debt load that no further accommodation from the banks was obtainable, a further issue of £5,000 was proposed, but had to be abandoned in the face of strong opposition.

MU-9

MU-10

Face Design: —/view of Kingston from Fort Henry/—
Colour: Black
Back Design: Plain
Issue Date: Partially engraved: ____184_; July 6, Oct. 13, 1842
Imprint: Rawdon, Wright & Hatch

Signatures

Left: mss. illegible **Right**:mss. illegible

Cat.No.	Denom.	Issue Date	G	VG	F	VF	EF	Unc
MU-9	$1 (5s.)	1842	200.	400.	600.	1,000.	2,000.	5,000.
MU-10	$2 (10s.)	1842	200.	400.	600.	1,000.	2,000.	5,000.

II. Municipal Council of the Midland District Issue 1860-62

Notes of this issue are found with the overprint "BANK OF THREE RIVERS" in red. Such a bank was actually established in 1841 as Banque des Trois Rivieres, but it was unable to complete its organization successfully, and its charter was never used.

MU-11

Face Design: —/oxen pulling haywagon/—
Colour: Black
Back Design: Plain

MU-12

Face Design: —/woman in ornate V/—
Colour: Black
Back Design: Plain
Issued Date: Partially engraved: ____18__, Jan. 7, 1860, Jan. 7, 1862
Imprint: Rawdon, Wright, Hatch & Edson, New York

Signatures

Left: mss. I. White or mss. D. Fox
Right: mss. T. Proudfoot, mss. D. Thomas

Overprint

$1 (5s.): "BANK OF THREE RIVERS" in red and "ONE" vertically at left in green.
£5: "BANK OF THREE RIVERS" in red and "FIVE" vertically at left in green.

Cat.No.	Denom.	Issue Date	G	VG	F	VF	EF	Unc
MU-11	$1 (5s.)	1860-62	150.	375.	500.	750.	1,200.	2,500.
MU-12a	£5	1860-62 o/p	150.	375.	500.	750.	1,200.	2,500.
MU-12b	£5	18__*	100.	200.	300.	525.	1,050.	2,500.

*Remainder note

LONDON

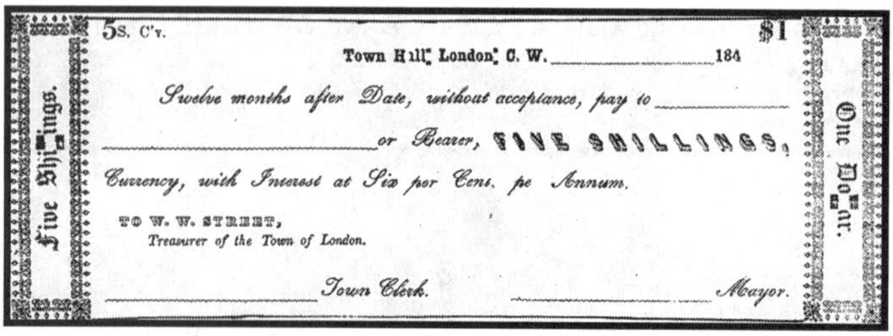

MU-13

Face Design: Text only
Colour: Black
Back Design: Plain
Issue Date: Partially engraved: _____ 184_
Imprint: None
Signatures: Unknown (Town Clerk); Unknown (Mayor)

Cat.No.	Denom.	Issue Date	G	VG	F	VF	EF	Unc
MU-13	5s. ($1)	184- One known, institutional collection						
MU-14	10s. ($2)	184- Surviving examples not confirmed						
MU-15	£1 ($4)	184- Surviving examples not confirmed			ALL VERY RARE			
MU-16	£1.5s ($5)	184- Surviving examples not confirmed			Estimate: G $750. VG $2,000.			
MU-17	£2.1s ($10)	184- Surviving examples not confirmed						

MONTREAL

POST OFFICE

These notes were probably issued to supply small change during the suspension of specie payments in 1837to 1938. They were redeemable in current Montreal bank notes when presented in sums of 5 shillings cy. ($1) or more.

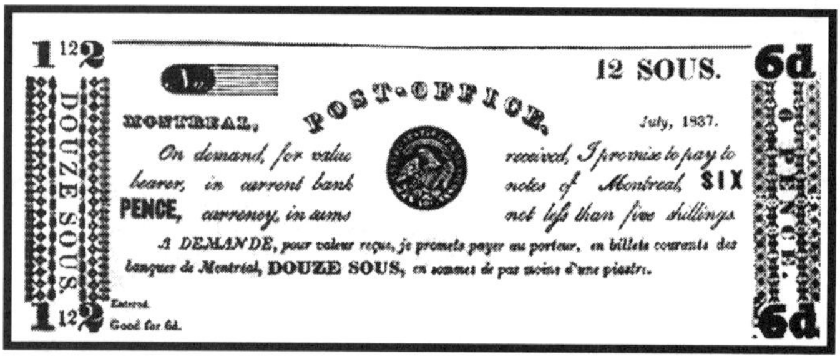

MU-18

6d. (12 sous)

Face Design: —//U.S. dime reverse/—
Colour: Black
Back Design: Plain
Issue Date: Partially engraved: _____ July 1837
Imprint: Unknown
Signatures: Unknown

Cat.No.	Denom.	Issue Date	G	VG	F	VF	EF	Unc
MU-18	6d. (12 sous)	1837	ALL VERY RARE Estimate: G $1,000. VG $3,000.					

NORTH VANCOUVER

WAGE PAYMENT CERTIFICATES

These notes were produced by letterpress. On the backs are listed various business firms in North Vancouver where presumably the notes would be honoured.

No. 45

The Corporation of the District of North Vancouver North Vancouver, B. C.

This Certificate is issued by the Corporation for the Payment of Wages, and entitles .... or any firm whose name is endorsed on the back hereof to whom this Certificate may be transferred, to be paid the sum of

FIVE DOLLARS

by presentment hereof to the Municipal Treasurer at the Municipal Hall, on or after the 31st July, 1913.

By Order of the Council,

$5.00

PAID AUG 4 1913

Treasurer

MU-20

Face Design: Wording only
Colour: Black with red border and denomination

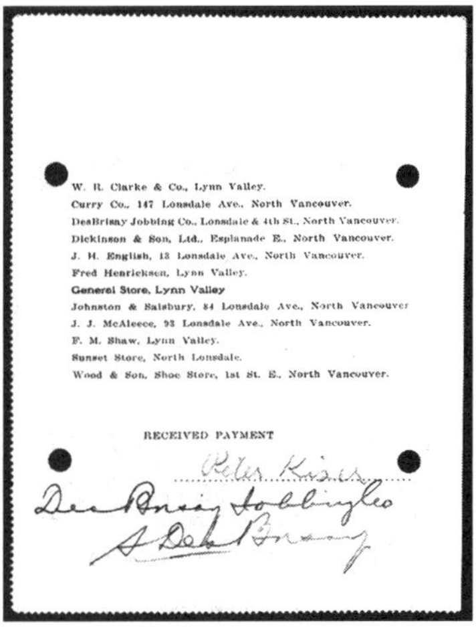
W. R. Clarke & Co., Lynn Valley.
Curry Co., 147 Lonsdale Ave., North Vancouver.
DesBrisay Jobbing Co., Lonsdale & 4th St., North Vancouver.
Dickinson & Son, Ltd., Esplanade E., North Vancouver.
J. H. English, 13 Lonsdale Ave., North Vancouver.
Fred Henrickson, Lynn Valley.
General Store, Lynn Valley
Johnston & Salsbury, 84 Lonsdale Ave., North Vancouver
J. J. McAleece, 93 Lonsdale Ave., North Vancouver.
F. M. Shaw, Lynn Valley.
Sunset Store, North Lonsdale.
Wood & Son, Shoe Store, 1st St. E., North Vancouver.

RECEIVED PAYMENT

MU-20

Back Design: List of North Vancouver businesses
Colour: Black
Issue Date: July 31, 1913
Imprint: None
Signatures: Stamped: P.L. Bayliss

Cat.No.	Denom.	Issue Date		G	VG	F	VF	EF	Unc
MU-19	$1	1913		30.	60.	100.	175.	300.	750.
MU-20	$5	1913		30.	60.	100.	175.	300.	750.
MU-21	$10	1913		SURVIVING EXAMPLES NOT CONFIRMED					
MU-21a	$10	1913	Raised from $5	40.	80.	120.	200.	350.	900.

PETERBOROUGH

DISTRICT OF COLBORNE

These crudely produced notes were issued under the authority of the building committee superintending the construction of a court house and jail for the "intended District of Colborne." They were repayable with interest 12 months after date. It is not certain whether these notes ever actually circulated; however, a numbered and signed example, with incomplete date 1847, first came to light in the February 1999 Jeffrey Hoare sale.

MU-22

Face Design: Standing Indian/stag/seated Justice figure
Colour: Black
Back Design: Plain
Issue Date: Partially Engraved:____18__; 1847
Imprint: None
Signatures: illegible - illegible

Cat.No.	Denom.	Issue Date	G	VG	F	VF	EF	Unc
MU-22	5s. ($1)	1847	150.	300.	500.	800.	—	—
MU-22R	5s. ($1)	18— unsigned remainder	75.	150.	250.	400.	800.	2,000.

PORTSMOUTH

Province of Canada

PHOTO NOT AVAILABLE

Face Design: Unknown
Colour: Black
Back Design: Unknown

Issue Date	Imprint	Signatures
Unknown	Unknown	Unknown

Cat.No.	Denom.	Issue Date	G	VG	F	VF	EF	Unc
MU-23	$1	1862	ALL VERY RARE Estimate: G $1,500. VG $5,000.					

QUEBEC CITY

CUSTOM HOUSE

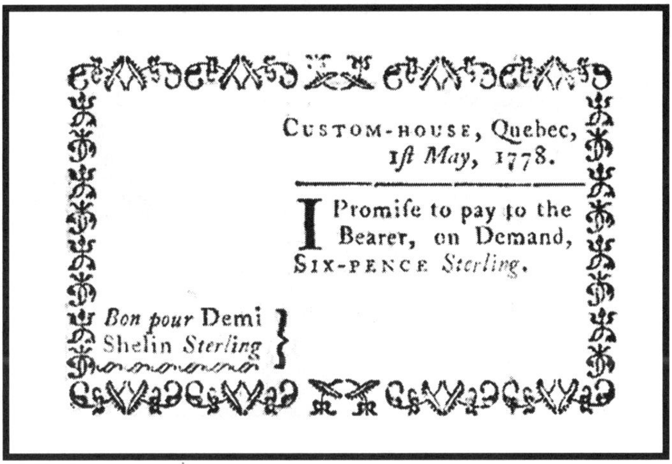

MU-24

Face Design: Wording only
Colour: Black
Back Design: Plain
Issue Date: Engraved: May 1, 1778
Imprint: Unknown
Signatures: Unknown

Cat.No.	Denom.	Issue Date	G	VG	F	VF	EF	Unc
MU-24	6d. (stg.)	1778	ALL VERY RARE Estimate: G $1,500. VG $5,000.					

CITY OF SAINT JOHN

I. First Issue

Notes of this issue measure approximately 1 3/4 by 3 inches.

MU-25 **Photo Not Available**

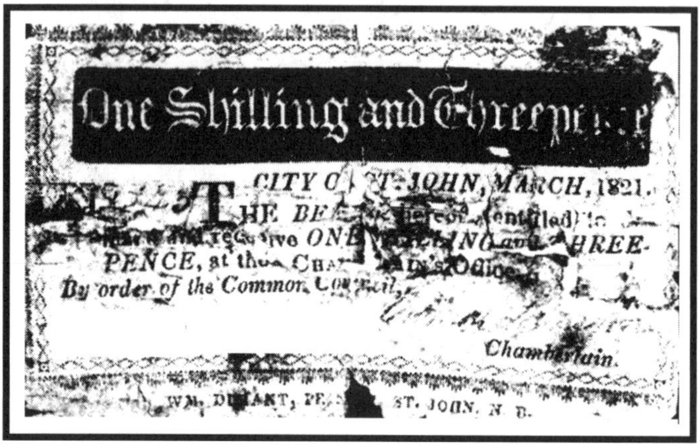

MU-26

Face Design: Wording only **Back Design:** Plain
Colour: Black

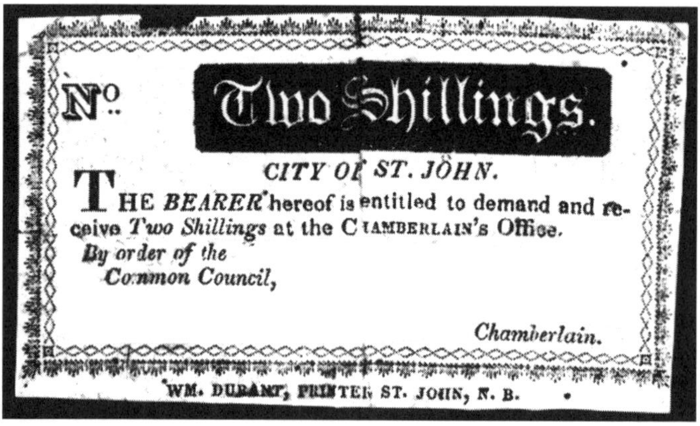

MU-27

Face Design: Wording only **Back Design:** Plain
Colour: Black
Issue Date: Undated or engraved: March, 1821 **Imprint:** Wm. Durant, Printer, St. John N.B.

Signatures

Left: Thomas A. Sancton **Right:** C.J. Peters

Cat.No.	Denom.	Issue Date	G	VG	F	VF	EF	Unc
MU-25	6d.	1821						
MU-26	1s.3d.	1821				ALL RARE		
MU-27	2s.	(1821)			Estimate: G $1,000. VG $5,000.			

II. Second Issue

This 1836 issue is unusual in that the denomination is not engraved on the notes, but is added in manuscript form in the space provided. Many of the surviving notes are remainders, in some cases partially completed. The lathework border reads “City of Saint John/Province of/New Brunswick/North America.”

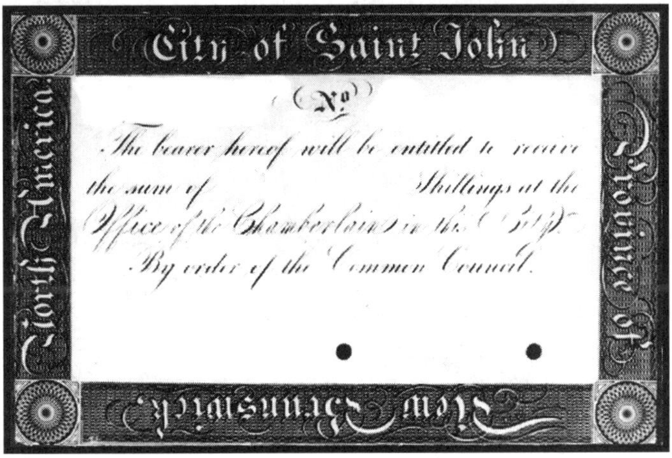

MU-28, 29

Face Design: Wording only
Colour: Black
Back Design: Plain
Issue Date: mss. May 26, 1836
Imprint: None

Signatures

Left: mss. various
Right: mss. various

Cat.No.	Denom.	Issue Date	G	VG	F	VF	EF	Unc
MU-28	2s.	1836				ALL RARE		
MU-29	4s.	1836		Estimate: G $1,000. VG $5,000.				

III. Third Issue 1837

Notes of this issue return to the normal printed denomination. The border consists of arcs and rays. Surviving notes that present a crude lithographed appearance are probably contemporary counterfeits.

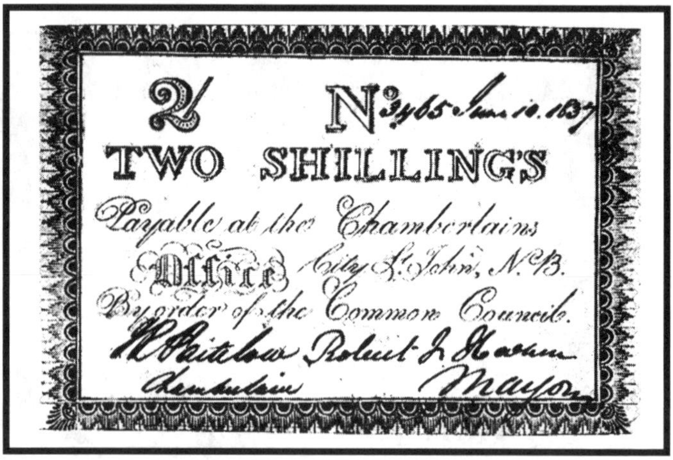

MU-30

Face Design: Wording only
Colour: Black
Back Design: Plain

MU-31

PHOTO NOT AVAILABLE

Face Design: Wording only
Colour: Black
Back Design: Plain
Issue Date: mss. June 10, 1837
Imprint: None

Signatures

Left: mss. various
Right: mss various

Cat.No.	Denom.	Issue Date	G	VG	F	VF	EF	Unc
MU-30	2s.	1837				ALL RARE		
MU-31	4s.	1837				Estimate: G $1,000. VG $5,000.		

CITY OF TORONTO

UPPER CANADA

The City of Toronto issued Corporation Notes, payable in one year with interest, to pay for public works projects. The notes were repaid with taxation revenue. The first issue, in 1837, was prompted by the refusal of the chartered and private banks to lend money to the city. New issues followed annually, and notes of the previous year were withdrawn and cancelled. In 1848 it was decided that better means of financing existed, and the gradual termination of the issue was planned. The last Corporation Notes were issued in 1852.

I. Fractional Issue of 1837

No notes of this first issue are known to have survived. The denomination, designs and imprint are unknown.

II. Burton, Gurley & Edmonds Printings 1837-c.1839

MU-32

Face Design: Crest/Royal Crest/Indian
Colour: Black
Back Design: Plain

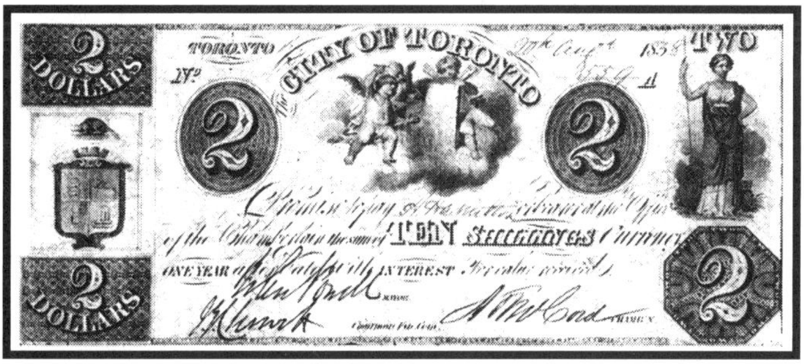

MU-33

Face Design: Crest/cherubs and tablet/woman with spear
Colour: Black
Back Design: Plain
Issue Date: Partially engraved: ____1837, Dec. 26, 1837
Partially engraved: ____183_, Aug. 20, 1838 (one or two)
Imprint: Burton, Gurley & Edmonds, New York

Signatures

Left: mss. various
Right: mss. A.T. McCord

Cat.No.	Denom.	Issue Date	G	VG	F	VF	EF	Unc
MU-32	$1	1837-1839	500.	1,200.	2,000.	3,000.	5,000.	7,000.
MU-33	$2	1837-1839	500.	1,200.	2,000.	3,000.	5,000.	7,000.

III. J. Ellis Printing c.1840-1847

Around 1840 it was decided to have the Corporation notes printed locally. The designs present a somewhat crude appearance. The illustration below is of a counterfeit $1 (5s.) note.

MU-34

Face Design: Crest/Royal Crest/Indian
Colour: Black
Back Design: Plain

MU-35

Face Design: Crest/woman, bales and ship/standing woman
Colour: Black
Back Design: Plain
Issue Date: Engraved:____184_ ; Various dates.
Imprint: J. Ellis Engraver, Toronto

Signatures

Left: mss. various
Right: A.T. McCord

Cat.No.	Denom.	Issue Date	G	VG	F	VF	EF	Unc
MU-34	$1	1841-1847	500.	1,200.	2,000.	3,000.	—	—
MU-35	$2	1841-1847	500.	1,200.	2,000.	3,000.	—	—

IV. J. Ellis Printing 1848-1852

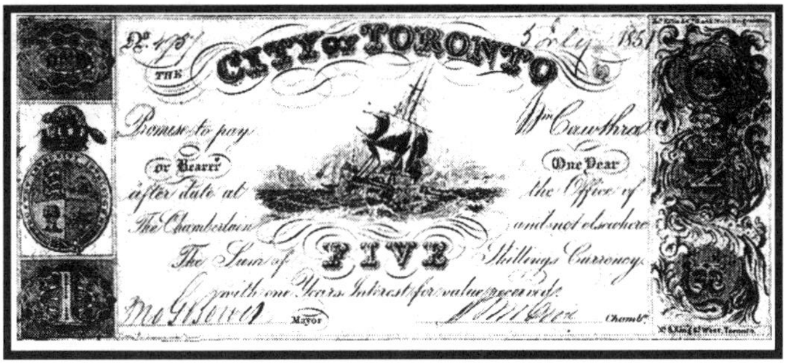

MU-36

Face Design: Crest/sailing ships/—
Colour: Black
Back Design: Plain

MU-37

Face Design: Crest/seated woman with plaque/—
Colour: Black
Back Design: Plain

MU-38

Face Design: Crest/city dockside scene/—
Colour: Black
Face Engraved: "Promise to pay to Wm Cawthra - - one year after date."
Back Design: Plain
Issue Date: Partially engraved: ____184_;
Partially engraved: ____185_; Various dates.
Imprint: Jno. Ellis & Co. Bank Note Engravers, 8 King St. West, Toronto

Signatures

Left: mss. various **Right:** mss. A.T. McCord

Cat.No.	Denom.	Issue Date	G	VG	F	VF	EF	Unc
MU-36	$1 (5s.)	1848-52	500.	1,200.	2,000.	3,000.	5,000.	7,000.
MU-37	$2 (10s.)	1848-52	500.	1,200.	2,000.	3,000.	5,000.	7,000.
MU-38	$4 (£1)	1848-52	500.	1,200.	2,000.	3,000.	5,000.	7,000.

Warning: Contemporary counterfeits probably outnumber genuine Corporation Notes. The counterfeits are usually badly faded, and in many cases, the imprint is omitted.

PROVINCE OF CANADA ISSUES

The Province of Canada was formed by the Act of Union of 1841, which united the former colonies of Upper Canada (Ontario) and Lower Canada (Quebec) under a single government. The seat of government was alternatively located in Kingston, Montreal, Toronto and Quebec, until Queen Victoria selected Ottawa to be the permanent capital. The Province was constantly searching for sources from which money could be borrowed to finance such public works as canal construction. Often the credit of the colony was exhausted and a government note issue was eyed as a means of raising an interest-free loan. The banks naturally united to resist this intrusion into what had been their exclusive preserve, until Edwin King, President of the Bank of Montreal and the "Napoleon of Canadian banking," brought his corporation into a brief partnership with the government. The Province of Canada was as unsatisfactory politically as it was financially, and it passed into history with Confederation in 1867.

PROVINCIAL DEBENTURES 1848-1850s

In 1848 the government of the Province of Canada, of which Francis Hincks was a member, had to raise funds to meet financial obligations contracted by the previous administration. Unable to borrow either from the financial houses of Great Britain or from the banks at home, the government with Hincks' guidance issued debentures bearing 6 percent interest. The debentures had the appearance of regular bank notes; they were of small, convenient denominations like bank notes, and they were transferable and reissuable. Although they were only payable in specie one year from the date of issue, they were accepted at any time in payment of accounts due the government.

These were effectively the first Province of Canada notes, and although they circulated but briefly, the success of the issue paved the way for future experiments in government-issued currency. Only face proofs are known to have survived. We list them here, although specific numbers are not assigned to them.

$1 (5s.)

Face Design: —/seated allegorical female with farm implements, highway and train in background/—
Colour: Black
Protector: Red
Back Design: Unknown
Colour: Unknown
Signatures: Unknown

$2 (10s.)

Face Design: —/two seated allegorical women with cornucopia and spear/—
Colour: Black
Protector: Red
Back Design: Unknown
Colour: Unknown
Signatures: Unknown

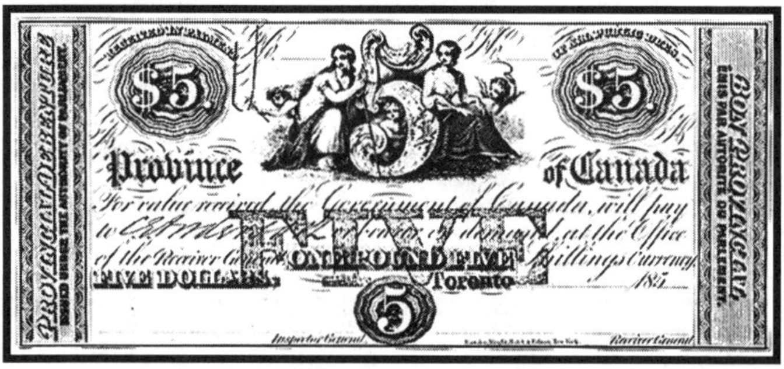

$5 (£1.50)

Face Design: —/three cherubs and two allegorical women surrounding the numeral five/—
Colour: Black,
Protector: Red five
Back Design: Plain
Colour: Unknown
Signatures: Unknown

$10 (£2.10)

Face Design: —/seated Britannia and Coat of Arms of the Province of Canada/—
Colour: Black
Protector: Red
Back Design: Unknown
Colour: Unknown
Signatures: Unknown

$20 (£5)

Face Design: —/Royal Crest/—
Colour: Black
Back Design: Unknown
Colour: Unknown
Issue Date: Paritally Engraved:____185_
Imprint: Rawdon, Wright, Hatch & Edson, New York
Signatures: Unknown

Denomination	Date	Unc
$1 (5s.)	185-	Face Proof $500.
$2 (10s.)	185-	Face Proof $500.
$5 (£1.5)	185-	Face Proof $1,000.
$10 (£2.10)	185-	Face Proof $500.
$20 (£5)	185-	Face Proof $500.

OVERPRINTED BANK OF MONTREAL NOTE ISSUE

In 1866 the Provincial Note Act was passed as a means to providing the government with funds, all other attempts to raise a loan at reasonable interest having failed. Under its terms, any chartered bank that agreed to surrender its own note issuing privileges could arrange with the government to be an issuing agent for the Provincial notes. Only the Bank of Montreal found the various inducements sufficiently attractive to participate in the plan.

Since the new Province of Canada notes had not yet been prepared in sufficient quantities, stocks of unissued Bank of Montreal notes were overprinted as a temporary measure. Denominations of $4, $5, $10, $20, $50 and $100 of various dates of issue from 1849 to 1862 were overprinted. The overprint, in green or blue, reads "PROVINCIAL NOTE/LEGAL TENDER" horizontally and "PAYABLE IN MONTREAL" or "PAYABLE IN TORONTO" and "FOR THE RECEIVER GENERAL" vertically. The notes were initialled by one of seven persons authorized by the Receiver General and signed by one of the officers of the bank.

These notes entered circulation from September to December 1866, when enough of the new Province of Canada notes were on hand to replace them. The overprinted "Legal Tenders" were then rapidly withdrawn. Three whole notes and some fragments produced during the process of cancelling others are known. For further details on the Bank of Montreal Issues please see *The Charlton Standard Catalogue of Canadian Bank Notes, Third Edition.*

Quantities of Bank of Monteal Notes Overprinted

Denomination	Payable at Montreal	Payable at Toronto
$4	119,000	36,000
$5	68,000	49,000
$10	77,500	41,000
$20	2,500	500
$50	2,500	1,100
$100	2,500	1,200

See Bank of Montreal Issues 505-20 to 505-32 in *The Charlton Standard Catalogue of Canadian Bank Notes* for information on designs, colours, issue dates, signatures and imprints.

Cat.No.	Denom.	Issue Date	G	VG	F	VF	EF	Unc
PC-1a to PC-1f	$4-$100	1849-62		ALL VERY RARE Estimate: $3,000. to $10,000.				

ISSUES OF 1866

The new notes issued in the name of the Province of Canada and dated at Ottawa entered circulation in January 1867, just a few months before Confederation, when the Province of Canada would disappear as a political entity. The notes however continued to be issued for several years and were the first issued by the government of the new Dominion of Canada.

Most of the plates were prepared by the American Bank Note Company in New York, but the government had arranged for a new Ottawa firm, the British American Bank Note Company, to do all of the printing. The latter company also engraved the plates for the higher denominations. The notes were printed in denominations of $1, $2, $5, $10, $20, $50, $100 and $500. The $1, $2, and $5 notes were each printed from 4/on plates with check letters A, B, C and D. The $10 and $20 notes were printed from a mixed plate, arranged 10.10.10.20 with check letters A, B, C, A. The $50 and $100 notes were each printed from 2/on plates with check letters A and B while the $500 note was printed from a 1/on plate with the check letter A. The $100 notes were never issued because the Bank of Montreal, still acting as the government's issuing agent, never asked for them, despite reminders that quantities of the notes were available.

The notes were domiciled; that is they were made redeemable in specie (gold) at specific branches of the Receiver General's Office. Originally such branches were set up in Montreal and Toronto. The notes were domiciled by having the location printed vertically in green using separate engraved plates up to the $20. Montreal notes have blue sheet numbers and Toronto notes have red sheet numbers.

All denominations were printed with the engraved signature of the Deputy Receiver General, T. D. Harington. The notes were countersigned at the left by Bank of Montreal personnel, in space designated "Countersigned for Provincial Agents." Plate numbers are present on most of the notes up to $20 and absent on the higher denominations.

All denominations are marked "Canada Bank Note Printing Tint" on the faces. This refers to the green tint used on all the Province of Canada notes. (Distinctive colours for each denomination were not a feature of Canadian government notes until after the printing contracts were taken from the British American Bank Note Co. in 1897.) This patented green ink was considered proof against photographic counterfeiting and was considered by some at the time to be a major development in bank note security.

Summary of Technical Details for 1866 Issues

Cat.No.	Denom.	Variety	Serial Numbers	Quantity Printed
PC-2a	$1	Montreal	000001 - 187500/A,B,C,D	750,000 (est.)
PC-2b	$1	Toronto	00001 - 22000	
			47001 - 62500/A,B,C,D	150,000 (est.)
PC-2c	$1	Toronto, o/p St. John	22001 - 47000/A,B,C,D	100,000
PC-3a	$2	Montreal	000001 - 187500/A,B,C,D	750,000 (est.)
PC-3b	$2	Toronto	00001 - 24000	
			36501 - 62500/A,B,C,D	200,000 (est.)
PC-3c	$2	Toronto, o/p St. John	24001 - 36500/A,B,C,D	50,000
PC-4a	$5	Montreal	000001 - 093750/A,B,C,D	375,000 (est.)
PC-4b	$5	Toronto	00001 - 17000	
			30751 - 31250/A,B,C,D	70,000
PC-4c	$5	Toronto, o/p St. John	17001 - 30750/A,B,C,D	55,000
PC-4d	$5	Halifax	00001 - 25000/A,B,C,D	100,000
PC-5a	$10	Montreal	000001 - 045000/A,B,C	135,000 (est.)
PC-5b	$10	Toronto	00001 - 12000/A,B,C	36,000
PC-5c	$10	Toronto, o/p St. John	12001 - 16000/A,B,C	12,000
PC-6a	$20	Montreal	000001 - 045000/A	45,000 (est.)
PC-6b	$20	Toronto	00001 - 12000/A	12,000 (est.)
PC-6c	$20	Toronto, o/p St. John	12001 - 16000/A	4,000
PC-7a	$50	Montreal	0001 - 4000/A,B	8,000 (est.)
PC-7b	$50	Toronto	0001 - 2000/A,B	4,000 (est.)
PC-7c	$50	Toronto, o/p St. John	2001 - 4000/A,B	4,000
PC-8a	$100	Montreal	0001 - 1250/A,B	2,500 (est.)
				(none issued)
PC-8b	$100	Toronto	0001 - 0875/A,B	1,750 (est.)
				(none issued)
PC-9a	$500	Montreal	0001 - 3000/A	3,000 (est.)
PC-9b	$500	Toronto	0001 - 2000/A	2,000 (est.)

$1 Issue — 1866

PC-2a

Face Design: Samuel de Champlain/Coat of Arms of the Province of Canada with sailor and farmer/Jacques Cartier (Riss portrait)
Colour: Black with green tint (See varieties)

PC-2a

Back Design: Lathework, counters and The Province of Canada
Colour: Green
Issue Date: Engraved: October 1st 1866
Imprint - Face: American Bank Note Co. New York;
British American Bank Note Co. Montreal and Ottawa
Back: American Bank Note Co. N.Y
Printer: British American Bank Note Company

Signatures

Left: mss. various **Right:** Engr.: T.D. Harington

Overprint

Toronto Notes: "ST. JOHN" in blue

It is possible that some notes were overprinted "ST. JOHN N.B.," but this has not been confirmed.

Varieties

Face Design: "PAYABLE AT MONTREAL" in green vertically flanking central vignette
"PAYABLE AT TORONTO" in green vertically flanking central vignette

Cat.No.	Denom.	Variety	G	VG	F	VF	EF	Unc
PC-2a	$1	Montreal	700.	1,200.	2,200.	3,100.	4,250.	—
PC-2b	$1	Toronto	800.	1,400.	2,500.	3,500.	5,000.	—
PC-2c	$1	Toronto, o/p St. John	2,500.	5,000.	7,500.	13,000.	—	—

$2 Issue — 1866

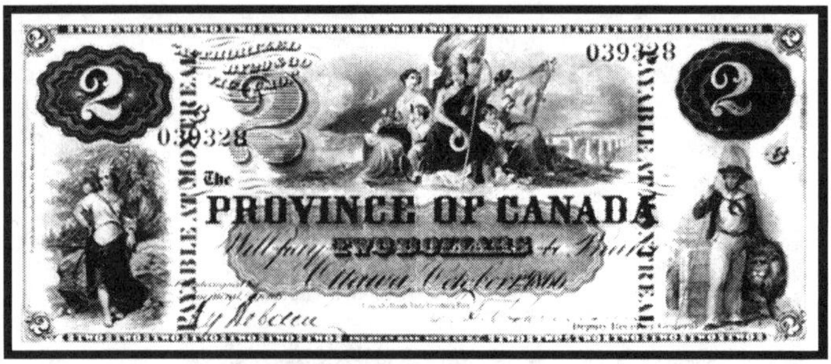

PC-3a

Face Design: Indian girl/seated Britannia with two allegorical women and boys, train and trestle in background/sailor holding flag, lion
Colour: Black with green tint (See varieties)

PC-3a

Back Design: Lathework, counters and Province of Canada
Colour: Green
Issue Date: Engraved: October 1st 1866
Imprint - Face: American Bank Note Co. N.Y. and
British American Bank Note Co. Montreal and Ottawa
Back: American Bank Note Co. N.Y
Printer: British American Bank Note Company

Signatures

Left: mss. various
Right: Engr.: T.D. Harington

Overprint

Toronto Notes: “ST. JOHN” in blue

It is possible that some notes were overprinted “ST. JOHN N.B.” but this has not been confirmed.

Varieties

Face Design: PAYABLE AT MONTREAL in green vertically flanking central vignette
PAYABLE AT TORONTO in green vertically flanking central vignette

Cat.No.	Denom.	Variety	G	VG	F	VF	EF	Unc
PC-3a	$2	Montreal	1,300.	2,500.	3,500.	4,500.	7,500.	—
PC-3b	$2	Toronto	1,500.	2,750.	4,000.	6,000.	—	—
PC-3c	$2	Toronto, o/p St. John	3,000.	5,000.	7,500.	—	—	—

$5 Issue — 1866

PC-4d

Face Design: Queen Victoria (Winterhalter portrait)/Coat of Arms of the Province of Canada with Indian Princess and lion/ship under sail
Colour: Black with green tint (See varieties)

PC-4

Back Design: Lathework, counters and "The Province of Canada"
Colour: Green
Issue Date: Engraved: Oct. 1, 1866
Imprint: American Bank Note Co. New York and British American Bank Note Co., Montreal and Ottawa
Printer: British American Bank Note Company

Signatures

Left: mss. various
Right: Engr.: T.D. Harington

Overprint

Toronto Notes: "ST. JOHN" in blue

It is possible that some notes were overprinted "ST. JOHN N.B." but this has not been confirmed.

Varieties

Face Design: PAYABLE AT HALIFAX/ONLY vertically flanking central vignette
PAYABLE AT MONTREAL vertically flanking central vignette
PAYABLE AT TORONTO vertically flanking central vignette

Cat.No.	Denom.	Variety	G	VG	F	VF	EF	Unc
PC-4a	$5	Montreal	2,500.	5,000.	10,000.	15,000.	—	—
PC-4b	$5	Toronto	2,500.	6,000.	11,000.	16,000.	—	—
PC-4c	$5	Toronto, o/p St. John	4,000.	7,500.	12,000.	18,000.	—	—
PC-4d	$5	Halifax	4,000.	7,500.	12,000.	18,000.	—	—

$10 Issue — 1866

PC-5a

Face Design: Columbus and sailors/lion, sheaf of wheat, train, anchor and sailing ships/two beavers
Colour: Black with green tint (See varieties)

PC-5

Back Design: Lathework, counters and Province of Canada
Colour: Green
Issue Date: Engraved: Oct. 1, 1866
Imprint - Face: American Bank Note Co. N.Y. and British American Bank Note Co. Montreal and Ottawa
Back: American Bank Note Co. New York
Printer: British American Bank Note Company

Signatures

Left: mss. various
Right: Engr.: T.D. Harington

Overprint

Toronto Notes: "ST. JOHN" in blue

It is possible that some notes were overprinted "ST. JOHN N.B." but this has not been confirmed.

Varieties

Face Design: PAYABLE AT MONTREAL in green vertically flanking central vignette
PAYABLE AT TORONTO in green vertically flanking central vignette

Cat.No.	Denom.	Variety	G	VG	F	VF	EF	Unc
PC-5a	$10	Montreal	8,000.	15,000.	18,000.	30,000.	—	—
PC-5bFP	$10	Toronto				Face Proof		$1,200.
PC-5c	$10	Toronto, o/p St. John			Surviving Examples Not Confirmed			

Note: No Toronto or overprinted St. John issued notes are known. Only three Montreal issued notes are known to exist.

$20 Issue — 1866

PC-6a

Face Design: Princess of Wales/four beavers building a dam/Prince Albert
Colour: Black with green tint (See varieties)

PC-6

Back Design: Lathework, counters and Province of Canada
Colour: Green
Issue Date: Engraved: October 1st 1866
Imprint - Face: American Bank Note Co. New York and British American Bank Note Co. Montreal & Ottawa
Back: American Bank Note Co. N.Y
Printer: British American Bank Note Company

Signatures

Left: mss. various **Right:** Engr.: T.D. Harington

Overprint: Toronto Notes: “ST. JOHN” in blue

It is possible that some notes were overprinted “ST. JOHN N.B.,” but this has not been confirmed.

Varieties

Face Design: PAYABLE AT MONTREAL in green vertically flanking central vignette
PAYABLE AT TORONTO in green vertically flanking central vignette

Cat.No.	Denom.	Variety	G	VG	F	VF	EF	Unc
PC-6FP	$20	Proof, No Tint				Face Proof		1,200.
PC-6a	$20	Montreal	10,000.	20,000.	30,000.			
PC-6b	$20	Toronto		Surviving Examples Not Confirmed				
PC-6c	$20	Toronto, o/p St. John		Surviving Examples Not Confirmed				

Note: No Toronto or overprinted St. John issued notes are known. Only one Montreal issued note is known.

$50 Issue — 1866

PC-7a

Face Design: —/Mercury holding map of British North America, harbour, ships, train/—
Colour: Black with green tint (See Varieties)

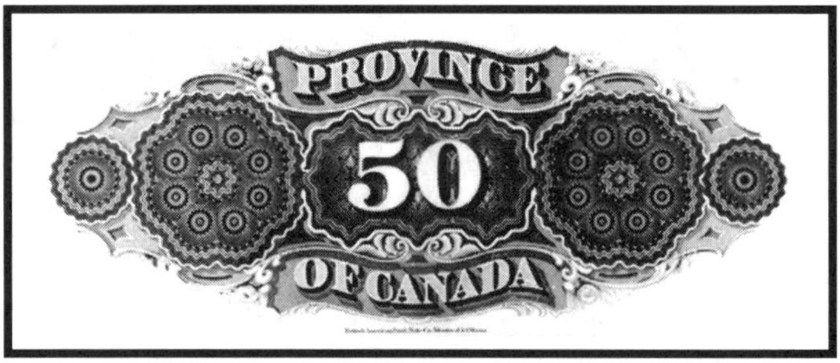

PC-7

Back Design: Lathework, counters and Province of Canada.
Colour: Green
Issue Date: Engraved: October 1st 1866
Imprint - Face: British American Bank Note Co.
Back: British American Bank Note Co. Montreal & Ottawa
Printer: British American Bank Note Company

Signatures

Left: mss. various
Right: Engr.: T.D. Harington

Overprint

Toronto Notes: "ST. JOHN" in blue

It is possible that some notes were overprinted "ST. JOHN N.B." but this has not been confirmed.

Varieties

Face Design: PAYABLE AT MONTREAL horizontally flanking central vignette
PAYABLE AT TORONTO horizontally flanking central vignette

Cat.No.	Denom.	Variety	G	VG	F	VF	EF	Unc
PC-7a	$50	Montreal		Only One Known				$30,000.
PC-7bFP	$50	Toronto				Face Proof		1,200.
PC-7c	$50	Toronto, o/p St. John				Surviving Examples Not Confirmed		

$100 Issue — 1866

PC-8a

Face Design: —/Queen Victoria (Chalon portrait)/—
Colour: Black with green tint (See varieties)

PC-8

Back Design: Lathework, counters and Province of Canada
Colour: Green
Issue Date: Engraved: October 1st 1866
Imprint: British American Bank Note Company
Printer: British American Bank Note Company

Signatures

Left: None
Right: Engr.: T.D. Harington

Varieties

Face Design: PAYABLE AT MONTREAL horizontally flanking central vignette
PAYABLE AT TORONTO horizontally flanking central vignette

Cat.No.	Denom.	Variety	G	VG	F	VF	EF	Unc
PC-8aFP	$100	Montreal			Face proof			1,200.
PC-8bFP	$100	Toronto			Face proof			1,200.

$500 Issue — 1866

PC-9a

Face Design: —/allegorical female and Coat of Arms of the Province of Canada with lion, wheat, bridge and Parliament Building in background/—
Colour: Black with green tint (See varieties)

PC-9

Back Design: Lathework, counters and Province of Canada.
Colour: Green
Issue Date: Engraved: October 1st 1866
Imprint - Face: British American Bank Note Co. Montreal & Ottawa
Back: British American Bank Note Co. Montreal & Ottawa
Printer: British American Bank Note Company

Signatures

Left: None
Right: Engr.: T.D. Harington

Varieties

Face Design: PAYABLE AT MONTREAL horizontally flanking central vignette
PAYABLE AT TORONTO horizontally flanking central vignette

Cat.No.	Denom.	Variety	G	VG	F	VF	EF	Unc
PC-9aFP	$500	Montreal			Face proof			1,200.
PC-9bFP	$500	Toronto			Face proof			1,200.

PROVINCIAL NOTES ISSUED BY THE DOMINION OF CANADA

Since Confederation took place only nine months after the Province of Canada notes began to enter circulation, large stockpiles were still on hand in the vaults of the Deputy Receiver General and the Bank of Montreal. It was decided to continue issuing these provincial notes under the authority of the Dominion of Canada, so that they effectively became the first issue of Dominion notes. This decision was given legal sanction by an act of May 1868 that virtually repeated the Provincial Note Act of 1866, with the term "Dominion" being substituted for "Provincial."

To avoid confusion, and since those notes issued under Provincial and Dominion authority are not completely separable, all will be listed here as Province of Canada issues, consistent with the name on the notes themselves.

With the addition of the provinces of New Brunswick and Nova Scotia to the federal union, provision had to be made to supply these provinces with government notes. Notes destined for issue in New Brunswick were overprinted "ST. JOHN" in large blue letters across the faces, and were issued through newly established Bank of Montreal branches in the province. These notes have red sheet numbers, since Toronto notes were used for overprinting.

Providing notes for Nova Scotia presented a special problem. The currency of Nova Scotia was not assimilated to that of the rest of Canada until 1871. The province was very attached to sterling and rated the pound sterling at $5.00 Nova Scotia currency, while it rated only $4.86 2/3 in Canada currency. Only $5 Province of Canada notes were sent for issue in Nova Scotia. These were not overprinted Toronto or Montreal notes, but a special printing expressly for use there with the legend "PAYABLE IN HALIFAX/ONLY" vertically in green. These had to be kept within Nova Scotia because they were worth only $4.86 2/3 in the rest of the country. Sheet numbers were black for this special issue. These notes and any others payable in Nova Scotia currency had to be withdrawn after July 1, 1871, when that province was put on a uniform currency basis with the rest of Canada.

The government gradually terminated its relationship with the Bank of Montreal from 1870 to 1871. Assistant Receiver General offices were set up in the provincial capitals to take over the government note issue and redemption functions which the Bank of Montreal had handled since 1866. The last few Province of Canada notes to be issued had come from the Receiver General's vault and had never been in the possession of the Bank of Montreal. These notes were signed by Bank of Montreal personnel prior to issue. After 1871 the provincial notes were withdrawn and replaced by Dominion notes. Some stocks of notes from the Receiver General's vault remained unissued and were destroyed.

DOMINION OF CANADA ISSUES

ISSUES OF 1870

The 1870 25¢ Fractional Note

At the time of the American Civil War, U.S. silver coin became depreciated by 5 percent relative to gold. The situation caused American silver, mostly of the 25-cent and 50-cent denominations, to pour into Canada, where it was still received at full face value. Banks and post offices would not accept these coins, so retailers sold them at a discount to brokers, who in turn derived their livelihoods by selling the depreciated silver back to manufacturers and buyers of grain and cattle. Thus the cycle repeated and the "American silver nuisance" resulted in hardship to farmers, merchants and factory workers who had no choice but to accept their losses. The government also suffered, because the $1 and $2 Province of Canada notes, issued by the Dominion government after Confederation, were being crowded out of circulation.

Sir Francis Hincks, minister of Finance in 1870, devised a three-pronged attack on the problem. The government would buy up the American silver at a discount progressing from 5 percent to 6 percent and export it, and then peg its legal value at an artificially low 80¢ on the dollar to ensure against its return to the country. To take its place, the first silver coins for the Dominion of Canada were ordered from the Royal Mint in London. Finally, as a temporary measure, 25-cent fractional notes were to be printed and issued to provide change while the new coinage was being prepared.

The banks were opposed to the introduction of the paper "shinplasters," but the fact that they were redeemable in gold when presented in quantity went a long way toward making the fractional notes acceptable.

Hincks' manoeuvres were eminently successful. Enough American silver was repatriated to New York to saturate the markets there, and the remainder was shipped to England as bullion. There was one unexpected outcome, however, far from being a temporary issue as planned, the fractional notes became popular with the public and persisted in circulation for the next 65 years.

Many attribute the expression "shinplaster" to the use of fractional U.S. notes by soldiers of the Revolutionary War period to prevent their boots from chafing. The term was first used in Canada with reference to the merchants' scrip which appeared in abundance from 1837 to 1838. Subsequently it came to be applied to 25-cent Dominion of Canada notes from the time of their first appearance in 1870.

Details of the Printing

The 25-cent fractionals were printed in sheets of ten (two across and five down), with no sheet numbers, no check letters and no plate numbers. Eight face plates, 14 tints and ten back plates were prepared, all in 1870. From these were printed three series of notes. The A series (letter A under the 1870 at the left), consisting of 2,000,000 notes with a total value of $500,000, was issued in 1870. Once the new Dominion silver coinage of 1870 arrived, the need for fractional notes diminished greatly. The B series, also consisting of 2,000,000 notes or $500,000, was printed by 1871 and issued slowly over the period 1871 to 1897, as needed. The plain or no letter series was printed in the 1890s from the old plates, which were modified by the removal of the series letter. Traces of the former series letter can be found on many of these notes. Only about 300,000 of these notes, or $75,000, were issued, but they remain the most readily available to collectors, having been issued most recently.

Summary of Technical Details

Cat.No.	Denom.	Date	Series	Serial Numbers	Quantity Printed
DC-1a	25¢	1870	A	None	2,000,000
DC-1b	25¢	1870	B	None	2,000,000
DC-1c	25¢	1870	Plain	None	300,000 (est.)

DC-1c

Face Design: —/Britannia/—
Colour: Black with green "25" tint

DC-1c

Back Design: Lathework and "redeemable on presentation at Montreal, Toronto or St. John"
Colour: Green
Issue Date: Engraved: March 1st 1870
Imprint: British American Bank Note Co. Montreal & Ottawa

Signatures

Left: Engr.: W. Dickinson
Right: Engr.: T.D. Harington

Varieties

This issue carried no serial numbers but had series letters which are immediately below the 1870 of the left hand date on the face of the note. The letter "B" below the left date shows considerable variation. On each sheet of ten notes, six notes present a large B and four notes a small B. Further subvariants are being researched.

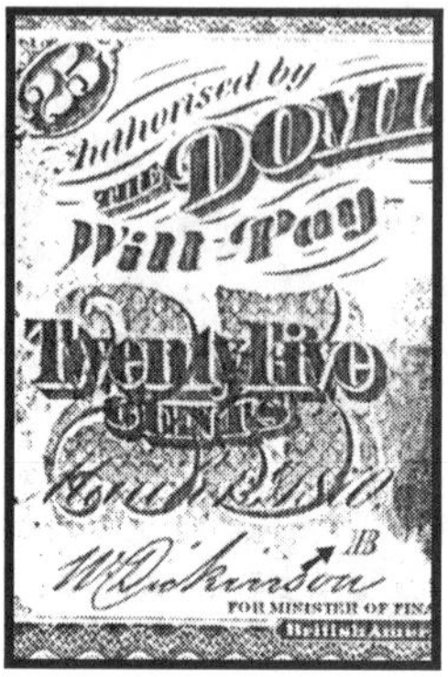

Large B

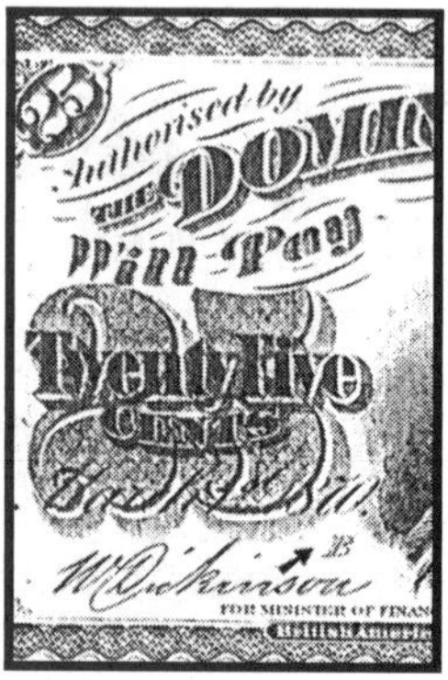

Small B

Series Letter A

Series Letter B

Plain (no series letter)

Cat.No.	Denom.	Series	G	VG	F	VF	EF	AU	Unc
DC-1a	25¢	A	150.	375.	600.	900.	1,400.	2,250.	3,000
DC-1a	25¢	A, sheet of 10	—	—	—	11,000.	17,000.	—	—
DC-1b	25¢	B	20.	55.	90.	160.	450.	750.	1,350.
DC-1b	25¢	B, uncut pair	—	—	250.	—	—	—	—
DC-1b	25¢	B, large letter B	20.	55.	90.	160.	450.	750.	1,350.
DC-1b-i	25¢	B, small letter B	20.	55.	90.	160.	450.	750.	1,350.
DC-1c	25¢	Plain	15.	35.	60.	125.	350.	600.	1,000.
DC-1c	25¢	Plain Uncut Pair	—	125.	175.	300.	650.	—	—
DC-1c	25¢	Plain Uncut strip/block of 4 notes	—	300.	450.	700.	1,400.	—	—

The 1870 $1 and $2 Notes

Apart from the fractionals, these are the only other denominations of this issue to enter ordinary circulation in quantity. Unlike the fractionals, which were redeemable in Montreal, Toronto or St. John, the $1 and $2 notes were specifically designated on their backs as being payable in Montreal, Toronto, St. John, Halifax or Victoria. The back design was different for each city. The only difference on the faces occurred in the sheet numbers, which were partially colour coded as follows:

Montreal	blue	6-digit numbers	Halifax	black	5-digit numbers
Toronto	red	6-digit numbers	Victoria	blue	5-digit numbers
St. John	black	5-digit numbers			

Special backs were not engraved for the notes issued by the Assistant Receiver General at Winnipeg. However, at least some of the notes were stamped MANITOBA vertically in black ink across the right end of the faces of Toronto and Montreal notes. The purpose behind rubber stamping these notes appears to have been to establish their migration pattern, rather than to indicate that they were payable at Winnipeg. Three $1 and two $2 notes with the MANITOBA stamp are known to have survived.

The engraved signatures are those of William Dickinson, Inspector General, on the space "For Minister of Finance" and T. D. Harington, Deputy Receiver General, in the space "For Receiver General." A third manuscript signature occurs vertically across the left end of the face, except for the Halifax notes, where it is sometimes found across the right end. These countersignatures were applied either in Ottawa or at the offices of the various Assistant Receivers General.

Both denominations are dated July 1st, 1870, although they were not released for circulation until well into 1871. The provincial notes were thereafter eventually withdrawn.

The $1 note has a fine portrait of Jacques Cartier at the left and an allegorical vignette called "Canada" at the centre. The Cartier portrait is taken from a painting by F. Riss (circa 1840-1866). It hangs in the Hotel de Ville of St. Malo, the port from which Cartier sailed on his memorable voyage to the New World in 1534. Riss is said to have taken as his model a pen drawing in the Bibliotheque Nationale, Paris, but this drawing has never been located. Of all the denominations of the first Dominion note issue, the $1 alone lacks any reference to the authorizing legislation (31 Vict. cap. 36).

The $2 note has at the left end a portrait of General Wolfe and at the right end a portrait of General Montcalm, both of whom were killed on the Plains of Abraham in 1759. The centre vignette, called "Civilization" or "Nor 'West" shows an Indian seated on a bluff, watching a train passing below.

The $1 Toronto notes were counterfeited extensively. The counterfeits can be identified by the presence of a coarse black dot for Cartier's eye.

The $1 and $2 notes were printed from 4/on plates, with check letter A, B, C and D. The $1 notes bear plate numbers at the right of the check letters, while the $2 notes have them at the right of, or below, the check letters, or have none at all.

Summary of Technical Details

Cat.No.	Denom.	Date	Variety	Series	Serial Numbers	Quantity Printed
DC-2a	$1	1870	Montreal	Plain	000001-650000/A,B,C,D	2,600,000 (est.)
DC-2b	$1	1870	Toronto	Plain	000001-587500/A,B,C,D	2,250,000 (est.)
DC-2c	$1	1870	St. John	Plain	00001-75000/A.B.C,D	300,000 (est.)
DC-2d	$1	1870	Halifax	Plain	00001-110000/A,B,C,D	440,000 (est.)
DC-2e	$1	1870	Victoria	Plain	00001-12500/A,B,C,D	50,000 (est.)
DC-3a	$2	1870	Montreal	Plain	000001-191000/A,B,C,D	764,000 (est.)
DC-3b	$2	1870	Toronto	Plain	000001-182000/A,B,C,D	728,000 (est.)
DC-3c	$2	1870	St. John	Plain	00001-37500/A,B,C,D	150,000 (est.)
DC-3d	$2	1870	Halifax	Plain	00001-100000/A,B,C,D	400,000 (est.)
DC-3e	$2	1870	Victoria	Plain	00001-06200/A,B,C,D	24,000 (est.)

$1 Issue — 1870

DC-2a

Face Design: Jacques Cartier (Riss portrait)/allegorical female pointing to Canada's location on a globe,"Canada"/—
Colour: Black with green tint

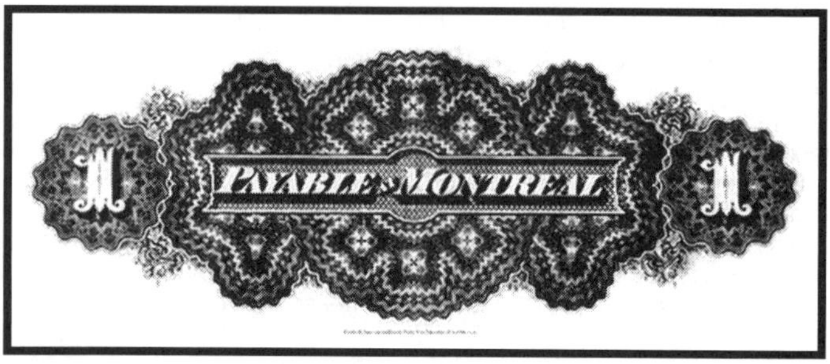

DC-2a

Back Design: Lathework, counters and "Payable at (city name)"
Colour: Green
Issue Date: July 1, 1870
Imprint: British American Bank Note Co. Montreal & Ottawa on the face and back

Signatures

Left: Engr.: W. Dickinson
Additional: mss. various (vertically), usually at the left end
Right: Engr.: T.D. Harington

Varieties

DC-2b

"Manitoba" Stamp

DC-2bii

DC-2c

DC-2d

DC-2e

Stamp: Stamped on the face, to the right of the central vignette, the word "MANITOBA" vertically in black

Back Design: Engraved in the lathework across the back is the location of the Assistant Receiver General's office at which the particular note was payable:
PAYABLE AT MONTREAL
PAYABLE AT TORONTO
PAYABLE AT ST. JOHN
PAYABLE AT HALIFAX
PAYABLE AT VICTORIA (2 known)

Small Date

Large Date

Engraved Date: The Montreal and Toronto notes have a small (SD) and large (LD) engraved date.

Cat.No.	Denom.	Variety	G	VG	F	VF	EF	AU	Unc
DC-2a	$1	Montreal, SD	400.	900.	1,750.	3,500.	5,000.	8,000.	—
DC-2ai	$1	Montreal, LD	400.	900.	1,750.	3,500.	5,000.	8,000.	—
DC-2aii	$1	Montreal, Manitoba	5,000.	—	—	—	—	—	—
DC-2b	$1	Toronto, SD	400.	900.	1,750.	3,500.	5,000.	8,000.	—
DC-2bi	$1	Toronto, LD	400.	900.	1,750.	3,500.	5,000.	8,000.	—
DC-2bii	$1	Toronto, Manitoba	5,000.	8,000.	15,000.	—	—	—	—
DC-2c	$1	St. John	2,000.	4,000.	6,000.	10,000.	—	—	—
DC-2d	$1	Halifax	2,000.	4,000.	6,000.	10,000.	—	—	—
DC-2e	$1	Victoria	5,000.	10,000.	18,000.	—	—	—	—

Note: A partial sheet (3 notes) of DC-2a is known to exist.

$2 Issue — 1870

DC-3a

Face Design: General Wolfe/Indian chief on bluff watching train below, "Nor'West"/General Montcalm
Colour: Black with green tint

DC-3a

Back Design: Lathework, counters and "Payable at (City name)"
Colour: Green
Issue Date: Engraved: July 1st 1870
Imprint: British American Bank Note Co. Montreal & Ottawa on the face and back

Signatures

Left: Engr.: W. Dickinson
Additional: mss. various (vertically), usually at the left end
Right: Engr.: T.D. Harington

DC-3b

"Manitoba" stamp

DC-3a-i

DC-3c

DC-3d

DC-3e

Stamp: Stamped on the face, to the right of the central vignette, the word "MANITOBA" vertically in black

Back Design: Engraved in the lathework across the back is the location of the Assistant Receiver General's office at which the particular note was payable:
PAYABLE AT MONTREAL
PAYABLE AT TORONTO
PAYABLE AT ST. JOHN
PAYABLE AT HALIFAX
PAYABLE AT VICTORIA

Cat.No.	Denom.	Variety	G	VG	F	VF	EF	AU	Unc
DC-3a	$2	Montreal	1,750.	3,500.	5,000.	10,000.	15,000.	—	—
DC-3a-i	$2	Montreal, Manitoba			Surviving Examples Not Confirmed				
DC-3b	$2	Toronto	1,750.	3,500.	5,000.	10,000.	15,000.	—	—
DC-3b-i	$2	Toronto, Manitoba	5,000.	10,000.	20,000.	—	—	—	—
DC-3c	$2	St. John	3,500.	7,000.	12,000.	20,000.	—	—	—
DC-3d	$2	Halifax	3,000.	5,500.	9,000.	15,000.	—	—	—
DC-3e	$2	Victoria			Surviving Examples Not Confirmed				

ISSUES OF 1871-1872

The first and only Dominion notes of $50 and $100 denominations are dated March 1, 1872, and the first $500 and $1000 Dominion notes are dated July 1, 1871. These denominations were primarily held by the chartered banks to secure their note circulation, but they were also legal tender for ordinary transactions. The $50 and $100 notes were too large to find much use among the public and were too small to be convenient for the banks. So small was the demand for them that no other Dominion note issues included these denominations.

Each of the higher denomination notes bears a single vignette at its centre. The vignette of Mercury on the $50 note had formerly been used on the Province of Canada $50. The newly built Parliament Buildings appear on the $100. The Chalon portrait of Queen Victoria is found on the $500 note while the $1000 notes uses the reclining woman and coat of arms vignette previously used on the Province of Canada $500.

Like the $1 and $2 notes of 1870, all of these notes were domiciled, with the city where the notes could be redeemed indicated on their backs. The $50 and $100 were payable in Montreal or Toronto only. The $500 and $1000 were payable originally in Montreal, Toronto, St. John and Halifax. Later, special backs were engraved for Victoria, Winnipeg and Charlottetown. Notes domiciled at the latter two cities were issued in 1891 and 1892 respectively.

The $50 and $100 notes were each printed from 2/on plates, with check letters A and B. The $500 and $1,000 were both printed from a single 2/on plate. The $500 was given check letter A, while the $1,000 had none. No plate numbers seem to have been used, and it is likely that only one set of plates was used in each case. The sheet numbers had only four digits. No signatures were engraved on the plates; all issued notes were signed and countersigned by hand. Proof notes, of course, have no signatures.

These notes are now extremely rare. One Montreal and one Toronto $50, as well as another partial Montreal $50, survive. One fragment of each of $100, $500 and $1,000 notes, all payable in Montreal, survive. All are in the Bank of Canada Currency collection. The last $100 Dominion note was turned in to the Department of Finance in 1918.

Summary of Technical Details

Cat.No.	Denom.	Date	Variety	Series	Serial Numbers	Quantity Printed
DC-4a	$50	1872	Montreal	Plain	0001-.../A,B	Unknown
DC-4b	$50	1872	Toronto	Plain	0001-.../A,B	—
DC-5a	$100	1872	Montreal	Plain	0001-.../A,B	—
DC-5b	$100	1872	Toronto	Plain	0001-.../A,B	—
DC-6a	$500	1871	Montreal	Plain	0001-.../A	—
DC-6b	$500	1871	Toronto	Plain	0001-.../A	—
DC-6c	$500	1871	St. John	Plain	0001-.../A	—
DC-6d	$500	1871	Halifax	Plain	0001-.../A	—
DC-6e	$500	1871	Victoria	Plain	0001-0420/A	420
DC-6f	$500	1871	Winnipeg	Plain	0001-0150/A	150
DC-6g	$500	1871	Charlottetown	Plain	0001-../A	
DC-7a	$1,000	1871	Montreal	Plain	0001	—
DC-7b	$1,000	1871	Toronto	Plain	0001	—
DC-7c	$1,000	1871	St. John	Plain	0001	—
DC-7d	$1,000	1871	Halifax	Plain	0001	—
DC-7e	$1,000	1871	Victoria	Plain	0001-0420	420
DC-7f	$1,000	1871	Winnipeg	Plain	0001-0150	150
DC-7g	$1,000	1871	Charlottetown	Plain	0001	—

$50 Issue — 1872

DC-4FP

Face Design: —/Mercury holding a map of British North America/—
Colour: Black with green tint

DC-4aBP

Back Design: Lathework, counters and "Payable at Montreal"
Colour: Green
Issue Date: Engraved: Mar. 1. 1872
Imprint: British American Bank Note Company

DC-4bBP

Back: Payable at Toronto

Signatures

Left: mss. various
Right: mss. various

Varieties

Engraved in the lathework across the back is the location of the Assistant Receiver General's office at which the particular note was payable:

PAYABLE AT MONTREAL PAYABLE AT TORONTO

These notes were also payable at the Receiver General's office in Ottawa. The word Ottawa is engraved in the left green "50" counter.

Cat.No.	Denom.	Variety	Series	G	VG	F	VF	EF	Unc
DC-4FP	$50	Ottawa	Plain						
DC-4aBP	$50	Montreal	Plain		Some proofs known in Institutions				
DC-4bBP	$50	Toronto	Plain						

$100 Issue — 1872

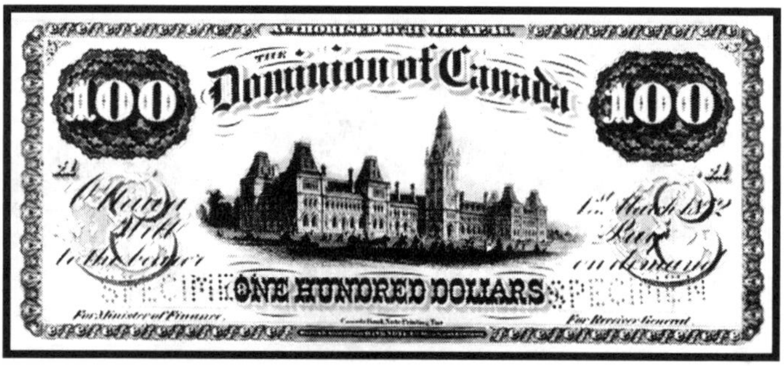

DC-5aFP

Face Design: —/Parliament Buildings/—
Colour: Black with green tint

DC-5aBP

Back Design: Lathework, counter and "Payable at Montreal"
Colour: Green
Issue Date: Engraved: 1st March 1872
Imprint: British American Bank Note Co. Montreal & Ottawa

DC-5bBP

Back: Payable at Toronto

Signatures

Left: mss. various
Right: mss. various

Varieties

Engraved in the lathework across the back is the location of the Assistant Receiver General's office at which the particular note was payable:

PAYABLE AT MONTREAL PAYABLE AT TORONTO

These notes were also payable at the Receiver General's office in Ottawa. The word Ottawa is engraved in the left green "C" counter.

Cat.No.	Denom.	Variety	Series	G	VG	F	VF	EF	Unc
DC-5FP	$100	Ottawa	Plain						
DC-5aBP	$100	Montreal	Plain		Some proofs known in Institutions				
DC-5bBP	$100	Toronto	Plain						

$500 Issue — 1871

DC-6bFP

Face Design: —/Queen Victoria (Chalon portrait)/—
Colour: Black with green tint

DC-6aBP

Back Design: Lathework, counters and "Payable at Montreal"
Colour: Green
Issue Date: July 1st 1871
Imprint: British American Bank Note Co. Montreal and Ottawa

DC-6bBP

Back: Payable at Toronto

DC-6cBP

Back: Payable at St. John

DC-6dBP

Back: Payable at Halifax

Signatures

Left: mss. various
Right: mss. various

Varieties

Engraved in the lathework across the back is the location of the Assistant Receiver General's office at which the particular note was payable:

PAYABLE AT MONTREAL
PAYABLE AT TORONTO
PAYABLE AT ST. JOHN
PAYABLE AT HALIFAX
PAYABLE AT VICTORIA
PAYABLE AT WINNIPEG
PAYABLE AT CHARLOTTETOWN

These notes were also payable at the Receiver General's office in Ottawa. The word Ottawa is engraved in the left green "D" counter.

Cat.No.	Denom.	Variety	Series	G	VG	F	VF	EF	Unc
DC-6FP	$500	Ottawa	Plain						
DC-6aBP	$500	Montreal	Plain						
DC-6bBP	$500	Toronto	Plain						
DC-6cBP	$500	St. John	Plain		Some proofs known in Institutions				
DC-6dBP	$500	Halifax	Plain						
DC-6eBP	$500	Victoria	Plain						
DC-6fBP	$500	Winnipeg	Plain						
DC-6gBP	$500	Charlottetown	Plain						

$1,000 Issue — 1871

DC-7FP

Face Design: —/Coat of Arms of the Dominion flanked by lion and woman/reclining woman
Colour: Black with green tint.

DC-7aBP

Back Design: Lathework, counters and "Payable at Montreal"
Colour: Green
Issue Date: Engraved: July 1st 1871
Imprint: British American Bank Note Co. Montreal & Ottawa

DC-7bBP

Back: Payable at Toronto

DC-7cBP

Back: Payable at St. John

DC-7dBP

Back: Payable at Halifax

Signatures

Left: mss. various
Right: mss. various

Varieties

Engraved in the lathework across the back is the location of the Assistant Receiver General's office at which the particular note was payable:

PAYABLE AT MONTREAL
PAYABLE AT TORONTO
PAYABLE AT ST. JOHN
PAYABLE AT HALIFAX
PAYABLE AT VICTORIA
PAYABLE AT WINNIPEG
PAYABLE AT CHARLOTTETOWN

These notes were also payable at the Receiver General's office in Ottawa. The word Ottawa is engraved to the right of the left "1,000" counter.

Cat.No.	Denom.	Variety	Series	G	VG	F	VF	EF	Unc
DC-7FP	$1,000	Ottawa	Plain						
DC-7aBP	$1,000	Montreal	Plain						
DC-7bBP	$1,000	Toronto	Plain						
DC-7cBP	$1,000	St. John	Plain		Some proofs known in Institutions				
DC-7dBP	$1,000	Halifax	Plain						
DC-7eBP	$1,000	Victoria	Plain						
DC-7fBP	$1,000	Winnipeg	Plain						
DC-7gBP	$1,000	Charlottetown	Plain						

ISSUES OF 1878

A plausible reason for preparing a new issue of $1 and $2 notes so soon after the introduction of the first Dominion note was the counterfeiting of the Toronto $1 notes. If the purpose of the 1878 issue was to improve security, it failed badly. The ones were "raised" to resemble $4 notes and the $2 notes were extensively counterfeited.

With this issue began the practice of placing the portraits of the Governor General and his wife on the faces of the Dominion notes. The Countess of Dufferin appears on the $1 note and the Earl of Dufferin, the eloquent and popular Governor General of Canada from 1872 to 1878, appears on the $2 denomination. The back designs of both denominations indicate the location of the Assistant Receiver General's office at which the note was payable, and portrays the Great Seal of Canada.

The 1878 $1 and $2 notes were domiciled at the same four cities as the 1870 issue, but this time bore the name of the city on the face, just above the countersignature, as well as on the back. Again the sheet numbers were colour coded, this time with:

Montreal — blue
Toronto — red
St. John — black
Halifax — green

The St. John and Halifax $2 notes had five-digit numbers; all others had six. The domiciling of notes ended with this issue.

The only engraved signature is that of T. D. Harington, the Deputy Receiver General, who had retired before any of the notes had actually entered circulation. The left signature space, "For Minister of Finance," was left blank for the manuscript countersignature so that it could be applied horizontally. About 1882 or 1883 the Finance Department hired women to countersign the notes, a task previously the preserve of men.

The new notes were not released until stocks of the old notes were used up, and did not enter circulation until August 1879. The initial $1 notes had a scalloped frame with a large "scallop" in each corner. The Finance Department was soon disturbed to find that some of the Toronto $1 notes were being "raised" to resemble $4"s by skillfully changing the large 1 counters to 4's with pen and ink, and altering the ONE's. The British American Bank Note Co. responded by making a number of design alterations, most of them intended to make raising more difficult. The scalloped border was replaced by a lettered border repeating the inscription "1 ONE DOLLAR," and "1" counters replaced the scallops in the corners. The word ONE was added across the large "1" counters at either end.

Both Montreal and Toronto $2 notes were extensively counterfeited, leading to the retirement of the Dufferin $2 note after 1887, while the lettered border $1's were issued for another decade. Many of the counterfeit notes are still in existence, outnumbering the genuine notes, and the collector should beware of them. The counterfeits usually contain at least one "1" digit in the sheet number, and it has a sloping top. Genuine notes of this issue have flat-topped "1's."

Flat-topped 1 (Genuine)

Curved-topped 1
(counterfeit)

As in 1870 the $1 and $2 "Dufferin" notes of 1878 were printed from 4/on plates, with check letters A, B, C and D. It was during this issue that the **series letter** was introduced, on the $1 denomination. After the printing of 1,000,000 sheets, the sheet numbering was started over at 000001 and a new series begun. Normally, and unlike the example of the fractionals, the first series was "plain", that is, had no series letter. The first sheets of $1 notes were of the scalloped border variety, and when the lettered border $1 was introduced, numbering resumed where it had left off with the scalloped border notes. When enough sheets were printed to reach number 1,000000, series A began, starting at 000001 and going up to 1,000000 again, then series B began, and so on.

Care must be taken to avoid confusion of the series letter with the check letter, particularly since the check letter was moved when the lettered border was adopted.

SCALLOPED BORDER $1 1878:

The check letter is the large solid black letter A, B, C, or D to the immediate left of the sheet number. There is no series letter ("plain").

LETTER BORDER $1 1878:

The check letter is the gothic letter below the sheet number. The series letter (A, B, C or plain) is the white faced letter to the left of the sheet number.

The face plate number, if it is present at all, is a tiny black number located as follows:
SCALLOPED BORDER $1's and all $2's: left of the left-hand check letter.
LETTERED BORDER $1's: above the D of DOMINION or above the last A of CANADA.

About 1889 the British American Bank Note Company moved from Montreal to Ottawa. This change was reflected in the imprint on the backs of the notes. The imprint on the face was not changed.

$1 Issue — 1878 Scalloped Border

Summary of Technical Details

Cat.No.	Denom.	Date	Variety	Series	Serial Numbers	Quantity Printed
DC-8a	$1	1878	Scalloped, Montreal	Plain	000001-200000/A,B,C,D	800,000
DC-8b	$1	1878	Scalloped, Toronto	Plain	000001-200000/A,B,C,D	800,000
DC-8c	$1	1878	Scalloped, St. John	Plain	000001-050000/A,B,C,D	200,000
DC-8d	$1	1878	Scalloped, Halifax	Plain	000001-050000/A,B,C,D	200,000

$1 Issue — 1878 Scalloped Border

Scalloped Border: No "1's" in the smaller corner counters and no overprint "ONE" on the large "1's" in the main right and left counters.

DC-8a

Face Design: —/Countess of Dufferin/—
Colour: Black with green tint

DC-8a

Back Design: —/Great Seal of Canada/—
Colour: Green
Issue Date: Engraved: June 1st 1878
Imprint - Face: British American Bank Note Co. Montreal
Back: British American Bank Note Co. Montreal or British American Bank Note Co. Ottawa

Signatures

Left: mss. various
Right: Engr.: T.D. Harington

Varieties

The various Assistant Receiver General office locations at which the note was payable appear around the Great Seal:

PAYABLE AT MONTREAL
PAYABLE AT TORONTO
PAYABLE AT ST. JOHN
PAYABLE AT HALIFAX

DC-8b

DC-8c

DC-8d

$1 Issue - 1878 Scalloped Border

Scalloped border dollar notes are frequently encountered with close cut margins, apparently as issued. It should not be assumed that all such notes have been trimmed in a misguided effort to improve their apparent condition. Inspect the edges carefully for evidence of fresh cutting if in doubt.

Cat.No.	Denom.	Variety	Series	G	VG	F	VF	EF	AU	Unc
DC-8a	$1	Montreal	Plain	300.	700.	1,250.	2,500.	4,000.	5,000.	—
DC-8b	$1	Toronto	Plain	300.	700.	1,250.	2,500.	4,000.	5,000.	—
DC-8c	$1	St. John	Plain	1,200.	2,500.	3,500.	5,000.	9,000.	—	—
DC-8d	$1	Halifax	Plain	1,200.	2,500.	3,500.	5,000.	9,000.	—	—
DC-8FP	$1	Face proof		—	—	—	—	—	—	1,000.
DC-8BP	$1	Back proof		—	—	—	—	—	—	300.

$1 Issue - 1878 Lettered Border

Summary of Technical Details

Cat.No.	Denom.	Date	Variety	Series	Serial Numbers	Quantity Printed
DC-8e	$1	1878	Lettered, Montreal	Plain	200001-1,000000/A,B,C,D	3,200,000
DC-8e-i	$1	1878	Lettered, Montreal	A	000001-1,000000/A,B,C,D	4,000,000
DC-8e-ii	$1	1878	Lettered, Montreal	B	000001-1,000000/A,B,C,D	4,000,000
DC-8e-iii-M	$1	1878	Lettered, Montreal	C, Montreal *	000001-800000/A,B,C,D	3,200,000 **
DC-8e-iii-O	$1	1878	Lettered, Montreal	C, Ottawa *	000001-800000*/A,B,C,D	3,200,000 **
DC-8f	$1	1878	Lettered, Toronto	Plain	200001-1,000000/A,B,C,D	3,200,000
DC-8f-i	$1	1878	Lettered, Toronto	A	000001-1,000000/A,B,C,D	4,000,000
DC-8g	$1	1878	Lettered, St. John	Plain	050001-075000/A,B,C,D	100,000
DC-8h	$1	1878	Lettered, Halifax	Plain	050001-1,00000/A,B,C,D	200,000

Note: * Back imprint BABN Montreal or BABN Ottawa
** an estimate, considered to be an upper maximum.

"1" and "ONE DOLLAR" are alternately repeated in the border. "1's" are placed in the four corner counters and the large "1's" in the main right and left counters have a "ONE" added.

DC-8f

Face Design: —/Countess of Dufferin/—
Colour: Black with green tint

DC-8h

Back Design: —/Great Seal of Canada/—
Colour: Green
Issue Date: Engraved: 1st June 1878
Imprint - Face: British American Bank Note Co. Montreal
Back: British American Bank Note Co. Montreal or Ottawa

Signatures

Left: mss. various **Right:** Engr.: T.D. Harington

Varieties

The various Assistant Receiver General office locations at which the note was payable appear around the Great Seal.

PAYABLE AT MONTREAL
PAYABLE AT TORONTO
PAYABLE AT ST. JOHN
PAYABLE AT HALIFAX

Cat.No.	Denom.	Variety	Series	G	VG	F	VF	EF	AU	Unc
DC-8e	$1	Montreal	Plain	100.	200.	400.	1,000.	1,750.	2,500.	3,250.
DC-8e-i	$1	Montreal	A	100.	200.	400.	1,000.	1,750.	2,500.	3,250.
DC-8e-ii	$1	Montreal	B	100.	200.	400.	1,000.	1,750.	2,500.	3,250.
DC-8e-iii-M	$1	Montreal	C Montreal *	150.	300.	550.	1,200.	2,100.	3,000.	4,200.
DC-8e-iii-O	$1	Montreal	C Ottawa *	100.	200.	400.	1,000.	1,750.	2,500.	3,250.
DC-8f	$1	Toronto	Plain	110.	225.	475.	1,050.	1,800.	2,750.	3,500.
DC-8f-i	$1	Toronto	A	110.	225.	475.	1,050.	1,800.	2,750.	3,500.
DC-8g	$1	St. John	Plain	1,000.	2,000.	3,500.	5,000.	—	—	—
DC-8h	$1	Halifax	Plain	1,000.	2,000.	3,500.	5,000.	—	—	—

Note: * Back imprint

$2 Issue — 1878

Summary of Technical Details

Cat.No.	Denom.	Date	Variety	Series	Serial Numbers	Quantity Printed
DC-9a	$2	1878	Montreal	Plain	000001-350000/A,B,C,D	1,400,000 (est.)
DC-9b	$2	1878	Toronto	Plain	000001-230000/A,B,C,D	920,000 (est.)
DC-9c	$2	1878	St. John	Plain	00001-12500/A,B,C,D	50,000
DC-9d	$2	1878	Halifax	Plain	00001-32500/A,B,C,D	130,000

$2 Issue — 1878

DC-9b

Face Design: —/Earl of Dufferin/—
Colour: Black with green tint

DC-9a

Back Design: —/Great Seal of Canada and "Payable at Montreal"
Colour: Green

DC-9b

Back: Payable at Toronto

DC-9c

Back: Payable at St. John

DC-9d

Back: Payable at Halifax

Issue Date: Engraved: June 1st 1878
Imprint - Face: British American Bank Note Co. Montreal
Back: British American Bank Note Co. Montreal

Signatures

Left: mss. various **Right:** Engr.: T.D. Harington

Varieties

The various Assistant Receiver General office locations at which the note was payable are engraved around the Great Seal on the back.

PAYABLE AT MONTREAL
PAYABLE AT TORONTO
PAYABLE AT ST. JOHN
PAYABLE AT HALIFAX

Genuine

Counterfeit
Type 1 — Toronto

Counterfeit
Type 2 — Montreal

COUNTERFEITS

Note: Beware of counterfeit notes of this issue. The counterfeits will have poor engraving of the portrait and lathework.

Cat.No.	Denom.	Variety	Series	G	VG	F	VF	EF	AU	Unc
DC-9a	$2	Montreal	Plain	1,200.	2,400.	4,700.	7,500.	13,000.	—	—
DC-9b	$2	Toronto	Plain	1,200.	2,500.	5,000.	8,000.	15,000.	—	—
DC-9c	$2	St. John	Plain	2,000.	4,000.	7,000.	12,000.	—	—	—
DC-9d	$2	Halifax	Plain	1,800.	3,500.	6,000.	9,000.	—	—	—

$4 ISSUE OF 1882

In 1880 the Dominion Government assumed the right to issue $4 notes, restricting the banks whose charters were coming up for renewal to the issue of denominations of $5 and its multiples. The first $4 Dominion notes entered circulation in October 1882.

The central vignette portrays the Marquis of Lorne, Governor General from 1878 to 1883. The Marquis married H.R.H. Princess Louise, the second daughter of Queen Victoria, but the match was not a happy one. He later succeeded his father as Duke of Argyll.

The green tint at the left consists of an ornate numeral 4 flanked by two cherubs and partially obscuring a view of Montreal's Victoria Bridge. At the right, the Great Seal of Canada, found on the backs of previous issues, occurs in orange ink.

The $4 note is dated at Ottawa, and represents the end of the policy of the Finance Department to make its notes payable at a specific Assistant Receiver General's office.

To provide additional security, the $4 notes were printed on watermarked paper, the only instance of such paper being used for Canadian government notes. The watermark consists of the words DOMINION OF CANADA on two intersecting bands, with a maple leaf, shamrock, rose and thistle at the intersection. The paper tended to tear along the watermark and was also too thin to hold up satisfactorily in circulation.

The engraved signature of J. M. Courtney, Deputy Minister of Finance from 1878 to 1906, is found at the right, while the Finance Department's clerks applied their manuscript signatures at the left, in the space marked "countersigned".

The notes of this issue never formed a very large component of the Dominion notes in circulation. The final stocks of these notes entered circulation in April, 1900.

The 1882 $4 notes were printed in sheets of four with check letters A, B, C and D. Four face plates, numbered 1, 2, 3 and 4, were laid down in March and April of 1882. The plate numbers are found just below the right-hand check letter. Additional plates were used for the tint, the seal and the back.

Summary of Technical Details for $4 Issue

Cat.No.	Denom.	Date	Variety	Series	Serial Numbers	Quantity Printed
DC-10	$4	1882	Plain	—	000001-300000/A,B,C,D	1,200,000

$4 Issue — 1882

DC-10

Face Design: Ornate 4, Cherubs, Victoria Bridge/Marquis of Lorne/Great Seal of Canada*
Colour: Black with green tint

*The Great Seal of Canada was originally orange in colour; however the ink is unstable and will vary in colour from orange to brown as a result of oxidation.

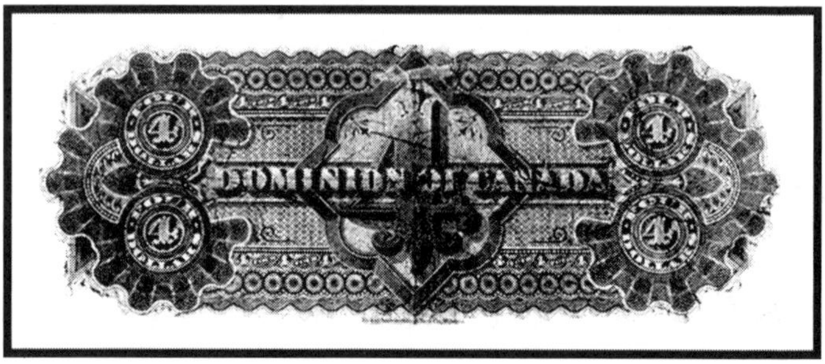

DC-10

Back Design: Lathework, counters and "Dominion of Canada"
Colour: Green
Issue Date: Engraved: May 1st, 1882
Imprint: British American Bank Note Co. Montreal on face and back

Signatures

Left: mms. various
Right: Engr.: J.M. Courtney

Cat.No.	Denom.	Series	G	VG	F	VF	EF	AU	Unc
DC-10	$4	Plain	600.	1,500.	2,500.	4,500.	6,500.	10,000.	—

$2 ISSUE OF 1887

A new issue of $2 notes was released in the fall of 1887 to replace the 1878 Dufferin notes, probably because of extensive counterfeiting of the latter.

Portraits of the Marquis and Marchioness of Lansdowne appear on the face of the note. The Marquis served as Governor General of Canada from 1883 to 1888. The back is unusual in that it is printed in two colours, black and green. Two printing runs, involving different plates, were needed to print such backs, making them more difficult to counterfeit. The back vignette, entitled "Quebec," shows Jacques Cartier and his men aboard ship.

Following the precedent established by the Lorne $4 notes, the Lansdowne $2 notes were not domiciled, but rather were dated at Ottawa for general use.

The notes bear the engraved signature of J. M. Courtney in the right-hand space designated "FOR MINISTER OF FINANCE," while the left-hand space contains the manuscript signature of any of various women employed by the Finance Department for the purpose of countersigning the notes.

The first, or "plain," series entered circulation between 1887 and 1896, when it was completed. The second series, designated "A," was then begun. The "A" series was discontinued late in 1897.

The notes were printed in sheets of four, with check letters A, B, C and D. The check letters are located above the portraits. The series letter, if there is one, is the solid black "A" below each sheet number. The face plate number occurs just above the right-hand check letter.

Summary of Technical Details

Cat.No.	Denom.	Date	Series	Serial Numbers	Qty. Printed
DC-11	$2	1887	Plain	000001-1000000/A,B,C,D	4,000,000
DC-11-i	$2	1887	A	000001-150000/A,B,C,D	600,000

$2 Issue — 1887

DC-11

Face Design: Marchioness of Lansdowne//Marquis of Lansdowne
Colour: Black with green tint

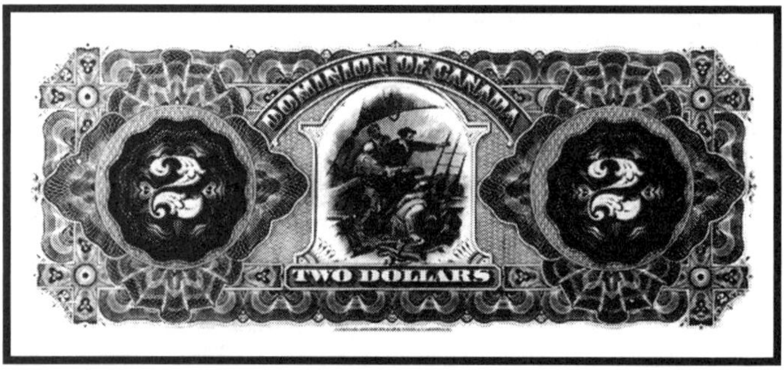

DC-11

Back Design: Lathework and counters with "Dominion of Canada" above Jacques Cartier's arrival at Quebec/
Colour: Black and green
Issue Date: Engraved: July 2nd, 1887
Imprint: British American Bank Note Co. Montreal on face and back

Signatures

Left: mss. various
Right: Engr.: J.M. Courtney

Cat.No.	Denom.	Series	G	VG	F	VF	EF	AU	Unc
DC-11	$2	Plain	350.	750.	1,200.	2,000.	3,500.	6,000.	8,000.
DC-11-i	$2	A	700.	1,500.	2,500.	4,000.	7,000.	10,000.	13,000.

ISSUES OF 1897 — 1898

In 1897 the Canadian government transferred its banknote printing business from the British American Bank Note Co. to the American Bank Note Co., New York. The American firm then established a branch plant in Ottawa, primarily to handle the government printing. This necessitated that new designs be prepared for all denominations of Dominion notes, although stocks on hand of the higher denominations were sufficient to last for several years.

The $1 notes dated 1897 portray the Countess and Earl of Aberdeen and a logging scene in the centre. The Earl was Governor General from 1893 to 1898. Lady Aberdeen founded the Victoria Order of Nurses in commemoration of Queen Victoria's Diamond Jubilee and was founding president of the National Council of Women. The backs depict the Centre Block of the Parliament Buildings, as seen from Wellington Street.

The $2 notes portray Edward, Prince of Wales, at the left. Following the death of Queen Victoria in 1901, he reigned as King Edward VII until his own death in 1910. A fishing scene vignette occupies the centre of the note. On the back of the note is a grain harvesting scene.

Both denominations of the first American Bank Note Co. issue of Dominion notes underwent modifications soon after the first deliveries were made to the Finance Department in August 1897. Both denominations were originally printed with green faces, so it was decided to change the $1 tint colour to light brown to better distinguish it from the $2. The issue dating was changed to March 31, 1898, although the first notes were not received by the Finance Department until September of that year. The lathework border was replaced by a lettered one. The large "1" counters on the backs of the 1897 $1 issue tended to show through the paper, disfiguring the portraits on the faces, so they were replaced by smaller counters.

The 1897 $1 notes have no series letter. The 1898 notes begin with series A, even though the plain series had not been completed, and continue to series S. This marks a change in procedure, for henceforth the Dominion note issues begin with the "A" series rather than a plain series.

Two varieties are found on the backs of the $1 1898 issue. Those received by the Finance Department between September 1898 and June 1903 have the "ONE" counters curved inward, and later notes have the "ONE" counters curved outward. The last sheet printed with the inward "ONE" was number 800000 in series D. A new series was not immediately begun, but series D resumed with sheet number 800001, with the outward "ONE." The last delivery of 1898 $1 notes was made to the Finance Department in May 1911.

The first printings of the 1897 $2 note have a red-brown back. After June 1898 all $2 notes were printed with a dark brown back. The red-brown backs were not discovered by collectors until recent years and are very scarce. Only sheets numbered 000001 to 175000 in the plain series have red-brown backs. Dark brown backs began with sheet number 175001 and continued to the end of the plain series and through series A to I. The last known delivery of the 1897 $2 notes was made to the Finance Department in June 1914, after which several years' records were destroyed.

The notes were printed in sheets of four with check letter A, B, C and D. The original engraved signature on the right was that of J. M. Courtney, Deputy Minister of Finance until 1906, when he retired and was succeeded by T. C. Boville. The signature changeover was not made immediately, and the delivery of Boville notes did not begin until August 1907 in the case of the $1 denomination and January 1908 for the $2's. The countersignatures at the right were applied by the women retained by the Finance Department for the exclusive purpose of signing notes.

The use of planchetted paper as an additional security device began during this issue of Dominion notes. The first $1 notes of the 1898 issue to contain these tiny embedded discs of coloured paper began with sheet number 046501 in the "C" series (delivered October 1901). Planchetted paper was also used for the 1897 dated $2 notes from sheet number 182501 in series "C" and onward.

The check letters are located on either side of the central vignettes on each denomination. The series letter, if there is one, is found below each sheet number on the $1 notes and below the central vignette on the $2 notes. The plate numbers were not printed on the notes, with the exception of some of the last Boville $2 1897 notes.

Checklist of Prefix Letters for 1897-1898 $1 Issues

Cat.No.	Denom.	Variety	Signature	Series Letters
DC-12	$1		Courtney	Plain
DC-13a	$1	ONEs Inward	Courtney	A B C D
DC-13b	$1	ONEs Outward	Courtney	D E F G H I J K
DC-13c	$1	ONEs Outward	Boville	L M N O P Q R S

Summary of Technical Details

Cat.No.	Denom.	Date	Variety	Series	Serial Numbers	Qty. Printed
DC-12	$1	1897		Plain	000001-600000/A,B,C,D	2,400,000
DC-13a	$1	1898	Courtney, ONEs	A	000001-1000000/A,B,C,D	4,000,000
			(Inward)	B	000001-1000000/A,B,C,D	4,000,000
				C	000001-1000000/A,B,C,D	4,000,000
				D	000001-800000/A,B,C,D	3,200,000
DC-13b	$1	1898	Courtney, ONEs	D	800001-1000000/A,B,C,D	800,000
			(Outward)	E	000001-1000000/A,B,C,D	4,000,000
				F	000001-1000000/A,B,C,D	4,000,000
				G	000001-1000000/A,B,C,D	4,000,000
				H	000001-1000000/A,B,C,D	4,000,000
				I	000001-1000000/A,B,C,D	4,000,000
				J	000001-1000000/A,B,C,D	4,000,000
				K	000001-1000000/A,B,C,D	4,000,000
DC-13c	$1	1898	Boville, ONEs	L	000001-1000000/A,B,C,D	4,000,000
			(Outward)	M	000001-1000000/A,B,C,D	4,000,000
				N	000001-1000000/A,B,C,D	4,000,000
				O	000001-1000000/A,B,C,D	4,000,000
				P	000001-1000000/A,B,C,D	4,000,000
				Q	000001-1000000/A,B,C,D	4,000,000
				R	000001-1000000/A,B,C,D	4,000,000
				S	000001-670000/A,B,C,D	2,680,000

$1 Issue — 1897

DC-12

Face Design: Countess of Aberdeen/logging on a Canadian river/ Earl of Aberdeen
Colour: Black with green tint

DC-12

Back Design: Lathework, counters and "Dominion of Canada" over the Parliament Building, view of the Centre Block from the front gate
Colour: Green
Issue Date: Engr.: July 2nd, 1897
Imprint: American Bank Note Co. Ottawa, face and back

Signatures

Left: mss. various
Right: Engr.: J.M. Courtney

Cat.No.	Denom.	Series	G	VG	F	VF	EF	AU	Unc
DC-12	$1	Plain	400.	700.	1,200.	2,400.	4,500.	7,000.	10,000.

$1 Issue — 1898

DC-13a

Face Design: Countess of Aberdeen/logging on a Canadian river/ Earl of Aberdeen
Colour: Black with light brown tint

DC-13a

ONEs curved inward

DC-13b & 13c

ONEs curved outward

Back Design: Lathework, counters and Parliament Building, view of the Centre block from the front gate/—
Colour: Green
Issue Date: Engr.: March 31st, 1898
Imprint: American Bank Note Company Ottawa on face and back

Signatures

Left: mss. various
Right: Engr.: J.M. Courtney, Engr.: T.C. Boville

Varieties

Two different back designs were used for the "ONE" counters at the left and right ends of the back of the note:

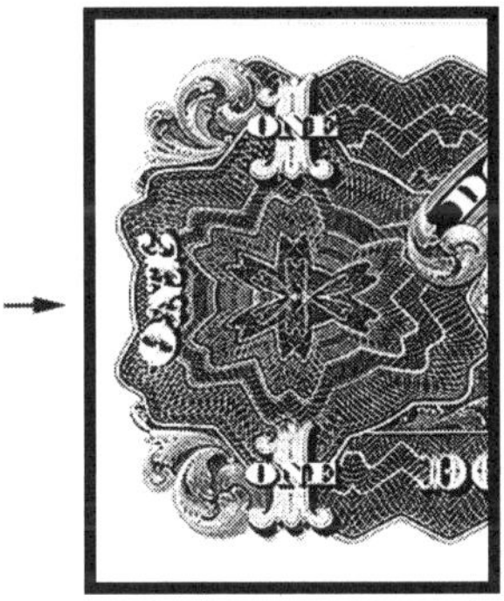

ONEs curved inward

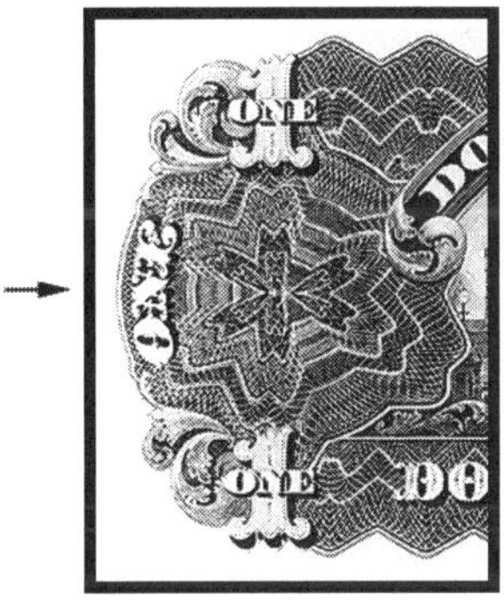

ONEs curved outward

Cat.No.	Denom.	Variety	Series	G	VG	F	VF	EF	AU	Unc
DC-13a	$1	Courtney, ONEs inward	A,B,C,D	80.	160.	375.	800.	1,600.	2,400.	3,500.
DC-13b	$1	Courtney, ONEs outward	D,E,F,G, H,I,J,K	70.	140.	275.	550.	1,200.	1,700.	2,400.
DC-13c	$1	Boville, ONEs outward	L,M,N,O, P,Q,R,S	60.	120.	225.	500.	1,100.	1,500.	2,000.

$2 Issue — 1897

Checklist of Prefix Letters for $2 Issues

Cat.No.	Denom.	Variety	Signature	Series Letters
DC-14a	$2	Red-brown back	Courtney	Plain
DC-14b	$2	Dark brown back	Courtney	Plain A B C
DC-14c	$2	Dark brown back	Boville	D E F G H I

Summary of Technical Details

Cat.No.	Denom.	Date	Variety	Series	Serial Numbers	Qty. Printed
DC-14a	$2	1897	Courtney, red-brown back	Plain	000001-175000/A,B,C,D	700,000
DC-14b	$2	1897	Courtney, dark brown back	Plain	175001-1000000/A,B,C,D	3,300,000
				A	000001-1000000/A,B,C,D	4,000,000
				B	000001-1000000/A,B,C,D	4,000,000
				C	000001-1000000/A,B,C,D	4,000,000
DC-14c	$2	1897	Boville, dark brown back	D	000001-1000000/A,B,C,D	4,000,000
				E	000001-1000000/A,B,C,D	4,000,000
				F	000001-1000000/A,B,C,D	4,000,000
				G	000001-1000000/A,B,C,D	4,000,000
				H	000001-1000000/A,B,C,D	4,000,000
				I	000001-242000/A,B,C,D*	968,000+

*Last recorded delivery. Records of shipments after June 1914 were destroyed.

$2 Issue — 1897

DC-14a

Face Design: Edward, Prince of Wales, six men in a fishing dory/—
Colour: Black with green tint

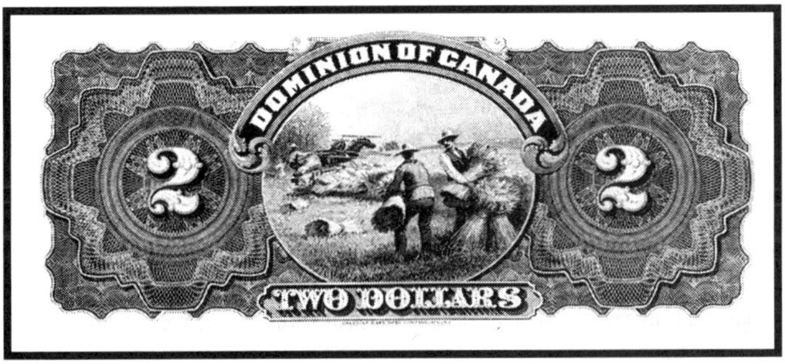

DC-14c

Back Design: Lathework and counters with "Dominion of Canada" over Agricultural scene
Colour: See varieties
Issue Date: July 2nd, 1897
Imprint: American Bank Note Co. Ottawa

Signatures

Left: mss. various
Right: Engr.: J.M. Courtney, Engr.: T.C. Boville

Varieties

$2 Back Colour: Red-brown; dark brown

Cat.No.	Denom.	Variety	Series	G	VG	F	VF	EF	AU	Unc
DC-14a	$2	Courtney, red-brown back	Plain	1,700.	3,000.	4,500.	8,000.	10,000.	13,000.	17,000.
DC-14b	$2	Courtney, dark brown back	Plain A,B,C	115.	225.	550.	1,100.	2,000.	3,000.	4,000.
DC-14c	$2	Boville, dark brown back	D,E,F,G, H,I	100.	200.	425.	900.	1,750.	2,500.	3,500.

ISSUES OF 1900 — 1902

In 1900 the American Bank Note Company added the 25-cent and $4 notes to the denominations of Dominion notes it was preparing on behalf of the government. These were only the second issues of each value to be released. Three major varieties are known for each.

25¢ Issue — 1900

The 1900 shinplasters portray a seated Britannia figure, with trident and shield. The vignette was engraved by Mr. Goodeve of the American Bank Note Company's engraving department in New York. The backs, consisting only of lathework and counters, omit any reference to cities where the notes were payable, consistent with the policy of no longer domiciling Dominion notes. A tint covers part of the face, the bottom consisting of a pantograph of "Dominion of Canada" and "25 cents" in a scrollwork design.

There is only a single engraved signature, that of the Deputy Minister of Finance. Initially the notes were signed by J. M. Courtney, Deputy Minister from 1878 to 1906. T. C. Boville followed from 1906 to 1920, and J. C. Saunders served as Deputy Minister from 1920 to 1929. The notes signed by Courtney have the word "OTTAWA" in large black letters to the right of the signature, but it does not appear on notes signed by his successors.

The 25-cent fractional notes were printed in sheets of ten until 1918. From 1918 they were printed in sheets of 20. There is no check letter or sheet number, consistent with the 1870 issue. There is also no series letter.

The first of the Courtney shinplasters were received by the Finance Department in July 1900. They were printed on paper differing from that used for the contemporary $1 and $2 notes. A strip of coloured planchettes was used as an added security feature.

Plate numbers did not appear on the Courtney notes, but may be found on notes bearing other signatures. The face plate number is located under the 25 counter at the upper left or upper right, and the back plate number is at the lower right. Plate number combinations seen in conjunction with the two signatures are as follows:

Plate Number Combinations for 1900 Issue Fractionals

A. Signed T.C. Boville		B. Signed J.C. Saunders	
Face Plate #'s	**Back Plate #'s**	**Face Plate #'s**	**Back Plate #'s**
None,13, 14, 15, 16	None	29	15, 16
17	None, 12	30	15, 16
18	None, 11, 12	31	17, 18
19	None, 9, 10, 11, 12	31	17, 18
20	None, 9, 10, 11, 12	32	17, 18
21	9, 10, 11, 12		
22	9, 10, 11, 12		
23	9, 10		
24	9, 10		
25	15, 16		
26	15, 16		

Unfortunately, bank note company records for note deliveries covering the period from mid 1914 to late 1921 were destroyed, so the total number of notes printed and issued is not available. However, it is known that between 1900 and mid 1914, 3,360,000 of the fractional notes were received. These had either the Courtney or the Boville signature. Another 1,960,000 of the 1900 type arrived at the Finance Department in 1922 and 1923, all presumably with the Saunders signature.

Summary of Technical Details

Cat.No.	Denom.	Date	Variety	Series	Serial Numbers	Qty. Printed
DC-15a	25¢	1900	Courtney	None	None	Unknown
DC-15b	25¢	1900	Boville	None	None	Unknown
DC-15c	25¢	1900	Saunders	None	None	Unknown

25¢ Issue — 1900

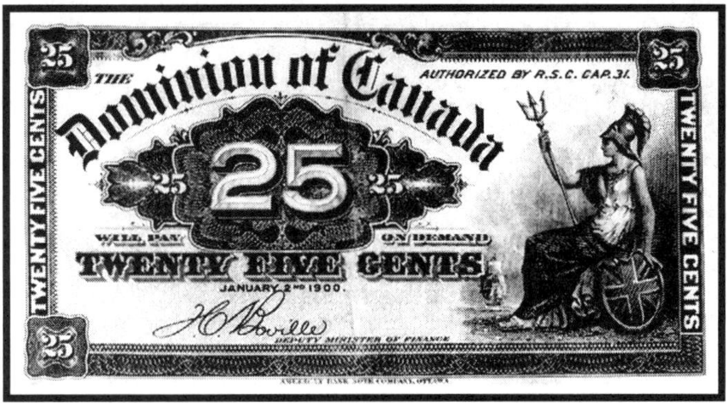

DC-15b

Face Design: —/—/Britannia seated with her shield and trident, sailing ship in background
Colour: Black with light brown tint

DC-15b

Back Design: Lathework and counters
Colour: Green
Issue Date: Engr.: January 2nd, 1900
Imprint: American Bank Note Company, Ottawa on face and back

Signatures

Left: Engr.: J.M. Courtney, Engr.: T.C. Boville, Engr.: J.C. Saunders
Right: None

Cat.No.	Denom.	Variety	G	VG	F	VF	EF	AU	Unc
DC-15a	25¢	Courtney	8.	12.	16.	27.	100.	140.	350.
DC-15a	25¢	Courtney Part sheet of 6	—	—	—	—	1,200.	—	—
DC-15b	25¢	Boville	7.	10.	12.	25.	100.	140.	350.
DC-15b	25¢	Boville Uncut Pair	—	—	110.	175.	300.	400.	—
DC-15b	25¢	Boville Uncut strip/block of 4	—	—	300.	450.	750.	1,150.	—
DC-15c	25¢	Saunders	8.	12.	16.	30.	115.	170.	400.

$4 ISSUE OF 1900 — 1902

The portraits on the $4 notes of 1900 and 1902 are those of the Countess and Earl of Minto, the latter being Governor General from 1898 to 1904. The central vignette features the Sault Ste. Marie locks, which connect Lake Superior and Lake Huron. Through an error, the United States side of the locks was shown on the 1900 issue instead of the Canadian side. The error was corrected on the 1902 issue. The backs of both issues depict the Parliament Buildings as seen from Nepean Point.

The 1900 $4 notes were delivered to the Finance Department from December 1900 to February 1902, at which time the 1902-dated issue became available. The initial 1902-dated notes have large "4" counters in the upper corners and "FOURs" in the lower corners. The last notes of this type were delivered in January 1903.

Thereafter no more $4 notes were printed until the summer of 1911, probably because the change to the $5 denomination was receiving active consideration . It was then that a sudden, unexpected need for large supplies of paper currency arose. New designs having "FOURs" in the corners had been ordered by the Finance Department late in 1902 to facilitate sorting. Models were submitted for government approval in 1910, and plates incorporating these changes and other slight changes in the tints were eventually engraved. With the urgent need for notes, they were pressed into service and additional plates engraved. The bank note company worked day and night, with all available presses running, to cope with the rush orders. Between June and September of 1911 the entire production of the final type of $4 notes was delivered to the Finance Department. No more $4 Dominion notes were ever ordered. The denomination, which was so important in colonial times because it was equivalent to one pound Halifax currency, had become obsolete.

Twenty-four face plates were engraved in 1911 and were used together with eight backs and eight tints, whereas eight of each could have been sufficient had production been carried out at a normal pace.

All varieties of the $4 notes of 1900 and 1902 were printed in sheets of four, with check letters A, B, C and D flanking the central vignette. Following the procedure established in 1898, all are designated "Series A," whereas the previous practice had been to begin a new issue with a plain (i.e. no letter) series, and begin the "A" series for the second million sheets. First, there was a 1900 series "A," with sheets numbered from 000001 to 105000, and then there was a 1902 Series "A", in which the sheet numbers started over at 000001. Sheets of this series had the large "4" counters at the top corners up to number 110000, after which "FOUR" counters appeared at the top corners. Plate numbers do not appear on any of the notes.

The 1900 issue, as well as the 1902 notes with the "4" counters on top, bear the engraved signature of J. M. Courtney at the right. The 1902-dated notes (actually printed in 1911) with the "FOUR" counters on top have the engraved signature of T. C. Boville. All received manuscript countersignatures on the left at the Department of Finance prior to issue.

By 1912 the $4 denomination was being withdrawn from circulation and replaced by $5 Dominion notes. Only small quantities of the outstanding $4 notes were turned in after the end of 1915, and by 1950 all but $29,000 worth of all dates of issue had been withdrawn, and most of those still outstanding have probably been lost through fire and decay.

Summary of Technical Details

Cat.No.	Denom.	Date	Variety	Series	Serial Numbers	Qty. Printed
DC-16	$4	1900	Courtney, U.S. Locks	A	000001 -105000/A,B,C,D	420,000
DC-17a	$4	1902	Courtney, 4s at top	A	000001 -110000/A,B,C,D	440,000
DC-17b	$4	1902	Boville, FOURs at top	A	110001 -519000/A,B,C,D	1,636,000

$4 Issue — 1900

DC-16

Face Design: Lady Minto/Sault Ste. Marie U.S. locks/Lord Minto
Colour: Black with green tint

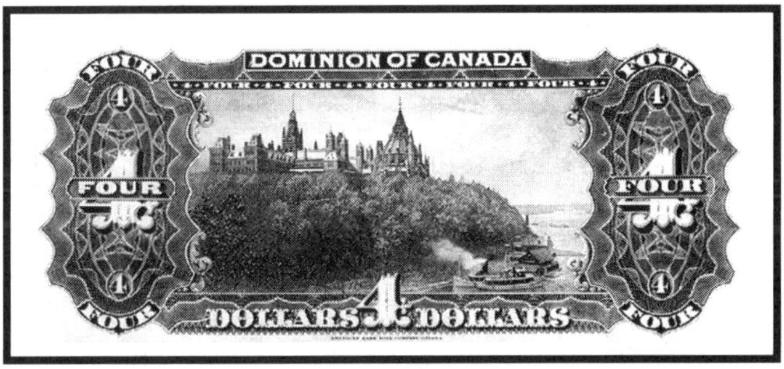

DC-16

Back Design: Lathework and counters with "Dominion of Canada" over Parliament Buildings and Library, view from the Ottawa River
Colour: Green
Issue Date: Engraved: July 2nd, 1900
Imprint: American Bank Note Company, Ottawa, on face and back

Signatures

Left: miss. various
Right: Engr.: J.M. Courtney

Cat.No.	Denom.	Variety	G	VG	F	VF	EF	AU	Unc
DC-16	$4	Courtney	400.	900.	1,750.	3,500.	4,500.	7,000.	12,000.

$4 Issue — 1902

The face of the $4 1902 issues used two designs on the upper left and right corner counters; large "4's" at top — large "FOURs" at top.

DC-17a

Face Design: Lady Minto/Sault Ste. Marie Canadian locks/ Lord Minto
Colour: Black with green tint

DC-17a

Back Design: Lathework and counters with "Dominion of Canada" over Parliament Buildings and Library, view from the Ottawa River
Colour: Green
Issue Date: Engraved: Jany 2nd, 1902
Imprint: American Bank Note Company, Ottawa, on face and back

Signatures

Left: mss. various
Right: Engr.: J.M. Courtney

Cat.No.	Denom.	Variety	G	VG	F	VF	EF	AU	Unc
DC-17a	$4	Courtney, 4's at top	500.	1,250.	2,250.	4,000.	6,000.	8,000.	14,000.

$4 Issue — 1902 (FOURS)

DC-17b

Face Design: Lady Minto/Sault Ste. Marie Canadian locks/Lord Minto
Colour: Black with green tint

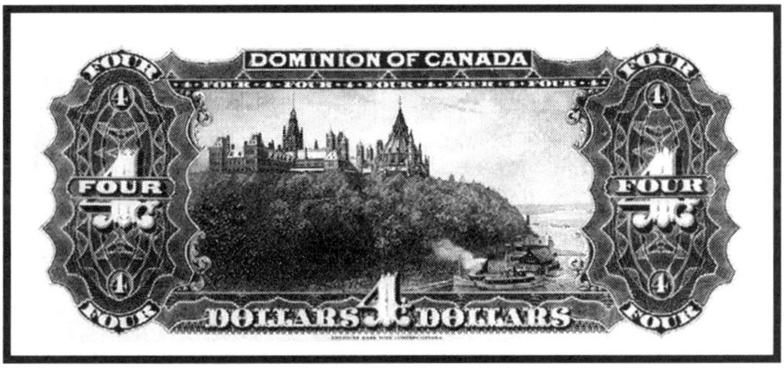

DC-17b

Back Design: Lathework and counters with "Dominion of Canada" over Parliament Buildings and Library, view from the Ottawa River
Colour: Green
Issue Date: Engraved: Jany. 2nd, 1902
Imprint: American Bank Note Company, Ottawa, on face and back

Signatures

Left: mss. various
Right: Engr.: T.C. Boville

Cat.No.	Denom.	Variety	G	VG	F	VF	EF	AU	Unc
DC-17b	$4	Boville, FOURs at top	375.	750.	1,500.	3,000.	4,000.	6,000.	10,000.

ISSUES OF 1911

$1 Issue — 1911

The $1 note issue dated 1911 began to be delivered to the Finance Department in May 1911, superseding the Aberdeen issue. Vignettes of Lord and Lady Grey occupy the centre of the notes. Earl Grey was Governor General from 1904 to 1911, a longer term than usual. The Greys were very popular and their period in office was extended at the request of the Canadian government. The backs were unchanged from the previous issue.

The early notes of this issue have a green lathework line along the top edge of the signature panel. On later issues the tint was modified by the removal of this line, and a black lathework line was added to the face plate. The bank note company made this change in its plates in mid 1914.

There was a good deal of experimentation with the series letter during the period of this issue. The first three series printed, series A, B and C, have the series letter engraved on both sides of the portraits just above the signature panel. The check letters are found near the upper corners. For series D, E, F and G, the engraved series letters and the check letters have interchanged positions. This change was made on the plates early in 1912. Thereafter, the series letter, printed by the letterpress method in red ink, follows the sheet number, while the check letters remain flanking the portraits. Series H, J, K and probably part of L occur in conjuction with the green lathework border on the signature panel, and the rest of series L through series Y were printed with the black lathework border. Series U, V, W, X and Y have the series letter separated from the sheet number by a hyphen Series letters I, O, Q and Z were not used.

All varieties bear the engraved signatures of T. C. Boville in the area designated "FOR MINISTER OF FINANCE, " and the manuscript signatures of various employees of the Finance Department in the area designated "COUNTERSIGNED". Face plate numbers when present are found below the second "1" in the top left border, and back plate numbers are found at the lower right corner. The notes were printed sometimes from 4/on plates, but more frequently from 8/on plates. In all cases check letters A, B, C and D were used. For 8/on plates, the sheets were arranged

A	A
B	B
C	C
D	D

with different numbers being used for each side of the sheet.

Checklist of Prefix Letters for 1911 $1 Dominion Notes

Cat.No.	Variety	Series Letter
DC-18a	Green line, series letter engraved above signature panel	A B C
DC-18b	Green line, series letter engraved near upper corners	D E F G
DC-18c	Green line, series letter follows sheet number, no hyphen	H J K L
DC-18d	Black line, series letter follows sheet number, no hyphen	LM N P R S T
DC-18d-i	Black line, series letter follows sheet number, with hyphen	U V W X Y

Summary of Technical Details

Cat.No.	Denom.	Date	Variety	Series	Serial Numbers	Qty. Printed
DC-18a	$1	1911	Green line, series	A	000001 -1000000/A,B,C,D	4,000,000
			Letter engr. bottom	B	000001 -1000000/A,B,C,D	4,000,000
				C	000001 -1000000/A,B,C,D	4,000,000
DC-18b	$1	1911	Green line, series	D	000001 -1000000/A,B,C,D	4,000,000
			Letter engr. top	E	000001 -1000000/A,B,C,D	4,000,000
				F	000001 -1000000/A,B,C,D	4,000,000
				G	000001 -1000000/A,B,C,D	4,000,000
DC-18c	$1	1911	Green line, series	H	000001 -1000000/A,B,C,D	4,000,000
			Letter after sheet no.	J	000001 -1000000/A,B,C,D	4,000,000
				K	000001 -1000000/A,B,C,D	4,000,000
				L	000001 -Unknown/A,B,C,D	Unknown
DC-18d	$1	1911	Black line, no hyphen	L	234411 -1000000/A,B,C,D	Unknown
				M	000001 -1000000/A,B,C,D	4,000,000
				N	000001 -1000000/A,B,C,D	4,000,000
				P	000001 -1000000/A,B,C,D	4,000,000
				R	000001 -1000000/A,B,C,D	4,000,000
				S	000001 -1000000/A,B,C,D	4,000,000
				T	000001 -1000000/A,B,C,D	4,000,000
DC-18d-i	$1	1911	Black line, hyphen	U	000001 -1000000/A,B,C,D	4,000,000
				V	000001 -1000000/A,B,C,D	4,000,000
				W	000001 -1000000/A,B,C,D	4,000,000
				X	000001 -1000000/A,B,C,D	4,000,000
				Y	000001 -1000000/A,B,C,D	4,000,000

$1 Issue — 1911

DC-18d

Face Design: —/Lord Grey, Lady Grey/—
See varieties
Colour: Black with green tint

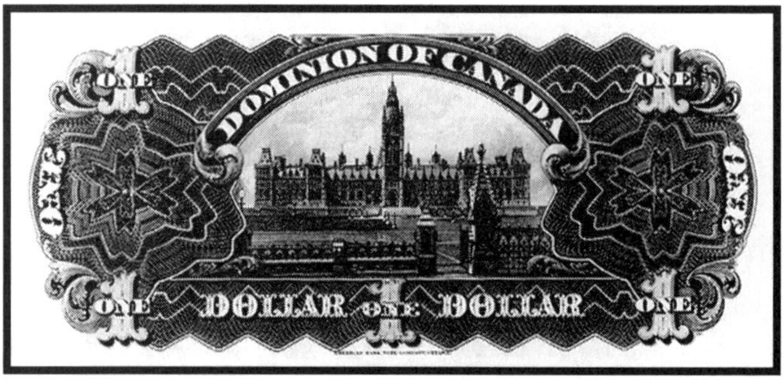

DC-18

Back Design: Lathework and counters with "Dominion of Canada" over Parliament Buildings, view of the Centre Block from the front gate
Colour: Green
Issue Date: Engraved: Jany. 3rd, 1911
Imprint: American Bank Note Company, Ottawa, on face and back

Signatures

Left: mss. various
Right: Engr.: T.C. Boville

Varieties

In the face design the line enclosing the microlettering and signatures, just below the large right and left counters, was printed in two colours, one all green, the other all black.

Green Line

Black Line

Cat.No.	Denom.	Variety	Series	G	VG	F	VF	EF	AU	Unc
DC-18a	$1	Green line, series letter engraved above signature panel	A,B,C	45.	90.	185.	400.	650.	1,350.	2,000.
DC-18b	$1	Green line, series letter engraved near upper corners	D,E,F,G	45.	90.	185.	400.	650.	1,350.	2,000.
DC-18c	$1	Green line, series letter follows sheet no., no hyphen	H,J,K,L	45.	90.	185.	400.	650.	1,350.	2,000.
DC-18d	$1	Black line, Series letter follows sheet no., no hyphen	L,M,N,P, R,S,T	45.	85.	175.	350.	550.	800.	1,300.
DC-18d-i	$1	Black line, Series letter follows sheet no., with hyphen	U,V,W, X,Y	45.	90.	185.	375.	650.	900.	1,400.

$500 and $1000 Issues of 1911

Consultations between the American Bank Note Co. and the Comptroller of Currency had taken place in 1902 concerning a new issue of $50 and $100 Dominion notes. No new issues of these denominations were ever printed, however, and the denominations were discontinued. New designs for $500 and $1000 notes had been ordered in February 1911, and by the spring of that year the stocks on hand of the 1871 issue were finally depleted. A 4/on plate was prepared for the $1000 note in August and one for the $500 note in December of 1911. There were no check letters A, B, C or D on the notes, the sheets being cut up and the notes numbered individually and consecutively before delivery to the Finance Department. Red six-digit serial numbers were used. Both denominations have "SERIES A" engraved upon the faces of the notes. They bore no engraved signatures, but were signed by hand at the Finance Department. The final delivery was made in 1924.

The central vignettes on the new $500 and $1000 Dominion notes were current portraits of Queen Mary and King George V respectively. To distinguish the higher denomination notes from the Bank Legals, or "specials," they were called "bearer notes" by government officials, because they were payable to the bearer.

Summary of Technical Details

Cat.No.	Denom.	Date	Series	Serial Numbers	Quantity Printed
DC-19	$500	1911	A	000001-044000	44,000
DC-20	$1000	1911	A	000001-034000	34,000

$500 Issue — 1911

DC-19S

Face Design: —/H.M. Queen Mary/—
Colour: Black with green tint

DC-19

Back Design: Lathework, counters and "Dominion of Canada"
Colour: Green
Issue Date: Engraved: Jany. 3rd, 1911
Imprint: American Bank Note Company, Ottawa, on face and back

Signatures

Left: mss. various
Right: mss. various

Cat.No.	Denom.	G	VG	F	VF	EF	AU	Unc.
DC-19	$500	10,000.	20,000.	30,000.	60,000.	—	—	—
DC-19S	$500				Specimen			3,000.

$1000 Issue — 1911

DC-20

Face Design: —/H.M. King George V/—
Colour: Black with blue tint

DC-20

Back Design: Lathework, counters and "Dominion of Canada"
Colour: Blue
Issue Date: Engraved: Jany. 3rd, 1911
Imprint: American Bank Note Co., Ottawa

Signatures

Left: mss. various
Right: mss. various

Cat.No.	Denom.	G	VG	F	VF	EF	AU	Unc
DC-20	$1000	10,000.	20,000.	30,000.	60,000.	—	—	—
DC-20S	$1000						Specimen	2,500.

ISSUE OF 1912

Work began on a $5 Dominion note issue as early as 1906. Some of the designs that were considered included a Nova Scotia mining scene, portraits of the Earl and Countess Grey and the train vignette, which was finally chosen for the issue of 1912. The coat of arms and the Great Seal of Canada were both contemplated for the back design, but were not used.

The issued note portrays an attractive vignette of a passenger train, the "Maritime Express," travelling through the Wentworth Valley in Nova Scotia. The back consists of lathework and Roman and Arabic numeral counters.

It occurred to officials of the Finance Deparment that hand signing of Dominion notes was not really necessary, and it was decided to acquire special presses for the application of the second signature. This change in procedure was made in 1922, with the first notes of the $5 denomination to be machine signed arriving in August. The word "COUNTERSIGNED" was removed from over the left signature space and was replaced by the words "COMPTROLLER OF CURRENCY" below the space. When the final signature was applied, a large blue Finance Department seal was added as an additional security device.

The original intention was to have the denominational counter at the right removed, making room for the seal, before machine signing any notes. However, difficulties were being experienced with the ink used for hand signing the notes. It did not adhere properly to the paper for some denominations. Accordingly it was decided to begin machine signing before the counters could be removed, creating the transitional "seal over" varieties.

The first series of the 1912 $5 issue had "SERIES A" engraved below the sheet numbers. The sheets were delivered to the Finance Department between June 1912 and January 1916. Despite the number issued, series "A" notes are now very scarce because no hoards have ever turned up.

With the beginning of the "B" series, the black engraved series letter was removed and, for a short time, was printed in red following the sheet number. Such notes are likewise very scarce. Soon the "B" series letter moved to precede the sheet number. These notes are now perhaps the most readily available variety since substantial hoards, all with check letter C and sheet numbers beginning 4650— and 4717—, have been placed on the market. All of the preceding notes bear the engraved signature of T. C. Boville and a manuscript countersignature.

A transitional variety follows, with the Finance Department seal applied over the right FIVE counter, and either the signature of T. C. Boville or J. C. Saunders engraved at the right. The left-hand signature, printed on the notes at the same time as the seal, is that of G. W. Hyndman. The "seal over FIVE" notes were delivered to the Finance Department between August 1922 and September 1923, with the signature changeover occurring in October 1922.

About September 1923 the right FIVE counter and lathework were removed, and the seal applied in the resulting space. The last of series "B" and all of series "C" were printed with this arrangement. The signature combination on nearly all of these "seal only" notes is Hyndman-Saunders, and the last notes with this signature combination were received in October 1924. No more $5 Dominion notes were printed until October 1931, when a few more were printed, still in series "C",with the McCavour-Saunders signatures.

The McCavour-Saunders note is rare; in fact only two examples have been discovered to date, of which one is in the Bank of Canada currency collection. The series "B" "seal only" note is very scarce. The series "C" Hyndman-Saunders note is easily obtainable, particularly because of the discovery of a hoard with check letter D and sheet numbers beginning 1443—.

In 1923 the American Bank Note Company, Ottawa, changed its name to the Canadian Bank Note Company, Limited. Accordingly, the imprints on both faces and backs were altered to reflect this change. Recent research indicates that the imprint changeover occurred with the introduction of the "seal only" variety, late in series B.

The $5 train notes were sometimes printed from 4/on plates, but usually from 8/on plates. The plate numbers are absent on the earlier varieties, but are found on later varieties just above and left of the last A in CANADA on the face and at the lower right on the back.

Checklist of Prefix Letter for 1912 $5 Dominion Notes

Cat.No.	Denom.	Variety	Signature(s)	Series Letters
DC-21a	$5	Engraved "SERIES A", no seal	Boville, r.	A
DC-21b	$5	Series letter "B" follows sheet number; no seal	Boville, r.	B
DC-21c	$5	Series letter, "B" precedes sheet number; no seal	Boville, r.	B
DC-21d	$5	Seal over FIVE	Hyndman-Boville	B
DC-21e	$5	Seal over FIVE	Hyndman-Saunders	B
DC-21f	$5	Seal only	Hyndman-Saunders	B C
DC-21g	$5	Seal only	McCavour-Saunders	C

Summary of Technical Details

Cat.No.	Denom.	Variety	Series	Serial Numbers	Qty. Printed
DC-21a	$5	Boville, r. (no seal)	A	000001-1000000/A,B,C,D	4,000,000
DC-21b	$5	Boville, r. ,B after sheet number (no seal)	B	000001- 389119*/A,B,C,D	Unknown
DC-21c	$5	Boville, r. B before sheet number (no seal)	B	443802*- 549000/A,B,C,D	2,196,000
DC-21d	$5	Hyndman-Boville (seal over FIVE)	B	549001-663287* /A,B,C,D	Unknown
DC-21e	$5	Hyndman-Saunders, (seal over FIVE)	B	669661*-805952*/A,B,C,D	Unknown
DC-21f	$5	Hyndman-Saunders (seal only)	B	836280*-1000000/A,B,C,D	Unknown
			C	000001-750000/A,B,C,D	3,000,000
DC-21g	$5	McCavour-Saunders (seal only)	C	750001-754750/A,B,C,D	19,000

Note: * denotes high and low numbers seen.

$5 Issue - 1912

DC-21f

Face Design: —/passenger train *Ocean Limited* of the Intercolonial Railway travelling through the Wentworth Valley in Nova Scotia/—
Colour: Black with blue tint

DC-21

Back Design: Lathework, counters and "Dominion of Canada"
Colour: Blue

Issue Date: Engraved: May 1st 1912
Imprint: American Bank Note Company, Ottawa or Canadian Bank Note Company Limited on face and back

Signatures

Left:		**Right:**	
	mss. various		Engr.: T. C. Boville
	Typed: G. W. Hyndman		Engr.: T. C. Boville
	Typed: G. W. Hyndman		Engr.: J. C. Saunders
	Typed: S. P. McCavour		Engr.: J. C. Saunders

Varieties

The seal of the Department of Finance is used during the middle of this issue and is overprinted on, or replaces the right FIVE of the right counter.

FIVE at right

Blue seal over FIVE at right

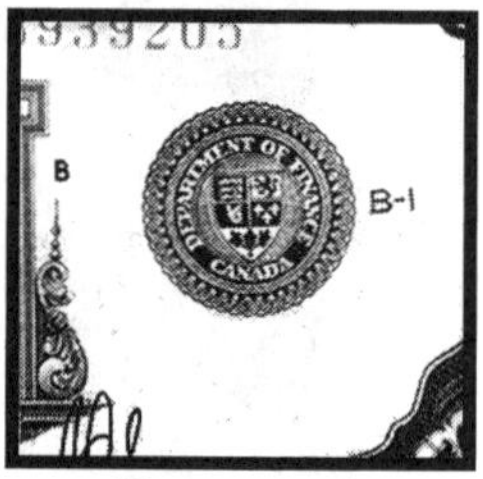

Blue seal only

Cat.No.	Denom.	Variety	Series	G	VG	F	VF	EF	AU	Unc
DC-21a	$5	No seal, Boville, r.	A	275.	550.	800.	1,250.	1,750.	2,500.	4,000.
DC-21b	$5	No seal, Boville, r., B after sheet no.	B	350.	700.	1,200.	1,600.	2,750.	4,000.	5,500.
DC-21c	$5	No seal, Boville, r., B before sheet no.	B	200.	400.	600.	900.	1,350.	2,000.	2,750.
DC-21d	$5	Hyndman-Boville, seal over FIVE	B	250.	500.	750.	1,200.	1,800.	2,500.	3,500.
DC-21e	$5	Hyndman-Saunders, seal over FIVE	B	300.	600.	900.	1,300.	2,000.	3,000.	4,500.
DC-21f	$5	Hyndman-Saunders, seal only	B	350.	700.	1,200.	1,600.	2,500.	3,500.	5,500.
DC-21f	$5	Hyndman-Saunders, seal only	C	200.	400.	600.	900.	1,400.	2,250.	3,000.
DC-21g	$5	McCavours-Saunders seal only	C	—	—	—	—	24,000.	—	—

ISSUE OF 1914

The 1897 "Prince of Wales" issue of $2 Dominion notes was finally replaced in 1914. Portraits of the Duke and Duchess of Connaught appear on the face of the new note and the back portrays the Canadian coat of arms surrounded by the provincial shields. The Duke, born Prince Arthur, was the third and favourite son of Queen Victoria. He came to Canada as a member of the Red River expedition of 1870, and Prince Arthur's Landing (later Port Arthur, and now part of Thunder Bay) was named in his honour. He was promoted to field marshal of the British Army in 1902, and was Governor General of Canada from 1911 to 1916. The Duke sometimes tended to make pronouncements upon Canadian military policy during World War I, which aroused some controversy. He organized the Canadian Patriotic Fund to assist dependants of servicemen.

The initial printings of the $2 Dominion notes of 1914 have the words "WILL PAY TO THE BEARER ON DEMAND" curved around the large 2 counter at the centre of the note. Two sub-varieties of this type exist. The series letter is found immediately after the sheet number, with no hyphen, for series A, B and C. A hyphen separates the sheet number from the series letter for series D, E, F, G, H, J and the low-numbered notes of series K.

In January 1920 the plates were modified so that "WILL PAY TO THE BEARER ON DEMAND" appears in a straight line. At the same time it was decided to put the series letter in front of the sheet number, retaining the hyphen. The signature engraved on the lower right side of these and the preceding notes is that of T. C. Boville, with various Finance Department employees countersigning on the left. The Boville signature continues for the remainder of the series K and for most of series L. Because of his retirement, Boville's signature was replaced on the plates by that of J. C. Saunders around the beginning of 1921. Before further changes were made series L was completed, together with series M, N and approximately half of series P, with the Saunders signature.

Late in 1922 it was thought best to begin immediately applying the second signature, that of G. W. Hyndman, by machine, simultaneously impressing the Finance Department seal, because of problems encountered with the ink being used for countersigning by hand. Thus it was that the seal was overprinted on the large TWO counter right of centre, because new plates with the counter removed to make space for the seal were not yet available. The last of series P and part of series R were of the "seal over TWO" variety.

In the spring of 1923 notes with the right hand TWO counter deleted began to be delivered to the Finance Department, where the Hyndman signature and seal were applied by typography. These are known as the "seal only" notes. The remainder of series R was of this type, as were all the notes of series S, which terminated at sheet number 742000. These final "Connaught" $2 notes were received in December 1923.

"Seal over TWO" notes are quite scarce, and care must be exercised in distinguishing them from the less scarce "seal only" notes, because the seal almost obliterates the TWO.

Checklist of Prefix Letters for 1914 $2 Dominion Notes

Cat.No.	Denom.	Variety	Signature	Series Letter
DC-22a	$2	"Will Pay.." curved; no hyphen	Boville, r.	A B C
DC-22a-i	$2	"Will Pay.." curved; with hyphen	Boville, r.	D E F G H J K
DC-22b	$2	"Will Pay.." straight	Boville, r.	K L
DC-22c	$2	"Will Pay.." straight	Saunders, r.	L M N P
DC-22d	$2	"Will Pay.." straight, seal over TWO	Hyndman-Saunders	P R
DC-22e	$2	"Will Pay.." straight, seal only	Hyndman-Saunders	R S

Summary of Technical Details

Cat.No.	Denom.	Variety	Series	Serial Numbers	Qty. Printed
DC-22a	$2	"Will Pay..." curved, no hyphen, Boville (no seal)	A	000001-1000000/A,B,C,D	4,000,000
			B	000001-1000000/A,B,C,D	4,000,000
			C	000001-1000000/A,B,C,D	4,000,000
DC-22a-i	$2	"Will Pay..." curved; with hyphen, Boville (no seal)	D	000001-1000000/A,B,C,D	4,000,000
			E	000001-1000000/A,B,C,D	4,000,000
			F	000001-1000000/A,B,C,D	4,000,000
			G	000001-1000000/A,B,C,D	4,000,000
			H	000001-1000000/A,B,C,D	4,000,000
			J	000001-1000000/A,B,C,D	4,000,000
			K	000001- 144113 /A,B,C,D	Unknown
DC-22b	$2	"Will Pay..." straight; Boville (no seal)	K	265726-1000000/A,B,C,D	Unknown
			L	000001- 831974/A,B,C,D	Unknown
DC-22c	$2	"Will Pay..." straight; Saunders (no seal)	L	927456-1000000/A,B,C D	Unknown
			M	000001-1000000/A,B,C,D	4,000,000
			N	000001-1000000/A,B,C,D	4,000,000
			P	000001- 598459/A,B,C,D	Unknown
DC-22d	$2	" Will Pay..." straight; Hyndman-Saunders (seal over TWO)	P	660097-1000000/A,B,C,D	Unknown
			R	000001- 708220/A,B,C,D	Unknown
DC-22e	$2	"Will Pay..." straight; Hyndman-Saunders, (seal only)	R	740064-1000000/A,B,C,D	Unknown
			S	000001- 742000/A,B,C,D	2,968,000

Note: Where quantity is given as "Unknown," the serial numbers shown are the highs and lows observed.

$2 Issue — 1914

DC-22a

Face Design: H.R.H. The Duke of Connaught/—/
H.R.H. The Duchess of Connaught (see varieties)
Colour: Black with brown and olive tint

DC-22a-i

Back Design: Royal coat of arms encircled by the shields of the nine provinces and maple leaves over the "Dominion of Canada"
Colour: Olive green

Issue Date: Engraved: Jan'y 2nd 1914
Imprint: American Bank Note Co. Ottawa on face and back

Signatures

Left:		Right:	
	mss. various		Engr.: T.C. Boville
	mss. various		Engr.: J.C. Saunders
	Typed: Geo. W. Hyndman		Engr.: J.C. Saunders

$2 Issue — 1914

Varieties

Over the black lathework of the centre counter is the wording "WILL PAY TO BEARER ON DEMAND" which appears two different ways:

Curved

Straight

"Will pay to bearer on demand"

The seal of the Department of Finance is used during the middle of this issue and is overprinted on, or replaces the right TWO of the centre counter.

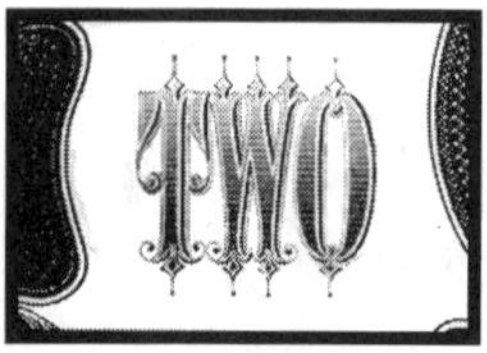
Two at right

Black seal over TWO at right

Black seal only

Cat.No.	Denom.	Variety	Series	G	VG	F	VF	EF	AU	Unc
DC-22a	$2	No seal, "Will pay..." curved, Boville	A,B,C	60.	125.	250.	550.	1,000.	1,500.	2,500.
DC-22a-i	$2	Same, but with hyphen	D,E,F,G, H,J,K	60.	125.	250.	550.	1,000.	1,500.	2,500.
DC-22b	$2	No seal, "Will Pay..." straight, Boville	K,L	90.	185.	375.	800.	1,300.	2,100.	3,100.
DC-22c	$2	Same, but Saunders	L,M,N,P	75.	150.	300.	650.	1,100.	1,800.	2,900.
DC-22d	$2	Seal over TWO; Hyndman-Saunders	P,R	100.	200.	400.	850.	1,400.	2,200.	3,250.
DC-22e	$2	Seal only, Hyndman-Saunders	R,S	100.	200.	400.	850.	1,400.	2,200.	3,250.

ISSUE OF 1917

The only new issue designed during World War I, the sixth issue of $1 Dominion notes not unexpectedly has several patriotic and military symbols. The centre of the note face portrays Princess Patricia (1886-1974), daughter of the former Governor General and his wife, T.R.H. the Duke and Duchess of Connaught. The lower part of the portrait is flanked by flags and maple leaves. Princess Patricia lent her name and assistance in raising a regiment designated the Princess Patricia's Canadian Light Infantry, designed the regiment's colours and became its Colonel-in-Chief. The issue date on the notes commemorates the sailing of the Princess Pat's for England. Upon her marriage to Admiral Sir Alexander Ramsay, the Princess assumed the name Lady Patricia Ramsay.

As on all $1 Dominion notes since 1897, the back depicts the Centre Block of the Parliament Buildings, although, unlike the previous issues, the view is from inside the front gate. However, the Centre Block no longer existed, having been destroyed by fire on February 3, 1916, with only the library being saved.

The first notes to be printed in this series have the engraved T. C. Boville signature in the right-hand signature space, with the countersignatures of various Finance Department employees at the left. The notes were printed by the American Bank Note Company, Ottawa, but the face and back imprints were omitted. However, their A. B. N. Co. logo was discreetly hidden away as part of the design on both sides. The logo can be found on the face on the left-hand side directly below the scroll, and on the back it is in the lower left corner close to the scroll work. The series letter follows the sheet number, from which it is separated by a hyphen. Notes of this type correspond to series A, B, C, D, E, F, G and the first part of series H.

It was in 1919, within series H, that the American Bank Note Company imprints were added on instructions from the Department of Finance, and this modified type continued into series J. In the latter part of series J, the series letter was placed ahead of the sheet number, from which it continued to be separated by a hyphen. These notes, still bearing the Boville signature, correspond to late series J, series K, L, M, N, P and part of series R. In September 1921 the Boville signature was removed from the plates and replaced by that of J. C. Saunders. With no other changes, the Saunders notes completed series R and continued through series S, T, U, V, W, X, Y and Z.

By September 1922, for the first time in an issue of Dominion notes, the alphabet had been exhausted for use as series letters, excepting the letters I, O and Q, which were avoided because of their resemblance to the digits 1 and 0. It was decided to start through the alphabet again, with the series letter still preceding the sheet number, but with the letter "A" following the sheet number with no hyphen, to indicate that the series letters were being used for the second time.

This procedure had just begun when it was decided to apply the second signature by machine, together with the Finance Department seal. The changeover occurred with sheet A-910500A in October 1922. Because is was considered desirable to begin machine signing immediately on notes of the first design, printed before the right-hand ONE counter could be removed from the plates, the transitional "seal over ONE" variety was created. The seal is in black ink, and the typographed signature is that of G. W. Hyndman, placed in the space designated "COUNTERSIGNED". These notes correspond to the last of series A, together with all of series B, C, D and E, and part of series F, all of course having the letter "A" after the sheet number. To the right of the seal, the series is repeated as A-1, B-1, etc.

In September 1923 notes of the second design appeared, having the right-hand ONE counter omitted. The space in which the typographed Hyndman signature was added was redesignated "FOR COMPTROLLER OF CURRENCY". The "seal only" notes occur in series F, G, H and J, the latter series ending at sheet J-855000A. The final deliveries of the 1917-dated Princess Pat issue were made to the Finance Department in October 1924, several months after the first 1923 King George V notes began to be received. Hoards of all the major varieties have turned up in excellent states of preservation.

Checklist of Prefix Letters for 1917 Dominion Notes

Cat.No.	Denom.	Variety	Signatures	Series Letters
DC-23a	$1	No seal, Boville r. series letter at end, no imprints	Boville	A B C D E F G H
DC-23a-i	$1	Imprints added	Boville	H J
DC-23a-ii	$1	Series letter at beginning	Boville	J K L M N P R
DC-23b	$1	As above	Saunders	R S T U V W X Y Z
DC-23b-i	$1	"A" after sheet numbers	Saunders	A
DC-23c	$1	Seal over ONE at right	Hyndman-Saunders	A B C D E F
DC-23d	$1	Seal only at right	Hyndman-Saunders	F G H J

Summary of Technical Details

Cat.No.	Denom.	Variety	Series	Serial Numbers	Quantity Printed
DC-23a	$1	No imprints; suffix letter; Boville	A	000001-1000000/A,B,C,D	4,000,000
			B	000001-1000000/A,B,C,D	4,000,000
			C	000001-1000000/A,B,C,D	4,000,000
			D	000001-1000000/A,B,C,D	4,000,000
			E	000001-1000000/A,B,C,D	4,000,000
			F	000001-1000000/A,B,C,D	4,000,000
			G	000001-1000000/A,B,C,D	4,000,000
			H	000001- 186774 /A,B,C,D	Unknown
DC-23a-i	$1	Imprints added, suffix letter, Boville	H	284718*-1000000/A,B,C,D	Unknown
			J	000001- 984901*/A,B,C,D	Unknown
DC-23a-ii	$1	Prefix letter, Boville	J	.....- 1000000/A,B,C,D	Unknown
			K	000001-1000000/A,B,C,D	4,000,000
			L	000001-1000000/A,B,C,D	4,000,000
			M	000001-1000000/A,B,C,D	4,000,000
			N	000001-1000000/A,B,C,D	4,000,000
			P	000001-1000000/A,B,C,D	4,000,000
			R	000001- 588044 /A,B,C,D	Unknown
DC-23b	$1	Prefix letter, Saunders	R	862635*-1000000/A,B,C,D	Unknown
			S	000001-1000000/A,B,C,D	4,000,000
			T	000001-1000000/A,B,C,D	4,000,000
			U	000001-1000000/A,B,C,D	4,000,000
			V	000001-1000000/A,B,C,D	4,000,000
			W	000001-1000000/A,B,C,D	4,000,000
			X	000001-1000000/A,B,C,D	4,000,000
			Y	000001-1000000/A,B,C,D	4,000,000
			Z	000001-1000000/A,B,C,D	4,000,000
DC-23b-i	$1	Prefix letter, Saunders suffix "A"	A	000001A-910500A/A,B,C,D	3,642,000
DC-23c	$1	Seal over ONE at right, Hyndman-Saunders	A	910501A-1000000A/A,B,C,D	358,000
			B	000001A-1000000A/A,B,C,D	4,000,000
			C	000001A-1000000A/A,B,C,D	4,000,000
			D	000001A-1000000A/A,B,C,D	4,000,000
			E	000001A-1000000A/A,B,C,D	4,000,000
			F	000001A- 213395A/A,B,C,D	Unknown
DC-23d	$1	Seal only at right, Hyndman-Saunders	F	282601A*-1000000A/A,B,C,D	Unknown
			G	000001A-1000000A/A,B,C,D	4,000,000
			H	000001A-1000000A/A,B,C,D	4,000,000
			J	000001A- 855000A/A,B,C,D	4,000,000

Note: * Denotes high and low numbers seen

$1 Issue — 1917

DC-23b

Face Design: —/H.R.H. Princess Patricia/—
Colour: Black with green tint

DC-23a

Back Design: Lathework and counters with "Dominion of Canada" over Parliament Building, view from inside the front gate
Colour: Green

Issue Date: Engraved: March 17th 1917
Imprint: American Bank Note Company Ottawa, face and back or no imprint, with A B N Co. logo

Signatures

Left:		Right:	
	mss. various		Engr.: T.C. Boville
	mss. various		Engr.: J.C. Saunders
	Typed: Geo. W. Hyndman		Engr.: J.C. Saunders

Varieties

The seal of the Department of Finance is used during the middle of this issue and is overprinted on, or replaces, the right ONE counter

ONE at right

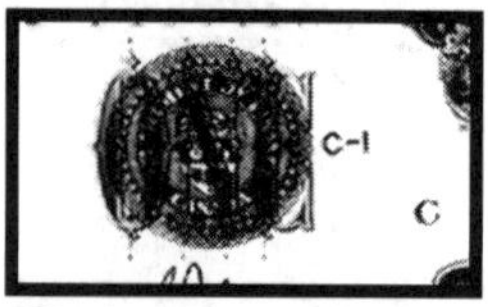

Black seal over ONE at right

Black seal only

Cat.No.	Denom.	Variety	Series	G	VG	F	VF	EF	AU	Unc
DC-23a	$1	No seal, no imprints, Boville, r.	A,B,C,D, E,F,G,H	30.	65.	100.	200.	400.	650.	1,500.
DC-23a-i	$1	No seal, imprints, Boville, Suffix letter	H,J	35.	80.	110.	225.	450.	700.	1,700.
DC-23a-ii	$1	No seal, imprints, Boville, Prefix letter	J,K,L, M,N,P,R	25.	55.	80.	175.	350.	600.	1,400.
DC-23b	$1	No seal, Saunders, r.	R,S,T,U, V,W,X,Y,Z	25.	55.	80.	175.	350.	600.	1,400.
DC-23b-i	$1	No seal, Saunders, r., Suffix "A"	A	35.	80.	110.	225.	450.	750.	1,700.
DC-23c	$1	Seal over ONE, suffix "A"	A	40.	85.	125.	250.	500.	850.	1,800.
DC-23c	$1	Seal over ONE, suffix "A"	B,C,D,E,F	30.	65.	110.	200.	400.	700.	1,500.
DC-23d	$1	Seal only, Suffix "A"	F,G,H,J	30.	65.	110.	200.	400.	700.	1,500.

ISSUE OF 1923

25¢ ISSUE — 1923

The face design of the 25-cent fractional note was considerably altered from the 1900 issue. The seated Britannia vignette was replaced by a head and torso vignette located in the centre of the note, with a large brown 25 counter at the left and the Department of Finance seal at the right. All notes of this issue correspond to an "A" series (A-1 at right of seal), which was never completed. Only in this third and final issue were the shinplasters provided with serial numbers. The second signature was restored. The backs remained unchanged from those of the 1900 issue.

On the first variety of this issue, the words "AUTHORIZED BY R. S. C. CAP. 31" are found above the left-hand signature space. They were issued by the Finance Department despite an earlier decision not to release any notes with this inscription. The notes were numbered in sheets of ten, using check letters A, B, C, D, E, H, J, K, L and M. The check letter is indicated in red prefixing the sheet number. The signatures are those of G. W. Hyndman, typographed at the left, and J. C. Saunders, engraved at the right. The notes were printed bearing the Saunders signature only. After delivery to the Finance Department the Hyndman signature and seal were added. The first plates for this issue were prepared in September 1923.

On the second and subsequent varieties, the words indicating the authorizing legislation were omitted. The red prefix check letter was removed, and replaced by a black letter engraved to the left of the large brown 25 counter. Three signature varieties exist: G. W. Hyndman-J. C. Saunders, delivered December 1924; S. P. McCavour-J. C. Saunders, delivered intermittently between April 1925 and March 1932; and C. E. Campbell-W. C. Clark, delivered in March 1932. On the final variety, the notes were printed without signatures as a result of the J. C. Saunders signature having been deleted from the plates. Both Campbell and Clark signatures were applied by the Finance Department.

A popular method of collecting these fractional notes is to acquire one of each check letter for each variety, making a total of 40 notes for this issue. Some specialists collect by plate numbers, which are found in the following combinations:

TABLE

PLATE NUMBER COMBINATIONS FOR 1923 ISSUE FRACTIONALS

A. "AUTHORIZED BY R. S. C. CAP. 31" PRESENT

Face Plate #	Back Plate #
1	1, 2
2	1, 2

B. "AUTHORIZED BY R. S. C. CAP. 31" OMITTED

1. Signed G. W. Hyndman

Face Plate #	Back Plate #
1	1, 2
2	1, 2

2. Signed S. P. McCavour

Face Plate #	Back Plate #'s
1	1, 2
2	1, 2
3	1, 2, 3, 4
4	1, 2, 3, 4
5	3, 4
6	3, 4

3. Signed C. E. Campbell

Face Plate #	Back Plate #'s
7	3, 4
8	3, 4

Summary of Technical Details for 1923

Cat.No.	Variety	Series	Serial Numbers	Qty. Printed
DC-24a	With "Authorized..," Hyndman-Saunders	A	000001-051000/A-M	510,000
DC-24b	Without "Authorized...,"Hyndman-Saunders	A	051001-092000/A-M	410,000
DC-24c	Without "Authorized...," McCavour-Saunders	A	092001-605000/A-M	5,130,000
DC-24d	Without "Authorized...," Campbell-Clark	A	605001-700000/A-M	950,000

25¢ Issue — 1923

DC-24b

Face Design: —/Britannia holding her trident/—
(see varieties)
Colour: Black with brown tint

DC-24b

Back Design: Lathework and counters
Colour: Green

Issue Date: Engraved: July 2nd 1923
Imprint: Canadian Bank Note Company Limited, on face and back

Signatures

Left:		Right:
Typed: Geo. W. Hyndman		Engr.: J.C. Saunders
Typed: S.P. McCavour		Engr.: J.C. Saunders
Typed: C.E. Campbell		Typed: W.C. Clark

Varieties

The early notes of this issue carried the supposed authorizing legislation, "Revised Statutes of Canada," above the left signature.

With AUTHORIZED BY R.S.C. CAP. 31.

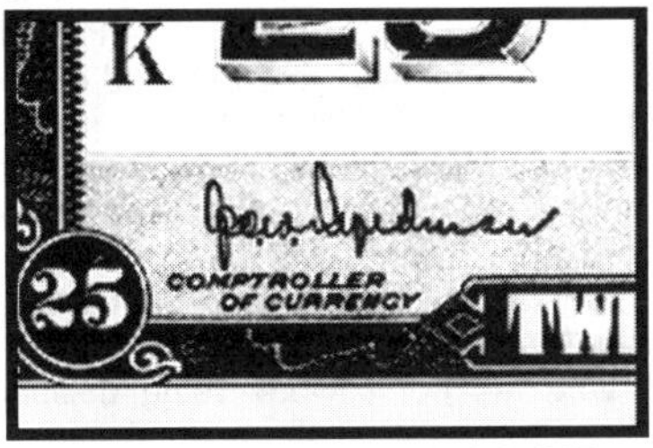

Without AUTHORIZED BY R.S.C. CAP.

Notes of the DC-24a issue come with red check letters A,B,C,D,E,H,J,K,L or M prefixing the sheet number. On catalogue numbers DC-24b, 24c and 24d, the check letter is black and is beside the large left counter.

Cat.No.	Denom.	Variety	G	VG	F	VF	EF	AU	Unc
DC-24a	25¢	AUTHORIZED, etc. Hyndman-Saunders	9.	17.	25.	40.	125.	225.	400.
DC-24b	25¢	No AUTHORIZED, Hyndman-Saunders	9.	17.	25.	40.	125.	225.	400.
DC-24c	25¢	No AUTHORIZED, McCavour-Saunders	6.	10.	14.	25.	60.	110.	220.
DC-24d	25¢	No AUTHORIZED, Campbell-Clark	6.	10.	14.	25.	60.	110.	220.

$1 Issue — 1923

The $1 Dominion notes of 1923 feature a large portrait of King George V, prepared from a photograph. The general layout of the other details on the face of the note bears some resemblance to that of the previous $1 issue. A space was left at the right for the application of the seal by the Finance Department. Various colours of seals were used to facilitate the sorting of notes as they were returned for redemption and destruction. The colours used for sealing were officially designated black, red, blue, green, bronze and purple, although collectors have long been accustomed to calling the latter two "purple-brown" and "lilac" respectively. The scarce purple seal was used to mark a very limited issue of notes printed on experimental paper, as will be explained in detail under the heading "Experimental Issues."

On the backs is found a vignette of the Library of Parliament, the only part of the Centre Block surviving the disastrous fire of February 3, 1916, having been saved by its steel doors. At the time the notes were being designed, however, reconstruction was substantially complete. The new structure resembles the old Centre Block in general outline but is a storey higher and fireproof. The corner stone of the Peace Tower was laid by the Prince of Wales in 1919. The Library of Parliament was badly damaged by fire in 1952 and was reopened in 1956. The printing of the notes was done by the Canadian Bank Note Company, formerly the Ottawa branch of the American Bank Note Company. This change of name seemed advisable in the face of growing Canadian nationalism.

VARIETIES

The notes of this issue are divided into four groups, the group number being found at the right of the seal and in the same colour. For group 1 notes, the 1 is preceded by the series letter, as A-1, B-1, etc. This is a continuation of the practice followed when sealing began on the previous issue. Subsequent groups are identified by a large 2, 3 or 4 found at the right of the seal, but with no letter. The groups are numbered in chronological order as issued, with the exception of the experimental purple seal notes.

The first notes of this issue, belonging to group 1, were delivered to the Finance Department in July 1924. The engraved J. C. Saunders signature was printed on the notes as part of the face plate detail. The typed G. W. Hyndman signature and black seal were applied by the Finance Department prior to distribution of the notes for circulation. Notes of this description were printed in series A, B and C, consisting of 1,000,000 sheets of four notes (distinguished by check letters A, B, C and D) in each series. The series letter is printed in red, prefixed to the sheet number by a hyphen.

In March 1925 the Hyndman signature typographed in the left-hand space was replaced by that of S. P. McCavour, and the seal colour was changed to red. Again, three series of one million sheets each were produced. This was followed by blue, green and bronze seals respectively, each appearing on three series of one million sheets.

The first notes of group 2 were delivered in the summer of 1927. The McCavour-Saunders signature combination was still in use. The application of seals of a particular colour was extended over four series, rather than three as previously. Black seals were used for the first four series of this group, series S, T, U and V, and red seals were used for the completion of the alphabet.

In 1927 a new $1 note design was being modelled by the Canadian Bank Note Company, which featured a portrait of Sir John A. Macdonald engraved from a photograph. Possibly it was intended to introduce this design after the series letters of the King George issue progressed to the end of the alphabet, a point which was actually reached in November 1928.

However, the problem of devising additional new serial numbers was solved without replacing the existing design and using a different procedure from that followed for the Princess Pat issue. The series letters began at "A" again, with the sheets numbered from 1000001 to 6000000 with the hyphen removed, so that each new series consisted of five million sheets of four notes, rather than one million as previously. Still within group 2 and with the McCavour-Saunders signature combination, delivery of the "A" series with a blue seal began in November 1928. This was followed by the "B" series with a bronze seal beginning in October

1929 and the "C" series with a green seal in May 1930. This brought to an end the group 2 part of the issue.

Group 1 reappeared briefly in May and June of 1931 with the release of the experimental purple seal notes. This time the numbering continued past 6000000, still within series "C." Most of the notes bear the McCavour-Saunders signature combination, although the Comptroller of Currency, C. E. Campbell, had instructed the bank note company to delete the engraved Saunders signature the previous February, Mr. Saunders having died in 1930. However the presses were shut down only one at a time to make the alteration on the plates, to avoid the temporary layoffs that would be brought on by idling all of the presses at once. Consequently a part of the new notes delivered as late as July 1931 continued to bear the obsolete Saunders signature, to the exasperation of Mr. Campbell.

Some of the purple seal notes were delivered without any signature to the Finance Department, where the signatures of C. E. Campbell and Watson Sellar, the Acting Deputy Minister of Finance, were applied by typography. The changeover number for this signature combination was 6386001. Surprisingly, the McCavour-Saunders signatures reappeared at some point. No documentation has been found indicating the precise changeover for this reversion, but an examination of the numbers of surviving notes indicated that it was 649——. The experimental purple seal issue ended at sheet number 6525000, and series "C" was terminated at the same time. These experimental notes mark the last time that seals coloured other than black were used on $1 Dominion notes.

In July 1931 the first notes of group 3 were supplied to the Finance Department. All notes of this group are in series "D", which consisted of nine million sheets numbered from 1000001 to 10000000. The first few sheets, up to number 1195000, have the McCavour-Saunders signatures, while all the others have the Campbell-Sellar signatures. The series "D" notes have black seals.

Delivery of the group 4 notes began in February 1933. This group is distinguished by the introduction of the Campbell-Clark signature combination. Again, the notes were delivered unsigned, with both signatures and the seal being typed on by the Finance Department. A full series "E", consisting of nine million sheets numbered 1000001 to 10000000, was issued. This was followed by only a half-million sheets in Series "F", numbered from 1000001 to 1500000. These were the final $1 Dominion notes, and the last delivery was made in January 1935. Series "F" was terminated at this point because the large Dominion notes were about to be superseded by the small-size notes of the newly formed Bank of Canada.

EXPERIMENTAL ISSUES

Before 1929, all Canadian bank notes and Dominion notes were being printed on paper supplied by Crane & Co. of Dalton, Massachusetts. A 1907 report on tests applied to the paper revealed that it was satisfactory and durable. During the First World War, difficulties arose with the Crane paper which led to a shorter circulation life of the notes. By 1925 some Crane paper of altered composition, having less linen and about 25 percent cotton, was used for Dominion notes on a trial basis, found satisfactory and approved for general use. With this change, the Canadian Bank Note Co. expected the notes to survive from one to one and a half years in circulation. This was considered quite acceptable, especially since the growing motor garage business was resulting in increased soiling of notes.

However, a Canadian paper source was considered desirable, and the government entered into discussions with the Howard Smith Paper Co. of Beauhamois, Quebec (subsequently known as Domtar Corp.). The company was given to understand that an order would be forthcoming when they could furnish a paper that could stand up reasonably well under mechanical tests.

Comparison tests performed on the Crane and Smith bank note papers revealed that they were essentially equal in terms of folding strength and resistance to rubbing. The Crane paper was almost white; Smith's was a cream shade. Crane's paper absorbed moisture more readily, making it easier to wet for printing. The Howard Smith paper seemed sufficiently promising to justify being tested in circulation. On March 14, 1928, the Finance Department instructed the Canadian Bank Note Company to prepare 100,000 sheets of $1 Dominion notes on Howard Smith paper. The 400,000 notes were to be distributed in various provinces for wear tests.

The number of notes was kept low to minimize the cost to the government if the test proved unsuccessful.

Whether the full order of 100,000 sheets was printed is uncertain, but it is known that at least 78,500 sheets were completed in June 1929 having sheet numbers 1000001-1078500 in series "B", group 2 (bronze seal). The paper was noted by the bank note company to take a better finish than Crane's paper, although it was darker in colour. There were some problems with the new paper. Bank note company employees had to sort the sheets to remove those containing knots or strings, comprising about 4 percent of the total. An extra step was required to wet the paper in preparation for printing because of its resistance to water. The Howard Smith company agreed to assume the resulting extra costs. The Finance Department early in 1931 pronounced itself satisfied with the results of the experiment, and it was considered even more appropriate to use the Canadian product to provide employment opportunities during the Depression.

A larger experimental test, consisting of 500,000 sheets to be printed on Howard Smith paper, was ordered before the final decision would be made. In fact 525,000 sheets were printed and delivered in the spring of 1931. These were identified with a purple seal, a colour not used on any other Dominion notes, to make them easier to sort out for the wear-test studies.

On the basis of all the tests, the Finance Department instructed the Canadian Bank Note Company to switch over to Howard Smith paper for all Dominion notes. The last sheet of $1 notes to be printed on Crane paper was number 1195000 in series "D" (group 3, black seal). This was the last sheet bearing the McCavour-Saunders signature combination.

Checklist of Prefix Letters for 1923 $1 Dominion Notes

GROUP 1

Cat.No.	Denom.	Signatures	Seal	Series Letters
DC-25a	$1	Hyndman-Saunders	Black	A B C
DC-25b	$1	McCavour-Saunders	Red	D E F
DC-25c	$1	McCavour-Saunders	Blue	G H J
DC-25d	$1	McCavour-Saunders	Green	K L M
DC-25e	$1	McCavour-Saunders	Bronze	N P R

GROUP 2

Cat.No.	Denom.	Signatures	Seal	Series Letters
DC-25f	$1	McCavour-Saunders	Black	S T U V
DC-25g	$1	McCavour-Saunders	Red	W X Y Z
DC-25h	$1	McCavour-Saunders	Blue	A
DC-25i	$1	McCavour-Saunders	Bronze	B
DC-25j	$1	McCavour-Saunders	Green	C

GROUP 1: EXPERIMENTAL

Cat.No.	Denom.	Signatures	Seal	Series Letters
DC-25k	$1	McCavour-Saunders	Purple	C
DC-25l	$1	Campbell-Sellar	Purple	C

GROUP 2: EXPERIMENTAL

Cat.No.	Denom.	Signatures	Seal	Series Letters
DC-25iT	$1	McCavour-Saunders	Bronze	B

Checklist of Prefix Letters for 1923 $1 Dominion Notes

GROUP 3

Cat.No.	Denom.	Signatures	Seal	Series Letters
DC-25m	$1	McCavour-Saunders	Black	D
DC-25n	$1	Campbell-Sellar	Black	D

GROUP 4

Cat.No.	Denom.	Signatures	Seal	Series Letters
DC-25o	$1	Campbell-Clark	Black	E F

Summary of Technical Details

Cat.No.	Group	Signatures	Seal	Series	Serial Numbers	Qty. Printed
DC-25a	1	Hyndman-Saunders	Black	A	000001- 1000000/A,B,C,D	4,000,000
DC-25a	1	Hyndman-Saunders	Black	B	000001- 1000000/A,B,C,D	4,000,000
DC-25a	1	Hyndman-Saunders	Black	C	000001- 1000000/A,B,C,D	4,000,000
DC-25b	1	McCavour-Saunders	Red	D	000001- 1000000/A,B,C,D	4,000,000
DC-25b	1	McCavour-Saunders	Red	E	000001- 1000000/A,B,C,D	4,000,000
DC-25b	1	McCavour-Saunders	Red	F	000001- 1000000/A,B,C,D	4,000,000
DC-25c	1	McCavour-Saunders	Blue	G	000001- 1000000/A,B,C,D	4,000,000
DC-25c	1	McCavour-Saunders	Blue	H	000001- 1000000/A,B,C,D	4,000,000
DC-25c	1	McCavour-Saunders	Blue	J	000001- 1000000/A,B,C,D	4,000,000
DC-25d	1	McCavour-Saunders	Green	K	000001- 1000000/A,B,C,D	4,000,000
DC-25d	1	McCavour-Saunders	Green	L	000001- 1000000/A,B,C,D	4,000,000
DC-25d	1	McCavour-Saunders	Green	M	000001- 1000000/A,B,C,D	4,000,000
DC-25e	1	McCavour-Saunders	Bronze	N	000001- 1000000/A,B,C,D	4,000,000
DC-25e	1	McCavour-Saunders	Bronze	P	000001- 1000000/A,B,C,D	4,000,000
DC-25e	1	McCavour-Saunders	Bronze	R	000001- 1000000/A,B,C,D	4,000,000
DC-25f	2	McCavour-Saunders	Black	S	000001- 1000000/A,B,C,D	4,000,000
DC-25f	2	McCavour-Saunders	Black	T	000001- 1000000/A,B,C,D	4,000,000
DC-25f	2	McCavour-Saunders	Black	U	000001- 1000000/A,B,C,D	4,000,000
DC-25f	2	McCavour-Saunders	Black	V	000001- 1000000/A,B,C,D	4,000,000
DC-25g	2	McCavour-Saunders	Red	W	000001- 1000000/A,B,C,D	4,000,000
DC-25g	2	McCavour-Saunders	Red	X	000001- 1000000/A,B,C,D	4,000,000
DC-25g	2	McCavour-Saunders	Red	Y	000001- 1000000/A,B,C,D	4,000,000
DC-25g	2	McCavour-Saunders	Red	Z	000001- 1000000/A,B,C,D	4,000,000
DC-25h	2	McCavour-Saunders	Blue	A	1000001- 6000000/A,B,C,D	20,000,000
DC-25iT	2	McCavour-Saunders	Bronze	B	1000001- 1078500/A,B,C,D	314,000
DC-25i	2	McCavour-Saunders	Bronze	B	1078501- 10000000/A,B,C,D	9,686,000
DC-25j	2	McCavour-Saunders	Green	C	1000001- 6000000/A,B,C,D	20,000,000
DC-25k	1	McCavour-Saunders	Purple	C	6000001- 6386000/A,B,C,D	
DC-25k	1	McCavour-Saunders	Purple	C	649... 6525000/A,B,C,D	1,644,000+
DC-25l	1	Campbell-Sellar	Purple	C	6386001- 6491046*/A,B,C,D	416,000+
DC-25m	3	McCavour-Saunders	Black	D	1000001- 1195000/A,B,C,D	780,000
DC-25n	3	Campbell-Sellar	Black	D	1195001- 10000000/A,B,C,D	35,220,000
DC-25o	4	Campbell-Clark	Black	E	1000001- 10000000/A,B,C,D	36,000,000
DC-25o	4	Campbell-Clark	Black	F	1000001- 1500000/A,B,C,D	2,000,000

Note: * Denotes high and low numbers seen.

$1 Issue — 1923

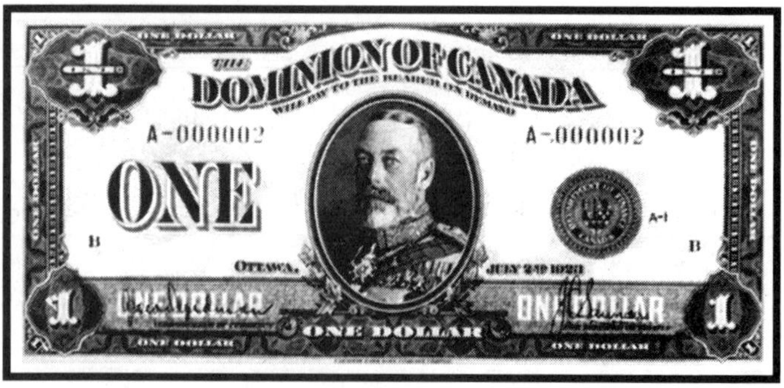

DC-25a

Face Design: —/King George V/—
Colour: Black with green tint

DC-25

Back Design: —/Library of Parliament/—
Colour: Green

Issue Date: Engraved: July 2nd 1923
Imprint: Canadian Bank Note Company Limited on face and back
Signatures: **Left:** Typed: Geo. W. Hyndman **Right:** Engr.: J.C. Saunders
Typed: S.P. McCavour Engr.: J.C. Saunders
Typed: C.E. Campbell Typed Watson Sellar
Typed: C.E. Campbell Typed W.C. Clark

Varieties

Seal Colour: The Seal of the Department of Finance was printed in the following colours: Black, red, blue, green, bronze or purple.

DC-25n

Purple Seal

DC-25l

Cat.No.	Denom.	Variety	Series	G	VG	F	VF	EF	AU	Unc
DC-25a	$1	Hyndman-Saunders, Black seal. Group 1.	A,B,C	30.	70.	100.	200.	500.	650.	1,100.
DC-25b	$1	McCavour-Saunders, Red seal. Group 1.	D,E,F	25.	60.	90.	200.	400.	500.	1,000.
DC-25c	$1	McCavour-Saunders, Blue seal. Group 1.	G,H,J	25.	60.	100.	225.	475.	750.	1,300.
DC-25d	$1	McCavour-Saunders, Green seal. Group 1.	K,L,M	20.	45.	75.	150.	275.	450.	950.
DC-25e	$1	McCavour-Saunders, Bronze seal. Group 1.	N,P,R	20.	45.	75.	150.	275.	450.	950.
DC-25f	$1	McCavour-Saunders, Black seal. Group 2.	S,T,U,V	20.	45.	75.	150.	275.	450.	850.
DC-25g	$1	McCavour-Saunders, Red seal. Group 2.	W,X,Y,Z	20.	35.	60.	100.	175.	375.	800.
DC-25h	$1	McCavour-Saunders, Blue seal, Group 2.	A	20.	45.	70.	120.	200.	425.	850.
DC-25i	$1	McCavour-Saunders, Bronze seal. Group 2.	B	20.	40.	60.	100.	175.	325.	600.
DC-25iT	$1	McCavour-Saunders Bronze seal. Group 2.	B*	450.	850.	1,700.	2,250.	3,300.	4,500.	—
DC-25j	$1	McCavour-Saunders, Green seal. Group 2.	C	20.	45.	70.	120.	200.	350.	700.
DC-25k	$1	McCavour-Saunders, Purple seal. Group 1.	C**	85.	175.	350.	700.	1,200.	2,000.	3,250.
DC-25l	$1	Campbell-Sellar, Purple seal. Group 1.	C**	200.	400.	750.	1,000.	1,800.	2,750.	3,750.
DC-25m	$1	McCavour-Saunders, Black seal. Group 3.	D***	200.	400.	700.	1,100.	1,900.	2,750.	4,000.
DC-25n	$1	Campbell-Sellar, Black seal. Group 3.	D	18.	35.	55.	90.	150.	250.	450.
DC-25o	$1	Campbell-Clark, Black seal. Group 4.	E	17.	32.	45.	80.	125.	175.	350.
DC-25o	$1	Campbell-Clark Black seal. Group 4.	F	30.	70.	140.	225.	350.	550.	900.

Notes: * Test notes, on Howard Smith paper, have sheet numbers 1000001-1078500 only.

** Do not confuse with the more common bronze seal. Purple seals only occur with C-1 to the right of the seal.

*** Do not confuse with the more common group 2 variety 25f. DC-25m notes only occur with the numeral 3 to the right of the seal.

$2 Issue — 1923

This denomination features as its central vignette the portrait of the Prince of Wales, who reigned briefly in 1936 as King Edward VIII. The photograph which was the basis of the portrait was selected in the summer of 1922, and proofs of the notes were approved in July 1923. The portrait was engraved by Mr. Savage of the American Bank Note Co. in New York City, who received praise from the Finance Department for the high quality of his work. In 1924 the photographer who took the picture from which the engraving was made threatened to sue for infringement of copyright. This was an oversight on the part of the Canadian Bank Note Co., and an amicable settlement was sought.

A different kind of controversy was aroused by the back of the note. The Dominion coat of arms was engraved from a photograph of an official drawing supplied by the Department of the Secretary of State. After the plates were engraved and a large quantity of notes issued, certain details were altered by the State Department. It was too late to make any changes in the notes. A Toronto newspaper discovered the discrepancy and criticized the Canadian Bank Note Co.

Like the $1 notes, the 1923 $2 notes are divided into four groups. Group 1 notes have the series letter and numeral 1, separated by a hyphen, following the seal and in the same colour as the seal. The other groups carry a large coloured numeral 2, 3 or 4, to the right of the seal. The groups are numbered in chronological order, as issued.

The first notes of group 1 were delivered to the Finance Department in November 1923. These have a black seal and bear the typed signature of G. W. Hyndman on the left and the engraved signature of J. C. Saunders on the right. These notes completed series "A" and "B", of 1,000,000 sheets each. The series letter is found in red, prefixing the sheet number, as well as to the right of the seal. In March 1925 the typed signature of G. W. Hyndman was replaced by that of S. P. McCavour. Two series of McCavour-Saunders notes were printed with red, blue, green and bronze seal colours, . By this point, ten million sheets (or 40 million notes) had been printed in group 1, which was then terminated.

Group 2 began in February 1929. Two series were printed with black, red and blue seal colours. In June 1931, during the production of blue seal notes in series "S", the J. C. Saunders signature was removed from the plates, and the notes were subsequently delivered unsigned to the Finance Department. There the typographed signatures of C. E. Campbell replacing S. P. McCavour, and Watson Sellar replacing J. C. Saunders, were applied along with the seal. The changeover began with sheet number S-194001. This signature change also coincided precisely with the changeover from Crane paper to Howard Smith paper for the $2 notes. Group 2 ended with series "S" in February 1932.

Group 3 notes, as well as those of group 4, were printed with black seals only. Group 3 contained three series on one million sheets, series T, U and V. During series V there was another signature change, with W. C. Clark replacing Watson Sellar, in the right-hand signature space. Again, both Campbell and Clark signatures were typographed.

Group 4 notes, consisting of series W and X only, were first delivered in June 1933. Series X was terminated after 850,000 sheets in January 1935, to make way for the introduction of the notes of the Bank of Canada.

Checklist of Prefix Letters for 1923 $2 Dominion Notes

GROUP 1

Cat.No.	Denom.	Signatures	Seal	Series Letters
DC-26a	$2	Hyndman-Saunders	Black	A B
DC-26b	$2	McCavour-Saunders	Red	C D
DC-26c	$2	McCavour-Saunders	Blue	E F
DC-26d	$2	McCavour-Saunders	Green	G H
DC-26e	$2	McCavour-Saunders	Bronze	J K

GROUP 2

Cat.No.	Denom.	Signatures	Seal	Series Letters
DC-26f	$2	McCavour-Saunders	Black	L M
DC-26g	$2	McCavour-Saunders	Red	N P
DC-26h	$2	McCavour-Saunders	Blue	R S
DC-26i	$2	Campbell-Sellar	Blue	S

GROUP 3

Cat.No.	Denom.	Signatures	Seal	Series Letters
DC-26j	$2	Campbell-Sellar	Black	T U V
DC-26k	$2	Campbell-Clark	Black	V

GROUP 4

Cat.No.	Denom.	Signatures	Seal	Series Letters
DC-26l	$2	Campbell-Clark	Black	W X

Summary of Technical Details

Cat.No.	Group	Signatures	Seal	Series	Serial Numbers	Qty. Printed
DC-26a	1	Hyndman-Saunders	Black	A	000001- 1000000/A,B,C,D	4,000,000
DC-26a	1	Hyndman-Saunders	Black	B	000001- 1000000/A,B,C,D	4,000,000
DC-26b	1	McCavour-Saunders	Red	C	000001- 1000000/A,B,C,D	4,000,000
DC-26b	1	McCavour-Saunders	Red	D	000001- 1000000/A,B,C,D	4,000,000
DC-26c	1	McCavour-Saunders	Blue	E	000001- 1000000/A,B,C,D	4,000,000
DC-26c	1	McCavour-Saunders	Blue	F	000001- 1000000/A,B,C,D	4,000,000
DC-26d	1	McCavour-Saunders	Green	G	000001- 1000000/A,B,C,D	4,000,000
DC-26d	1	McCavour-Saunders	Green	H	000001- 1000000/A,B,C,D	4,000,000
DC-26e	1	McCavour-Saunders	Bronze	J	000001- 1000000/A,B,C,D	4,000,000
DC-26e	1	McCavour-Saunders	Bronze	K	000001- 1000000/A,B,C,D	4,000,000
DC-26f	2	McCavour-Saunders	Black	L	000001- 1000000/A,B,C,D	4,000,000
DC-26f	2	McCavour-Saunders	Black	M	000001- 1000000/A,B,C,D	4,000,000
DC-26g	2	McCavour-Saunders	Red	N	000001- 1000000/A,B,C,D	4,000,000
DC-26g	2	McCavour-Saunders	Red	P	000001- 1000000/A,B,C,D	4,000,000
DC-26h	2	McCavour-Saunders	Blue	R	000001- 1000000/A,B,C,D	4,000,000
DC-26h	2	McCavour-Saunders	Blue	S	000001- 194000/A,B,C,D	776,000
DC-26i	2	Campbell-Sellar	Blue	S	194001- 1000000/A,B,C,D	3,224,000
DC-26j	3	Campbell-Sellar	Black	T	000001- 1000000/A,B,C,D	4,000,000
DC-26j	3	Campbell-Sellar	Black	U	000001- 1000000/A,B,C,D	4,000,000
DC-26j	3	Campbell-Sellar	Black	V	000001- 261515/A,B,C,D	Unknown
DC-26k	3	Campbell-Clark	Black	V	336663 - 1000000/A,B,C,D	Unknown
DC-26l	4	Campbell-Clark	Black	W	000001- 1000000/A,B,C,D	4,000,000
DC-26l	4	Campbell-Clark	Black	X	000001- 850000/A,B,C,D	3,400,000

$2 Issue — 1923

DC-26L

Face Design: —/ H.R.H. Prince of Wales in uniform of the Welsh Guards/—
(See varieties)
Colour: Black with olive green tint

DC-26

Back Design: Lathework and counters with "Dominion of Canada" over the Coat of Arms of Canada
Colour: Olive green

Issue Date: Engraved: June 23rd 1923
Imprint: Canadian Bank Note Company Limited on face and back

Signatures

Left:	Right:
Typed: Geo. W. Hyndman	Engr.: J.C. Saunders
Typed: S.P. McCavour	Engr.: J.C. Saunders
Typed: C.E. Campbell	Typed: Watson Sellar
Typed: C.E. Campbell	Typed: W.C. Clark

Varieties

Seal Colour: The Seal of the Department of Finance was printed in black, red, blue, green or bronze.

Cat.No.	Denom.	Variety	Series	G	VG	F	VF	EF	AU	Unc
DC-26a	$2	Hyndman-Saunders Black seal. Group 1.	A,B	45.	95.	160.	325.	550.	950.	1,400.
DC-26b	$2	McCavour-Saunders Red seal. Group 1.	C,D	40.	85.	150.	300.	500.	750.	1,000.
DC-26c	$2	McCavour-Saunders Blue seal. Group 1.	E,F	50.	110.	200.	350.	700.	1,100.	1,600.
DC-26d	$2	McCavour-Saunders Green seal. Group 1.	G,H	50.	100.	180.	300.	600.	900.	1,300.
DC-26e	$2	McCavour-Saunders Bronze seal. Group 1.	J,K	40.	85.	150.	300.	550.	850.	1,200.
DC-26f	$2	McCavour-Saunders Black seal. Group 2.	L,M	40.	85.	150.	300.	550.	850.	1,200.
DC-26g	$2	McCavour-Saunders Red seal. Group 2.	N,P	40.	85.	150.	300.	500.	700.	950.
DC-26h	$2	McCavour-Saunders Blue seal. Group 2.	R	40.	85.	150.	300.	550.	850.	1,200.
DC-26h	$2	McCavour-Saunders Blue seal, Group 2.	S	55.	110.	200.	400.	750.	1,100.	1,600.
DC-26i	$2	Campbell-Sellar Blue seal. Group 2.	S	55.	90.	175.	300.	600.	850.	1,200.
DC-26j	$2	Campbell-Sellar Black seal. Group 3.	T,U	35.	70.	100.	200.	300.	600.	900.
DC-26j	$2	Campbell-Sellar Black seal, Group 3	V	50.	100.	150.	300.	400.	700.	1,000
DC-26k	$2	Campbell-Clark Black seal. Group 3.	V	40.	85.	125.	250.	350.	650.	950.
DC-26l	$2	Campbell-Clark Black seal. Group 4.	W,X	40.	85.	125.	250.	350.	650.	950.

ISSUE OF 1924

Queen Mary (1867-1953) was the wife of King George V. She was originally engaged to his elder brother, the wayward Duke of Clarence, but married George after the Duke's untimely death. She lived to see the reigns of two of her sons, Edward VIII and George VI, and grandaughter Queen Elizabeth II.

Work on the engraving of the portrait of Queen Mary was in progress in March 1924, when the difficulty with the copyright protecting the Prince of Wales portrait used on the $2 note erupted. The Finance Department wished to avoid a recurrence of the problem with the $5 denomination, so the legal question was carefully checked before further work was done on the portrait. The engraver was probably Mr. Woodhull of the American Bank Note Co. in New York City, where all Canadian Bank Note Co. portrait engraving for Dominion notes was being done at that time. The note is dated May 26th, 1924, in honour of Queen Mary's birthday.

The back depicts the East Block of the Parliament Buildings, engraved from a photograph. The general layout of the $5 note conforms to the 1923 $1 and $2 notes. They were printed in blue, distinguishing them from the other denominations.

The Department of Finance had little need for $5 notes on a continuing basis, the needs of commerce for that denomination being largely met by the chartered bank issues. When, in October 1931, an order was given for stocks of $5 notes, it was after a seven year hiatus. Only then were the plates for the Queen Mary $5 notes prepared, there having been no previous orders for the notes. The die for the vignette had been put away since being engraved in 1924. The immediate need for the notes was met in 1931 by running off a small final batch of the 1912 "train" notes. Production of the Queen Mary $5 notes began as soon as the plates were ready. Altogether 500,000 sheets of Queen Mary $5 notes were printed, all in series "A". The total production was completed and delivered between late October 1931 and February 1932. The signatures, those of C. E. Campbell and Watson Sellar, were both typed onto the notes along with the (black) seal by the Finance Department. They were the same signatures as those being applied to the $1 and $2 notes at that time.

The Finance Department delayed release of the Queen Mary notes, possibly because a new issue of small-size Dominion notes was then being contemplated (which never became a reality). They were finally put into circulation in 1934, just before the introduction of the Bank of Canada notes and the withdrawal of Dominion notes.

A survey of the sheet numbers of existing notes suggests that only about a third of the modest total printed were ever released for circulation. It is not surprising then that collectors have long found the Queen Mary $5 to be a very elusive note. Those notes which have turned up are generally in the more attractive grades.

Summary of Technical Details

Cat.No.	Denom.	Series	Serial Numbers	Qty. Printed*
DC-27	$5	A	000001- 500000/A,B,C,D	2,000,000

*Approximately one-third of these were issued for circulation.

$5 Issue — 1924

DC-27

Face Design: —/H.M. Queen Mary in official court dress of consort /Department of Finance seal

Colour: Black with blue tint

DC-27

Back Design: Lathework, counters and "Dominion of Canada" over Parliament Buildings, view of the East Block

Colour: Blue

Issue Date: Engraved: May 26th 1924

Imprint: Canadian Bank Note Company, Limited on face and back

Signatures

Left: Typed: C.E. Campbell **Right:** Typed: Watson Sellar

Cat.No.	Denom.	Series	G	VG	F	VF	EF	AU	Unc
DC-27	$5	A	1,600.	2,750.	3,750.	5,000.	6,500.	8,500.	11,000.

ISSUES OF 1925

In March 1925 the Department of Finance was experiencing difficulties related to the circulation of the 1911 issue $500 and $1000 notes. It was decided to proceed quickly with a new issue and to withdraw the old notes for accounting.

The portraits of King George V and Queen Mary used on the $500 and $1000 notes were the same as those on the $1 and $5 notes respectively, being from the same dies. The portrait-denomination combinations were interchanged from the 1911 issue, possibly to facilitate sorting. The notes were called bearer notes, since they were inscribed "Will pay to the bearer," to distinguish them from the bank legals. The backs have no vignettes, consisting essentially of lathework and counters.

No seal was applied to these high denomination notes, and the area at the right of the portrait reserved on the lower values for the departmental seal was occupied by an additional large counter. Neither engraved nor typed signatures were printed on the notes. Both the signature and countersignature were applied by hand in Ottawa by various officials of the Finance Department.

The previous issue of these denominations had "SERIES A" engraved on the faces on both sides of the vignette. This was deleted on the 1925 issue, but the series letter was continued as a prefix to the serial number. There were no check letters either, the notes being numbered individually rather than by the sheet.

Only one 4/on face plate was engraved for each denomination, in May 1925. An order for 40,000 notes of the $500 denomination and 30,000 of the $1,000 value had been placed the previous March. In July all of the $500 notes and 6,000 of the $1,000 notes were delivered to the Finance Department. It may be supposed that the remaining $1,000 notes followed in due course, but the delivery date is not known.

When the new notes became available the Finance Department instructed its Assistant Receivers General to withdraw the 1911 issue notes immediately, and to ask the banks to exchange any notes in their possession.

Summary of Technical Details

Cat.No.	Denom.	Series	Serial Numbers	Quantity Printed
DC-28	$500	A	000001-040000	40,000
DC-29	$1000	A	000001-030000	30,000*

*Assumed, on the basis of order of March 7, 1925.

$500 Issue — 1925

DC-28

Face Design: —/H.M. King George V/—
Colour: Black with brown tint

DC-28

Back Design: Lathework, counters and Dominion of Canada
Colour: Brown

Issue Date: Engraved: Jany 2nd 1925
Imprint: Canadian Bank Note Company, Limited on face and back

Signatures

Left: mms. various **Right:** mss. various

Cat.No.	Denom.	Series	G	VG	F	VF	EF	AU	Unc
DC-28	$500	A	6,000.	12,000.	15,000.	25,000.	35,000.	—	—
DC-28S	$500	A				Specimen			4,000.

$1,000 Issue — 1925

DC-29

Face Design: —/H.M. Queen Mary/—
Colour: Black with orange tint

DC-29

Back Design: Lathework, counters and Dominion of Canada
Colour: Orange

Issue Date: Engraved: Jany 2nd 1925
Imprint: Canadian Bank Note Company, Limited, on face and back

Signatures

Left: mss. various   **Right:** mss. various

Cat.No.	Denom.	Series	G	VG	F	VF	EF	AU	Unc
DC-29	$1,000.	A	6,000.	12,000.	15,000.	25,000.	35,000.	—	—
DC-29S	$1,000.	A					Specimen		4,000.

BANK LEGALS

Bank legals were very large denomination notes, which were not issued for general circulation. Sometimes referred to as bank specials, these notes were held by the chartered banks as a convenient form for the Dominion note reserves required by the bank act in lieu of gold. They were exchanged between banks in settlement of their cash balances due to each other.

When the Bank of Canada began its operations in 1934, the cash deposits each chartered bank was required to lodge with the central bank, replacing Dominion note reserves, were made with the bank legals. The bank legals thereafter ceased to have any purpose and were withdrawn.

The wording on the face of the bank legals restricted their use solely to banks.

The issues of 1896, 1901 and 1918 carried the following authorizations and restrictions:

"AUTHORIZED BY CHAP. 31 OF REVISED STATUTES OF CANADA
LEGAL TENDER NOTE FOR USE BY BANKS ONLY

THE
DOMINION OF CANADA
WILL PAY

ON DEMAND TO BEARER, BEING A BANK TO WHICH THE BANK ACT OF CANADA APPLIES ON THE CONDITIONS MENTIONED BELOW AT THE OFFICE OF ANY ASSISTANT RECEIVER GENERAL OF CANADA. THIS NOTE IS GOOD ONLY IN THE HANDS OF A BANK TO WHICH THE BANK ACT OF CANADA APPLIES AND WILL BE REDEEMED ONLY WHEN PRESENTED BY ONE OF SUCH BANKS."

The issues of 1924 carried:

"AUTHORIZED BY 5 GEORGE V CAP. 4 1914"

and then the restrictions as above.

$500 Issue — 1896

DC-30

Face Design: Vignette of "Genius" with part of Library of Parliament / Marquis of Lorne / Parliament Buildings, East Block
Colour: Black on white with peach tint

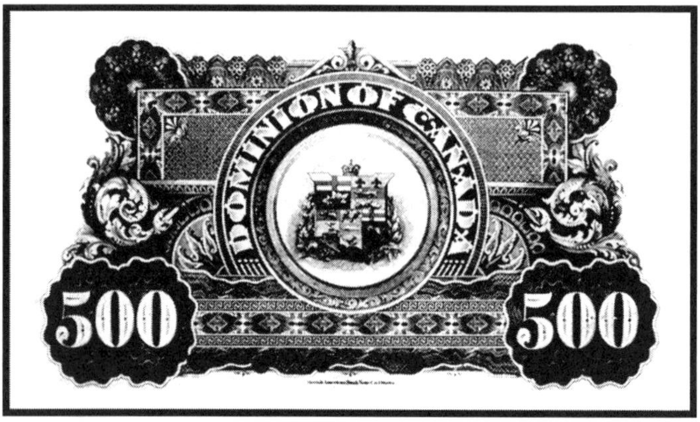

Back Design: "Dominion of Canada" arched over the seal of Canada, lathework and counters
Colour: Blue

Issue Date: Engraved: July 2nd 1896
Imprint: British American Bank Note Co. Ottawa, on face and back

Signatures

Left: mss. various **Right:** mss. various

Cat.No.	Denom.	VF	EF	AU	Unc
DC-30FP	$500	Face Proof $2,500. to $5,000.			
DC-30BP	$500	Back Proof $250. to $750.			
DC-30S	$500	Specimen $2,500. to $5,000.			
DC-30C	$500	Cancelled $3,500. to $7,000.			

$1000 Issue — 1896

DC-31

Face Design: Queen Victoria (Die "No. 11") / — / —
Colour: Black on white with terra cotta numeral "1000"

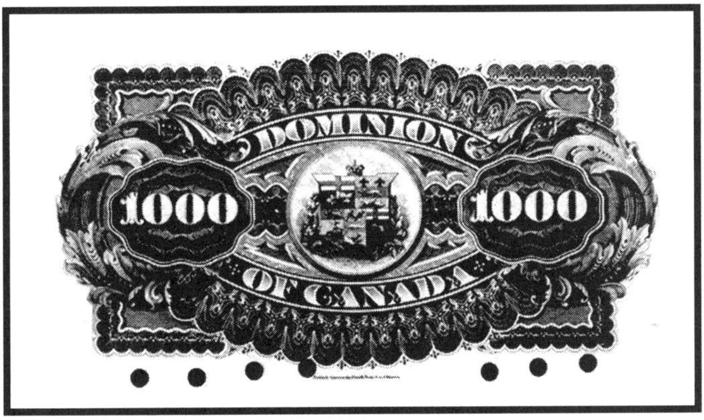

Back Design: "Dominion of Canada" around seal of Canada, lathework and counters
Colour: Dark brown
Issue Date: July 2nd 1896
Imprint: British American Bank Note Co. Ottawa on face and back

Signatures

Left: mss. various **Right:** mss. various

Cat.No.	Denom.	VF	EF	AU	Unc
DC-31FP	$1000	Face Proof $3,000. to $4,000.			
DC-31BP	$1000	Back Proof $250. to $500.			
DC-31S	$1000	Specimen $3,000. to $5,000.			
DC-31C	$1000	Cancelled $3,500. to $6,000.			

$5000 Issue — 1896

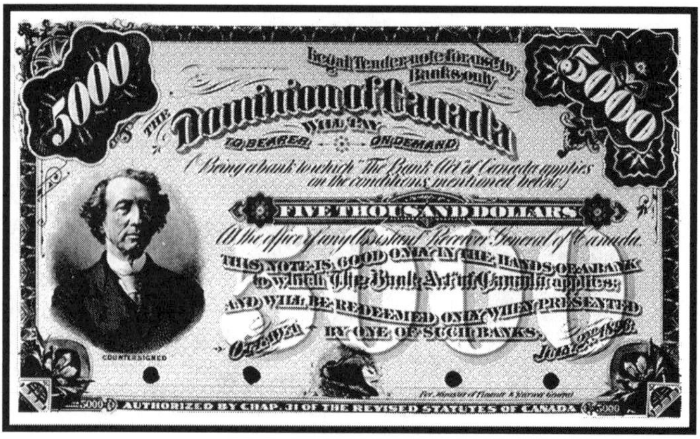

DC-32

Face Design: John A. Macdonald/Small vignette of a beaver/—
Colour: Black and white with yellow-orange tint outlining numeral "5000"

Back Design: "Dominion of Canada" surrounding Canadian seal with lathework and counters, bottom centre panel with classical motif
Colour: Red brown

Issue Date: July 2nd 1896
Imprint: British American Bank Note Co. Ottawa

Signatures

Left: mss. various **Right:** mss. various

Cat.No.	Denom.	VF	EF	AU	Unc
DC-32FP	$5000	Face Proof $3,000. to $4,000.			
DC-32BP	$5000	Back Proof $250. to $500.			
DC-32S	$5000	Specimen $3,000. to $5,000.			
DC-32C	$5000	Cancelled $3,500. to $6,000.			

Note: A face proof exists with overall yellow tint, and a blue back proof exists. (Ex BABN Archives, sold by Spink America in December 1997).

$1000 Issue — 1901

DC-33

Face Design: Lord Roberts (die no. “Canada-A-8”)/—/—
Colour: Black on white with green tint

Back Design: “Dominion of Canada” in a semi-circle over central “1000” counter, “One Thousand Dollars” twice horizontally near the bottom, lathework and counters.
Colour: Green

Issue Date: 2nd Jany 1901
Imprint: American Bank Note Co. Ottawa

Signatures

Left: mss. various
Engraved: J.C. Saunders
Engraved: J.M. Courtney

Right: Engraved: T.C. Boville

Cat.No.	Denom.	VF	EF	AU	Unc
DC-33FP	$1000	Face Proof $3,000. to $4,000.			
DC-33BP	$1000	Back Proof $250. to $500.			
DC-33S	$1000	Specimen $3,000. to $5,000.			
DC-33C	$1000	Cancelled $3,500. to $6,000.			

$5000 Issue — 1901

DC-34S

Face Design: Queen Victoria (Die No. “Canada-A-9”) / — / —
Colour: Yellow-brown

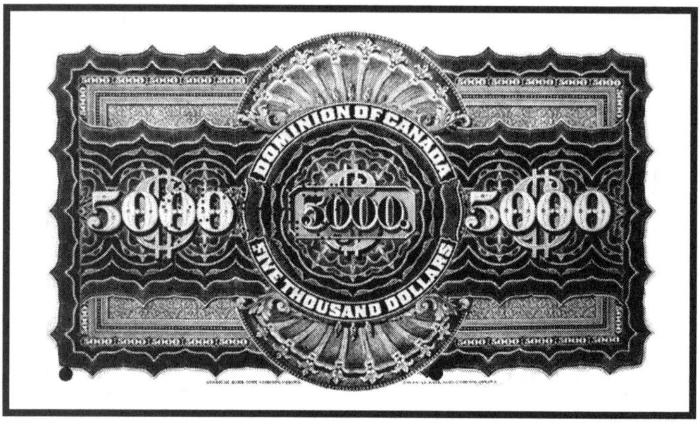

Back Design: “Dominion of Canada”, “Five Thousand Dollars” around central counter with lathework and counters.
Colour: Brown

Issue Date: 2nd Jany 1901
Imprint: American Bank Note Co. Ottawa on face and back

Signatures:

Left: mss. various **Right:** Engraved: T.C. Boville
Engraved: J.C. Saunders
Engraved: J.M. Courtney

Cat.No.	Denom.	VF	EF	AU	Unc
DC-34FP	$5000	Face Proof $3,000. to $4,000.			
DC-34BP	$5000	Back Proof $250. to $500.			
DC-34S	$5000	Specimen $3,500. to $6,000.			
DC-34C	$5000	Cancelled $4,000. to $6,000.			

$5000 Issue — 1918

DC-35S

Face Design: Queen Victoria facing left/—/—
Colour: Black on white with brown tint panel at bottom

Back Design: "Dominion of Canada" "Five Thousand Dollars" around central counter with lathework and counters
Colour: Yellow-brown

Issue Date: Jany 2nd 1918
Imprint: ABN Co. Logo hidden in design

Signatures

Left: mss. various **Right:** Engraved: T.C. Boville
Engraved: J.C. Saunders

Cat.No.	Denom.	VF	EF	AU	Unc
DC-35FP	$5000	Face Proof $3,000. to $4,000.			
DC-35BP	$5000	Back Proof $500. to $1,000.			
DC-35S	$5000	Specimen $3,000. to $7,500.			
DC-35C	$5000	Cancelled $3,500. to $6,000.			

$50000 Issue — 1918

DC-36S

Face Design: —/HM King George V (Die No. "Special-C-362"/"A.B.N. Co. N.Y.") and HM Queen Mary (Die No. "Special-A-13-Canada"/"A.B.N. Co. Ottawa") /—

Colour: Black on white with olive green tint panel at bottom

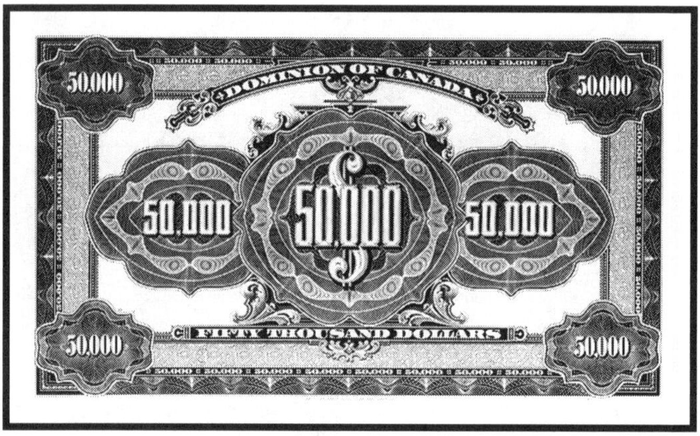

Back Design: Central counter "50,000", with "Dominion of Canada" above and "Fifty Thousand Dollars" below, counters and lathework either side

Colour: Dark olive green

Issue Date: Jany 2nd 1918

Imprint: ABN Co. Logo hidden in design

Signatures

Left: mss. various **Right:** Engraved: T.C. Boville
Engraved: J.C. Saunders

Cat.No.	Denom.	VF EF AU Unc
DC-36FP	$50000	Face Proof $5,800. to $7,800.
DC-36BP	$50000	Back Proof $500. to $1,000.
DC-36S	$50000	Specimen $6,500. to $9,750.
DC-36C	$50000	Cancelled $6,500. to $10,500.

$1000 Issue — 1924

DC-37S

Face Design: Lord Roberts (Die No. "Canada-A-8")/—/—
Colour: Black on white with green tint

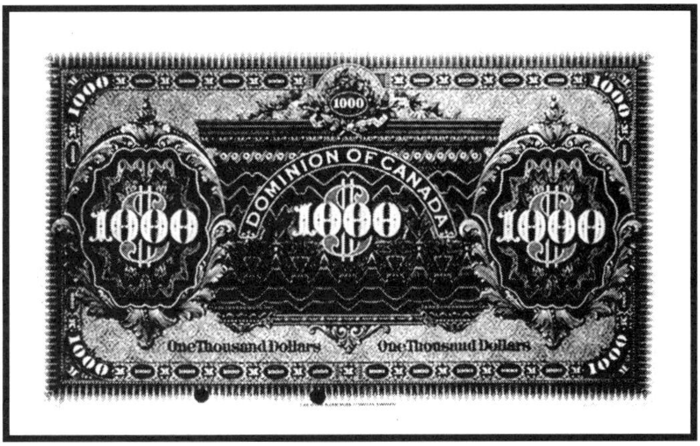

Back Design: "Dominion of Canada" in a semi-circle over central "1000" counter. "One Thousand Dollars" twice horizontally near the bottom, lathework and counters
Colour: Green

Issue Date: 2nd Jany 1924
Imprint: Canadian Bank Note Company, Limited on face and back

Signatures

Left: mss. various **Right:** Engraved: J.C. Saunders

Cat.No.	Denom.	VF EF AU Unc
DC-37FP	$1000	Face Proof $3,900. to $5,200.
DC-37BP	$1000	Back Proof $325. to $650.
DC-37S	$1000	Specimen $3,900. to $6,500.
DC-37C	$1000	Cancelled $4,500. to $7,800.

$5000 Issue — 1924

DC-38S

Face Design: Queen Victoria facing left/—/—
Colour: Black on white with brown tint panel at bottom

Back Design: "Dominion of Canada" curved near the top with "Five Thousand Dollars" horizontally near the bottom, lathework and counters
Colour: Yellow brown

Issue Date: Jany 2nd 1924
Imprint: Canadian Bank Note Company, Limited on face and back

Signatures

Left: mss. various **Right:** Engraved: J.C. Saunders

Cat.No.	Denom.	VF	EF	AU	Unc
DC-38FP	$5000	Face Proof $3,900. to $5,200.			
DC-38BP	$5000	Back Proof $325. to $650.			
DC-38S	$5000	Specimen $3,900. to $6,500.			
DC-38C	$5000	Cancelled $4,500. to $7,800.			

$50000 Issue — 1924

DC-39

Face Design: —/HM King George V (Die No. "Special-C-362") and HM Queen Mary (Die No. "Special-A-13-Canada")/—

Colour: Black on white with dark olive green tint panel at bottom

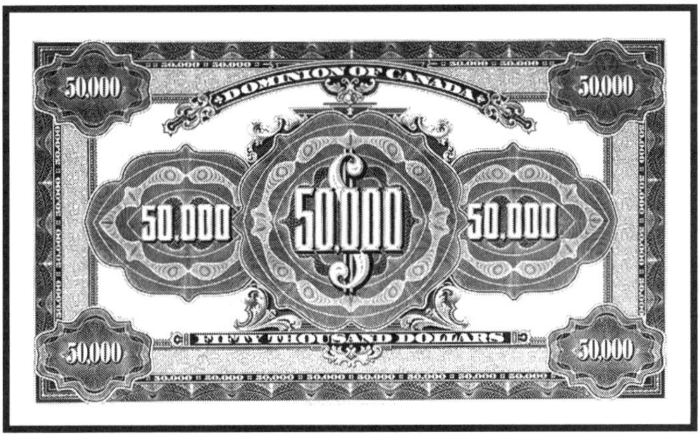

Back design: Central counter "50,000", with "Dominion of Canada" above and "Fifty Thousand Dollars" below, counters and lathework either side

Colour: Olive green

Issue Date: Jany 2nd, 1924

Imprint: Canadian Bank Note Company, Limited on face and back

Signatures

Left: mss. various **Right:** Engraved: J.C. Saunders

Cat.No.	Denom.	VF	EF	AU	Unc
DC-39FP	$50000	Face Proof $10,000. to $15,000.			
DC-39BP	$50000	Back Proof $750. to $1,500.			
DC-39S	$50000	Specimen $10,000. to $15,000.			
DC-39C	$50000	Cancelled $10,000. to $16,000.			

THE PROPOSED SMALL SIZE DOMINION NOTE ISSUE

In January 1931 the Comptroller of Currency, C. E. Campbell, inquired of the Canadian Bank Note Company what savings might be expected if the size of Dominion notes was reduced to the dimensions adopted by the United States in 1928. Economic considerations had prompted the American move, bank note paper being very costly. In March a model of the $1 face was assembled, and a projected cost of $49.75 per thousand notes was worked out.

The following January the reduction in Dominion note size was again being considered, and models of a $2 face and backs of both $1 and $2 denominations were ordered. The distinctive colours of each denomination were to be retained, and the date line was specified to read "OTTAWA 2nd July 1932" on the tint. Then further work was suddenly ordered to be suspended, to permit the notes to be redesigned on a shorter and wider format than the U.S. notes. In February 1932 a further alteration was requested, to bilingual notes. The bank note company feared that greatly increasing the amount of information to be printed on a note would reduce its protection against counterfeiting, which depended on large, well-executed portraits.

The project of another Dominion note issue was shelved as the establishment of a central bank was coming under active consideration. Such a bank would eventually assume all of the note issuing functions.

BANK OF CANADA ISSUES

The Bank of Canada came into being through the work of a typically Canadian institution, a Royal Commission. The majority report of the Royal Commission on Banking and Currency, brought down in September 1933, favoured the establishment of a central bank in Canada. The chartered banks were not enthusiastic but pledged their co-operation. The bill to incorporate the Bank of Canada was brought in by the Conservative government of R. B. Bennett during the 1934 session of Parliament. The capital of the bank was set at $5,000,000, divided into shares of $50 each which were offered for sale to the public in September 1934 and largely oversubscribed despite the fact that no individual or corporation was allowed to hold more than fifty shares.

The Liberals under W. L. M. King were returned to power in 1935. They had opposed private ownership of the bank from the start and promised to "nationalize" it as part of their election platform. This King typically proceeded to do by halves. In 1936 he had an additional $5,100,000 in class "B" shares created and sold to the Finance Department, giving the government majority ownership and effective control. In 1938 King "nationalized" the bank again. This time the class "A" shares held by the public were bought up by the government for $59.20 each plus accrued dividends. The capital was reduced to the original $5,000,000, with all of the shares now owned by the government.

Although the government owns all of the shares in the Bank of Canada, it remains relatively free of political interference and is prepared to offer the government skilled and impartial advice on monetary policy. However, monetary policy in a democratic country must conform to the wishes of the elected government, which has the power to issue orders to the bank. This was illustrated by the celebrated dispute of J. E. Coyne with the Diefenbaker administration, which culminated in the resignation of the governor.

The Bank of Canada was not established to engage in ordinary banking business with the public in competition with the chartered banks. The central bank accepts deposits from other banks and will if necessary lend them money. When the Bank of Canada was set up, the chartered banks were required to deposit 5% of their own deposit liabilities with the central bank, replacing the reserves formerly held in gold and Dominion notes. The old Bank Legals and gold previously held as part of their reserves were paid in to the Bank of Canada to comply with this regulation.

The Bank of Canada was originally required to hold gold reserves equal to 25% of its note and bank deposit liabilities. This requirement disappeared early in World War II since the existing gold available was inadequate to cover the necessary expansion of the money supply. Since then the Bank of Canada notes have not had any gold backing.

The bank commenced business on March 11, 1935. The first set of officers, appointed by the government, included G. F. Towers, formerly with the Royal Bank of Canada, as Governor; J. A. C. Osborne, on loan from the Bank of England, as Deputy Governor; and L. P. St. Amour, formerly with La Banque Canadienne Nationale, as Assistant Deputy Governor. The bank was given responsibility for management of the currency and the national debt. The head office was established in Ottawa, with agencies in every province. The bank assumed liability for the Dominion notes in circulation, which it undertook to replace by its own small-size notes in denominations of $1, $2, $5, $10, $20, $25, $50, $100, $500 and $1000.

The chartered banks were required to reduce their note circulation to 25% of their paid-up capital over the next ten years. The 1944 revision of the bank act then prohibited the issue or reissue of any chartered bank's own notes after January 1, 1945. The last issue by a chartered bank was the $5 Royal Bank issue of 1943. The notes of the chartered banks were withdrawn and as of January 1, 1950, liability for all outstanding chartered bank notes was assumed by the Bank of Canada. The issue of chartered bank notes for circulation outside of Canada was still permitted to a maximum of 10% of the paid-up capital under the 1944 act, but even that was ended under the 1954 revision of the bank act. During January 1950 the ten Canadian chartered banks paid over to the Bank of Canada the balances outstanding in their note circulation accounts as at December 31, 1949, amounting to $13,302,046.60. (Since that time over $5,000,000 in notes of the chartered banks have been turned in for redemption, leaving about $8,000,000 outstanding). This was the final step in the 15-year program under which the Bank of Canada assumed the entire issuing function of the country and wrote "finis" to an important, sometimes tempestuous, chapter of Canadian banking history.

ISSUES OF 1935

When the Bank of Canada opened for business on March 11, 1935, it issued its own notes in denominations of $1, $2, $5, $10, $20, $50, $100, $500 and $1000. The notes were of the small 6 x 2 7/8 inch format which resulted in a saving of both bank note paper and ink. This Bank of Canada issue consisted of separate unilingual English and French notes. As might be expected, most of the French notes were sent to the Bank of Canada agency in Montreal for distribution, although most of the other agencies received a small supply as well.

For the first time since 1897 the British American Bank Note Company received a contract for printing government paper currency. British American printed the $2, $5 and $10 notes while the Canadian Bank Note Company printed the remaining denominations, including the $25 commemorative note. Thereafter both security printers participated in the production of Bank of Canada notes.

The regular issue notes up to the $100 denomination feature different members of the Royal Family on the left, with a large numeral counter in the middle and the Bank of Canada seal on the right. The $500 and $1000 notes portray former Prime Ministers Macdonald and Laurier respectively. The backs of all denominations of these regular issue notes depict various allegorical scenes.

Details Of The Printing

The lower denominations were printed from 24/on plates, with the last few sheets needed to complete an order, called make-up sheets, being from 4/on plates. The higher denominations were printed 12/on, with make-ups again being 4/on. Howard Smith bank note paper was used, in which green planchettes were embedded as a security device. The paper composition was 75% high grade flax and 25% cotton.

Sheets were numbered in red, twice on the face of each note, in groups of four notes each with the same number. For each sheet number there were four distinguishing black check letters, A, B C and D. For the most part there was only a single series for each denomination in each language, Series "A" for English and series "F" for French. However, the "A" series of English $1 notes, consisting of ten million "sheets" of four notes, was completed and a "B" series begun.

The notes were delivered by the bank note companies without signatures and seals. These were added by the letterpress method by Bank of Canada personnel, using plates prepared by the Royal Canadian Mint. The signatures applied were those of J. A. C. Osborne, Deputy Governor, and G. F. Towers, Governor. Because the signing was done after the notes were printed, the positions of the signatures tend to vary. Black seals only were used, and in all cases the numeral 1 appears to the right of the seal, identifying the notes as being from Group 1. Since the notes were issued over a relatively short time span, the group number never progressed beyond 1. Large seals were used on the $1, $2, $5, $10, $25 and the lower numbered $20 notes, while the higher numbered $20 notes and the denominations of $50 and up had small seals.

Circulation And Withdrawal

The $25 commemorative note was the first to be withdrawn from circulation. On May 18, 1937, it was decided to cancel both new and issued $25 notes as they were acquired by the Bank of Canada agencies. By August 1942 only 1,920 of these notes had escaped withdrawal and cancellation. In the summer of 1937 it was intended to continue issuing the other denominations until all of the stocks on hand had been used up. Shortly afterwards, there arose some trouble with the 1935 $2 notes which were being confused with the 1937 $5 notes because both were blue in colour. Consequently the 1935 $2 note was ordered withdrawn from circulation as quickly as possible and on September 18, 1937 about 3,900,000 new, unissued $2 notes were taken out of stock for destruction. In February 1938 stocks of unissued notes of other denominations, except for the $1000 notes, were also destroyed, with 824,500 unissued $5 and 356,500 unissued $10 notes consigned to the furnaces. The withdrawal of $1, $5 and $10 notes began that month, and the $20, $50, $100 and $500 notes began to be withdrawn the following July. The $500 denomination was permanently retired, and at the time of preparation of this edition only 46 of these were outstanding.

The $1000 notes enjoyed by far the greatest longevity. It was not until January 1952 that the old 1935-dated $1000 notes were superseded by 1937-dated notes. This denomination was used primarily by the chartered banks. The old notes were not recalled from the banks but neither were they reissued from the Bank of Canada agencies.

Summary of Technical Details

Cat.No.	Denom.	Variety	Printer	Series	Serial Numbers	Qty. Printed
BC-1a	$1	English	CBN	A	0000001- 10000000/A,B,C,D	40,000,000
BC-1b	$1	English	CBN	B	000001- 5078000/A,B,C,D	20,312,000
BC-2	$1	French	CBN	F	0000001-3799000/A,B,C,D	15,196,000
BC-3	$2	English	BABN	A	000001- 5585000/A,B,C,D	22,340,000
BC-4	$2	French	BABN	F	000001- 1325000/A,B,C,D	5,300,000
BC-5	$5	English	BABN	A	000001- 1535000/A,B,C,D	6,140,000
BC-6	$5	French	BABN	F	000001- 750000/A,B,C,D	3,000,000
BC-7	$10	English	BABN	A	000001-1250000/A,B,C,D	5,000,000
BC-8	$10	French	BABN	F	000001- 387500/A,B,C,D	1,550,000
BC-9	$20	English (large seal)	CBN	A	000001- *049284/A,B,C,D	(est.) 200,000
BC-9b	$20	English (small seal)	CBN	A	052325*- 250675/A,B,C,D	(est.) 802,700
BC-10	$20	French	CBN	F	000001-050625/A,B,C,D	202,500
BC-11	$25	English	CBN	A	000001- 035000/A,B,C,D	140,000
BC-12	$25	French	CBN	F	000001- 005000/A,B,C,D	20,000
BC-13	$50	English	CBN	A	00001-32750/A,B,C,D	131,000
BC-14	$50	French	CBN	F	00001-08125/A,B,C,D	32,500
BC-15	$100	English	CBN	A	00001-21875/A,B,C,D	87,500
BC-16	$100	French	CBN	F	00001-04375/A,B,C,D	17,500
BC-17	$500	English	CBN	A	00001-05225/A,B,C,D	20,900
BC-18	$500	French	CBN	F	00001-01250/A,B,C,D	5,000
BC-19	$1000	English	CBN	A	00001-16625/A,B,C,D	66,500
BC-20	$1000	French	CBN	F	00001-01900/A,B,C,D	7,600

* Refers to high and low numbers seen

$1 Issue — 1935

BC-1

Face Design: H.M. King George V/—/—
Portrait Imprint: H.M. King George V/Bank of Canada/X-V-114/ Canadian Bank Note Co. Ltd.
Portrait Photograph: Reduction of die "CANADA-A-21" which used original photographs by Vandyk and by Lafayette Ltd., London, England
Portrait Engraver: Robert Savage
Pantograph Panel:
English: Bank of Canada, One Dollar
French: Banque du Canada, Un Dollar
Colour: Black with green tint (42 green)

BC-1

Back Design: —/Agriculture allegory: seated female with agricultural tools and produce/—
Vignette Imprint: Agriculture/V-71428/American Bank Note Company
Vignette Design: Original Painting by A. E. Foringer
Vignette Engraver: Wm. Ford
Colour: Green (42 green)
Issue Date: Engraved: 1935
Imprint: Canadian Bank Note Company, Limited on face and back
Signatures: **Left:** Typed: J.A.C. Osborne **Right:** Typed: G.F. Towers

Cat.No.	Denom.	Variety	Series	G	VG	F	VF	EF	AU	Unc
BC-1	$1	English	A	15.	35.	55.	100.	160.	300.	450.
BC-1	$1	English	B	18.	40.	60.	110.	225.	350.	550.
BC-2	$1	French	F	25.	55.	85.	150.	250.	425.	600.

$2 Issue — 1935

BC-3

Face Design: Queen Mary/—/—
Portrait Imprint: Die No. 24
Portrait Engraver: H. P. Dawson
Colour: Black with blue tint

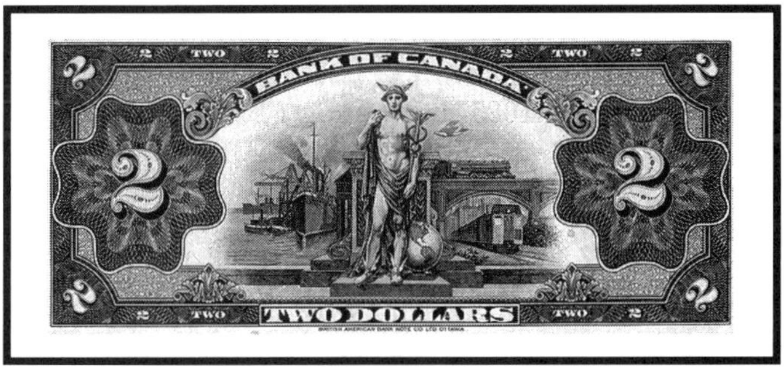

BC-3

Back Design: —/Transportation allegory: Mercury with ships trains, and planes/—
Vignette Imprint: Unknown
Vignette Design: Unknown
Vignette Engraver: H. P. Dawson and G. Gundersen
Colour: Blue
Issue Date: Engraved: 1935
Imprint: British American Bank Note Co Ltd Ottawa on face and back

Signatures

Left: Typed J.A.C. Osborne **Right:** Typed G.F. Towers

Cat.No.	Denom.	Variety	Series	G	VG	F	VF	EF	AU	Unc
BC-3	$2	English	A	30.	50.	90.	175.	400.	750.	1,000.
BC-4	$2	French	F	55.	100.	200.	450.	900.	1,900.	2,800.

$5 Issue — 1935

BC-6

Face Design: Prince of Wales/—/—
Portrait Imprint: Unknown
Portrait Engraver: H. P. Dawson
Colour: Black with orange tint

BC-5

Back Design: —/Electric Power allegory: Seated male with symbols of electricity/—
Vignette Imprint: Unknown
Vignette Design: Original painting, artist unknown
Vignette Engraver: H. P. Dawson
Colour: Orange

Issue Date: Engraved: 1935
Imprint: British American Bank Note Co Ltd Ottawa on face and back

Signatures

Left: Typed J.A.C. Osborne **Right:** Typed G.F. Towers

Cat.No.	Denom.	Variety	Series	G	VG	F	VF	EF	AU	Unc
BC-5	$5	English	A	40.	75.	125.	275.	600.	1000.	1,750.
BC-6	$5	French	F	55.	100.	200.	500.	1,200.	1,900.	2,700.

$10 Issue — 1935

BC-7

Face Design: Princess Mary /—/—
Portrait Imprint: Unknown
Portrait Engraver: H. P. Dawson
Colour: Black with dark purple tint

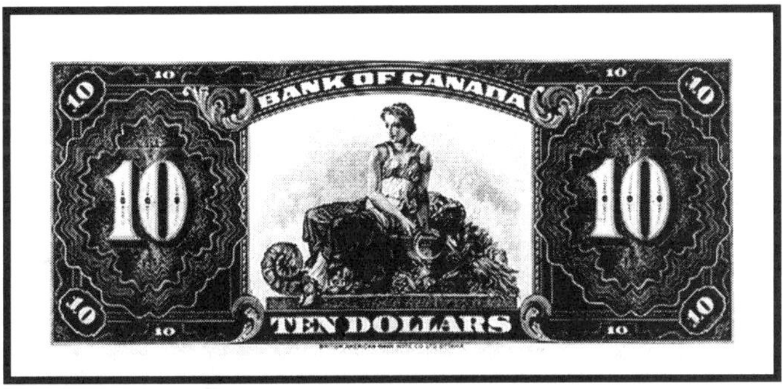

BC-7

Back Design: —/Harvest allegory: Seated female with fruits of harvest
Vignette Imprint: Unknown/—
Vignette Design: Original paintings, artist unknown.
Vignette Engraver: H. P. Dawson
Colour: Dark purple

Issue Date: Engraved: 1935
Imprint: British American Bank Note Co Ltd Ottawa on face and back

Signatures

Left: Typed J.A.C. Osborne **Right:** Typed G.F. Towers

Cat.No.	Denom.	Variety	Series	G	VG	F	VF	EF	AU	Unc
BC-7	$10	English	A	40.	75.	125.	300.	550.	1,000.	1,600.
BC-8	$10	French	F	55.	100.	200.	400.	700.	1,500.	2,400.

$20 Issue — 1935

BC-9a

Face Design: H.R.H. Princess Elizabeth/—/—
(See varieties)
Portrait Imprint: H.R.H. Princess Elizabeth/Bank of Canada/X-V-125/
Canadian Bank Note Co. Ltd.
Portrait Engraver: Edwin Gunn
Pantograph Panel:
English: Bank of Canada, Twenty Dollars, 20
French: Banque du Canada, Vingt Dollars, 20
Portrait Source: Photograph by Bertram Park, Marcus Adams Ltd.,
Yvonne Gregory, London, England
Colour: Black with rose tint (80A Rose)

BC-9

Back Design: —/Agriculture allegory: Kneeling male exhibiting the produce of the field to female Agriculture figure/—
Vignette Imprint: Testing Grain/V-58827/American Bank Note Company
Vignette Design: Original painting by A. E. Foringer
Vignette Engraver: Edwin Gunn
Colour: Rose (80A Rose)

Issue Date: Engraved: 1935
Imprint: Canadian Bank Note Company, Limited on face and back

Signatures

Left: Typed J.A.C. Osborne **Right:** Typed G.F. Towers

Varieties

$20 English Issue Face Design:

Large Bank of Canada Seal

Small Bank of Canada Seal

Cat.No.	Denom.	Variety	Series	G	VG	F	VF	EF	AU	Unc
BC-9a	$20	English, (large seal)	A	150.	400.	800.	1,750.	3,500.	5,000.	8,500.
BC-9b	$20	English, (small seal)	A	125.	300.	500.	1,200.	2,750.	4,000.	6,500.
BC-10	$20	French	F	225.	500.	1,000.	2,500.	4,500.	6,500.	10,000.

The $25 Commemorative Note

The $25 note was a special commemorative issue marking the Silver Jubilee of the reign of King George V. These notes were printed in separate English and French versions like the regular issue notes of 1935, but they do not, strictly speaking, form part of the first issue. They have a different issue date, May 6, 1935, whereas the other denominations are simply dated ISSUE OF 1935. The regnal dates 1910-1935 appear at the top, and under the portraits appear the inscription TWENTY-FIFTH ANNIVERSARY OF THE ACCESSION OF H.M. KING GEORGE V. This denomination is the only one having two portraits, those of King George V and Queen Mary, and these are located in the centre, with the large denominational counter occurring on the left. Instead of an allegorical vignette, the back depicts Windsor Castle as seen from across the Thames River.

Some difficulty was experienced with the King's crown, which was too large to fit in the frame. This was solved by allowing the upper part of the crown to cross over the frame, from which it protrudes so far as to divide the words PAY and TO. The Bank of Canada agencies were instructed to release the notes on May 2, four days before their printed issue date.

Of the 160,000 $25 notes issued, a total of 1,840 were still outstanding at the time of preparation of this edition.

$25 Issue — 1935

BC-12

Face Design: —/H.M. King George V and H.M. Queen Mary/—
Portrait Imprint: H.M. King George V/Bank of Canada/X-V-126/ Canadian Bank Note Co. Ltd.
Portrait Engraver: Edwin Gunn
Portrait Imprint: H.M. Queen Mary/Bank of Canada/X-V-127/ Canadian Bank Note Co. Ltd.
Portrait Engraver: Will Ford
Portrait Source: Photograph by Vandyk, London, England
Pantograph Panel:
English: Bank of Canada/Twenty-five dollars/25
French: Banque du Canada/Vingt-Cinq Dollars/25
Colour: Black with royal purple tint (85 Royal purple)

BC-11

Back Design: —/Windsor Castle/—
Vignette Imprint: Windsor Castle/Bank of Canada/X-V-128/ Canadian Bank Note Co. Ltd.
Vignette Design: Photograph by Raphael Tuck & Son, London.
Vignette Engraver: Louis Delnoce
Colour: Royal Purple (85 Royal purple)

Issue Date: Engraved: May 6th 1935 or 6 Mai 1935
Imprint: Canadian Bank Note Company, Limited on face and back
Signatures: **Left:** Typed J.A.C. Osborne **Right:** Typed G.F. Towers

Cat.No.	Denom.	Variety	Series	G	VG	F	VF	EF	AU	Unc
BC-11	$25	English	A	800.	1,200.	2,000.	3,000.	4,500.	5,500.	7,500.
BC-12	$25	French	F	950.	1,500.	2,500.	3,500.	5,000.	7,000.	10,000.

$50 Issue — 1935

BC-14

Face Design: Prince Albert, Duke of York/—/—
Portrait Imprint: H.R.H. Duke of York/Bank of Canada/X-V-119/ Canadian Bank Note Co. Ltd.
Portrait Engraver: Robert Savage
Portrait Source: Photographed by Bertram Park, Marcus Adams Ltd., Yvonne Gregory, London, England
Pantograph Panel:
English: Bank of Canada/Fifty Dollars/50
French: Banque du Canada/Cinquante Dollars/50
Colour: Black with brown tint (15 Brown)

BC-14

Back Design: —/Modern inventions allegory: Seated female with symbols of radio broadcasting/—
Vignette Imprint: "Allegory Radio"
Vignette Design: Painting by A. E. Foringer
Vignette Engraver: R. Savage
Colour: Brown (15 Brown)

Issue Date: Engraved: 1935
Imprint: Canadian Bank Note Company, Limited on face and back
Signatures: **Left:** Typed J.A.C. Osborne **Right:** Typed G.F. Towers

Cat.No.	Denom.	Variety	Series	G	VG	F	VF	EF	AU	Unc
BC-13	$50	English	A	400.	700.	1,200.	2,000.	3,250.	5,000.	8,000.
BC-14	$50	French	F	650.	1,100.	1,800.	3,250.	4,500.	7,000.	11,000.

$100 Issue — 1935

BC-15

Face Design: Prince Henry, Duke of Gloucester/—/—
Portrait Imprint: H.R.H. Duke of Gloucester/Bank of Canada/X-V-124/ Canadian Bank Note Co. Ltd.
Portrait Engraver: Will Ford
Portrait Source: Photograph by Vandyk, London, England
Pantograph Panel:
English: Bank of Canada/One Hundred Dollars/100
French: Banque du Canada/Cent Dollars/100
Colour: Black with dark brown tint (11 Brown)

BC-15

Back Design: —/Commerce and Industry allegory: Seated male showing ship to child, dock and industrial scene in background/—
Vignette Imprint: Original die V-43076 and die V-43246; Altered die V-73316
Vignette Design: Painting by A. E. Foringer
Vignette Engraver: Original by Wm. Adolf; Re-engraved by E. Loizeaux, S. Smith and W. Hauck
Colour: Dark brown (#11 Brown)

Issue Date: Engraved: 1935
Imprint: Canadian Bank Note Company, Limited on face and back
Signatures: **Left:** Typed J.A.C. Osborne **Right:** Typed G.F. Towers

Cat.No.	Denom.	Variety	Series	G	VG	F	VF	EF	AU	Unc
BC-15	$100	English	A	275.	600.	850.	1,400.	2,250.	3,300.	5,000.
BC-16	$100	French	F	650.	1,100.	1,800.	3,250.	4,500.	7,000.	11,000.

$500 Issue — 1935

BC-17

Face Design: Sir John A. Macdonald/—/—
Vignette Imprint: Sir John Macdonald/Bank of Canada/X-V-118/ Canadian Bank Note Co. Ltd.
Vignette Engraver: Will Ford
Portrait Source: Unknown
Pantograph Panel:
English: Bank of Canada/Five Hundred Dollars/500
French: Banque du Canada/Cinq Cents Dollars/500
Colour: Black with brown tint (13 brown)

BC-17

Back Design: —/Fertility allegory: Seated female with sickle/—
Vignette Imprint: V-58826
Vignette Design: Painting by A. E. Foringer
Vignette Engraver: Robert Savage
Colour: Brown (13 brown)

Issue Date: Engraved: 1935
Imprint: Canadian Bank Note Company Limited on face and back

Signatures

Left: Typed J. A. C. Osborne **Right:** Typed G. F. Towers

Cat.No.	Denom.	Variety	Series	G	VG	F	VF	EF	AU	Unc
BC-17	$500	English	A	8,000.	12,000.	18,000.	25,000.	35,000.	—	—
BC-18	$500	French	F		Extremely Rare. Market value not established					

$1000 Issue — 1935

BC-19

Face Design: Sir Wilfrid Laurier/—/—
Vignette Imprint: Sir Wilfrid Laurier/Bank of Canada/X-V-117/ Canadian Bank Note Co. Ltd.
Vignette Engraver: Edwin Gunn
Portrait Source: Unknown
Pantograph Panel:
English: Bank of Canada/One Thousand Dollars/1000
French: Banque du Canada/Mille Dollars/1000
Colour: Black with olive green tint (85 olive)

BC-19

Back Design: —/Security allegory: Kneeling female shielding her child/—
Vignette Imprint: "Protection," V-74811 - No. 2/reduction of V-43281/ American Bank Note Company
Vignette Design: Painting by A. E. Foringer
Vignette Engraver: Wm. Jung
Colour: Olive green (85 olive)
Issue Date: Engraved: 1935
Imprint: Canadian Bank Note Company, Limited on face and back

Signatures

Left: Typed J.A.C. Osborne **Right:** Typed G.F. Towers

Cat.No.	Denom.	Variety	Series	G	VG	F	VF	EF	AU	Unc
BC-19	$1000	English	A	1,100.	1,400.	1,700.	2,200.	2,500.	3,000.	4,500.
BC-20	$1000	French	F	1,500.	2,000.	3,000.	5,000.	7,000.	9,000.	12,000.

PROOF AND SPECIMEN NOTES OF THE 1935 ISSUE

Some face and back proofs of the 1935 Bank of Canada notes exist in private collections. In November 1999 the bank made available quantities of specimen notes that were surplus to its operations. These were sold at public auction. The specimen notes have been perforated diagonally with the word "SPECIMEN" three times, and often have two to four round holes punched in the signature area. Most are also overprinted once or twice with the word "SPECIMEN", in red, in the signature area. The specimen notes were generally described in the auction catalogue as AU, with glue and paper tape residue on the back in the right margin area. Specimen notes impaired by staining or thinning will transact at reduced prices.

Prior to the Bank of Canada sale only the $1 denomination of this issue was listed in this catalogue in specimen form (both English and French).

Cat. No.	Denom.	Variety	Quantity Sold Bank of Canada Sale		AU	Unc
BC-1FP	$1	English	Face Proof	n/a	—	800.
BC-1BP	$1	English	Back Proof	n/a	—	275.
BC-1S	$1	English	Specimen	(9)	600.	—
BC-2FP	$1	French	Face Proof	n/a	—	900.
BC-2BP	$1	French	Back Proof	n/a	—	350.
BC-2S	$1	French	Specimen	(9)	1,000.	—
BC-3S	$2	English	Specimen	(9)	500.	—
BC-4S	$2	French	Specimen	(9)	900.	—
BC-5S	$5	English	Specimen	(8)	700.	—
BC-6S	$5	French	Specimen	(8)	900.	—
BC-7S	$10	English	Specimen	(9)	600.	—
BC-8S	$10	French	Specimen	(8)	800.	—
BC-9FP	$20	English	Face Proof	n/a	—	1,000.
BC-9BP	$20	English	Back Proof	n/a	—	450.
BC-9S	$20	English	Specimen	(9)	900.	—
BC-10FP	$20	French	Face Proof	n/a	—	1,100.
BC-10BP	$20	French	Back Proof	n/a	—	450.
BC-10S	$20	French	Specimen	(9)	2,000.	—
BC-11FP	$25	English	Face Proof	n/a	—	1,750.
BC-11BP	$25	English	Back Proof	n/a	—	450.
BC-11S	$25	English	Specimen	(7)	3,500.	—
BC-12FP	$25	French	Face Proof	n/a	—	2,000.
BC-12BP	$25	French	Back Proof	n/a	—	450.
BC-12S	$25	French	Specimen	(9)	3,500.	—
BC-13FP	$50	English	Face Proof	n/a	—	1,000.
BC-13BP	$50	English	Back Proof	n/a	—	350.
BC-13S	$50	English	Specimen	(9)	800.	—
BC-14FP	$50	French	Face Proof	n/a	—	1,200.
BC-14BP	$50	French	Back Proof	n/a	—	350.
BC-14S	$50	French	Specimen	(9)	1,400.	—
BC-15FP	$100	English	Face Proof	n/a	—	900.
BC-15BP	$100	English	Back Proof	n/a	—	350.
BC-15S	$100	English	Specimen	(9)	800.	—
BC-16FP	$100	French	Face Proof	n/a	—	1,000.
BC-16BP	$100	French	Back Proof	n/a	—	350.
BC-16S	$100	French	Specimen	(9)	1,200.	—
BC-17FP	$500	English	Face Proof	n/a	—	2,000.
BC-17BP	$500	English	Back Proof	n/a	—	800.
BC-17S	$500	English	Specimen	(9)	4,500.	—
BC-18FP	$500	French	Face Proof	n/a	—	2,000.
BC-18BP	$500	French	Back Proof	n/a	—	800.
BC-18S	$500	French	Specimen	(9)	5,500.	—

Cat. No.	Denom.	Variety	Quantity Sold Bank of Canada Sale		AU	Unc
BC-19FP	$1,000	English	Face Proof	n/a	—	1,500.
BC-19BP	$1,000	English	Back Proof	n/a	—	750.
BC-19S	$1,000	English	Specimen	(9)	2,800.	—
BC-20FP	$1,000	French	Face Proof	n/a	—	1,500.
BC-20BP	$1,000	French	Back Proof	n/a	—	750.
BC-20S	$1,000	French	Specimen	(9)	3,000.	—
Set of ten, $1 to $1,000		English	Specimen		16,500.	—
Set of ten, $1 to $1,000		French	Specimen		22,500.	—

ISSUES OF 1937

The 1937 issue of the Bank of Canada was the first to be bilingual. It had proven too expensive to prepare separate English and French emissions of the 1935 issue. The denominations and text are in English on the left side and French on the right. All notes are the same size as those of the 1935 issue (6" long by 2 7/8" wide). Denominations in this issue consist of $1, $2, $5, $10, $20, $50, $100 and $1000, and although there was some feeling on the part of the public that there should also be a 25-cent fractional note, it was not sufficiently widespread to receive serious consideration from Bank officials. Both the Canadian and British American Bank Note Companies were receiving orders for 1937 notes as early as October 1936, during the reign of King Edward VIII. At least some of the denominations being prepared would have borne his portrait. The new prefix system of numbering explained below (see "Serial Numbers and Signatures") was to go into effect for this issue. When Edward VIII abdicated in December 1936, he was succeeded by his brother, the Duke of York, who reigned as King George VI. King Edward's portrait was replaced by that of King George, using the same vignette as on the $50 note of 1935. The King's portrait was moved from the left to the centre of the note, and was used on all denominations from $1 to $50. The portrait of Sir John A. Macdonald used at the left of the 1935 $500 note was moved to the centre of the $100 denomination, while Sir Wilfrid Laurier continued to appear on the $1000 note, also being moved to the centre.

Like the portraits on the faces, the allegorical vignettes on the backs of the notes of the 1937 issue were the same as those used in 1935, although in some cases they were used on different denominations. The old $20 back vignette was abandoned and replaced on the new $20 notes by that of the former $500 denomination. The $2 and $10 back vignettes were interchanged from their 1935 situations. The backs were also made bilingual, English on the left and French on the right; the counters were made larger and the lathework was altered. A number of denominations also underwent colour changes.

The 1937 issue was released for circulation on July 21, 1937 in denominations from $1 to $100. Originally it was intended to put all remaining stocks of the 1935 issue into circulation except for the $25 denomination, and to withhold notes of the 1937 issue except when they were specifically requested. This plan was scuttled by the confusion which arose between the 1935 $2 and the 1937 $5, both of which were blue, causing the destruction of the reserves of the 1935 $2 notes. Most other denominations of the 1935 issue were phased out by July 1938. Thus the 1937 issue displaced the former issue somewhat earlier than had been anticipated, increasing the cost to the Bank of Canada. To replace the stocks of unused 1935 notes which had been destroyed, the British American Bank Note Company printed $2, $5 and $10 notes at a much reduced cost. The 1937 $1000 notes were the last to be released for circulation, when they finally superseded the 1935 $1000 notes in January 1952. The "new" $1000 notes had been printed in 1937 and had been kept in the reserve stockpile of the Bank of Canada over the years, as indicated by the Osborne-Towers signatures.

The paper used for the issue was again supplied by Howard Smith Paper Co. of Montreal. The bank note paper used in 1937 was composed of 75% highest grade linen and 25% cotton. Its ability to withstand the stresses of circulation was so great the the notes were usually withdrawn because of having become excessively soiled rather than because of wear. The use of watermarked paper was contemplated but rejected. As with the previous issue, the paper was manufactured containing green planchettes to increase the security of the notes against counterfeiting. Planchettes were also used in the production of notes for the chartered banks with a different colour assigned for the use of each bank. In 1941 the linen content was reduced to 50%, because of the necessity of conservation during wartime. For the same reason the use of chlorine in bleaching the paper was reduced, as was the amount of titanium oxide, a paper brightener. This resulted in a decrease in overall brightness of the paper. The paper composition was further reduced to 25% flax and 75% cotton, to conserve linen for the production of war uniforms.

Serial Numbers And Signatures

Beginning with the 1937 issue, the Bank of Canada adopted a two-letter prefix, written as a fraction. The lower letter was the denominational letter, reserved for use on one specific denomination. The upper letter designated the series and could be used on any denomination. Within each series, notes were numbered from 0000001 to 10000000 with the number printed twice in red on the face of each note. Since each note on the sheet had a different number, there was no need for using check letters.

Ordinarily the series letters used were A,B,C,D,E,H,J,K,L,M,N,O,R,S,T,U,W,X,Y and Z, a total of twenty letters, corresponding to 20 series of 10,000,000 notes each. Occasionally letters were added to this list or deleted (see checklist of prefix letters). Thus each denominational letter could usually be used for 200,000,000 notes.

If more notes were needed, a new denominational letter was chosen. By September 1941 it was clear that the end of the use of the "A" denominational letter for the $1 notes was imminent. It was decided to give the next twenty series the denominational letter "L", which in turn lasted until the end of 1946 when the letter "M" was begun. The "M" group contained series F and G, letters which had apparently not been authorized, so this group consisted of 22 series. The final $1 group, the "N" group, probably began in 1951. The only other denominations for which the demand exceeded twenty series of 10,000,000 notes each, the $2, $5 and $10, all exhausted their first denominational letters (B, C and D) in 1949 and were then assigned letters R, S and T respectively.

The lower denominations were printed from 24/on plates (3 across, 8 down) and 12/on plates were used for the higher denominations. To print the small quantities required to finish the last few notes of an order, 4/on plates were used. The notes were not numbered consecutively on each sheet but were "skip-numbered". This means that the notes on a given sheet received numbers which differed by 1,000, so that when a stock of 1,000 sheets was cut, the notes automatically formed "bricks" of 1,000 consecutively-numbered notes. From 1937 to 1940 the Canadian Bank Note Company "skipped" $1 sheets by five thousands, which made bricks of 5,000 $1 notes, but then began printing in limits of 1,000 as for the other denominations.

The 1937 issue consists of three sets of signatures. The first Deputy Governor of the Bank of Canada, J. A. C. Osborne, resigned on September 14, 1938. He had been "on loan" from the Bank of England since 1934. His successor was Donald Gordon, whose signature was applied on notes printed from November 1938. The unused numbers in series which were in progress when the signature change occurred were cancelled, so that Gordon's signature appeared together with the new series prefix letters. In the case of the $1 and $2 notes however, the last series receiving the Osborne signature had been completed so that no discontinuity occurred in the numbering of these denominations.

James E. Coyne was appointed Deputy Governor on January 1, 1950 to replace Donald Gordon who had resigned to become President of Canadian National Railways. This time the last series of each denomination to receive the Gordon signature was not terminated, but instead completed with the Coyne signature. The changeover occurred within each series of numbers which are listed in the Summary of Technical Details. Graham F. Towers remained Governor of the Bank of Canada throughout the entire issue, and his signature is found in the right hand space on all of the notes.

The $1 Face Plate Modification

All notes of the 1937 issue were delivered to the Bank of Canada without signatures. There the signatures were applied by letterpress using a plate prepared from signature dies made by the Royal Canadian Mint. Considerable difficulty was encountered in 1937 with the $1 notes with respect to registration of the signatures. Because the signatures and the signature panel were almost the same height, there was little margin for error if the signatures were not to appear either too high or too low. The Canadian Bank Note Company suggested a reduction in the size of the signatures, an option which did not appeal to Bank of Canada officials. They in turn felt that if the sheets were trimmed with very uniform margins the problem would be eliminated. Although the bank note company tried to improve its margins, the necessary precision was difficult to attain because the notes were printed wet and shrank during drying.

Finally in mid-1938 a suggestion was made to rearrange the $1 note leaving about 3/32" more space in the signature panel. The proposal was approved because it would solve the problem of signing the notes while not being noticeable to the general public. The face plate was modified accordingly and specimens of the new $1 notes with the wide signature panel were approved in November 1938. The first of these notes produced for circulation were given prefix letters K/A and were probably released early in 1939.

Checklist of Prefix Letters

Cat.No.	Denom.	Signatures	Denom. Letter	Series Letter
BC-21a	$1	Osborne-Towers	A	A B C D E
BC-21b	$1	Gordon-Towers (NP)	A	H J
BC-21c	$1	Gordon-Towers (WP)	A	K L M N O R S T U W X Y Z
BC-21c	$1	Gordon-Towers (WP)	L	A B C D E H J K L M N O R S T U W X Y Z
BC-21c	$1	Gordon-Towers (WP)	M	A B C D E F G H J K L M N O
BC-21d	$1	Coyne-Towers	M	O R S T U W X Y Z
BC-21d	$1	Coyne-Towers	N	A B C D E H J K L M N O R S T U W
BC-22a	$2	Osborne-Towers	B	A B
BC-22b	$2	Gordon-Towers	B	C D E H J K L M N O R S T U W X Y Z
BC-22c	$2	Coyne-Towers	B	Z
BC-22c	$2	Coyne-Towers	R	A B C D E H J K L
BC-23a	$5	Osborne-Towers	C	A
BC-23b	$5	Gordon-Towers	C	B C D E H J K L M N O R S T U W X
BC-23c	$5	Coyne-Towers	C	X Y Z
BC-23c	$5	Coyne-Towers	S	A B C D E H
BC-24a	$10	Osborne-Towers	D	A
BC-24b	$10	Gordon-Towers	D	B C D E H J K L M N O R S T U W X Y Z
BC-24c	$10	Coyne-Towers	D	Z
BC-24c	$10	Coyne-Towers	T	A B C D E H J K L M
BC-25a	$20	Osbourne-Towers	E	A
BC-25b	$20	Gordon-Towers	E	B C D E H
BC-25c	$20	Coyne-Towers	E	H J K L
BC-26a	$50	Osbourne-Towers	H	A
BC-26b	$50	Gordon-Towers	H	B
BC-26c	$50	Coyne-Towers	H	B
BC-27a	$100	Osbourne-Towers	J	A
BC-27b	$100	Gordon-Towers	J	B
BC-27c	$100	Coyne-Towers	J	B
BC-28	$1000	Osborne-Towers	K	A

Summary of Technical Details

Cat.No.	Denom.	Variety	Printer	Prefixes	Numbers	Qty.Printed
BC-21a	$1	Osborne-Towers	CBN	A/A-E/A	0000001-10000000	50,000,000
BC-21b	$1	Gordon-Towers (NP)	CBN	H/A-J/A	0000001-10000000	20,000,000
BC-21c	$1	Gordon-Towers (WP)	CBN	K/A-Z/A	0000001-10000000	130,000,000
BC-21c	$1	Gordon-Towers (WP)	CBN	A/L-Z/L	0000001-10000000	200,000,000
BC-21c	$1	Gordon-Towers (WP)	CBN	A/M- N/M	0000001-10000000	130,000,000
BC-21c	$1	Gordon-Towers (WP)	CBN	O/M	0000001-2840000	2,840,000
BC-21d	$1	Coyne-Towers	CBN	O/M	2840001-10000000	7,160,000
BC-21d	$1	Coyne-Towers	CBN	R/M-Z/M	0000001-10000000	80,000,000
BC-21d	$1	Coyne-Towers	CBN	A/N-U/N	0000001-10000000	160,000,000
BC-21d	$1	Coyne-Towers	CBN	W/N	0000001-2408000	2,408,000
BC-22a	$2	Osborne-Towers	BABN	A/B-B/B	0000001-10000000	20,000,000
BC-22b	$2	Gordon-Towers	BABN	C/B-Y/B	000001-10000000	170,000,000
BC-22b	$2	Gordon-Towers	BABN	Z/B	0000001-4000000	4,000,000
BC-22c	$2	Coyne-Towers	BABN	Z/B	4000001-10000000	6,000,000
BC-22c	$2	Coyne-Towers	BABN	A/R-K/R	0000001-10000000	80,000,000
BC-22c	$2	Coyne-Towers	BABN	L/R	0000001-5668000	5,668,000
BC-23a	$5	Osborne-Towers	BABN	A/C	0000001-8824500(est.)	8,824,500(est.)
BC-23b	$5	Gordon-Towers	BABN	B/C-W/C	0000001-10000000	160,000,000
BC-23b	$5	Gordon-Towers	BABN	X/C	0000001-5200000	5,200,000
BC-23c	$5	Coyne-Towers	BABN	X/C	5200001-10000000	4,800,000
BC-23c	$5	Coyne-Towers	BABN	Y/C-Z/C	0000001-10000000	20,000,000
BC-23c	$5	Coyne-Towers	BABN	A/S-E/S	0000001-10000000	50,000,000
BC-23c	$5	Coyne-Towers	BABN	H/S	0000001-8000000(est.)	8,000,000 (est.)
BC-24a	$10	Osborne-Towers	BABN	A/D	0000001-6400000(est.)	6.400,000(est.)
BC-24b	$10	Gordon-Towers	BABN	B/D-Y/D	0000001-10000000	180,000,000
BC-24b	$10	Gordon-Towers	BABN	Z/D	0000001-0470356*	500,000(est.)
BC-24c	$10	Coyne-Towers	BABN	Z/D	0541805*-10000000	9,500,000 (est.)
BC-24c	$10	Coyne-Towers	BABN	A/T-L/T	0000001-10000000	90,000,000
BC-24c	$10	Coyne-Towers	BABN	M/T	0000001-2960000	2,960,000
BC-25a	$20	Osborne-Towers	CBN	A/E	0000001-1622000	1,622,000
BC-25b	$20	Gordon-Towers	CBN	B/E-E/E	000001-10000000	40,000,000
BC-25b	$20	Gordon-Towers	CBN	H/E	0000001-1600000	1,600,000 (est.)
BC-25c	$20	Coyne-Towers	CBN	H/E	1600001-10000000	8,400,000 (est.)
BC-25c	$20	Coyne-Towers	CBN	J/E-K/E	0000001-10000000	20,000,000
BC-25c	$20	Coyne-Towers	CBN	L/E	0000001-1416000	1,416,000
BC-26a	$50	Osborne-Towers	CBN	A/H	0000001-0100000	100,000 (est.)
BC-26b	$50	Gordon-Towers	CBN	B/H	0000001-4200000	4,200,000
BC-26c	$50	Coyne-Towers	CBN	B/H	4200001-5300000	1,100,000
BC-27a	$100	Osborne-Towers	CBN	A/J	0000001-0070000	70,000 (est.)
BC-27b	$100	Gordon-Towers	CBN	B/J	0000001-4160000	4,160,000 (est.)
BC-27c	$100	Coyne-Towers	CBN	B/J	4160001-5070000	910,000(est.)
BC-28	$1000	Osborne-Towers	CBN	A/K	0000001-0015000	15,000

$1 Issue — 1937

BC-21d

Face Design: —/King George VI/—
(See varieties)
Portrait Imprint: H.M. King George VI/Bank of Canada/X-V-119/
Canadian Bank Note Co. Ltd.
Portrait Engraver: Robert Savage
Portrait Source: Photograph by Bertram Park, Marcus Adams Ltd., Yvonne Gregory, London, England
Pantograph Panel:
Left: One Dollar, 1 **Right:** Un Dollar, 1
Colour: Black with green tint

BC-21

Back Design: —/Agriculture allegory: Seated female with agricultural products/—
Vignette Imprint: Agriculture/V-71428/American Bank Note Company
Vignette Design: Painting by A. E. Foringer
Vignette Engraver: Wm. Ford
Colour: Green

Issue Date: Engraved: 2nd JAN 1937
Imprint: Canadian Bank Note Company, Limited on face and back

Signatures

Left	Right
Typed: J.A.C. Osborne	Typed: G.F. Towers
Typed: D. Gordon	Typed: G.F. Towers
Typed: J.E. Coyne	Typed: G.F. Towers

Varieties

The face design with the narrow and wide signature panel can be easily identified by the spacing of the King's portrait medallion from the note's border. The narrow signature variety has a wider space between the top of the Kings' portrait and the top border. The wide signature panel variety has a very narrow space in the same area.

BC-21b-i Narrow Signature Panel

Wide Space

Narrow signature panel

BC-21c Wide Signature Panel

Narrow Space

Wide signature panel

Cat.No.	Denom.	Variety	VG	F	VF	EF	AU	Unc
BC-21a	$1	Osborne-Towers	12.	18.	27.	50.	150.	225.
BC-21b	$1	Gordon-Towers (NP) H/A	90.	150.	300.	400.	600.	800.
BC-21b-i	$1	Gordon-Towers (NP) J/A	225.	350.	700.	1,000.	1,300.	1,600.
BC-21c	$1	Gordon-Towers (WP)	8.	10.	12.	20.	35.	55.
BC-21d	$1	Coyne-Towers	8.	10.	12.	18.	30.	50.

$2 Issue — 1937

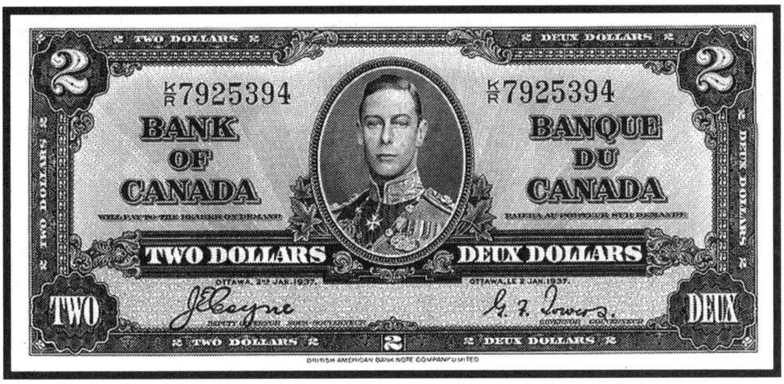

BC-22c

Face Design: —/King George VI/—
Portrait Details: See $1 note BC-21 page number 191
Pantograph Panel:
Left: Two Dollars, 2 **Right:** Deux Dollars, 2
Colour: Black with red-brown tint

BC-22

Back Design: —/Harvest allegory: Seated female with fruits of harvest/—
Vignette Imprint: Unknown
Vignette Design: Original painting, artist unknown.
Vignette Engraver: H. P. Dawson
Colour: Red-brown

Issue Date: Engraved: 2nd JAN 1937
Imprint: British American Bank Note Company Limited on face and back

Signatures

Left:	Right:
Typed: J.A.C. Osborne	Typed: G.F. Towers
Typed: D. Gordon	Typed: G.F. Towers
Typed: J.E. Coyne	Typed: G.F. Towers

Cat.No.	Denom.	Variety	VG	F	VF	EF	AU	Unc
BC-22a	$2	Osborne-Towers	22.	35.	80.	160.	300.	475.
BC-22b	$2	Gordon-Towers	12.	17.	22.	40.	100.	140.
BC-22c	$2	Coyne-Towers	12.	17.	22.	40.	100.	140.

$5 Issue — 1937

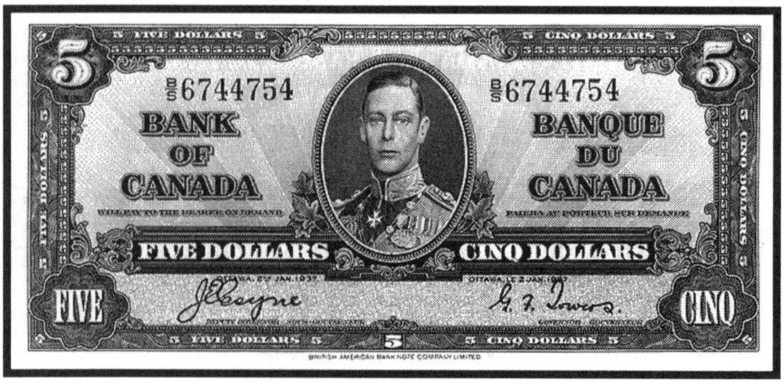

BC-23c

Face Design: —/King George VI/—
Portrait Details: See $1 note BC-21 page number 191
Pantograph Panel:
Left: Five Dollars, 5V5 **Right:** Cinq Dollars, 5V5
Colour: Black with blue tint

BC-23

Back Design: —/Electric Power allegory: Seated male with symbols of electricity/—
Vignette Imprint: Unknown
Vignette Design: Original painting, artist unknown.
Vignette Engraver: H. P. Dawson
Colour: Blue

Issue Date: Engraved: 2nd JAN 1937
Imprint: British American Bank Note Company Limited on face and back

Signatures

Left: Typed: J.A.C. Osborne **Right:** Typed: G.F. Towers
Typed: D. Gordon Typed: G.F. Towers
Typed: J.E. Coyne Typed: G.F. Towers

Cat.No.	Denom.	Variety	VG	F	VF	EF	AU	Unc
BC-23a	$5	Osborne-Towers	65.	100.	175.	400.	1,000.	1,600.
BC-23b	$5	Gordon-Towers	15.	20.	30.	50.	80.	130.
BC-23c	$5	Coyne-Towers	15.	20.	25.	50.	80.	130.

$10 Issue — 1937

BC-24a

Face Design: —/King George VI/—
Portrait Details: See $1 note BC-21 page number 191
Pantograph Panel:
Left: Ten Dollars, 10 Dollars, 10, Ten.
Right: Dix Dollars, X Dollars, X, Dix.
Colour: Black with purple tint

BC-24

Back Design: —/Transportation allegory: Mercury with ships, trains and planes/—
Vignette Imprint: Unknown
Vignette Design: Unknown.
Vignette Engraver: H. P. Dawson and G. Gundersen
Colour: Purple

Issue Date: Engraved: 2nd JAN 1937
Imprint: British American Bank Note Company Limited on face and back

Signatures

Left:		Right:
Typed: J.A.C. Osborne		Typed: G.F. Towers
Typed: D. Gordon		Typed: G.F. Towers
Typed: J.E. Coyne		Typed: G.F. Towers

Cat.No.	Denom.	Variety	VG	F	VF	EF	AU	Unc
BC-24a	$10	Osborne-Towers	50.	65.	100.	275.	750.	1,100.
BC-24b	$10	Gordon-Towers	15.	18.	20.	25.	60.	100.
BC-24c	$10	Coyne-Towers	15.	18.	20.	25.	60.	100.

$20 Issue — 1937

BC-25b

Face Design: —/King George VI/—
Portrait Details: See $1 note BC-21 page number 191
Pantograph Panel:
Left: Twenty Dollars **Right:** Vingt Dollar
Colour: Black with olive green tint

BC-25

Back Design: —/Fertility allegory: Seated female with sickle/—
Vignette Imprint: V-58826
Vignette Design: Painting by A.E. Foringer
Vignette Engraver: Robert Savage
Colour: Olive green

Issue Date: Engraved: 2nd JAN 1937
Imprint: Canadian Bank Note Company, Limited on face and back

Signatures

Left: Typed: J.A.C. Osborne — **Right:** Typed: G.F. Towers
Typed: D. Gordon — Typed: G.F. Towers
Typed: J.E. Coyne — Typed: G.F. Towers

Cat.No.	Denom.	Variety	VG	F	VF	EF	AU	Unc
BC-25a	$20	Osborne-Towers	50.	80.	150.	450.	900.	1,300.
BC-25b	$20	Gordon-Towers	25.	27.	30.	35.	75.	150.
BC-25c	$20	Coyne-Towers	25.	27.	30.	35.	75.	150.

$50 Issue — 1937

BC-26c

Face Design: —/King George VI/—
Portrait Details: See $1 note BC-21 page number 191

Pantograph Panel:
Left: Fifty Dollars, 50 **Right:** Cinquante Dollars, 50
Colour: Black with orange tint

BC-26

Back Design: —/Modern Inventions allegory: Seated female with symbols of radio broadcasting/—
Vignette Imprint: "Allegory Radio"
Vignette Design: Painting by A. E. Foringer
Vignette Engraver: R. Savage
Colour: Orange

Issue Date: Engraved: 2nd JAN 1937
Imprint: Canadian Bank Note Company, Limited on face and back

Signatures

Left:		Right:	
	Typed: J.A.C. Osborne		Typed: G.F. Towers
	Typed: D. Gordon		Typed: G.F. Towers
	Typed: J.E. Coyne		Typed: G.F. Towers

Cat.No.	Denom.	Variety	VG	F	VF	EF	AU	Unc
BC-26a	$50	Osborne-Towers	350.	600.	1,200.	2,000.	3,500.	6,000.
BC-26b	$50	Gordon-Towers	75.	100.	125.	250.	500.	700.
BC-26c	$50	Coyne-Towers	75.	100.	125.	250.	500.	700.

$100 Issue — 1937

BC-27c

Face Design: —/Sir John A. Macdonald/—
Portrait Details: See $500 note BC-17, page number 183
Pantograph Panel:
Left: One Hundred Dollars, 100 **Right:** Cent Dollars, 100
Colour: Black with sepia tint

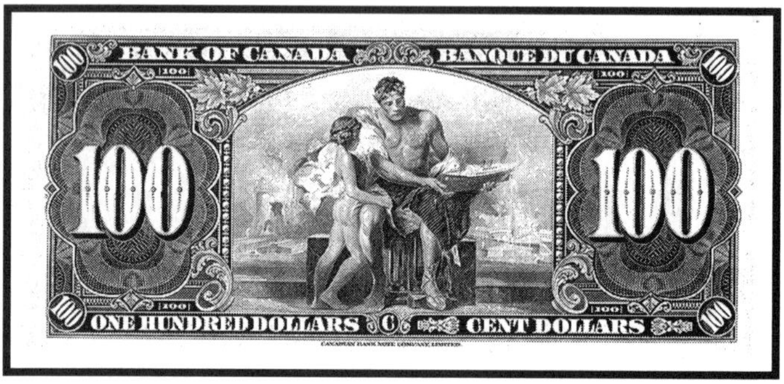

BC-27

Back Design: Commerce and Industry allegory: Seated male showing ship to child, dock and industrial scene in background
Vignette Imprint: Original die V-43076 and die V-43246; Altered die V-73316
Vignette Design: Painting by A. E. Foringer
Vignette Engraver: Original by Wm. Adolf; Re-engraved by E. Loizeaux,
Colour: Sepia

Issue Date: Engraved: 2nd JAN 1937
Imprint: Canadian Bank Note Company, Limited on face and back

Signatures

Left:	Right:
Typed:J.A.C. Osborne	Typed: G.F. Towers
Typed: D. Gordon	Typed: G.F. Towers
Typed: J.E. Coyne	Typed: G.F. Towers

Cat.No.	Denom.	Variety	VG	F	VF	EF	AU	Unc
BC-27a	$100	Osborne-Towers	250.	300.	400.	650.	1,250.	2,000.
BC-27b	$100	Gordon-Towers	125.	135.	150.	200.	350.	600.
BC-27c	$100	Coyne-Towers	125.	135.	150.	200.	350.	600.

$1000 Issue — 1937

BC-28

Face Design: —/Sir Wilfrid Laurier/—
Portrait Details: See $1,000 note BC-19 page number 184
Pantograph Panel:
Left: One Thousand Dollars, 1000 **Right:** Mille Dollars, 1000
Colour: Black with rose pink tint

BC-28

Back Design: —/Security allegory: Kneeling female shielding her child/—
Vignette Imprint: “Protection”, V-74811 - No. 2/reduction of V43281/ American Bank Note Company
Vignette Design: Painting by A. E. Foringer
Vignette Engraver: Wm. Jung
Colour: Rose pink

Issue Date: Engraved: 2nd JAN 1937
Imprint: **Canadian Bank Note Company, Limited on face and back**

Signatures

Left: Typed: J.A.C. Osborne **Right:** Typed: G.F. Towers

Cat.No.	Denom.	Variety	VG	F	VF	EF	AU	Unc
BC-28	$1000	Osborne-Towers	1,300.	1,350.	1,450.	1,650.	3,000.	4,300.

PROOF AND SPECIMEN NOTES OF THE 1937 ISSUE

Some face and back proofs of the 1937 Bank of Canada notes exist in private collections. All specimen notes of this issue available to collectors were sold by public auction in November 1999 by the Bank of Canada. These specimen notes have been perforated diagonally with the word "SPECIMEN" three times. Denominations printed by Canadian Bank Note Co. ($1, $20, $50, $100, $1,000) also have four round holes punched in the signature area, but the British American Bank Note Co. printings ($2, $5, $10) do not. The 1937 specimens are overprinted twice with the word "SPECIMEN", in red, in the signature area, and often twice more, vertically, at the sides. The specimen notes were generally described in the auction catalogue as AU, with glue residue on the back, usually in the right margin area. Specimen notes impaired by staining or thinning will transact at reduced prices.

Specimens of this issue have been released with various prefixes, except the $1,000 which has prefix A/K only.

Cat. No.	Denom.	Variety	Quantity Sold Bank of Canada Sale		AU	Unc
BC-21FPNT-i	$1	Narrow Panel	Face Proof Without Tint	n/a	—	500.
BC-21FP-i	$1	Narrow Panel	Face Proof With Tint	n/a	—	500.
BC-21S-i	$1	Narrow Panel	Specimen	(12)	650.	—
BC-21FPNT-ii	$1	Wide Panel	Face Proof Without Tint	n/a	—	500.
BC-21FP-ii	$1	Wide Panel	Face Proof With Tint	n/a	—	500.
BC-21S-ii	$1	Wide Panel	Specimen	(35)	550.	—
BC-21BP	$1		Back Proof	n/a	—	350.
BC-22S	$2		Specimen	(48)	500.	—
BC-23S	$5		Specimen	(47)	500.	—
BC-24S	$10		Specimen	(48)	500.	—
BC-25FP	$20		Face Proof	n/a	—	600.
BC-25BP	$20		Back Proof	n/a	—	300.
BC-25S	$20		Specimen	(47)	500.	—
BC-26FP	$50		Face Proof	n/a	—	800.
BC-26BP	$50		Back Proof	n/a	—	350.
BC-26S	$50		Specimen	(47)	500.	—
BC-27FP	$100		Face Proof	n/a	—	800.
BC-27BP	$100		Back Proof	n/a	—	325.
BC-27S	$100		Specimen	(48)	500.	—
BC-28FP	$1,000		Face Proof	n/a	—	1,000.
BC-29BP	$1,000		Back Proof	n/a	—	450.
BC-28S	$1,000		Specimen	(48)	2,200.	—
Set of eight, $1 (WP) to $1,000			Specimen		5,750.	—

ISSUES OF 1954

The third issue of the Bank of Canada, and the second to have a bilingual format, was prepared following the untimely death in 1952 of King George VI and released in 1954. The new notes measured 6 x 2 3/4 inches, slightly narrower than the issue they replaced. The portrait of Queen Elizabeth II, appearing on the faces of all denominations from $1 to $1000, was placed at the right-hand side where it was less susceptible to wear caused by folding than the previous centrally placed portrait. George Gundersen of the British American Bank Note Company engraved the portrait.

The allegorical vignettes on the backs of the previous issues were abandoned in favour of Canadian landscapes. The rural scene on the $2 back and the Rocky Mountain scene on the $10 back were engraved by H. P. Dawson. Gordon Yorke engraved the northern river scene on the $5 back. The latter two engravers were also employed by the British American Bank Note Company.

The printing contracts were again divided between the Canadian Bank Note Company, which produced $1, $5, $20, $50, $100 and $1,000 notes, and the British American Bank Note Company which printed $1, $2, $5 and $10 notes. The issue was terminated over the interval 1970 to 1976 because the alphabet had practically been exhausted as a source of denominational letters, every letter but Q having been employed for this purpose. In addition, dangerous counterfeits had become a serious problem, particularly affecting the $50 and $100 denominations. The final signature varieties of these denominations were quickly replaced by the new multi-coloured notes, resulting in their present scarcity.

The "Devil's Face" Notes

On the earliest notes of the 1954 issue, highlighted areas of the Queen's hair produced the illusion of a leering demonic face behind her ear. This was not the result of an error, nor was it, as some have asserted, the prank of an IRA sympathizer at the bank note company. It was merely the faithful reproduction of the original photograph. The portrait of the Queen with the "Devil's Face" outlined in her hair generated almost instant controversy. The portrait was modified by darkening the highlights in the hair and thus removing the shading which had resulted in the "devil". The modification of the face plates was made for most denominations in 1956, except for the $1000 denomination which was modified several years later.

Devil's Face Portrait

Modified Portrait

Prefixes And Numbering

The procedure for numbering notes which was initiated on the 1937 issue was continued, with slight modifications, on the 1954 issue. Once again the number was preceded by two prefix letters, written as a fraction. The upper letter was the series letter, with all letters except Q being used. The numbers within each series originally began at 0000001 and ended at 10000000, so that each series consisted of 10,000,000 notes. About 1968 the numbering was altered to begin at 0000000 and end at 9999999, the zero note being removed and destroyed.

The lower letter, or denominational letter, was used for only one specific denomination. For each denominational letter, twenty-five series letters could be used, so that a denominational letter could be used for up to 250,000,000 notes. Nevertheless, the issue was so extensive that every possible denominational letter except Q was eventually used.

When the 1954 issue was being designed it was proposed that the check letters A, B, C and D be restored so that one series of ten million sheet numbers would comprise forty million notes. The effect would have been the more economical use of prefix letters and thus a delay in the exhaustion of possible prefix letter combinations. However the suggestion narrowly missed being acted upon and no check letters were used.

The 1954 "Devil's Face" notes were printed in sheets of 24. The modified portrait notes introduced in 1956 were printed in sheets of 32 until 1968 when the printing of sheets of 40 began. In all cases the notes were "skip-numbered" as in 1937, so that the sheets when stacked could be cut into bricks of consecutively-numbered notes.

Some variation has been reported in the size of numbers on $1, $2 and $10 notes printed by the British American Bank Note Company. This change in the size and style of the numbering head type apparently corresponds closely with the changeover to engraved signatures in 1968.

Signatures Of 1954 Notes

Before 1968, notes were delivered unsigned by the bank note companies to the Bank of Canada. The signatures were then applied by letterpress by Bank of Canada employees. Because they were printed in a separate process, the signatures show some variation in position. In 1968 the signatures began to be engraved on the face plates starting with the lower denominations so that the notes were printed fully signed. Naturally there can be no variation in the positions of the signatures on these notes.

Signatures of the following Bank of Canada officials occur on notes of the 1954 issue:

Senior Deputy Governor	*Term of Office*
James E. Coyne	Jan. 1, 1950 to Dec. 31, 1954
John Robert Beattie	Jan. 1, 1955 to Dec. 31, 1971
Gerald K. Bouey	Jan. 1, 1972 to Feb. 1, 1973
R. William Lawson	Mar. 1, 1973 to Feb. 29, 1984
Gordon G. Thiessen	Oct. 27, 1987 to Jan. 31, 1994

Governor	*Term of Office*
Graham F. Towers	Sept. 10, 1934 to Sept. 10, 1954
James E. Coyne	Jan. 1, 1955 to July 24, 1961
Louis Rasminsky	July 24, 1961 to Feb. 1, 1973
Gerald K. Bouey	Feb. 1, 1973 to Jan. 31, 1987
John W. Crow	Feb. 1, 1987 to Jan. 31, 1994

There are six signature combinations which occur on the 1954 issue. The Coyne-Towers signature combination appears only on the "Devil's Face" notes while the Beattie-Coyne signatures occur on both "Devil's Face" and modified portrait notes. Later combinations are Beattie-Rasminsky, Bouey-Rasminsky, Lawson-Bouey and Thiessen-Crow (on the $1,000 note). For denominations of $5 and up, some of the later signature combinations were not always printed.

Imprints Of 1954 Notes

Both the Canadian Bank Note Company and the British American Bank Note Company participated in the printing of the 1954 issue of notes. At the outset each printer had the contract for the same denominations as for the 1935 and 1937 issues; namely, the British American Bank Note Company printed $2, $5 and $10 while the Canadian Bank Note Company printed the others. In 1959 the Canadian Bank Note Company assumed all further production of the $5 denominations while the British American Bank Note Company shared in the printing of the $1 notes. In the case of the $1 notes, different denominational prefix letters were assigned to each printer. The imprints of the bank note companies are found at the bottom centre of the notes.

1954 Asterisk Notes

Prior to the 1954 issue, identical notes were made up to replace notes which were spoiled by the bank note companies during printing or by Bank of Canada employees during signing. Parcels containing defective notes had to be set aside in the Bank's examining room until replacement notes were received from the printer. Because of this delay, and the nuisance of having to supply individually numbered notes to match those which had been spoiled, a new scheme was devised in 1953 for the issue then in preparation. Independently numbered replacement notes were printed with an asterisk preceding the serial number, and stocks of these were maintained to replace defective notes. No asterisk notes were printed for the $50, $100 or $1000 denominations.

It is believed that the asterisk notes were block-numbered. That is, they were not numbered continuously but in blocks with serial number gaps in between, the numbering of each block beginning at some arbitrarily chosen point.

When the two bank note companies began sharing the production of $1 notes in 1959, the asterisk notes were made interchangeable when substitution of defective notes was made at Bank of Canada. A $1 BABN asterisk note could be used to replace a defective note in a CBN bundle, and vice-versa. Asterisk notes are designated in the Charlton numbering system with a capital "A" added to the normal number.

Experimental Issues

In the 1960's and early 1970's mysterious batches of $2 notes with a prefix S/R were released for circulation. These were experimental notes circulated for testing purposes. The S/R $2 numbered up to 2339999 (est.) were signed Beattie-Rasminsky, as were the $2 notes in all of the other series within the R group. The next lot, numbered from 2340000 (est.) to 2679999 (est.) were signed Bouey-Rasminsky, and the last lot, from 2680000 to 2919999 (est.) were signed Lawson-Bouey. There the S/R series ended, rather than after the usual ten million notes. These notes are designated with a letter "T" following the catalogue number. It has recently been made known that certain $2 notes of series G/R are also test notes. Only notes numbered 0000001 - 0079999, 5280000 - 5359999, 5360000 - 5367999 and 5400001 - 5480000 were employed as test notes. These were subjected to a treatment, which, it was hoped, would improve their durability in circulation.

Anomalies Of The 1954 Issue

The 1954 issue was more extensive and complicated than any previous emission of the Bank of Canada. A number of intriguing problems arose.

One such problem is the asterisk notes with a denominational letter belonging to a different denomination. A *V/V $1 is known, but the lower V was assigned for use on $10 notes. Similarly, *Z/Z $2 notes are known, but the lower Z letter was supposed to be reserved for $1 notes only. Both of these curiosities may be the result of mistakes made by the bank note company when numbering the asterisk notes.

Checklist of Prefix Letters for 1954 Devil's Face Issues

Cat.No.	Denom.	Signatures	Printer	Denom. Letter	Series Letters
BC-29a	$1	Coyne-Towers	CBN	A	A B C D E F G H
BC-29aA	$1	Coyne-Towers	CBN	A	A
BC-29b	$1	Beattie-Coyne	CBN	A	H I J K L M N O P R S T
BC-29bA	$1	Beattie-Coyne	CBN	A	A
BC-30a	$2	Coyne-Towers	BABN	B	A B C D
BC-30aA	$2	Coyne-Towers	BABN	B	A
BC-30b	$2	Beattie-Coyne	BABN	B	D E F G H I
BC-30bA	$2	Beattie-Coyne	BABN	B	A
BC-31a	$5	Coyne-Towers	BABN	C	A B C
BC-31aA	$5	Coyne-Towers	BABN	C	A
BC-31b	$5	Beattie-Coyne	BABN	C	C D E F G H I
BC-31bA	$5	Beattie-Coyne	BABN	C	A
BC-32a	$10	Coyne-Towers	BABN	D	A B C D E
BC-32aA	$10	Coyne-Towers	BABN	D	A
BC-32b	$10	Beattie-Coyne	BABN	D	E F G H I J
BC-32bA	$10	Beattie-Coyne	BABN	D	A
BC-33a	$20	Coyne-Towers	CBN	E	A B
BC-33aA	$20	Coyne-Towers	CBN	E	A
BC-33b	$20	Beattie-Coyne	CBN	E	B C D E
BC-33bA	$20	Beattie-Coyne	CBN	E	A
BC-34a	$50	Coyne-Towers	CBN	H	A
BC-34b	$50	Beattie-Coyne	CBN	H	A
BC-35a	$100	Coyne-Towers	CBN	J	A
BC-35b	$100	Beattie-Coyne	CBN	J	A
BC-36	$1000	Coyne-Towers	CBN	K	A

A = Asterisk replacement note

Summary of Technical Details for 1954 Devil's Face Issue

Cat.No.	Denom.	Variety	Printer	Prefixes	Numbers	Qty.Printed	
BC-29a	$1	Coyne-Towers	CBN	A/A-G/A	0000001-10000000	70,000,000	
BC-29a	$1	Coyne-Towers	CBN	H/A	0000001-7200000	7,200,000	
BC-29aA	$1	Coyne-Towers	CBN	A/A	0000001-0013622*	14,000	(est.)
BC-29b	$1	Beattie-Coyne	CBN	H/A	7200001-10000000	2,800,000	
BC-29b	$1	Beattie-Coyne	CBN	I/A-S/A	0000001-10000000	100,000,000	
BC-29b	$1	Beattie-Coyne	CBN	T/A	0000001-3940000	3,940,000	
BC-29bA	$1	Beattie-Coyne	CBN	A/A	0014508-0021479*	7,000	(est.)
BC-30a	$2	Coyne-Towers	BABN	A/B-C/B	0000001-10000000	30,000,000	
BC-30a	$2	Coyne-Towers	BABN	D/B	0000001-7200000	7,200,000	
BC-30aA	$2	Coyne-Towers	BABN	A/B	0000001-0003244*	3,600	(est.)
BC-30b	$2	Beattie-Coyne	BABN	D/B	7200001-10000000	2,800,000	
BC-30b	$2	Beattie-Coyne	BABN	E/B-H/B	0000001-10000000	40,000,000	
BC-30b	$2	Beattie-Coyne	BABN	I/B	0000001-8600000	8,600,000	
BC-30bA	$2	Beattie-Coyne	BABN	A/B	0004822-0009082*	4,800	(est.)
BC-31a	$5	Coyne-Towers	BABN	A/C-B/C	0000001-10000000	20,000,000	
BC-31a	$5	Coyne-Towers	BABN	C/C	0000001-7600000	7,600,000	
BC-31aA	$5	Coyne-Towers	BABN	A/C	0000001-0001143*	1,200	(est.)
BC-31b	$5	Beattie-Coyne	BABN	C/C	7600001-10000000	2,400,000	
BC-31b	$5	Beattie-Coyne	BABN	D/C-H/C	0000001-10000000	50,000,000	
BC-31b	$5	Beattie-Coyne	BABN	I/C	0000001-9014816*	unknown	
BC-31bA	$5	Beattie-Coyne	BABN	A/C	0002453-0006575*	4,800	(est.)
BC-32a	$10	Coyne-Towers	BABN	A/D-D/D	0000001-10000000	40,000,000	
BC-32a	$10	Coyne-Towers	BABN	E/D	0000001-7200000	7,200,000	
BC-32aA	$10	Coyne-Towers	BABN	A/D	0000001-0002396*	2,400	(est.)
BC-32b	$10	Beattie-Coyne	BABN	E/D	7200001-10000000	2,800,000	
BC-32b	$10	Beattie-Coyne	BABN	F/D-I/D	0000001-10000000	40,000,000	
BC-32b	$10	Beattie-Coyne	BABN	J/D	0000001-7800000	7,800,000	
BC-32bA	$10	Beattie-Coyne	BABN	A/D	0004932-0008617*	4,800	(est.)
BC-33a	$20	Coyne-Towers	CBN	A/E	0000001-10000000	10,000,000	
BC-33a	$20	Coyne-Towers	CBN	B/E	0000001-7173417*	7,200,000	(est.)
BC-33aA	$20	Coyne-Towers	CBN	A/E	0000001-0001811*	2,400	(est.)
BC-33b	$20	Beattie-Coyne	CBN	B/E	7271414*-10000000	2,800,000	(est.)
BC-33b	$20	Beattie-Coyne	CBN	C/E-D/E	0000001-10000000	20,000,000	
BC-33b	$20	Beattie-Coyne	CBN	E/E	0000001-2523271	2,550,000	
BC-33bA	$20	Beattie-Coyne	CBN	A/E	0007332-0009129*	3,000	(est.)
BC-34a	$50	Coyne-Towers	CBN	A/H	0000001-1440000	1,440,000	
BC-34b	$50	Beattie-Coyne	CBN	A/H	1440001-2396825*	unknown	(est.)
BC-35a	$100	Coyne-Towers	CBN	A/J	0000001-1752000	1,752,000	(est.)
BC-35b	$100	Beattie-Coyne	CBN	A/J	1752001-2392000	640,000	
BC-36	$1000	Coyne-Towers	CBN	A/K	0000001-0030000	30,000	

A=Asterisk Replacement Note

Note: Printing estimates for low and high serial numbers seen may be higher than the actual number of notes printed. Many times large numbers of notes between the low and high number were not printed.

$1 Issue — 1954

"DEVIL'S FACE" PORTRAIT

BC-29a

Face Design: —/—/Queen Elizabeth II
Colour: Black with green tint
Micro Lettering: Green
Diagonal lines: Grey

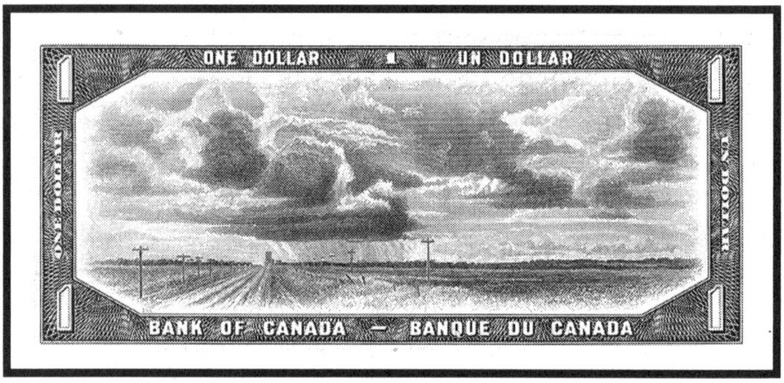

BC-29

Back Design: —/Western prairie and sky/—
Colour: Green

Issue Date: Engraved: 1954
Imprint: Canadian Bank Note Company Limited

Signatures

Left: Typed: J.E. Coyne
Typed: J.R. Beattie

Right: Typed: G.F. Towers
Typed: J.E. Coyne

Cat.No.	Denom.	Variety	VG	F	VF	EF	AU	Unc
BC-29a	$1	Coyne-Towers	10.	14.	18.	25.	50.	80.
BC-29aA	$1	Coyne-Towers * A/A	500.	750.	1,100.	1,500.	2,500.	3,200.
BC-29b	$1	Beattie-Coyne	6.	9.	12.	20.	40.	65.
BC-29bA	$1	Beattie-Coyne * A/A	375.	550.	750.	1,100.	1,750.	2,250.

A=Asterisk replacement note

$2 Issue — 1954

"DEVIL'S FACE" PORTRAIT

BC-30b

Face Design: —/—/Queen Elizabeth II
Colour: Black with terracotta (red-brown) tint
Micro Lettering: Brick red
Diagonal Lines: Chartreuse (yellow green)

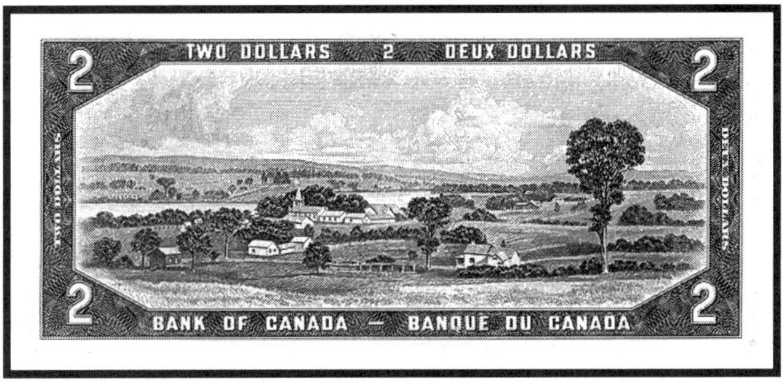

BC-30

Back Design: —/Landscape from the Upper Melbourne, Richmond, Quebec/—
Colour: Terracotta (red-brown)

Issue Date: Engraved: 1954
Imprint: British American Bank Note Company Limited

Signatures

Left:	Typed: J.E. Coyne	**Right:**	Typed: G.F. Towers
	Typed: J.R. Beattie		Typed: J.E. Coyne

Cat.No.	Denom.	Variety	VG	F	VF	EF	AU	Unc
BC-30a	$2	Coyne-Towers	14.	20.	30.	60.	125.	200.
BC-30aA	$2	Coyne-Towers * A/B	750.	1,000.	1,400.	2,250.	3,300.	5,000.
BC-30b	$2	Beattie-Coyne	10.	15.	20.	40.	80.	120.
BC-30bA	$2	Beattie-Coyne * A/B	600.	800.	1,200.	2,000.	2,800.	4,000.

A=Asterisk replacement note

$5 Issue — 1954

"DEVIL'S FACE" PORTRAIT

BC-31b

Face Design: —/—/Queen Elizabeth II
Colour: Black with blue tint
Micro Lettering: Blue
Diagonal Lines: Light purple

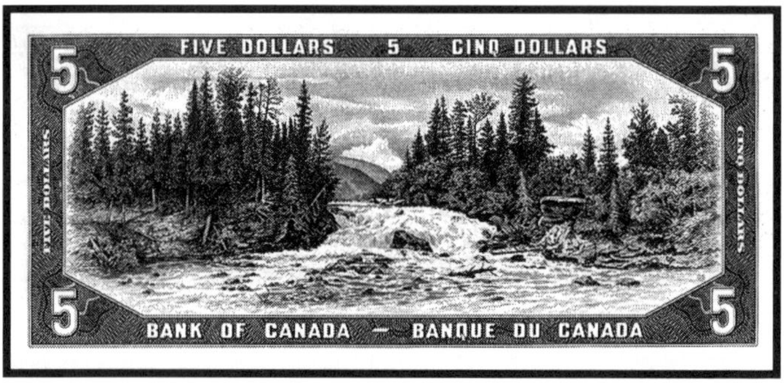

BC-31

Back Design: —/Otter Falls, mile 996, Alaska Highway/—
Colour: Blue

Issue Date: Engraved: 1954
Imprint: British American Bank Note Company Limited

Signatures

Left: Typed: J.E. Coyne
Typed: J.R. Beattie

Right: Typed: G.F. Towers
Typed: J.E. Coyne

Cat.No.	Denom.	Variety	VG	F	VF	EF	AU	Unc
BC-31a	$5	Coyne-Towers	20.	25.	35.	75.	135.	200.
BC-31aA	$5	Coyne-Towers * A/C	2,500.	4,000.	4,500.	5,500.	7,500.	11,000.
BC-31b	$5	Beattie-Coyne	15.	20.	30.	70.	100.	150.
BC-31bA	$5	Beattie-Coyne * A/C	1,400.	1,800.	2,300.	3,500.	4,500.	7,000.

A=Asterisk replacement note

$10 Issue — 1954

"DEVIL'S FACE" PORTRAIT

BC-32b

Face Design: —/—/Queen Elizabeth II
Colour: Black with purple tint
Micro Lettering: Purple
Diagonal Lines: Salmon pink

BC-32

Back Design: —/Mount Burgess, B.C./—
Colour: Purple

Issue Date: Engraved: 1954
Imprint: British American Bank Note Company Limited

Signatures

Left:	Typed: J.E. Coyne	**Right:**	Typed: G.F. Towers
	Typed: J.R. Beattie		Typed: J.E. Coyne

Cat.No.	Denom.	Variety	VG	F	VF	EF	AU	Unc
BC-32a	$10	Coyne-Towers	17.	22.	32.	55.	100.	150.
BC-32aA	$10	Coyne-Towers * A/D	700.	850.	1,200.	2,000.	2,750.	4,500.
BC-32b	$10	Beattie-Coyne	15.	20.	30.	50.	80.	140.
BC-32bA	$10	Beattie-Coyne * A/D	500.	650.	800.	1,400.	1,800.	3,000.

A=Asterisk replacement note

$20 Issue — 1954

"DEVIL'S FACE" PORTRAIT

BC-33a

Face Design: —/—/Queen Elizabeth II
Colour: Black with olive tint
Micro Lettering: Olive
Diagonal Lines: Grey

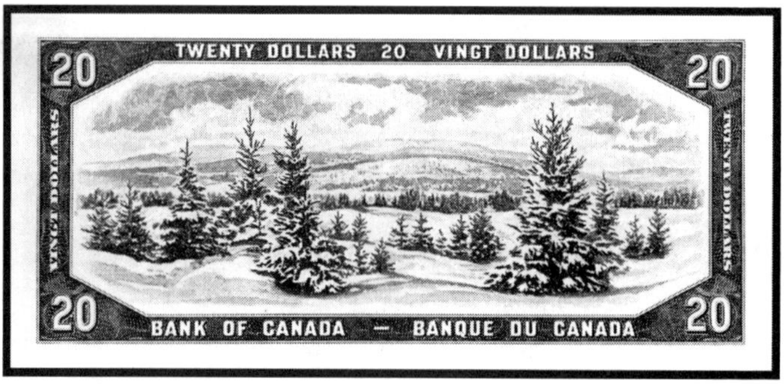

BC-33

Back Design: —/Laurentian hills in winter/—
Colour: Olive

Issue Date: Engraved: 1954
Imprint: Canadian Bank Note Company Limited

Signatures

Left: Typed: J.E. Coyne
Typed: J.R. Beattie

Right: Typed: G.F. Towers
Typed: J.E. Coyne

Cat.No.	Denom.	Variety	VG	F	VF	EF	AU	Unc
BC-33a	$20	Coyne-Towers	25.	30.	40.	75.	125.	250.
BC-33aA	$20	Coyne-Towers * A/E	1,000.	1,200.	1,800.	2,800.	3,800.	5,500.
BC-33b	$20	Beattie-Coyne	22.	25.	35.	60.	90.	190.
BC-33bA	$20	Beattie-Coyne * A/E	800.	1,000.	1,500.	2,500.	3,500.	4,500.

A=Asterisk replacement note

$50 Issue — 1954

"DEVIL'S FACE" PORTRAIT

BC-34a

Face Design: —/—/Queen Elizabeth II
Colour: Black with orange tint
Micro Lettering: Orange
Diagonal Lines: Grey

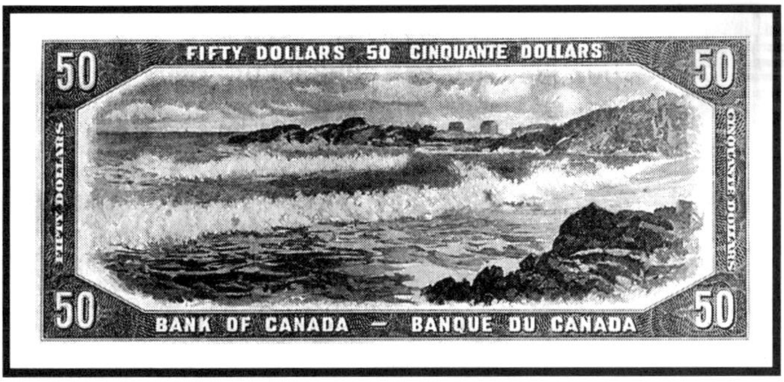

BC-34

Back Design: —/Beach and Breakers Lockeport, N.S./—
Colour: Orange

Issue Date: Engraved: 1954
Imprint: Canadian Bank Note Company Limited

Signatures

Left: Typed: J.E. Coyne; Typed: J.R. Beattie
Right: Typed: G.F. Towers; Typed: J.E. Coyne

Cat.No.	Denom.	Variety	VG	F	VF	EF	AU	Unc
BC-34a	$50	Coyne-Towers	65.	70.	85.	125.	275.	375.
BC-34b	$50	Beattie-Coyne	65.	70.	100.	150.	300.	550.

$100 Issue — 1954

"DEVIL'S FACE" PORTRAIT

BC-35a

Face Design: —/—/Queen Elizabeth II
Colour: Black with sepia tint
Micro Lettering: Sepia
Diagonal Lines: Grey

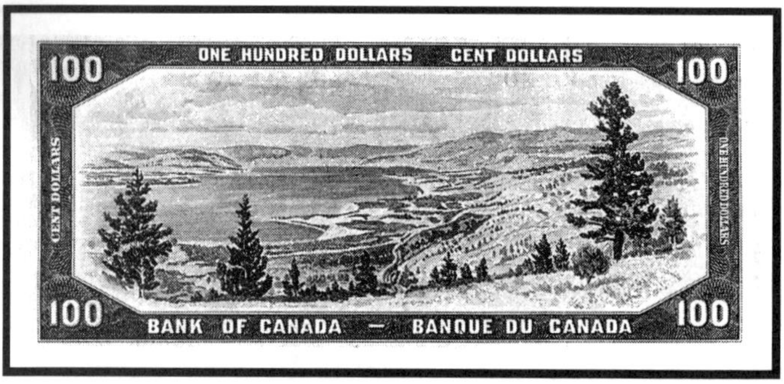

BC-35

Back Design: —/Okanagan Lake, B.C./—
Colour: Sepia

Issue Date: Engraved: 1954
Imprint: Canadian Bank Note Company Limited

Signatures

Left: Typed: J.E. Coyne
Typed: J.R. Beattie

Right: Typed: G.F. Towers
Typed: J.E. Coyne

Cat.No.	Denom.	Variety	F	VF	EF	AU	Unc.
BC-35a	$100	Coyne-Towers	110.	120.	140.	175.	350.
BC-35b	$100	Beattie-Coyne	110.	120.	175.	250.	550.

$1000 Issue — 1954

"DEVIL'S FACE" PORTRAIT

BC-36

Face Design: —/—/Queen Elizabeth II
Colour: Black with rose pink tint
Micro Lettering: Rose pink
Diagonal Lines: Grey

BC-36

Back Design: —/Anse St. Jean on the Saguenay River, Quebec/—
Colour: Rose pink

Issue Date: Engraved: 1954
Imprint: Canadian Bank Note Company Limited

Signatures

Left: Typed: J.E. Coyne **Right:** Typed: G.F. Towers

Cat.No.	Denom.	Variety	F	VF	EF	AU	Unc
BC-36	$1000	Coyne-Towers	1,750.	2,500.	3,000.	4,500.	6,500.

SPECIMEN NOTES OF THE 1954 DEVIL'S FACE ISSUE

No specimen notes of this issue are known to have been available to collectors prior to the November 1999 Bank of Canada sale. These specimen notes have been overprinted twice with the word "SPECIMEN", in red, in the signature area and may have two punch holes in the same area. Usually "SPECIMEN" is stamped once, in red, on the back as well. The specimen notes were generally described in the auction catalogue as AU, with glue residue on the back, usually in the right margin area, except most of the $5 and $10 specimens which were free of glue spots. All have manuscript "set" numbers on the back. Specimen notes impaired by staining or thinning will transact at reduced prices.

Specimens of each denomination occur with only one prefix.

Cat. No.	Denom.	Quantity Sold Bank of Canada Sale		AU
BC-29s	$1	Specimen	(9)	600.
BC-30S	$2	Specimen	(9)	550.
BC-31S	$5	Specimen	(110)	150.
BC-32S	$10	Specimen	(110)	150.
BC-33S	$20	Specimen	(9)	550.
BC-34S	$50	Specimen	(9)	550.
BC-35S	$100	Specimen	(9)	650.
BC-36S	$1,000	Specimen	(7)	2,700.
Set of eight, $1 to $1,000		Specimen		6,400.

Checklist of Prefix Letters for 1954 Modified Portrait Issues

Cat.No.	Denom.	Signature	Printer	Denom. Letter	Series Letter
BC-37a	$1	Beattie-Coyne	CBN	A	T U V W X Y Z
BC-37a	$1	Beattie-Coyne	CBN	L	A B C D E F G H I J K L M N O P R S T U V W X Y Z
BC-37a	$1	Beattie-Coyne	CBN	N	A B C D E F
BC-37aA	$1	Beattie-Coyne	CBN	A	A
BC-37a-i	$1	Beattie-Coyne	BABN	M	A B C D E F G H
BC-37b	$1	Beattie-Rasminsky	CBN	N	F G H I J K L M N O P R S T U V W X Y Z
BC-37b	$1	Beattie-Rasminsky	CBN	O	A B C D E F G H I J K L S T U V W X Y Z
BC-37b	$1	Beattie-Rasminsky	CBN	Y	A B C D E F G H I J K L M N O P R S T U
BC-37bA	$1	Beattie-Rasminsky	CBN	A	A
BC-37bA	$1	Beattie-Rasminsky	CBN	O	D I S
BC-37bA	$1	Beattie-Rasminsky	CBN	Y	A H M N O
BC-37b-i	$1	Beattie-Rasminsky	BABN	M	H I J K L M N O P R S T U V W X Y Z
BC-37b-i	$1	Beattie-Rasminsky	BABN	P	A B C D E F M N O P R S T U V W X Y Z
BC-37b-i	$1	Beattie-Rasminsky	BABN	Z	A B C D E F G H I J K L M N O P R S T U V W X Y Z
BC-37b-i	$1	Beattie-Rasminsky	BABN	F	A B C D E F G H
BC-37bA-i	$1	Beattie-Rasminsky	BABN	M	A B
BC-37bA-i	$1	Beattie-Rasminsky	BABN	F	A
BC-37c	$1	Bouey-Rasminsky	BABN	F	H I J K L M N O P R S T U V
BC-37cA	$1	Bouey-Rasminsky	BABN	F	C H
BC-37cA	$1	Bouey-Rasminsky	BABN	V	V
BC-37d	$1	Lawson-Bouey	BABN	F	V W X Y Z
BC-37d	$1	Lawson-Bouey	BABN	I	A B C D E
BC-37dA	$1	Lawson-Bouey	BABN	F	X
BC-37dA	$1	Lawson-Bouey	BABN	I	C
BC-38a	$2	Beattie-Coyne	BABN	B	I J K L M N O P R S T U V W X Y Z
BC-38a	$2	Beattie-Coyne	BABN	R	A
BC-38aA	$2	Beattie-Coyne	BABN	B	A
BC-38b	$2	Beattie-Rasminsky	BABN	R	A B C D E F G H I J K L MN O P R T U V W X Y Z
BC-38b	$2	Beattie-Rasminsky	BABN	U	A B C D E F G H I J K L M N O P R S T U V W X Y Z
BC-38bT	$2	Beattie-Rasminsky	BABN	R	G S (Test note)
BC-38b	$2	Beattie-Rasminsky	BABN	G	A
BC-38bA	$2	Beattie-Rasminsky	BABN	B	A B
BC-38bA	$2	Beattie-Rasminsky	BABN	R	R
BC-38c	$2	Bouey-Rasminsky	BABN	G	AB C D E F G H I J K L
BC-38cT	$2	Bouey-Rasminsky	BABN	R	S (Test note)
BC-38cA	$2	Bouey-Rasminsky	BABN	G	A
BC-38cA	$2	Bouey-Rasminsky	BABN	Z	Z
BC-38d	$2	Lawson-Bouey	BABN	G	L M N O P R S T U V
BC-38dT	$2	Lawson-Bouey	BABN	R	S (Test note)
BC-38dA	$2	Lawson-Bouey	BABN	G	K O

Note: The letter "T" added to the catalogue number denotes a "Test Note"

Checklist of Prefix Letters for 1954 Modified Portrait Issues (Cont'd)

Cat.No.	Denom.	Signature	Printer	Denom.Letter	Series Letter
BC-39a	$5	Beattie-Coyne	BABN	C	I J K L M N O P R
BC-39aA	$5	Beattie-Coyne	BABN	C	A
BC-39a-i	$5	Beattie-Coyne	CBN	C	R S T U V W X Y
BC-39aA-i	$5	Beattie-Coyne	CBN	C	R
BC-39b	$5	Beattie-Rasminsky	CBN	C	Y Z
BC-39b	$5	Beattie-Rasminsky	CBN	S	A B C D E F G H I J K L M N O P R S T U V W X Y Z
BC-39b	$5	Beattie-Rasminsky	CBN	X	A B C D E F G H I J K L M N O P R
BC-39bA	$5	Beattie-Rasminsky	CBN	C	R
BC-39bA	$5	Beattie-Rasminsky	CBN	S	L N S V W
BC-39bA	$5	Beattie-Rasminsky	CBN	X	I N
BC-39c	$5	Bouey-Rasminsky	CBN	X	R S T U V
BC-39cA	$5	Bouey-Rasminsky	CBN	X	R
BC-40a	$10	Beattie-Coyne	BABN	D	J K L M N O P R S T U V W X Y Z
BC-40a	$10	Beattie-Coyne	BABN	T	A B C D E
BC-40aA	$10	Beattie-Coyne	BABN	D	A
BC-40b	$10	Beattie-Rasminsky	BABN	T	E F G H I J K L M N O P R S T U V W X Y Z
BC-40b	$10	Beattie-Rasminsky	BABN	V	A B C D E F G H I J K L M N O P R S T
BC-40bA	$10	Beattie-Rasminsky	BABN	D	A B
BC-40bA	$10	Beattie-Rasminsky	BABN	T	U
BC-40bA	$10	Beattie-Rasminsky	BABN	V	B
BC-41a	$20	Beattie-Coyne	CBN	E	E F G H I J K L M
BC-41aA	$20	Beattie-Coyne	CBN	E	A
BC-41b	$20	Beattie-Rasminsky	CBN	E	M N O P R S T U V W X Y Z
BC-41b	$20	Beattie-Rasminsky	CBN	W	A B C D E F G
BC-41bA	$20	Beattie-Rasminsky	CBN	E	A V
BC-42a	$50	Beattie-Coyne	CBN	H	A
BC-42b	$50	Beattie-Rasminsky	CBN	H	A B
BC-42c	$50	Lawson-Bouey	CBN	H	B C
BC-43a	$100	Beattie-Coyne	CBN	J	A
BC-43b	$100	Beattie-Rasminsky	CBN	J	A B
BC-43c	$100	Lawson-Bouey	CBN	J	B C
BC-44a	$1000	Beattie-Coyne	CBN	K	A
BC-44b	$1000	Beattie-Rasminsky	CBN	K	A
BC-44c	$1000	Bouey-Rasminsky	CBN	K	A
BC-44d	$1000	Lawson-Bouey	CBN	K	A
BC-44e	$1000	Thiessen-Crow	CBN	K	A

Summary of Technical Details for 1954 Modified Portrait Issues

Cat.No.	Denom.	Signature	Printer	Prefixes	Numbers	Qty.Printed
BC-37a	$1	Beattie-Coyne	CBN	T/A	3940001-10000000	6,060,000
BC-37a	$1	Beattie-Coyne	CBN	U/A-Z/A	0000001-10000000	60,000,000
BC-37a	$1	Beattie-Coyne	CBN	A/L-Z/L	0000001-10000000	250,000,000
BC-37a	$1	Beattie-Coyne	CBN	A/N-E/N	0000001-10000000	50,000,000
BC-37a	$1	Beattie-Coyne	CBN	F/N	0000001-5920000	5,920,000
BC-37aA	$1	Beattie-Coyne	CBN	A/A	0030714-0090565*	64,000 (est.)
BC-37a-i	$1	Beattie-Coyne	BABN	A/M-G/M	0000001-10000000	70,000,000
BC-37a-i	$1	Beattie-Coyne	BABN	H/M	0000001-6848000	6,848,000
BC-37b	$1	Beattie-Rasminsky	CBN	F/N	5920001-10000000	4,080,000
BC-37b	$1	Beattie-Rasminsky	CBN	G/N-Z/N	0000001-10000000	190,000,000
BC-37b	$1	Beattie-Rasminsky	CBN	A/O-K/O	0000001-10000000	110,000,000
BC-37b	$1	Beattie-Rasminsky	CBN	L/O	0000001-7000000	7,000,000
BC-37b	$1	Beattie-Rasminsky	CBN	S/O	7900001-10000000	2,100,000
BC-37b	$1	Beattie-Rasminsky	CBN	T/O	0000001-10000000	10,000,000
BC-37b	$1	Beattie-Rasminsky	CBN	U/O-Z/O	0000000-9999999	60,000,000
BC-37b	$1	Beattie-Rasminsky	CBN	A/Y-T/Y	0000000-9999999	190,000,000
BC-37b	$1	Beattie-Rasminsky	CBN	U/Y	0000000-6439999	6,440,000
BC-37bA	$1	Beattie-Rasminsky	CBN	A/A	0091262-0466167*	400,000 (est.)
BC-37bA	$1	Beattie-Rasminsky	CBN	D/O	0469266-0547933	80,000 (est.)
BC-37bA	$1	Beattie-Rasminsky	CBN	I/O	0601491-0673530*	80,000 (est.)
BC-37bA	$1	Beattie-Rasminsky	CBN	S/O	0000001-0399529*	400,000 (est.)
BC-37bA	$1	Beattie-Rasminsky	CBN	A/Y	0000000-0399273*	400,000 (est.)
BC-37bA	$1	Beattie-Rasminsky	CBN	H/Y	0000000-0398018*	400,000 (est.)
BC-37bA	$1	Beattie-Rasminsky	CBN	M/Y	0000000-0198132*	200,000 (est.)
BC-37bA	$1	Beattie-Rasminsky	CBN	N/Y	0680581-0751629*	80,000 (est.)
BC-37bA	$1	Beattie-Rasminsky	CBN	O/Y	0001875-0196135*	200,000 (est.)
BC-37b-i	$1	Beattie-Rasminsky	BABN	H/M	6848001-10000000	3,152,000
BC-37b-i	$1	Beattie-Rasminsky	BABN	I/M-Z/M	0000001-10000000	170,000,000
BC-37b-i	$1	Beattie-Rasminsky	BABN	A/P-E/P	0000001-10000000	50,000,000
BC-37b-i	$1	Beattie-Rasminsky	BABN	F/P	0000001-7160000	7,160,000
BC-37b-i	$1	Beattie-Rasminsky	BABN	M/P	2720001-10000000	7,280,000
BC-37b-i	$1	Beattie-Rasminsky	BABN	N/P	0000001-10000000	10,000,000
BC-37b-i	$1	Beattie-Rasminsky	BABN	O/P-Z/P	0000000-9999999	110,000,000
BC-37b-i	$1	Beattie-Rasminsky	BABN	A/Z-Z/Z	0000000-9999999	250,000,000
BC-37b-i	$1	Beattie-Rasminsky	BABN	A/F-G/F	0000000-9999999	70,000,000
BC-37b-i	$1	Beattie-Rasminsky	BABN	H/F	0000000-7239999	7,240,000
BC-37bA-i	$1	Beattie-Rasminsky	BABN	A/M	0000001-0007953*	8000 (est.)
BC-37bA-i	$1	Beattie-Rasminsky	BABN	B/M	0000001-1159710*	1,160,000 (est.)
BC-37bA-i	$1	Beattie-Rasminsky	BABN	B/M	1768049-4261089*	2,520,000 (est.)
BC-37bA-i	$1	Beattie-Rasminsky	BABN	B/M	0000001-4261089*	3,640,000 (est.)
BC-37bA-i	$1	Beattie-Rasminsky	BABN	A/F	0202371-0565225*	380,000 (est.)
BC-37c	$1	Bouey-Rasminsky	BABN	H/F	7240000-9999999	2,760,000
BC-37c	$1	Bouey-Rasminsky	BABN	I/F-U/F	0000000-9999999	120,000,00
BC-37c	$1	Bouey-Rasminsky	BABN	V/F	0000000-8559999	8,560,000
BC-37cA	$1	Bouey-Rasminsky	BABN	C/F	0600566-0999073*	400,000 (est.)
BC-37cA	$1	Bouey-Rasminsky	BABN	H/F	0760000-0796334*	40,000 (est.)
BC-37cA	$1	Bouey-Rasminsky	BABN	V/V	3000000-5674999*	**120 (est.)
BC-37d	$1	Lawson-Bouey	BABN	V/F	8560000-9999999	1,440,000
BC-37d	$1	Lawson-Bouey	BABN	W/F-Z/F	0000000-9999999	40,000,000
BC-37d	$1	Lawson-Bouey	BABN	A/I-D/I	0000000-9999999	40,000,000
BC-37d	$1	Lawson-Bouey	BABN	E/I	0000000-4119999	4,120,000
BC-37dA	$1	Lawson-Bouey	BABN	X/F	0100570-0334335*	240,000 (est.)
BC-37dA	$1	Lawson-Bouey	BABN	C/I	9578799*	40 (est.)

*Denotes low and high serial numbers seen

**Only seven of these notes have been verified

Summary of Technical Details for 1954 Modified Portrait Issues

Cat.No.	Denom.	Signature	Printer	Prefixes	Numbers	Qty.Printed
BC-38a	$2	Beattie-Coyne	BABN	I/B	8600001-10000000	1,400,000
BC-38a	$2	Beattie-Coyne	BABN	J/B-Z/B	0000001-10000000	160,000,000
BC-38a	$2	Beattie-Coyne	BABN	A/R	0000001-5952000	5,952,000
BC-38aA	$2	Beattie-Coyne	BABN	A/B	0012714-0033284*	22,400 (est.)
BC-38b	$2	Beattie-Rasminsky	BABN	A/R	5952001-10000000	4,048,000
BC-38b	$2	Beattie-Rasminsky	BABN	B/R-F/R	0000001-9999999	50,000,000
BC-38b	$2	Beattie-Rasminsky	BABN	G/R	0080000-5279999	5,200,000
BC-38b	$2	Beattie-Rasminsky	BABN	G/R	5368000-5400000	32,001
BC-38b	$2	Beattie-Rasminsky	BABN	G/R	5480001-10000000	4,520,000
BC-38b	$2	Beattie-Rasminsky	BABN	H/R-R/R	0000001-9999999	100,000,000
BC-38bT	$2	Beattie-Rasminsky	BABN	G/R	0000001-0079999	79,999
BC-38bT	$2	Beattie-Rasminsky	BABN	G/R	5280000-5367999	88,000
BC-38bT	$2	Beattie-Rasminsky	BABN	G/R	5400001-5480000	80,000
BC-38bT	$2	Beattie-Rasminsky	BABN	S/R	0000001-2339999*	2,400,000
BC-38b	$2	Beattie-Rasminsky	BABN	T/R-Z/R	0000001-10000000	70,000,000
BC-38b	$2	Beattie-Rasminsky	BABN	A/U-D/U	0000001-10000000	40,000,000
BC-38b	$2	Beattie-Rasminsky	BABN	E/U-Z/U	0000000-9999999	210,000,000
BC-38b	$2	Beattie-Rasminsky	BABN	A/G	0000000-5119999	5,120,000
BC-38bA	$2	Beattie-Rasminsky	BABN	A/B	0036398-0197720*	166,400 (est.)
BC-38bA	$2	Beattie-Rasminsky	BABN	B/B	0000001-3272533*	3,280,000 (est.)
BC-38bA	$2	Beattie-Rasminsky	BABN	R/R	0242813-0300328*	60,000 (est.)
BC-38c	$2	Bouey-Rasminsky	BABN	A/G	5120000-9999999	4,880,000
BC-38c	$2	Bouey-Rasminsky	BABN	B/G-K/G	0000000-9999999	100,000,000
BC-38c	$2	Bouey-Rasminsky	BABN	L/G	0000000-7959999	7,960,000
BC-38cT	$2	Bouey-Rasminsky	BABN	S/R	2340000-2679999*	340,000
BC-38cA	$2	Bouey-Rasminsky	BABN	A/G	0323000-0379036*	460,000 (est.)
BC-38cA	$2	Bouey-Rasminsky	BABN	A/G	3200129-3592128*	460,000 (est.)
BC-38cA	$2	Bouey-Rasminsky	BABN	Z/Z	6248000-8889999	160 (est.)
BC-38d	$2	Lawson-Bouey	BABN	L/G	7960000-9999999	2,040,000
BC-38d	$2	Lawson-Bouey	BABN	M/G-U/G	0000000-9999999	80,000,000
BC-38d	$2	Lawson-Bouey	BABN	V/G	0000000-8559999	8,559,999
BC-38dT	$2	Lawson-Bouey	BABN	S/R	2680000-2919999	240,000 (est.)
BC-38dA	$2	Lawson-Bouey	BABN	K/G	0200004-0392976*	200,000 (est.)
BC-38dA	$2	Lawson-Bouey	BABN	O/G	0000000-0318646*	320,000 (est.)
BC-39a	$5	Beattie-Coyne	BABN	I/C	9526925*-10000000	Unknown
BC-39a	$5	Beattie-Coyne	BABN	J/C-P/C	0000001-10000000	70,000,000
BC-39a	$5	Beattie-Coyne	BABN	R/C	0000001-0088000	90,000
BC-39aA	$5	Beattie-Coyne	BABN	A/C	0011108-0025515*	16,000 (est.)
BC-39a-i	$5	Beattie-Coyne	CBN	R/C	0088001-10000000*	9,910,000 (est.)
BC-39a-i	$5	Beattie-Coyne	CBN	S/C-X/C	0000001-10000000	60,000,000
BC-39a-i	$5	Beattie-Coyne	CBN	Y/C	0000001-8256000	8,256,000
BC-39aA-i	$5	Beattie-Coyne	CBN	R/C	0000001-0007385*	8,000 (est.)
BC-39b	$5	Beattie-Rasminsky	CBN	Y/C	8256001-10000000	1,744,000
BC-39b	$5	Beattie-Rasminsky	CBN	Z/C	0000001-10000000	10,000,000
BC-39b	$5	Beattie-Rasminsky	CBN	A/S-Z/S	0000001-10000000	250,000,000
BC-39b	$5	Beattie-Rasminsky	CBN	A/X-P/X	0000000-9999999	160,000,000
BC-39b	$5	Beattie-Rasminsky	CBN	R/X	0000000-7083999	7,084,000
BC-39bA	$5	Beattie-Rasminsky	CBN	R/C	0016094-0143574*	128,000 (est.)
BC-39bA	$5	Beattie-Rasminsky	CBN	L/S	0145598*-0175877*	32,000 (est.)
BC-39bA	$5	Beattie-Rasminsky	CBN	N/S	0201956-0238459*	40,000 (est.)
BC-39bA	$5	Beattie-Rasminsky	CBN	S/S	0001322-0399170*	400,000 (est.)
BC-39bA	$5	Beattie-Rasminsky	CBN	V/S	0001008-0399170*	400,000 (est.)
BC-39bA	$5	Beattie-Rasminsky	CBN	W/S	0240987-0315596*	80,000 (est.)
BC-39bA	$5	Beattie-Rasminsky	CBN	I/X	0002299-0088051*	100,000 (est.)
BC-39bA	$5	Beattie-Rasminsky	CBN	N/X	0000000-0144345*	160,000 (est.)

Summary of Technical Details for 1954 Modified Portrait Issue (Cont'd.)

Cat.No.	Denom.	Signature	Printer	Prefixes	Numbers	Qty. Printed
BC-39c	$5	Bouey-Rasminsky	CBN	R/X	7084000-9999999	2,916,000
BC-39c	$5	Bouey-Rasminsky	CBN	S/X-U/X	0000000-9999999	30,000,000
BC-39c	$5	Bouey-Rasminsky	CBN	V/X	0000000-7999999	8,000,000
BC-39cA	$5	Bouey-Rasminsky	CBN	R/X	0162692-0359872*	200,000 (est.)
BC-39cA	$5	Bouey-Rasminsky	CBN	R/X	7646367-7756505*	120,000 (est.)
BC-40a	$10	Beattie-Coyne	BABN	J/D	7800001-10000000	2,200,000
BC-40a	$10	Beattie-Coyne	BABN	K/D-Z/D	0000001-10000000	150,000,000
BC-40a	$10	Beattie-Coyne	BABN	A/T-D/T	0000001-10000000	40,000,000
BC-40a	$10	Beattie-Coyne	BABN	E/T	0000001-4688000	4,688,000
BC-40aA	$10	Beattie-Coyne	BABN	A/D	0009617-0031412*	25,600 (est.)
BC-40b	$10	Beattie-Rasminsky	BABN	E/T	4688001-10000000	5,312,000
BC-40b	$10	Beattie-Rasminsky	BABN	F/T-M/T	0000001-10000000	80,000,000
BC-40b	$10	Beattie-Rasminsky	BABN	N/T-Z/T	0000000-9999999	120,000,000
BC-40b	$10	Beattie-Rasminsky	BABN	A/V-S/V	0000000-9999999	180,000,000
BC-40b	$10	Beattie-Rasminsky	BABN	T/V	0000000-1719999	1,720,000
BC-40bA	$10	Beattie-Rasminsky	BABN	A/D	0038669-0193843*	160,000 (est.)
BC-40bA	$10	Beattie-Rasminsky	BABN	B/D	0336460-2502690	2,520,000 (est.)
BC-40bA	$10	Beattie-Rasminsky	BABN	B/V	0282875*-0345126*	60,000 (est.)
BC-40bA	$10	Beattie-Rasminsky	BABN	U/T	0201296*-0279329*	80,000 (est.)
BC-41a	$20	Beattie-Coyne	CBN	E/E	2550000-10000000	7,450,000 (est.)
BC-41a	$20	Beattie-Coyne	CBN	F/E-L/E	0000001-10000000	70,000,000
BC-41a	$20	Beattie-Coyne	CBN	M/E	0000001-2400000	2,400,000
BC-41aA	$20	Beattie-Coyne	CBN	A/E	0012984-0025527*	12,800 (est.)
BC-41b	$20	Beattie-Rasminsky	CBN	M/E	2400001-10000000	7,600,000
BC-41b	$20	Beattie-Rasminsky	CBN	N/E-T/E	0000001-10000000	60,000,000
BC-41b	$20	Beattie-Rasminsky	CBN	U/E-Z/E	0000000-9999999	60,000,000
BC-41b	$20	Beattie-Rasminsky	CBN	A/W-F/W	0000000-9999999	60,000,000
BC-41b	$20	Beattie-Rasminsky	CBN	G/W	0000000-8799999	8,800,000
BC-41bA	$20	Beattie-Rasminsky	CBN	A/E	0029050-0142763*	114,000 (est.)
BC-41bA	$20	Beattie-Rasminsky	CBN	V/E	0161721-0234262*	80,000 (est.)
BC-42a	$50	Beattie-Coyne	CBN	A/H	2513090*- 9492000	7,000,000 (est.)
BC-42b	$50	Beattie-Rasminsky	CBN	A/H	9492001-10000000	508,000
BC-42b	$50	Beattie-Rasminsky	CBN	B/H	0000000-8071999	8,072,000
BC-42c	$50	Lawson-Bouey	CBN	B/H	8072000-9999999	1,928,000
BC-42c	$50	Lawson-Bouey	CBN	C/H**	0000000-2015999*	2,016,000 (est.)
BC-43a	$100	Beattie-Coyne	CBN	A/J	2392001-8308000	5,916,000
BC-43b	$100	Beattie-Rasminsky	CBN	A/J	8308001-10000000	1,692,000
BC-43b	$100	Beattie-Rasminsky	CBN	B/J	0000000-8007999	8,008,000
BC-43c	$100	Lawson-Bouey	CBN	B/J	8008000-9999999	1,992,000
BC-43c	$100	Lawson-Bouey	CBN	C/J	0000000-3711999	3,712,000
BC-44a	$1000	Beattie-Coyne	CBN	A/K	0030001-0062000	32,000
BC-44b	$1000	Beattie-Rasminsky	CBN	A/K	0062001-0122400	60,400
BC-44c	$1000	Bouey-Rasminsky	CBN	A/K	0122401-0218000	96,000
BC-44d	$1000	Lawson-Bouey	CBN	A/K	0218001-1949400	1,731,400
BC-44e	$1000	Thiessen-Crow	CBN	A/K	1949401-2189400	240,000

Note: * Denotes low and high serial numbers seen
**It is believed that most of prefix C/H was destroyed and very few, if any, were circulated.

$1 Issue — 1954

MODIFIED PORTRAIT

BC-37b

Face Design: —/—/Queen Elizabeth II
Colour: Black with green tint

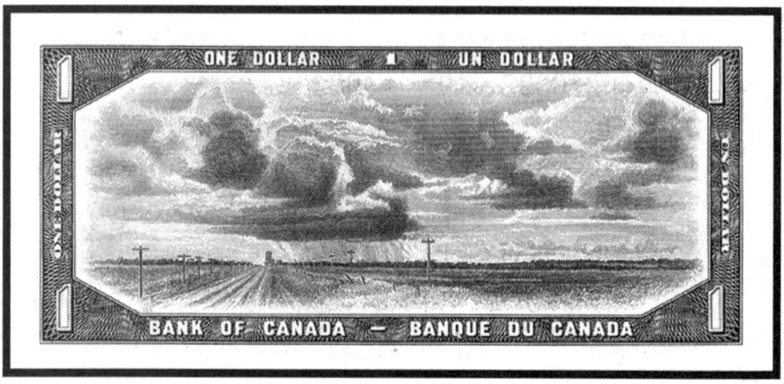

BC-37

Back Design: —/Western prairie and sky/—
Colour: Green

Issue Dated: Engraved: 1954
Imprint: Canadian Bank Note Company, Limited or British American Bank Note Company Limited

Signatures

The signatures were printed until 1968, then engraved on plates.

Left:	Right:
Typed: J.R. Beattie	Typed: J.E. Coyne
Typed: J.R. Beattie	Typed: L. Rasminsky
Engr.: J.R. Beattie	Engr.: L. Rasminsky
Engr.: G.K. Bouey	Engr.: L. Rasminsky
Engr.: R.W. Lawson	Engr.: G.K. Bouey

Cat.No.	Denom.	Signature	Printer	VG	F	VF	EF	AU	Unc
BC-37a	$1	Beattie-Coyne	CBN	1.25	1.50	2.00	3.00	5.00	10.00
BC-37aA	$1	Beattie-Coyne	*A/A	4.00	7.00	10.00	18.00	45.00	90.00
BC-37a-i	$1	Beattie-Coyne	BABN	1.25	1.50	2.00	10.00	15.00	20.00
BC-37b	$1	Beattie-Rasminsky	CBN	1.25	1.50	2.00	3.00	5.00	10.00
BC-37bA	$1	Beattie-Rasminsky	*A/A	2.00	3.00	5.00	8.00	12.00	18.00
BC-37bA	$1	Beattie-Rasminsky	*D/O	7.00	10.00	20.00	30.00	50.00	100.00
BC-37bA	$1	Beattie-Rasminsky	*I/O	6.00	8.00	12.00	20.00	40.00	80.00
BC-37bA	$1	Beattie-Rasminsky	*S/O	4.00	5.00	6.00	12.00	25.00	40.00
BC-37bA	$1	Beattie-Rasminsky	*A/Y	4.00	5.00	6.00	12.00	25.00	40.00
BC-37bA	$1	Beattie-Rasminsky	*H/Y	5.00	6.00	9.00	17.00	30.00	60.00
BC-37bA	$1	Beattie-Rasminsky	*M/Y	4.00	5.00	6.00	12.00	25.00	40.00
BC-37bA	$1	Beattie-Rasminsky	*N/Y	4.00	5.00	6.00	12.00	27.00	50.00
BC-37bA	$1	Beattie-Rasminsky	*O/Y	7.00	10.00	12.00	20.00	40.00	80.00
BC-37b-i	$1	Beattie-Rasminsky	BABN	1.25	1.50	2.00	3.00	5.00	10.00
BC-37bA-i	$1	Beattie-Rasminsky	*A/M	25.00	40.00	60.00	100.00	150.00	250.00
BC-37bA-i	$1	Beattie-Rasminsky	*B/M	2.50	3.00	5.00	7.00	14.00	20.00
BC-37bA-i	$1	Beattie-Rasminsky	*A/F	3.00	3.50	5.00	8.00	18.00	30.00
BC-37c	$1	Bouey-Rasminsky	BABN	1.25	1.50	2.00	3.00	5.00	10.00
BC-37cA	$1	Bouey-Rasminsky	*C/F	3.50	4.00	5.00	9.00	18.00	30.00
BC-37cA	$1	Bouey-Rasminsky	*H/F	8.00	12.00	25.00	50.00	75.00	150.00
BC-37cA	$1	Bouey-Rasminsky	*V/V	400.00	650.00	900.00	1,500.00	2,200.00	3,000.00
BC-37d	$1	Lawson-Bouey	BABN	1.25	1.50	2.00	3.00	6.00	11.00
BC-37dA	$1	Lawson-Bouey	*X/F	5.00	7.00	10.00	20.00	35.00	70.00
BC-37dA	$1	Lawson-Bouey	*C/I	500.00	900.00	1,200.00	1,800.00	3,000.00	4,000.00

A=Asterisk replacement note

$2 Issue — 1954

MODIFIED PORTRAIT

BC-38bT

Face Design: —/—/Queen Elizabeth II
Colour: Black with red-brown tint

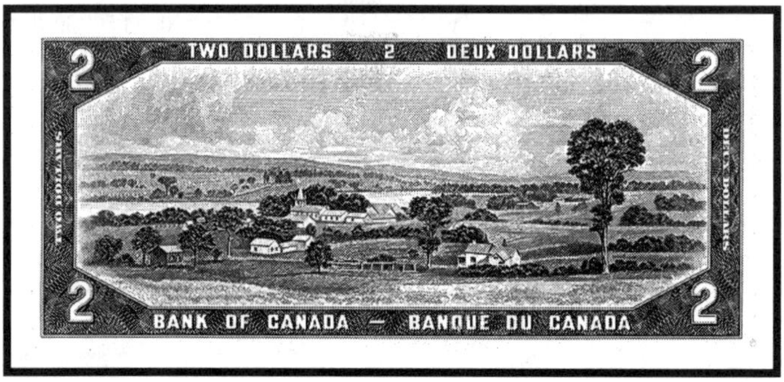

BC-38

Back Design: —/Landscape from the Upper Melbourne, Richmond, Quebec/—
Colour: Red-brown

Issue Date: Engraved: 1954
Imprint: British American Bank Note Company Limited

Signatures

The signatures were printed until 1968, then engraved on plates.

Left:	Typed: J.R. Beattie	**Right:**	Typed: J.E. Coyne
	Typed: J.R. Beattie		Typed: L. Rasminsky
	Engr.: G.K. Bouey		Engr.: L. Rasminsky
	Engr.: R.W. Lawson		Engr.: G.K. Bouey

Cat.No.	Denom.	Signature	Prefix	VG	F	VF	EF	AU	Unc
BC-38a	$2	Beattie-Coyne		2.50	5.00	7.00	12.00	24.00	40.00
BC-38aA	$2	Beattie-Coyne	*A/B	22.00	28.00	35.00	75.00	150.00	250.00
BC-38b	$2	Beattie-Rasminsky		2.25	2.50	3.50	4.50	6.50	12.00
BC-38b	$2	Beattie-Rasminsky	**G/R	7.00	10.00	15.00	20.00	35.00	60.00
BC-38bA	$2	Beattie-Rasminsky	*A/B	4.00	6.00	8.00	16.00	25.00	40.00
BC-38bA	$2	Beattie-Rasminsky	*B/B	2.50	4.50	5.50	9.00	16.00	30.00
BC-38bA	$2	Beattie-Rasminsky	*R/R	10.00	20.00	50.00	100.00	150.00	200.00
BC-38bT*	$2	Beattie-Rasminsky	G/R		Rare. Market value not yet established				
BC-38bT	$2	Beattie-Rasminsky	S/R	60.00	90.00	175.00	300.00	700.00	1,200.00
BC-38c	$2	Bouey-Rasminsky		2.25	2.50	4.00	5.00	7.00	15.00
BC-38cA	$2	Bouey-Rasminsky	*A/G	2.50	3.50	5.00	8.00	15.00	30.00
BC-38cA	$2	Bouey-Rasminsky	*Z/Z	300.00	400.00	600.00	900.00	1,600.00	2,600.00
BC-38cT	$2	Bouey-Rasminsky	S/R	50.00	80.00	125.00	225.00	550.00	850.00
BC-38d	$2	Lawson-Bouey		2.25	2.50	4.00	5.00	7.00	15.00
BC-38dA	$2	Lawson-Bouey	*K/G	3.00	7.50	10.00	14.00	30.00	50.00
BC-38dA	$2	Lawson-Bouey	*O/G	3.00	7.50	10.00	14.00	25.00	45.00
BC-38dT	$2	Lawson-Bouey	S/R	90.00	120.00	185.00	300.00	500.00	800.00

* **CAUTION!** Only notes in series G/R with numbers 0000001-0079999, 5280000-5367999 and 5400001-5480000 are test notes.

Note: *Z/Z pricing is for this prefix only
** non-test
A=Asterisk replacement note

$5 Issue — 1954

MODIFIED PORTRAIT

BC-39b

Face Design: —/—/Queen Elizabeth II
Colour: Black with blue tint

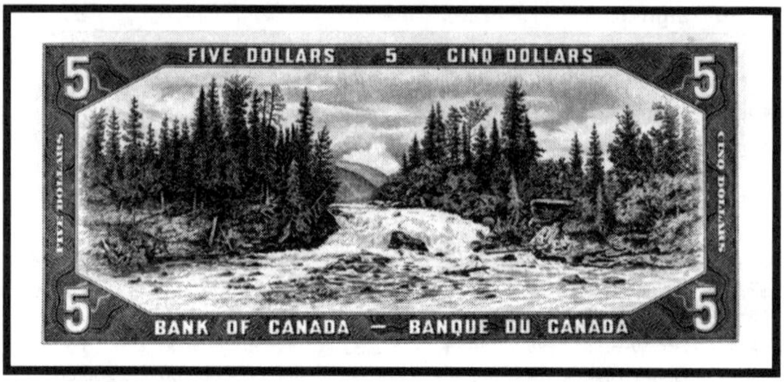

BC-39

Back Design: —/Otter Falls, mile 996, Alaska Highway/—
Colour: Blue
Issue Date: Engraved: 1954
Imprint: British American Bank Note Company, Limited and Canadian Bank Note Company, Limited

Signatures

The signatures were printed until 1968, then engraved on plates.

Left:	**Right:**
Typed: J.R. Beattie	Typed: J.E. Coyne
Typed: J.R. Beattie	Typed: L. Rasminsky
Engr.: J.R. Beattie	Engr.: L. Rasminsky
Engr.: G.K. Bouey	Engr.: L. Rasminsky

Cat.No.	Denom.	Signature	Printer	VG	F	VF	EF	AU	Unc
BC-39a	$5	Beattie-Coyne	BABN	6.50	7.50	9.00	12.00	25.00	60.00
BC-39a	$5	Beattie-Coyne	BABN	15.00	30.00	75.00	150.00	225.00	300.00
			prefix I/C only						
BC-39aA	$5	Beattie-Coyne	*A/C	20.00	25.00	30.00	50.00	175.00	275.00
BC-39a-i	$5	Beattie-Coyne	CBN	6.50	7.50	9.00	12.00	20.00	55.00
BC-39aA-i	$5	Beattie-Coyne	*R/C	30.00	40.00	50.00	100.00	200.00	275.00
BC-39b	$5	Beattie-Rasminsky	CBN	6.50	7.50	9.00	12.00	20.00	35.00
BC-39bA	$5	Beattie-Rasminsky	*R/C	7.50	11.00	16.00	24.00	60.00	100.00
BC-39bA	$5	Beattie-Rasminsky	*L/S	25.00	40.00	75.00	125.00	200.00	300.00
BC-39bA	$5	Beattie-Rasminsky	*N/S	10.00	15.00	25.00	45.00	75.00	150.00
BC-39bA	$5	Beattie-Rasminsky	*S/S	7.00	10.00	14.00	20.00	50.00	100.00
BC-39bA	$5	Beattie-Rasminsky	*V/S	7.00	10.00	14.00	20.00	50.00	100.00
BC-39bA	$5	Beattie-Rasminsky	*W/S	10.00	20.00	30.00	50.00	100.00	200.00
BC-39bA	$5	Beattie-Rasminsky	*I/X	8.00	12.00	20.00	25.00	50.00	100.00
BC-39bA	$5	Beattie-Rasminsky	*N/X	7.00	10.00	14.00	20.00	45.00	95.00
BC-39c	$5	Bouey-Rasminsky	CBN	6.50	7.50	9.00	12.00	16.00	35.00
BC-39cA	$5	Bouey-Rasminsky	*R/X	7.00	9.00	11.00	16.00	40.00	90.00

A=Asterisk replacement note

$10 Issue — 1954

MODIFIED PORTRAIT

BC-40a

Face Design: —/—/Queen Elizabeth II
Colour: Black with purple tint

BC-40

Back Design: —/Mount Burgess, B.C./—
Colour: Purple

Issue Date: Engraved: 1954
Imprint: British American Bank Note Company Limited

Signatures
The signatures were printed until 1968, then engraved on plates.

Left:	Typed: J.R. Beattie	**Right:**	Typed: J.E. Coyne
	Typed: J.R. Beattie		Typed: L. Rasminsky
	Engr.: J.R. Beattie		Engr.: L. Rasminsky

Cat.No.	Denom.	Signature	Printer	VG	F	VF	EF	AU	Unc
BC-40a	$10	Beattie-Coyne	BABN	12.	12.	13.	15.	30.	55.
BC-40aA	$10	Beattie-Coyne	*A/D	20.	25.	30.	40.	100.	250.
BC-40b	$10	Beattie-Rasminsky	BABN	12.	12.	13.	15.	20.	40.
BC-40bA	$10	Beattie-Rasminsky	*A/D	25.	50.	75.	100.	175.	225.
BC-40bA	$10	Beattie-Rasminsky	*B/D	12.	15.	20.	30.	60.	100.
BC-40bA	$10	Beattie-Rasminsky	*B/V	60.	100.	150.	200.	300.	500.
BC-40bA	$10	Beattie-Rasminsky	*U/T	100.	150.	200.	450.	600.	1,000.

A=Asterisk replacement note

$20 Issue — 1954

MODIFIED PORTRAIT

BC-41a

Face Design: —/—/Queen Elizabeth II
Colour: Black with olive green tint

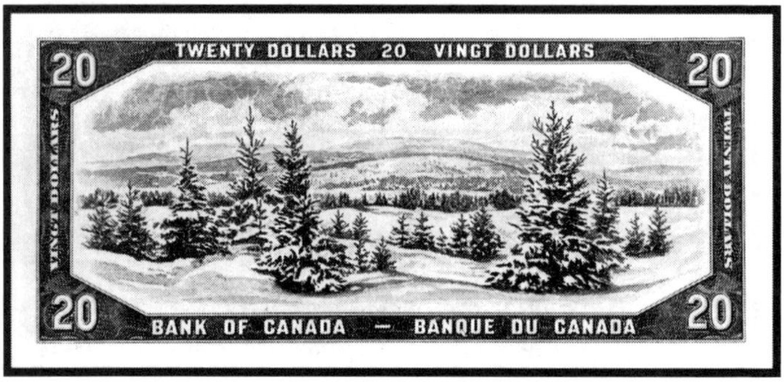

BC-41

Back Design: —/Laurentians in winter/—
Colour: Olive green

Issue Date: Engraved: 1954
Imprint: Canadian Bank Note Company Limited

Signatures
The signatures were printed until 1968, then engraved on plates.

Left:		Right:	
	Typed: J.R. Beattie		Typed: J.E. Coyne
	Typed: J.R. Beattie		Typed: L. Rasminsky
	Engr.: J.R. Beattie		Engr.: L. Rasminsky

Cat.No.	Denom.	Signature	Printer	VG	F	VF	EF	AU	Unc
BC-41a	$20	Beattie-Coyne	CBN	22.	22.	22.	25.	75.	120.
BC-41aA	$20	Beattie-Coyne	*A/E	30.	40.	50.	75.	200.	550.
BC-41b	$20	Beattie-Rasminsky	CBN	22.	22.	22.	25.	50.	80.
BC-41bA	$20	Beattie-Rasminsky	*A/E	30.	40.	50.	75.	250.	500.
BC-41bA	$20	Beattie-Rasminsky	*V/E	75.	100.	175.	250.	600.	1,200.

A=Asterisk replacement note

$50 Issue — 1954

MODIFIED PORTRAIT

BC-42a

Face Design: —/—/Queen Elizabeth II
Colour: Black with orange tint

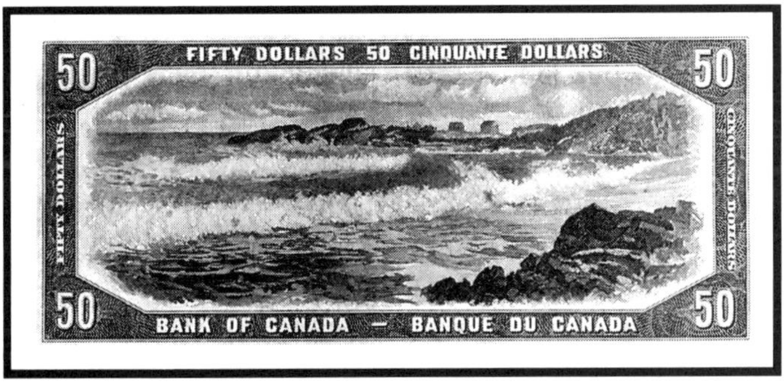

BC-42

Back Design: —/Beach and Breakers, Lockeport N.S./—
Colour: Orange

Issue Date: Engraved: 1954
Imprint: Canadian Bank Note Company Limited

Signatures
The signatures were printed until 1968, then engraved on plates.

Left:		Right:
	Typed: J.R. Beattie	Typed: J.E. Coyne
	Typed: J.R. Beattie	Typed: L. Rasminsky
	Engr.: J.R. Beattie	Engr.: L. Rasminsky
	Engr.: R.W. Lawson	Engr.: G.K. Bouey

Cat.No.	Denom.	Signature	Printer	VG	F	VF	EF	AU	Unc
BC-42a	$50	Beattie-Coyne	CBN	50.	50.	65.	85.	125.	200.
BC-42b	$50	Beattie-Rasminsky	CBN prefix A/H only	50.	55.	75.	125.	200.	300.
BC-42b	$50	Beattie-Rasminsky	CBN prefix B/H	50.	50.	65.	85.	125.	225.
BC-42c	$50	Lawson-Bouey	CBN	50.	50.	75.	100.	150.	275.

$100 Issue — 1954

MODIFIED PORTRAIT

BC-43b

Face Design: —/—/Queen Elizabeth II
Colour: Black with brown tint

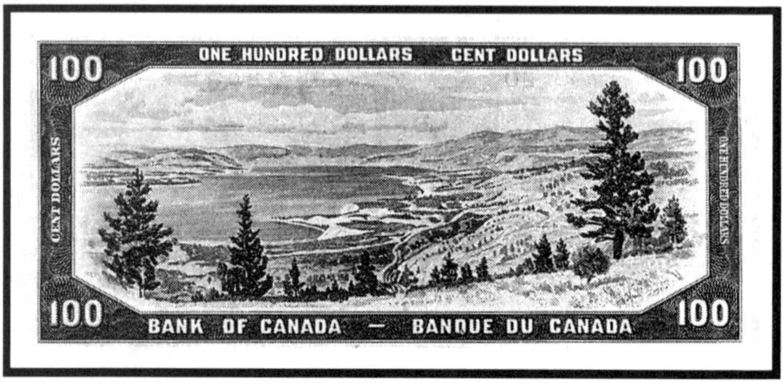

BC-43

Back Design: —/Okanagan Lake, B.C./—
Colour: Brown

Issue Date: Engraved: 1954
Imprint: Canadian Bank Note Company Limited

Signatures
The signatures were printed until 1968, then engraved on plates.

Left: Typed: J.R. Beattie
Typed: J.R. Beattie
Engr.: J.R. Beattie
Engr.: R.W. Lawson

Right: Typed: J.E. Coyne
Typed: L. Rasminsky
Engr.: L. Rasminsky
Engr.: G.K. Bouey

Cat.No.	Denom.	Signature	Printer	VG	F	VF	EF	AU	Unc
BC-43a	$100	Beattie-Coyne	CBN	100.	100.	110.	130.	165.	275.
BC-43b	$100	Beattie-Rasminsky	CBN	100.	100.	110.	120.	130.	225.
BC-43c	$100	Lawson-Bouey	CBN	100.	100.	110.	120.	150.	275.

Note: Lower grade notes are not collectable and command no premium.

$1000 Issue — 1954

MODIFIED PORTRAIT

BC-44c

Face Design: —/—/Queen Elizabeth II
Colour: Black with rose pink tint

BC-44

Back Design: —/Anse St. Jean on the Saguenay River, Quebec/—
Colour: Rose pink

Issue Date: Engraved: 1954
Imprint: Canadian Bank Note Company Limited

Signatures
The signatures were printed until 1968, then engraved on plates.

Left:		Right:
Typed: J.R. Beattie		Typed: J.E. Coyne
Typed: J.R. Beattie		Typed: L. Rasminsky
Engr.: J.R. Beattie		Engr.: L. Rasminsky
Engr.: G.K. Bouey		Engr.: L. Rasminsky
Engr.: R.W. Lawson		Engr.: G.K. Bouey
Engr.: G.G. Thiessen		Engr.: J.W. Crow

Cat.No.	Denom.	Signature	Printer	VG	F	VF	EF	AU	Unc
BC-44a	$1000	Beattie-Coyne	CBN	1,000.	1,000.	1,100.	1,150.	1,500.	2,750.
BC-44b	$1000	Beattie-Rasminsky	CBN	1,000.	1,000.	1,100.	1,150.	1,250.	2,000.
BC-44c	$1000	Bouey-Rasminsky	CBN	1,000.	1,000.	1,100.	1,150.	1,250.	2,000.
BC-44d	$1000	Lawson-Bouey	CBN	1,000.	1,000.	1,100.	1,150.	1,250.	1,600.
BC-44e	$1000	Thiessen-Crow	CBN	1,000.	1,000.	1,250.	1,400.	1,500.	2,000.

Note: The majority of BC-44e notes were not issued and later destroyed.

SPECIMEN NOTES OF THE 1954 MODIFIED ISSUE

No specimen notes of this issue are known to have been available to collectors prior to the November 1999 Bank of Canada sale. These specimen notes have been overprinted twice with the word "SPECIMEN", in red, in the signature area and may have several punch holes in the same area. Usually "SPECIMEN" is stamped once, in red, on the back as well. A few have been perforated diagonally with the word "SPECIMEN" three times.

The specimen notes were generally described in the auction catalogue as AU, with glue from tape on the face, usually in the left margin area, excepting most of the $2 and $5 specimens which were free of glue spots. All have manuscript "set" numbers on the back. Specimen notes impaired by staining or thinning will transact as reduced prices.

Specimens of each denomination are available with either of two prefixes.

Cat. No.	Denom.	Quantity Sold Bank of Canada Sale		AU
BC-37S	$1	Specimen	(12)	600.
BC-38S	$2	Specimen	(108)	150.
BC-39S	$5	Specimen	(109)	150.
BC-40S	$10	Specimen	(12)	600.
BC-41S	$20	Specimen	(12)	600.
BC-42S	S50	Specimen	(12)	700.
BC-43S	$100	Specimen	(12)	800.
Set of seven, $1 to $100		Specimen		3,600.

$1 CENTENNIAL ISSUE OF 1967

Special $1 notes were issued in 1967 to commemorate the centennial of Confederation. The face of the note resembles that of the 1954 $1 issue, except for the maple leaf centennial symbol at the left and references to the centennial along the top and bottom. The back vignette portrays the original Centre Block of the Parliament buildings, which was destroyed by fire in 1916. The same vignette was used on the face of the 1872 $100 Dominion note. Restoration of the original die was done by Gordon Yorke. He also re-engraved the sky and added landscaping to both sides of the building and to the foreground.

Deliveries of the 1954 $1 notes to the chartered banks were suspended through 1967, and the commemorative notes were distributed exclusively. A special collector's issue was prepared with the dates "1867 1967" replacing the serial numbers. These notes were available only from the Bank of Canada but soon began to enter circulation. Because they were hoarded by the public, these special notes remain very common, while the regular serial number notes have to a greater extent disappeared.

Both bank note companies were involved in the printing of these notes but their imprints were omitted. The Canadian Bank Note Co. printed the notes in group "O", series L, M, N, O, P, R and S, and the British American Bank Note Co. printed the notes in group "P", series F, G, H, J, K, L and M. Because there are no imprints, the notes of the special collector's issue produced by the two companies are not given separate catalogue numbers.

The serial numbers of these notes conform to gaps in the numbering of the 1954 $1 notes which occurred between 1966 and 1968.

Checklist of Prefix Letters for 1967 Issues

Cat.No.	Denom.	Variety	Printer	Denom. Letter	Series Letter
BC-45a	$1	Commemorative Serial No	CBN	None	None
BC-45a	$1	Commemorative Serial No	BABN	None	None
BC-45b	$1	Regular Serial No	CBN	O	L M N O P R S
BC-45bA	$1	Asterisk	CBN	O	L N
BC-45b-i	$1	Regular Serial No	BABN	P	F G H I J K L M
BC-45bA-i	$1	Asterisk	BABN	M	B
BC-45bA-i	$1	Asterisk	BABN	P	F

A=Asterisk replacement note

Summary of Technical Details

Cat.No.	Denom.	Variety	Printer	Prefixes	Numbers	Qty.Printed
BC-45a	$1	1867 1967 in place of serial number	CBN or BABN	None	None	12,000,000
BC-45b	$1	Regular serial number	CBN	L/O	7000001-10000000	3,000,000
BC-45b	$1	Regular serial number	CBN	M/O-R/O	0000001-10000000	50,000,000
BC-45b	$1	Regular serial number	CBN	S/O	0000001- 7900000	7,900,000
BC-45bA	$1	Regular serial number	CBN	L/O	7000084- 7039926*	40,000 (est.)
BC-45bA	$1	Regular serial number	CBN	N/O	0000001- 0175031*	176,000 (est.)
BC-45b-i	$1	Regular serial number	BABN	F/P	7160001-10000000	2,840,000
BC-45b-i	$1	Regular serial number	BABN	G/P-L/P	0000001-10000000	60,000,000
BC-45b-i	$1	Regular serial number	BABN	M/P	0000001- 2720000	2,720,000
BC-45bA-i	$1	Regular serial number	BABN	B/M	1161540- 1756581*	600,000 (est.)
BC-45bA-i	$1	Regular serial number	BABN	F/P	8001010- 8060571*	64,000 (est.)

$1 Issue — 1967

BC-45a

Face Design: Centennial symbol/—/Queen Elizabeth II. The Centennial symbol is a stylized Maple Leaf divided into eleven triangles.
Colour: Black with green tint

BC-45

Back Design: —/Old Parliament Buildings/—
Colour: Green

Issue Date: Engraved: 1967
Imprint: None
Printer: British American Bank Note Company or Canadian Bank Note Co.

Signatures

Left: Engr.: J. R. Beattie **Right:** Engr.: L. Rasminsky

Combinations of Face and Back Plate Numbers of the Special 1867 1967 Issue

Face Plate Number	Back Plate Numbers
2	4, 5, 6, 7
3	4, 5, 6, 7
4	4, 5, 6, 7
6	4, 5, 6, 7, 8, 14, 16, 17
7	9, 10, 11, 12, 13
8	8, 10, 12, 13
9	12, 14, 15
10	8, 9, 10, 11
11	14, 15, 16, 17
12	14, 15, 16, 17
13	16, 17
14	14, 15, 16, 17
15	11, 16, 17, 18, 19, 21
16	11, 16, 17, 18, 19

Combinations of Face and Back Plate Numbers of the Centennial Regular Issues: CBN

Prefix	Face Plate Number	Back Plate Numbers
L/O	1	1, 2
	2	1, 2
	3	1, 2
M/O	1	2
	2	1, 2, 3, 4, 5,
	3	1, 3, 4, 5, 7
N/O	2	4, 5, 6
	3	5, 6
	4	5, 6
O/O	2	4, 5, 6
	3	4, 5, 6, 7
	4	4, 5, 6, 7
	6	4, 7
P/O	2	4, 5, 6, 7
	3	5, 6, 7
	4	5, 6
	5	5
	6	4, 5, 6, 7
R/O	2	4, 5, 6, 7
	3	4
	4	4, 5, 6, 7
	6	4, 5, 6, 7
	8	7
S/O	2	4, 5, 6, 7
	3	4, 5, 6, 7
	4	4, 5
	6	5, 6, 7
	8	4
*L/O	1	1, 2, 3
	2	1, 2
*N/O	2	5, 6
	3	5, 6

Combinations of Face and Back Plate Numbers of the Specimen Issues: CBN

Prefix	Face Plate Number	Back Plate Numbers
I/P	5	8
	6	10
1867-1967	6	8, 10

Combinations of Face and Back Plate Numbers of the Centennial Regular Issues: BABN

Prefix	Face Plate Number	Back Plate Numbers
F/P	2	2, 4, 5
	4	2, 4, 5
	5	6, 7
G/P	2	2, 3, 5, 6, 7
	4	2, 3, 5
	5	3, 5, 6, 7, 8, 10
	6	6, 7, 8, 10
	7	8, 10
	10	8
H/P	5	8, 10
	6	8, 10
	7	8, 9, 10, 11
	8	10
	10	8, 9, 10, 11, 12
	11	14
I/P	7	8, 9, 10, 11, 12, 13
	8	12, 13
	9	12, 13
	10	8, 9, 10, 11
	11	15
	12	15
J/P	8	12, 13, 15
	9	12, 13, 14, 15
	11	14, 15
	12	14, 15
K/P	6	14, 16
	11	14, 15, 17
	12	14, 15, 17
	13	17
	14	14, 17
	15	11, 18
	16	11, 18, 19
L/P	13	16, 17
	14	16, 17

Centennial Regular Issues BABN (cont.)

Prefix	Face Plate Number	Back Plate Numbers							
L/P	15			11,	16,	17,	18,	19,	
	16			11,	16,	17,	18,	19	
	17							19,	21
	18								21
M/P	15			11,			18,	19	
	16			11,	16,		18,	19	
*B/M	6		10,						
	7	8,	10						
	10	8,	10						
	15			11,			18		
	16			11,			18		
*F/P	7	8,	10						
	10	8							

Varieties

Special Commemorative Serial Number 1867-1967

Regular Serial Number

Asterisk Serial Number

Cat.No.	Variety	VG	F	VF	EF	AU	Unc
BC-45a	No serial number	1.50	2.00	2.25	2.50	4.00	5.00
BC-45b	Prefix L/O	1.50	2.00	3.00	5.00	8.00	12.00
BC-45b	Prefix M/O	1.50	1.75	2.50	3.50	5.00	7.00
BC-45b	Prefix N/O	1.50	1.75	2.50	3.50	5.00	8.00
BC-45b	Prefix O/O	1.50	2.00	3.00	4.00	6.00	12.00
BC-45b	Prefix P/O	1.50	1.75	2.50	3.50	5.00	8.00
BC-45b	Prefix R/O	1.50	2.00	3.00	5.00	8.00	12.00
BC-45b	Prefix S/O	1.50	2.00	3.00	5.50	9.00	14.00
BC-45b-i	Prefix F/P	1.50	1.75	2.50	3.50	5.00	9.00
BC-45b-i	Prefix G/P, H/P, I/P, J/P	1.50	1.75	2.50	3.50	5.00	8.00
BC-45b-i	Prefix K/P	1.50	2.00	3.00	5.00	8.00	12.00
BC-45b-i	Prefix L/P	1.50	2.00	3.00	4.50	7.00	10.00
BC-45b-i	Prefix M/P	5.00	10.00	15.00	20.00	30.00	60.00
BC-45bA	Prefix *L/O	6.00	12.00	18.00	35.00	60.00	140.00
BC-45bA	Prefix *N/O	4.00	8.00	12.00	25.00	40.00	80.00
BC-45bA-i	Prefix *B/M	3.00	7.00	10.00	15.00	20.00	30.00
BC-45bA-i	Prefix *F/P	7.00	15.00	20.00	40.00	70.00	150.00

SPECIMEN NOTES OF THE 1967 CENTENNIAL ISSUE

No specimen notes of this issue are known to have been available to collectors prior to the November 1999 Bank of Canada sale. These specimen notes have been overprinted twice with the word "SPECIMEN", in red, in the signature area and have four punch holes in the same area. They have also been perforated diagonally with the word "SPECIMEN" three times.

The specimen notes were generally described in the auction catalogue as AU. All have manuscript "set" numbers on the back. Specimen notes impaired by margin tears, staining or thinning will transact at reduced prices.

They occur with 1867 1967 or I/P 0000000 in the serial number location. the 1967 Centennial $1 specimens are the first to be printed with signatures engraved in the face plates, and all are signed Beattie-Rasminsky. Previously signatures had been applied (to regular issuable notes) in a separate printing operation.

Cat. No.	Denom.	Variety	Quantity Sold Bank of Canada Sale		AU
BC-45aS	$1	1867 1967	Specimen	(246)	175.
BC-45bS	$1	prefix I/P	Specimen	(246)	175.

ISSUES OF 1969 - 1975

The 1969-1975 issue, unlike the previous Bank of Canada issues, does not have a common date for all denominations. The issue dates span the years 1969 to 1975. Termination of the 1954 issue was necessary for two reasons. Almost all prefix letter combinations had been used up, and counterfeiting was rampant, particularly affecting the intermediate and higher denominations. Advanced security features were incorporated into the new multicolour issue. These have been so successful that there has been to date no counterfeit problem involving the new notes. The $1000 denomination was not included in this issue.

The traditional promise "will pay to the bearer on demand" was finally replaced by the words "this note is legal tender", reflecting the fact that government paper currency had long since ceased to be redeemable in gold.

George Gundersen engraved the portrait of Queen Elizabeth used on the $1, $2 and $20 notes, as well as the portraits of Sir John A. Macdonald on the $10 and William Lyon Mackenzie King on the $50. He also engraved the Rocky Mountain scene on the back of the $20 note. Gordon Yorke engraved the portraits of Sir Wilfrid Laurier on the $5 and Sir Robert Borden on the $100 note. Yorke also engraved the scenes on the backs of the $2, $5 and $100. Paper composition was altered from a linen (flax) - cotton combination to 100% cotton in 1983, to comply with Quebec environmental laws.

Prefixes And Numbering

Printing was in sheets of 40, with the notes in the sheet "skip-numbered" in jumps of 1000, so that a stack of 1000 sheets when cut yielded bricks of 1000 consecutively-numbered notes. The serial numbers were in red at the left and in blue at the right.

In a departure from previous practice, the prefix letters were no longer arranged in the form of the fraction. Instead, the denominational letter appeared first, followed by the series letter. The series letters included all letters from "A" to "Z" excepting I, O, and Q because of their resemblance to numerals. Thus any given denomational letter may accommodate twenty-three series, or 230,000,000 notes. Each series was numbered from 0000000 to 9999999, with the zero note being removed and destroyed prior to issue.

With the imminent exhaustion of the possible prefix letter combinations, the triple letter prefix was introduced in 1981. The first letter designates the printer and the next two letters indicate the series. Four first letters have been employed: A and B for BABN and E and F for CBN.

Lithographed Backs

In 1984 a change was initiated in the printing technique used for the backs of Bank of Canada notes, from the intaglio steel engraved process to the lithographic process. This cost-cutting measure was begun with the $1 and $2 notes, and gradually extended to include the $5, $10 and $20 notes dated 1979. The changeover numbers are:

Denom.	Printer	Last Note with Engraved Back	First Note with Lithographed Back
$1	BABN	AFF3799999	AFF3800000
$1	BABN Replacement	AAX2159999	AAX2160000
$1	CBN	EAK1199999	EAK1200000
$1	CBN Replacement	EAX0619999	EAX0620000
$2		AGJ9999999	AGK0000001
$2	Replacement	ABX1119999	ABX1120000
$10		EEV4999999	EEV5000000
$10	Replacement	EDX2639999	EDX2640000

Signatures

Signatures of the following Bank of Canada officials occur on notes of the 1969-1975 issues: in all cases the signatures are engraved on the face plates.

Senior Deputy Governor	*Term of Office*
John Robert Beattie	Jan. 1, 1955 to Dec. 31, 1971
Gerald K. Bouey	Jan. 1, 1972 to Feb. 1, 1973
R. William Lawson	March 1, 1973 to Feb. 29, 1984
John W. Crow	March 1, 1984 to Jan. 31, 1987
Gordon G, Thiessen	Oct. 27, 1987 to Jan. 31, 1994
Governor	*Term of Office*
Louis Rasminsky	July 24, 1961 to Feb. 1, 1973
Gerald K. Bouey	Feb. 1, 1973 to Jan. 31, 1987
John W. Crow	Feb. 1, 1987 to Jan. 31, 1994

Imprints

Both the British American and Canadian Bank Note companies have participated in the printing of the multicoloured notes, but there are no imprints. The work of the two companies can be distinguished by the styles of type used in the serial numbers, which show slight differences.

Asterisk Replacement Notes

Replacement of defective notes by asterisk notes was continued when the 1969-1975 issue was introduced. The highest denomination of the 1954 issue to be printed with asterisks was the $20; however, all denominations in the 1969-1975 issue including the $50 and $100 notes occur with asterisks in front of the two letter prefix type.

When the triple letter prefix notes were introduced in 1981, the use of asterisk notes was discontinued. For triple letter prefix notes, a replacement note is designated by the use of an "X" for the third letter.

Asterisk Notes BC-46aA

"X" Replacement Notes BC-46A-i

Experimental Notes

The rule that the first prefix letter on double prefix notes may only be associated with one specific denomination was violated once in the 1969-1975 issue. The denominational letter "R" was used for both $2 and $5 notes. The RS $2 and $5 notes are believed to be experimental, placed in circulation in limited quantity to test the durability of new innovations in ink or paper composition or some other changes. This prefix corresponds to the prefix S/R which was used on some experimental $2 notes of the 1954 issue. The $2 with the RS prefix appeared in circulation long before the other $2 notes in the R group. It has been reported that some of the $2 RS notes are of an unusually dark colour.

Experimental issues have also appeared in the triple letter prefix notes. For the $1 (1973 issue) the prefixes AXA and EXA have been used on experimental notes.

$2 Experimental Note BC-47aT

$5 Experimental Note BC-48bT

$1 Experimental Note BC-46aT-i

$1 Experimental Note BC-46bT-i

Anomalies Of The 1969-1975 Issues

$10 notes of the 1971 issue changed from the Lawson-Bouey signature combination to Crow-Bouey at note 9000000 in series EEP. For the rest of series EEP, all of series EER and EES, up to number EET 93599999, all $10 notes were signed Crow-Bouey. However the Lawson-Bouey signatures made a surprising reappearance on notes EET 9360000 to EET 9999999, when 640,000 Lawson-Bouey notes were salvaged from defective sheets and assigned these numbers.

Early in 1990 $50 notes of the 1975 issue appeared in circulation with prefix EFA, following the release of prefix EHN. Prefix EFA would normally have been reserved for $1 notes, although the latter were no longer being issued. It was speculated that stocks of the new 1988 $50's had been printed, beginning with prefix EHP, but delays associated with the optical security device occurred. A final series of the old design $50 notes was produced with prefix EFA to meet requirements for the denomination until the new technology could be perfected.

Checklist of Prefix Letters for 1969-1975 Issues

Cat.No.	Denom.	Date	Variety	Denom. Letter	Series Letters
BC-46a	$1	1973	Lawson-Bouey; 2 letters	A	A B C D E F G H J K L M N P R S T U V W X Y Z
BC-46aA				A	A B L N (Asterisk note)
BC-46a				F	A B C D E F G H J K L M N P R S T U V W X Y Z
BC-46aA				F	A B G H N V (Asterisk note)
BC-46a				G	A B C D E F G H J K L M N P R S T U V W X Y Z
BC-46aA				G	F L U Y (Asterisk note)
BC-46a				I	A B C D E F G H J K L M N P R S T U V W X Y Z
BC-46aA				I	A G L V (Asterisk note)
BC-46a				L	A B C D E F G H J K L M N P R S T U V W X Y Z
BC-46a				M	A B C D E F G H J K L M N P R S T U V W X Y Z
BC-46-aA				M	C D M R Z (Asterisk note)
BC-46a				N	A B C D E F G H J K L M N P R S T U V W X Y Z
BC-46aA				N	P (Asterisk note)
BC-46a				O	A D C D E F G H J K L M N P R S T U V
BC-46aA				O	G L (asterisk note)
BC-46a				P	A
BC-46a-i	$1	1973	Lawson-Bouey; 3 letters (steel engraved back)	AA	A B C D E F G H J K L M N P R S T U V WYZ
BC-46aA-i				AA	X (Replacement note)
BC-46a-i				AC	A B C D E F G H J K L M N P R S T U V W Y Z
BC-46a-i				AF	A B C D E F
BC-46aT-i				AX	A (Test note)
BC-46a-i				EA	A B C D E F G H J K
BC-46aA-i				EA	X (Replacement note)
BC-46a-i	$1	1973	Lawson-Bouey; 3 letter (lithographed back)	AF	F G H J K L M N P R S T U V W Y Z
BC-46a-i				AL	A B C D F G H J K L M
BC-46a-i				EA	K L M N
BC-46aA-i				AA	X (Replacement note)
BC-46aA-i				EA	X (Replacement note)
BC-46b	$1	1973	Crow-Bouey	EA	N P R S T U V W Y Z
BC-46bA				EA	X (Replacement note)
BC-46b				AL	M N P R S T U V W Y Z
BC-46b				AM	A B C D E F G H J K L M N P R S T U V W Y Z
BC-46b	$1	1973	Crow-Bouey	EC	A B C D E F G H J K L M N P R S T U V W
BC-46bT	$1	1973	Crow-Bouey	EX	A (Test note)
BC-46bA	$1	1973	Crow-Bouey	AA	X (Replacement note)
BC-46b				BA	A B C D E F G H J K L M N P R S T U V W Y Z
BC-46b				BC	A B C D E F G H J K L M N P R S T U V W Y Z
BC-46b				BF	A B C D E F G H J K L
BC-46bA				BA	X (Replacement Note)

Checklist of Prefix Letters for 1969-1975 Issues (Cont'd.)

Cat.No.	Denom.	Date	Variety	Denom. Letter	Series Letters
BC-47a	$2	1974	Lawson-Bouey; 2 letters	B	A B C D E F G H J K L M N P R S T U V W X Y Z
BC-47aA				B	A C J M X (Asterisk note)
BC-47a				R	A B C D E F G H J K L M N P R T U V W Y Z
BC-47aA				R	A E W (Asterisk note)
BC-47aT				R	S (Test note)
BC-47a				U	A B C D E F G H J K L M
BC-47aA				U	G (Asterisk note)
BC-47a-i	$2	1974	Lawson-Bouey; 3 letters	AB	A B C D E F G H J K L M N P R S T U V W Y Z
BC-47a-i				AG	A B C D E F G H J
BC-47aA-i				AB	X (Replacement note)
BC-47b	$2	1974	Crow-Bouey	AG	K L M N P R S T U V W Y Z
BC-47b				AR	A B C D E
BC-47bA				AB	X (Replacement note)
BC-48a	$5	1972	Bouey-Rasminsky	C	A B C D E F G H J K L M N P
BC-48aA				C	A C D (Asterisk note)
BC-48b	$5	1972	Lawson-Bouey; 2 letters	C	P R S T U V W X Y Z
BC-48bA				C	S U V (Asterisk note)
BC-48bT				R	S (Test note)
BC-48b				X	A
BC-48b				S	A B C D E F G H J K L M N P R S T U V W X Y Z
BC-48bA	$5	1972	Lawson-Bouey	S	B F L P W (Asterisk note)
BC-49a	$10	1971	Beattie-Rasminsky	D	A B C D E F G H J K L
BC-49aA				D	A B E G (Asterisk note)
BC-49b	$10	1971	Bouey-Rasminsky	D	L M N P R S T U V W X
BC-49bA				D	K R X(Asterisk note)
BC-49c	$10	1971	Lawson-Bouey; 2 letters	D	X Y Z
BC-49cA	$10	1971	Lawson-Bouey; 2 letters	D	Y (Asterisk note)
BC-49c	$10	1971	Lawson-Bouey; 2 letters	T	A B C D E F G H J K L M N P R S T U V W X Y Z
BC-49cA				T	C G L T (Asterisk note)
BC-49c				V	A B C D E F G H J K L M N P R S T U V W X
BC-49cA				V	A J L T (Asterisk note)
BC-49c-i	$10	1971	Lawson-Bouey; 3 letters (steel engraved back)	ED	A B C D E F G H J K L M N P R S T U V W Y Z
BC-49cA-i				ED	X (Replacement note)
BC-49c-i				EE	A B C D E F G H J K L M N P
BC-49c-i	$10	1971	Lawson-Bouey; 3 letters (anomaly)	EE	T
BC-49d	$10	1971	Crow-Bouey (steel engraved back)	EE	P R S T U V
BC-49d	$10	1971	Crow-Bouey (lithographed back)	EE	V W Y Z
BC-49d				ET	A B C D E F G H J K L M N P R S T U V W Y Z
BC-49d				FD	A B C
BC-49dA				ED	X (Replacement note)

Checklist of Prefix Letters for 1969-1975 Issues (Cont'd.)

Cat.No.	Denom.	Date	Variety	Denom. Letter	Series Letters
BC-49e	$10	1971	Thiessen-Crow	FD	C D E F G H J K L M N P R S
BC-49eA	$10	1971	Thiessen-Crow	ED	X (Replacement note)
BC-50a	$20	1969	Beattie-Rasminsky	E	A B C D E F G H J K L M N P R S T U V W Y Z
BC-50aA				E	A B H M V X (Asterisk note)
BC-50b	$20	1969	Lawson-Bouey; 2 letters	E	Z
BC-50bA				E	Z (Asterisk note)
BC-50b				W	A B C D E F G H J K L M N P R S T U V W X Y Z
BC-50bA				W	A E F L N V (Asterisk note)
BC-50b				Y	A B C D E F G H
BC-50bA	$20	1969	Lawson-Bouey; 2 letters	Y	A (Asterisk note)
BC-51a	$50	1969	Lawson-Bouey; 2 letters	H	A B C D
BC-51aA				H	B C (Asterisk note)
BC-51a-i	$50	1975	Lawson-Bouey; 3 letters	EH	A B C D E F
BC-51aA-i				EH	X (Replacement note)
BC-51b	$50	1975	Crow-Bouey	EH	F G H J K L M N
BC-51b	$50	1975	Crow-Bouey	EF	A
BC-51bA				EH	X (Replacement note)
BC-52a	$100	1975	Lawson-Bouey; 2 letters	J	A B C D
BC-52aA				J	A C (Asterisk note)
BC-52a-i	$100	1975	Lawson-Bouey; 3 letters	AJ	A B C
BC-52aA-i				AJ	X (Replacement note)
BC-52b	$100	1975	Crow-Bouey	AJ	C D E F G H J K L M
BC-52bA				AJ	X (Replacement note)

Summary of Technical Details

Cat.No.	Denom.	Date	Variety	Prefixes	Numbers	Qty.Printed
BC-46a	$1	1973	Lawson-Bouey; 2 letters	AA-AZ	0000000-9999999	230,000,000
BC-46a				FA-FZ	0000000-9999999	230,000,000
BC-46a				GA-GZ	0000000-9999999	230,000,000
BC-46a				IA-IZ	0000000-9999999	230,000,000
BC-46a				LA-LZ	0000000-9999999	230,000,000
BC-46a				MA-MZ	0000000-9999999	230,000,000
BC-46a				NA-NZ	0000000-9999999	230,000,000
BC-46a				OA-OV	0000000-9999999	190,000,000
BC-46a				PA	0000000-9399999	9,400,000
BC-46aA	$1	1973	Asterisk note	AA	1600000-7112000*	1,000,000 (est.)
BC-46aA				AB	1994000-2005000*	40 (est.)
BC-46aA				AB	3035499*	40 (est.)
BC-46aA				AB	3393499-3398499*	40 (est.)
BC-46aA				AB	4123500*	40 (est)
BC-46aA				AB	5164999-5471999*	Unknown
BC-46aA				AL	6326887-6799723*	480,000 (est.)
BC-46aA				AN	1681495-3184685*	1,520,000 (est.)
BC-46aA				FA	2880635-3516966*	640,000 (est.)
BC-46aA				FB	3478500-3946499*	80 (est.)
BC-46aA				FG	3120163-3595420*	480,000 (est.)
BC-46aA				FH	3423500-4910999	120 (est.)
BC-46aA				FN	3121892-3511249*	400,000 (est.)
BC-46aA				FV	6120232-7066450*	960,000 (est.)
BC-46aA				GF	6417330-6798108*	400,000 (est.)

Summary of Technical Details (Cont'd.)

Cat.No.	Denom.	Date	Variety	Prefixes	Numbers	Qty.Printed
BC-46aA	$1	1973	Asterisk note	GL	3508504-3898117*	400,000 (est.)
BC-46aA				GU	2802038-3194209*	400,000 (est.)
BC-46aA				GY	5703227-6097120*	400,000 (est.)
BC-46aA				IA	2120062-2519017*	400,000 (est.)
BC-46aA				IG	8325303-8471368*	140,000 (est.)
BC-46aA				IL	1651526-2119999*	480,000 (est.)
BC-46aA				IV	1640000-2039999	400,000 (est.)
BC-46aA				MC	6408367-6794477*	400,000 (est.)
BC-46aA				MD	3644999-Unknown*	4 Known
BC-46aA				MM	6641557-7033914*	400,000 (est.)
BC-46aA				MR	6401791-6799491*	400,000 (est.)
BC-46aA				MZ	7204295-7639732*	440,000 (est.)
BC-46aA				NP	6244041-6635993*	400,000 (est.)
BC-46aA				OG	6244041-6637078*	400,000 (est.)
BC-46aA				OL	2120004-2199999*	80,000 (est.)
BC-46a-i	$1	1973	Lawson-Bouey; 3 letters (steel engraved back)	AAA-AAZ	0000000-9999999	220,000,000
BC-46a-i				ACA-ACZ	0000000-9999999	220,000,000
BC-46a-i				AFA-AFE	0000000-9999999	50,000,000
BC-46a-i				AFF	0000000-3799999	3,800,000
BC-46a-i				EAA-EAJ	0000000-9999999	90,000,000
BC-46a-i				EAK	0000000-1199999	1,200,000
BC-46aA-i	$1	1973	Replacement Note	AAX	0000000-2159999	2,160,000
BC-46aA-i			Replacement Note	EAX	0000000-0619999	620,000
BC-46aT-i	$1	1973	Test Note	AXA	0001082-1305299*	400,000 (est.)
BC-46a-i			Lawson-Bouey; 3 letters (lithographed back)	AFF	3800000-9999999	6,200,000
BC-46a-i				AFG-AFZ	0000000-9999999	160,000,000
BC-46a-i			(ALE not issued)	ALA-ALL	0000000-9999999	100,000,000
BC-46a-i				ALM	0000000-1399999	1,400,000
BC-46a-i				EAK	1200000-9999999	8,800,00
BC-46a-i				EAL-EAM	0000000-9999999	20,000,000
BC-46a-i				EAN	0000000-8919999	8,920,000
BC-46aA-i	$1	1973	Replacement Note	AAX	2160000-3218078*	1,060,000 (est.)
BC-46aA-i			Replacement Note	EAX	0620000-1059999	440,000
BC-46b	$1	1973	Crow-Bouey	ALM	1400000-9999999	8,600,000
BC-46b				ALN-ALZ	0000000-9999999	100,000,000
BC-46b				AMA-AMZ	0000000-9999999	220,000,000
BC-46b				BAA-BAZ	0000000-9999999	220,000,000
BC-46b				BCA-BCZ	0000000-9999999	220,000,000
BC-46b				BFA-BFK	0000000-9999999	100,000,000
BC-46b				BFL	0000000-1599999	1,600,000
BC-46b				EAN	8920000-9999999	1,080,000
BC-46b				EAP-EAZ	0000000-9999999	90,000,000
BC-46b				ECA-ECU	0000000-9999999	180,000,000
BC-46b				ECV	7300000-8999999	1,700,000 (est.)
BC-46b				ECW	0000000-4699999	4,700,000
BC-46bA			Replacement Note	AAX	3220000-4256959*	1,040,000 (est.)
BC-46bA			Replacement Note	BAX	0000000-1559999	1,560,000
BC-46bA			Replacement Note	EAX	1060000-2579999	1,520,000
BC-46bT			Test Note	EXA	1104720-1692242*	600,000 (est.)

Summary of Technical Details (Cont'd.)

Cat.No.	Denom.	Date	Variety	Prefixes	Numbers	Qty.Printed
BC-47a	$2	1974	Lawson-Bouey; 2 letters, Modified Tint	BA-BB	0000000-9999999	20,000,000
BC-47a			Original Tint	BC	0000000-8599999	8,600,000
BC-47a			Modified Tint	BC	8600000-9999999	1,400.000
BC-47a			Modified Tint	BD-BN	0000000-9999999	100,000,000
BC-47a			Modified Tint	BP	0000000-7719999	7,720,000
BC-47a			Original Tint	BP	7720000-9999999	2,280,000
BC-47a			Original Tint	BR-BZ	0000000-9999999	90,000,000
BC-47a				RA-RZ	0000000-9999999	230,000,000
BC-47a				UA-UL	0000000-9999999	110,000,000
BC-47a				UM	0000000-9520000	9,520,000
BC-47aA	$2	1974	Asterisk Note	BA	0320000-0799573*	480,000 (est.)
BC-47aA				BC	0320000-0437510*	120,000 (est.)
BC-47aA				BC	2000000*	40 (est.)
BC-47aA				BC	5001500-5003500*	40 (est.)
BC-47aA				BJ	6353385-6386330*	200,000 (est.)
BC-47aA				BM	4400635-4739436*	400,000 (est.)
BC-47aA				BX	6324371-6514974*	200,000 (est.)
BC-47aA				RA	6519679-6591484*	80,000 (est.)
BC-47aA				RE	6641714-7036039*	400,000 (est.)
BC-47aA				RW	5246209-5638545*	400,000 (est.)
BC-47aA				UG	5763743-5949068*	200,000 (est.)
BC-47aT	$2	1974	Test Note	RS	0000041-3195324*	3,200,000 (est.)
BC-47a-i	$2	1974	Lawson-Bouey; 3 letters	ABA-ABZ	0000000-9999999	220,000,000
BC-47a-i				AGA-AGJ	0000000-9999999	90,000,000
BC-47aA-i	$2	1974	Replacement Note	ABX	0000001-1015463*	1,120,000 (est.)
BC-47b	$2	1974	Crow-Bouey	AGK-AGZ	0000000-9999999	130,000,000
BC-47b				ARA-ARD	0000000-9999999	40,000,000
BC-47b				ARE	0000000-8799999	8,800,000
BC-47bA	$2	1974	Replacement Note	ABX	1120000-1652005*	560,000 (est.)
BC-48a	$5	1972	Bouey-Rasminsky	CA-CN	0000000-9999999	130,000,000 (est.)
BC-48a				CP	0000000-4199999	4,200,000
BC-48aA	$5	1972	Asterisk Note	CA	2800104-3279444*	480,000 (est.)
BC-48aA			Asterisk Note	CC	2884982-3270586*	400,000 (est.)
BC-48aA			Asterisk Note	CD	2881164-3268670*	400,000 (est.)
BC-48b	$5	1972	Lawson-Bouey; 2 letters	CP	4200000-9999999	5,800,000
BC-48b				CR-CZ	0000000-9999999	90,000,000
BC-48b				SA-SZ	0000000-9999999	230,000,000
BC-48b				XA	0000000-5519999	5,520,000
BC-48bT	$5	1972	Test Note	RS	8007162-8436478*	440,000 (est.)
BC-48bA	$5	1972	Asterisk Note	CS	0320000-0395185*	80,000 (est.)
BC-48bA				CU	2880164-3036160*	160,000 (est.)
BC-48bA				CV	2884994-3234077*	350,000 (est.)
BC-48bA				SB	1120000-1586821*	480,000 (est.)
BC-48bA				SB	-4138000*-	40 (est)
BC-48bA				SF	2121124-2519882*	400,000 (est.)
BC-48bA				SL	2124958-2314945*	200,000 (est.)
BC-48bA				SP	2121676-2591999*	400,000 (est.)
BC-48bA				SW	2126372-2315681*	200,000 (est.)

Summary of Technical Details (Cont'd.)

Cat.No.	Denom.	Date	Variety	Prefixes	Numbers	Qty.Printed
BC-49a	$10	1971	Beattie-Rasminsky	DA-DK	0000000-9999999	100,000,00
BC-49a				DL	0000000-0799999	800,000
BC-49aA	$10	1971	Asterisk Note	DA	2369944-2764006*	440,000 (est.)
BC-49aA				DB	2814719-3184778*	380,000 (est.)
BC-49aA				DE	9604518-9611441*	80 (est.)
BC-49aA				DG	2361237-2519161*	160,000 (est.)
BC-49b	$10	1971	Bouey-Rasminsky	DL	0800000-9999999	9,200,000
BC-49b				DM-DW	0000000-9999999	90,000,000
BC-49b				DX	0000000-0439999	440,000
BC-49bA				DK	2810322-3279697*	460,000 (est.)
BC-49bA				DR	2905202*-3221355*	320,000 (est.)
BC-49bA			Asterisk	DX	-0338663*-	40 (est.)
BC-49c	$10	1971	Lawson-Bouey; 2 letters	DX	0440000-9999999	9,560,000
BC-49c				DY-DZ	0000000-9999999	20,000,000
BC-49c				TA-TZ	0000000-9999999	230,000,000
BC-49c				VA-VW	0000000-9999999	200,000,000
BC-49c				VX	0000000-7239999	7,240,000
BC-49cA			Asterisk	DY	2896587-3353085*	460,000 (est.)
BC-49cA				TC	1128995-1514422*	400,000 (est.)
BC-49cA				TG	1128995-1298446*	180,000 (est.)
BC-49cA				TL	1102708-1513275*	420,000 (est.)
BC-49cA				TT	2120482-2526409*	420,000 (est.)
BC-49cA				VA	2120717-2516272	400,000 (est.)
BC-49cA				VJ	2122809-2237141*	120,000 (est.)
BC-49cA				VL	2061892-2419260*	360,000 (est.)
BC-49cA				VT	2044384-2189223*	160,000 (est.)
BC-49c-i	$10	1971	Lawson-Bouey; 3 letters (steel engraved)	EDA-EDZ	0000000-9999999	220,000,000
BC-49c-i				EEA-EEN	0000000-9999999	130,000,000
BC-49c-i				EEP	0000000-8999999	9,000,000
BC-49cA-i	$10	1971	Replacement Note	EDX	0000001-2159911	2,160,000 (est.)
BC-49c-i	$10	1971	Lawson-Bouey; 3 letters (lithographed back)	EET	9360000-9999999	640,000
BC-49d	$10	1971	Crow-Bouey (steel engraved)	EEP	9000000-9999999	1,000,000
BC-49d	$10	1971	Crow-Bouey (steel engraved)	EER-EES	0000000-9999999	20,000,000
BC-49d				EET	0000000-9359999	9,360,000
BC-49d				EEU-	0000000-9999999	10,000,000
BC-49d				EEV	0000000-4999999	5,000,000
BC-49dA	$10	1971	Replacement Note	EDX	2169349*-2639999	480,000 (est.)
BC-49d	$10	1971	Crow-Bouey (lithographed back)	EEV	5000000-9999999	5,000,000
BC-49d				EEW-EEZ	0000000-9999999	30,000,000
BC-49d				ETA-ETZ	0000000-9999999	220,000,000
BC-49d				FDA-FDB	0000000-9999999	20,000,000
BC-49d				FDC	0000000-4819999	4,820,000
BC-49dA	$10	1971	Replacement Note	EDX	2640000-4589750*	1,960,000 (est.)
BC-49e	$10	1971	Thiessen-Crow	FDC	4820000-9999999	5,180,000
BC-49e				FDD-FDR	0000000-9999999	120,000,000
BC-49e				FDS	0000000-3139999	3,140,000
BC-49eA	$10	1971	Replacement Note	EDX	4601105-5543079*	1,000,000 (est.)

Summary of Technical Details (Cont'd.)

Cat.No.	Denom.	Date	Variety	Prefixes	Numbers	Qty.Printed
BC-50a	$20	1969	Beattie-Rasminsky	EA-EY	0000000-9999999	220,000,000
BC-50a				EZ	0000000-4519999	4,520,000
BC-50aA	$20	1969	Asterisk Note	EA	1400937-1871972*	480,000 (est.)
BC-50aA				EB	1887101-2314515*	480,000 (est.)
BC-50aA				EH	2360720-2827049*	480,000 (est.)
BC-50aA				EM	2840150-3235765*	400,000 (est.)
BC-50aA				EV	0005918-0115269*	120,000 (est.)
BC-50aA				EX	3130562-3340531*	220,000 (est.)
BC-50b	$20	1969	Lawson-Bouey; 2 letters	EZ	4520000-9999999	5,480,000 (est.)
BC-50b				WA-WZ	0000000-9999999	230,000,000
BC-50b	$20	1969		YA-YG	0000000-9999999	70,000,000
BC-50b				YH	0000000-9749999	9,750,000
BC-50bA	$20	1969	Asterisk Note	EZ	9281722-9930878*	660,000 (est.)
BC-50bA				WA	- 7498999 -	40 (est.)
BC-50bA				WE	9293324-9464054*	200,000 (est.)
BC-50bA				WF	3122767-3518103*	400,000 (est.)
BC-50bA				WL	3122258-3238274*	120,000 (est.)
BC-50bA				WN	1133823-1504152*	400,000 (est.)
BC-50bA				WV	1120793-1514665*	400,000 (est.)
BC-50bA				YA	2121349-2479018*	400,000 (est.)
BC-51a	$50	1975	Lawson-Bouey; 2 letters	HA-HC	0000000-9999999	30,000,000
BC-51a				HD	0000000-6455999	6,456,000
BC-51aA	$50	1975	Asterisk Note	HB	3121438-3355134*	240,000 (est.)
BC-51aA				HC	1132142-2599999	150,000 (est.)
BC-51a-i	$50	1975	Lawson-Bouey; 3 letters	EHA-EHE	0000000-9999999	50,000.000
BC-51a-i				EHF	0000000-6439999	6,440,000
BC-51aA-i	$50	1975	Replacement Note	EHX	0000001-0343124*	400,000 (est.)
BC-51b	$50	1975	Crow-Bouey	EHF	6440000-9999999	3,560,000
BC-51b				EHG-EHN	0000000-9999999	70,000,000
BC-51b				EFA	0000000-6818999	6,819,000
BC-51bA	$50	1975	Replacement Note	EHX	0420471-0854434*	460,000 (est.)
BC-51bA			Replacement Note	EHX	1709086-2159999*	460,000 (est.)
BC-52a	$100	1975	Lawson-Bouey; 2 letters	JA-JC	0000000-9999999	30,000,000
BC-52a				JD	0000000-5399999	5,400,000
BC-52aA	$100	1975	Asterisk Note	JA	6400000-6553394*	160,000 (est.)
BC-52aA			Asterisk Note	JC	1404516-1479999*	80,000 (est.)
BC-52a-i	$100	1975	Lawson-Bouey; 3 letters	AJA-AJB	0000000-9999999	20,000,000
BC-52a-i				AJC	0000000-2399999	2,400,000
BC-52aA-i	$100	1975	Replacement Note	AJX	0000001-0154321*	200,000 (est.)
BC-52b	$100	1975	Crow-Bouey	AJC	2400000-9999999	7,600,000
BC-52b				AJD-AJM	0000000-9999999	90,000,000
BC-52bA	$100	1975	Replacement Note	AJX	0200001-1059999	860,000

*Denotes low and high serial numbers seen

Note: $1 notes with the prefix ECV and ECW are believed to have originally appeared in sheets. Most are thought to have been destroyed.

$1 Issue — 1973

BC-46a-i

Face Design: Coat of Arms of Canada/—/Queen Elizabeth II
Colour: Green multicoloured tint

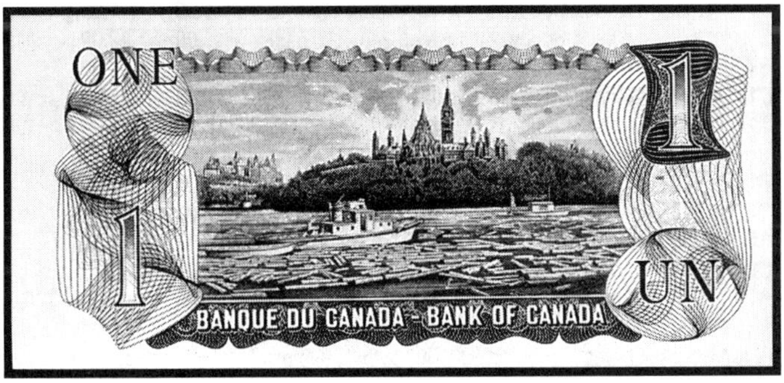

BC-46

Back Design: —/Parliament Hill, across the Ottawa River/—
Colour: Green, blue tint
Issue Date: Engraved: 1973
Printer: CBN Co. and BABN Co.
Imprint: None

Signatures

Left: Engr. R.W. Lawson / Engr. J.W. Crow
Right: Engr. G.K. Bouey / Engr. G.K. Bouey

Official First Day of Issue: June 3, 1974
Official Last Day of Issue: June 30, 1989

Cat.No.	Den.	Date	Variety	VG	F	VF	EF	AU	Unc
BC-46a	$1	1973	Lawson-Bouey; 2 letters	1.00	1.00	1.25	1.50	3.00	5.00
BC-46a	$1	1973	Lawson-Bouey; prefix PA only	8.00	15.00	30.00	75.00	100.00	150.00
BC-46aA	$1	1973	Lawson-Bouey; *AA	2.50	3.00	3.50	4.00	7.00	16.00
BC-46aA	$1	1973	Lawson-Bouey; *AB	80.00	100.00	200.00	400.00	1,000.00	2,500.00
BC-46aA	$1	1973	Lawson-Bouey, *AL	2.50	3.00	4.00	5.00	12.00	20.00
BC-46Aa	$1	1973	Lawson-Bouey, *AN	2.50	3.00	3.50	4.50	10.00	18.00
BC-46aA	$1	1973	Lawson-Bouey, *FA	2.50	3.00	4.00	5.00	10.00	20.00
BC-46aA	$1	1973	Lawson-Bouey, *FB	350.00	600.00	900.00	1,200.00	1,750.00	3,000.00
BC-46aA	$1	1973	Lawson-Bouey, *FG	2.50	3.00	3.25	4.00	7.00	16.00
BC-46aA	$1	1973	Lawson-Bouey; *FH	300.00	500.00	800.00	1,000.00	1,500.00	2,500.00
BC-46aA	$1	1973	Lawson-Bouey, *FN	2.50	3.00	4.00	7.50	15.00	30.00
BC-46aA	$1	1973	Lawson-Bouey, *FV	2.50	3.00	3.50	4.50	10.00	18.00

Cat. No.	Den.	Date	Variety	VG	F	VH	EF	AU	Unc
BC-46aA	$1	1973	Lawson-Bouey, *GF	2.50	3.00	4.00	7.50	15.00	30.00
BC-46aA	$1	1973	Lawson-Boury, *GL	2.50	3.00	4.00	8.00	16.00	32.00
BC-46aA	$1	1973	Lawson-Bouey, *GU	2.50	3.00	5.00	9.00	18.00	35.00
BC-46aA	$1	1973	Lawson-Bouey, *GY	2.50	3.00	4.00	7.50	15.00	30.00
BC-46aA	$1	1973	Lawson-Bouey, *IA	2.50	3.00	3.75	6.00	13.00	25.00
BC-46aA	$1	1973	Lawson-Bouey, *IG	2.50	3.00	4.00	5.00	8.00	18.00
BC-46aA	$1	1973	Lawson-Bouey, *IL	2.50	3.00	3.50	4.50	9.00	18.00
BC-46aA	$1	1973	Lawson-Bouey, *IV	2.50	3.00	4.00	5.00	11.00	22.00
BC-46aA	$1	1973	Lawson-Bouey, *MC	2.50	3.00	4.00	5.00	11.00	22.00
BC-46aA	$1	1973	Lawson-Bouey; *MD	1,000.	1,200.	1,800.	2,200.	3,200.	5,000.
BC-46aA	$1	1973	Lawson-Bouey, *MM	2.50	3.00	4.00	5.00	11.00	22.00
BC-46aA	$1	1973	Lawson-Bouey, *MR	2.50	3.00	3.50	4.50	10.00	20.00
BC-46aA	$1	1973	Lawson-Bouey, *MZ	2.50	3.00	4.50	6.00	12.00	24.00
BC-46aA	$1	1973	Lawson-Bouey, *NP	2.50	3.00	3.50	4.50	10.00	20.00
BC-46aA	$1	1973	Lawson-Bouey, *OG	2.50	3.00	4.50	6.00	12.00	24.00
BC-46aA	$1	1973	Lawson-Bouey; *OL	25.00	35.00	50.00	90.00	135.00	275.00
BC-46a-i	$1	1973	Lawson-Bouey; 3 letters	1.00	1.00	1.00	1.25	3.00	4.00
BC046aA-i	$1	1973	Lawson-Bouey; AAX, steel	4.00	5.00	6.00	12.00	18.00	25.00
BC-46aA-i	$1	1973	Lawson-Bouey; AAX, litho	5.00	7.00	8.00	15.00	24.00	35.00
BC-46aA-i	$1	1973	Lawson-Bouey; EAX,steel	4.00	4.50	8.00	15.00	60.00	120.00
BC-46aA-i	$1	1973	Lawson-Boury, EAX, litho	4.50	5.00	10.00	20.00	100.00	175.00
BC-46aT-i	$1	1973	Lawson-Bouey; AXA	20.00	25.00	50.00	90.00	150.00	300.00
BC-46b	$1	1973	Crow-Bouey; 3 letters	1.00	1.00	1.00	1.00	1.50	4.00
BC-46bA	$1	1973	Crow-Bouey; AAX	4.00	5.00	6.00	12.00	18.00	25.00
BC-46bA	$1	1973	Crow-Bouey, BAX	2.50	3.00	3.00	4.00	7.00	15.00
BC-46bA	$1	1973	Crow-Bouey, EAX	2.50	3.00	3.00	4.00	7.00	15.00
BC-46bT	$1	1973	Crow-Bouey; EXA	20.00	30.00	60.00	100.00	165.00	325.00

BC-46A-i EAX replacement notes numbered 0000000 to 0619999 have steel engraved backs; those numbered 0620000 to 1059999 have lithographed backs.

BC-46aA-i AAX replacement notes numbered 0000000 to 2159999 have steel engraved backs; those numbered 2160000 and higher have lithographed backs.

One Dollar Bank Note Sheet

The first official public sale of uncut bank note sheets (40 x $1 notes) began at the Bank of Canada agencies across Canada on December 12th, 1988. These sheets were printed by the British American Bank Note Company (BABN) in a 5 x 8 note format (five notes across, eight deep) and were offered either across the counter or by mail at $50 each, plus $5 postage and provincial sales tax where applicable.

With the success of the BABN sheet a second was introduced on May 8th, 1989. These sheets were printed by the Canadian Bank Note Company (CBN), in a 4 x 10 note format.

The sheets were available to the public until June 30th, 1989, the day the $1 note was retired from circulation.

The last sheet of regular and replacement notes for the BABN and CBN are:

	Regular	Replacement
BABN	BFL1540499-1559999	BAX1540498-1559998
CBN	ECW4680499-4689999	EAX2560120-2579620

These four sheets must be considered the last of the “one dollar” notes. They are lodged in the National Currency Collection at the Bank of Canada, Ottawa.

Quantities Issued

A total of 114,516 sheets were sold during the period December 1988 to June 1989, having the following breakdown.

Printer	Sheet	Quantity
BABN	Regular	88009
(5 x 8 format)	Replacement	Included above
CBN	Regular	26507
(4 x 10 format)	Replacement	Included above

Cat.No.	Den.	Date	Variety	AU
BC-46b	$1	1973	BABN Sheet Regular, BFD, BFK, BFL	275.
BC-46bA	$1	1973	BABN Sheet Replacement, BAX	900.
BC-46b	$1	1973	CBN Sheet Regular, ECP, ECR, ECV	300.
BC-46b	$1	1973	CBN Sheet Regular, ECW	400.
BC-46bA	$1	1973	CBN Sheet Replacement, EAX	1,000.

Note: These sheets generally show some minor signs of handling and are normally found in AU condition. Uncirculated perfect sheets may command a premium.

$2 Issue — 1974

BC-47aA-i

Face Design: Coat of Arms of Canada/—/Queen Elizabeth II
Colour: Terra Cotta, multicoloured tint

BC-47

Back Design: —/Inuit hunting scene, Baffin Island/—
Colour: Terra Cotta, multicoloured tint

Issue Date: Engraved: 1974
Printer: BABN Co.
Imprint: None

Signatures

Left:	Engr.: R.W. Lawson	**Right:**	Engr.: G.K. Bouey
	Engr.: J.W. Crow		Engr.: G.K. Bouey

Official First Day of Issue: August 5, 1975

Cat.No.	Den.	Date	Variety	VG	F	VF	EF	AU	Unc
BC-47a	$2	1974	Lawson-Bouey; 2 letters	2.00	2.00	2.50	4.00	8.00	16.00
BC-47aA	$2	1974	Lawson-Bouey; *BA	2.50	4.00	7.00	12.00	25.00	50.00
BC-47aA	$2	1974	Lawson-Bouey; *BC	6.00	10.00	20.00	40.00	60.00	100.00
BC-47aA	$2	1974	Lawson-Bouey; *BJ	3.00	6.00	10.00	20.00	30.00	60.00
BC-47aA	$2	1974	Lawson-Bouey, *BM	2.50	4.00	7.00	12.00	25.00	50.00
BC-47aA	$2	1974	Lawson-Bouey; *BX	8.00	12.00	20.00	40.00	60.00	120.00
BC-47aA	$2	1974	Lawson-Bouey; *RA	6.00	12.00	20.00	40.00	80.00	135.00
BC-47aA	$2	1974	Lawson-Bouey; *RE	2.50	4.00	7.00	12.00	25.00	50.00
BC-47aA	$2	1974	Lawson-Bouey; *RW	2.50	4.00	7.00	12.00	25.00	50.00
BC-47aA	$2	1974	Lawson-Bouey; *UG	4.00	8.00	12.00	24.00	40.00	80.00
BC-47aT	$2	1974	Lawson-Bouey; RS	60.00	80.00	150.00	225.00	450.00	800.00
BC-47a-i	$2	1974	Lawson-Bouey; 3 letters	2.00	2.00	2.50	4.00	7.00	14.00
BC-47aA-i	$2	1974	Lawson-Bouey; ABX	8.00	12.00	33.00	50.00	100.00	200.00
BC-47b	$2	1974	Crow-Bouey; 3 letters	2.00	2.00	2.50	4.00	7.00	14.00
BC-47bA	$2	1974	Crow-Bouey; 3 ABX	15.00	25.00	60.00	120.00	200.00	400.00

$5 Issue — 1972

BC-48a

Face Design: Coat of Arms of Canada/—/Sir Wilfrid Laurier
Colour: Blue with multicoloured tint

BC-48

Back Design: —/Salmon seiner, Johnston Strait, Vancouver Island/—
Colour: Blue with multicoloured tint

Issue Date: Engraved: 1972
Printer: CBN Co.
Imprint: None

Signatures

Left:	Engr.: G.K. Bouey	**Right:**	Engr.: L. Rasminsky
	Engr.: R.W. Lawson		Engr.: G.K. Bouey

Official First Day of Issue: December 4, 1972

Cat.No.	Den.	Date	Variety	VG	F	VF	EF	AU	Unc
BC-48a	$5	1972	Bouey-Rasminsky; 2 letters	5.00	5.00	9.00	15.00	30.00	45.00
BC-48aA	$5	1972	Bouey-Rasminsky; *CA	6.00	7.00	12.00	20.00	40.00	80.00
BC-48aA	$5	1972	Bouey-Rasminsky; *CC	6.00	7.00	12.00	20.00	40.00	80.00
BC-48aA	$5	1972	Bouey-Rasminsky; *CD	10.00	12.00	15.00	25.00	50.00	100.00
BC-48b	$5	1972	Lawson-Bouey; 2 letters	5.00	5.00	8.00	12.00	20.00	40.00
BC-48b	$5	1972	Lawson-Bouey; prefix XA only	8.00	10.00	25.00	40.00	60.00	80.00
BC-48bA	$5	1972	Lawson-Bouey; *CS	15.00	18.00	35.00	100.00	225.00	400.00
BC-48bA	$5	1972	Lawson-Bouey; *CU	10.00	12.00	25.00	45.00	90.00	175.00
BC-48bA	$5	1972	Lawson-Bouey; *CV	10.00	12.00	20.00	40.00	70.00	130.00
BC-48bA	$5	1972	Lawson-Bouey; *SB	6.00	10.00	14.00	25.00	50.00	90.00
BC-48bA	$5	1972	Lawson-Bouey; *SF	6.00	10.00	14.00	28.00	55.00	110.00
BC-48bA	$5	1972	Lawson-Bouey; *SL	15.00	18.00	35.00	75.00	175.00	400.00
BC-48bA	$5	1972	Lawson-Bouey; *SP	6.00	10.00	14.00	25.00	50.00	100.00
BC-48bA	$5	1972	Lawson-Bouey; *SW	10.00	15.00	20.00	40.00	100.00	200.00
BC-48bT	$5	1972	Lawson-Bouey; Prefix RS	600.00	800.00	1,500.00	2,500.00	3,200.00	4,500.00

$10 Issue — 1971

BC-49a

Face Design: Coat of Arms of Canada/—/Sir John A. Macdonald
Colour: Purple with multicoloured tint

BC-49

Back Design: —/Industrial scene, Sarnia, Ontario/—
Colour: Purple with multicoloured tint
Issue Date: Engraved:1971
Printer: CBN Co. **Imprint:** None

Signatures

Left:	Right:
Engr.: J.R. Beattie	Engr.: L. Rasminsky
Engr.: G.K. Bouey	Engr.: L. Rasminsky
Engr.: R.W. Lawson	Engr.: G.K. Bouey
Engr.: J.W. Crow	Engr.: G.K. Bouey
Engr.: G.G. Thiessen	Engr.: J.W. Crow

Official First Day of Issue: November 8, 1971

Cat.No.	Den.	Date	Variety	VG	F	VF	EF	AU	Unc
BC-49a	$10	1971	Beattie-Rasminsky; 2 letters	10.00	10.00	12.00	18.00	40.00	85.00
BC-49aA	$10	1971	Beattie-Rasminsky; *DA	15.00	17.00	18.00	35.00	65.00	150.00
BC-49aA	$10	1971	Beattie-Rasminsky; *DB	20.00	21.00	22.00	40.00	75.00	175.00
BC-49aA	$10	1971	Beattie-Rasminsky; *DE (2 Known)			—	—	3,500.00	—
BC-49aA	$10	1971	Beattie-Rasminsky; *DG	18.00	20.00	25.00	45.00	85.00	175.00
BC-49b	$10	1971	Bouey-Rasminsky; 2 letters	10.00	10.00	12.00	16.00	36.00	65.00
BC-49bA	$10	1971	Bouey-Rasminsky; *DK	15.00	17.00	18.00	35.00	65.00	125.00
BC-49bA	$10	1971	Bouey-Rasminsky; *DR	15.00	20.00	25.00	40.00	75.00	150.00
BC-49bA	$10	1971	Bouey-Rasminsky; *DX	400.00	500.00	600.00	900.00	1,200.00	2,000.00
BC-49c	$10	1971	Lawson-Bouey; 2 letters	10.00	10.00	10.00	10.00	15.00	50.00
BC-49cA	$10	1971	Lawson-Bouey; *DY	15.00	17.00	18.00	24.00	40.00	80.00
BC-49cA	$10	1971	Lawson-Bouey; *TC	15.00	17.00	18.00	20.00	38.00	75.00
BC-49cA	$10	1971	Lawson-Bouey; *TG	15.00	18.00	20.00	28.00	50.00	90.00
BC-49cA	$10	1971	Lawson-Bouey; *TL	15.00	17.00	19.00	25.00	45.00	85.00
BC-49cA	$10	1971	Lawson-Bouey; *TT	15.00	17.00	20.00	28.00	50.00	90.00
BC-49cA	$10	1071	Lawson-Bouey; *VA	15.00	17.00	18.00	24.00	40.00	80.00
BC-49cA	$10	1971	Lawson-Bouey; *VJ	15.00	18.00	20.00	28.00	50.00	90.00
BC-49cA	$10	1971	Lawson-Bouey; *VL	15.00	17.00	18.00	24.00	40.00	80.00
BC-49cA	$10	1971	Lawson-Bouey; *VT	15.00	17.00	20.00	28.00	50.00	90.00
BC-49c-i	$10	1971	Lawson-Bouey; 3 letters	10.00	10.00	10.00	12.00	20.00	45.00
BC-49c-i	$10	1971	Lawson-Bouey; EET	350.00	400.00	500.00	700.00	1,200.00	2,000.00
BC-49cA-i	$10	1971	Lawson-Bouey; EDX	225.00	275.00	350.00	500.00	1,000.00	1,750.00
BC-49d	$10	1971	Crow-Bouey; 3 letters	10.00	10.00	10.00	11.00	20.00	45.00
BC-49dA	$10	1971	Crow-Bouey; EDX, steel	30.00	40.00	55.00	110.00	200.00	350.00
BC-49dA	$10	1971	Crow-Bouey; EDX, litho	20.00	25.00	35.00	65.00	120.00	200.00
BC-49e	$10	1971	Thiessen-Crow, 3 letters	10.00	10.00	10.00	11.00	20.00	40.00
BC-49eA	$10	1971	Thiessen-Crow, EDX	20.00	24.00	28.00	32.00	65.00	120.00

BC-49dA EDX replacement notes numbered below 2640000 have steel engraved backs; those numbered 2640000 and higher have lithographed backs.

$20 Issue — 1969

BC-50a

Face Design: Coat of Arms of Canada/—/Queen Elizabeth II
Colour: Olive green with multicoloured tint

BC-50

Back Design: —/Moraine Lake, Alberta/—
Colour: Olive green with multicoloured tint

Issue Date: Engraved: 1969
Printer: CBN Co.
Imprint: None

Signatures

Left:	Engr.: J.R. Beattie	**Right:**	Engr.: L. Rasminsky
	Engr.: R.W. Lawson		Engr.: G.K. Bouey

Official First Day of Issue: June 22, 1970

Cat.No.	Den.	Date	Variety	VG	F	VF	EF	AU	Unc
BC-50a	$20	1969	Beattie-Rasminsky; 2 letters	20.00	20.00	20.00	25.00	50.00	120.00
BC-50aA	$20	1969	Beattie-Rasminsky; *EA	25.00	30.00	35.00	60.00	100.00	200.00
BC-50aA	$20	1969	Beattie-Rasminsky; *EB	25.00	30.00	40.00	65.00	125.00	225.00
BC-50aA	$20	1969	Beattie-Rasminsky; *EH	40.00	75.00	175.00	275.00	350.00	500.00
BC-50aA	$20	1969	Beattie-Rasminsky, *EM	35.00	60.00	100.00	150.00	225.00	375.00
BC-50aA	$20	1969	Beattie-Rasminsky; *EV	60.00	125.00	225.00	300.00	400.00	600.00
BC-50aA	$20	1969	Beattie-Rasminsky; *EX	25.00	35.00	50.00	100.00	175.00	300.00
BC-50b	$20	1969	Lawson-Bouey; 2 letters	20.00	20.00	20.00	25.00	45.00	95.00
BC-50bA	$20	1969	Lawson-Bouey; *EZ	25.00	30.00	35.00	65.00	125.00	250.00
BC-50bA	$20	1969	Lawson-Bouey, *WA			Only one known; sold for $7000 (Unc) in 1999			
BC-50bA	$20	1969	Lawson-Bouey; *WE	25.00	35.00	50.00	90.00	175.00	275.00
BC-50bA	$20	1969	Lawson-Bouey; *WF	25.00	30.00	40.00	65.00	125.00	225.00
BC-50bA	$20	1969	Lawson-Bouey;*WL	25.00	35.00	50.00	80.00	175.00	300.00
BC-50bA	$20	1969	Lawson-Bouey; *WN	25.00	35.00	40.00	65.00	125.00	225.00
BC-50bA	$20	1969	Lawson-Bouey; *WV	25.00	35.00	50.00	90.00	175.00	275.00
BC-50bA	$20	1969	Lawson-Bouey; *YA	25.00	30.00	35.00	60.00	100.00	200.00

$50 Issue — 1975

BC-51b

Face Design: Coat of Arms of Canada/—/
William Lyon Mackenzie King
Colour: Red with multicoloured tint

BC-51

Back Design: —/R.C.M.P. Musical Ride dome formation/—
Colour: Red with multicoloured tint

Issue Date: Engraved: 1975
Printer: CBN Co.
Imprint: None

Signatures

Left: Engr.: R.W. Lawson
Engr.: J.W. Crow

Right: Engr.: G.K. Bouey
Engr.: G.K. Bouey

Official First Day of Issue: March 31, 1975

Cat.No.	Den.	Date	Variety	VG	F	VF	EF	AU	Unc
BC-51a	$50	1975	Lawson-Bouey; 2 letters	50.00	50.00	75.00	100.00	150.00	250.00
BC-51aA	$50	1975	Lawson-Bouey; *HB	60.00	75.00	150.00	300.00	600.00	1,000.00
BC-51aA	$50	1975	Lawson-Bouey *HC	65.00	90.00	175.00	400.00	750.00	1,200.00
BC-51a-i	$50	1975	Lawson-Bouey; 3 letters	50.00	50.00	75.00	100.00	175.00	275.00
BC-51aA-i	$50	1975	Lawson-Bouey, 3 letters EHX	125.00	250.00	600.00	900.00	1,500.00	2,400.00
BC-51b	$50	1975	Crow-Bouey; 3 letters	50.00	50.00	75.00	100.00	125.00	200.00
BC-51bA	$50	1975	Crow-Bouey; 3 letters EHX	60.00	75.00	90.00	125.00	175.00	300.00

$100 Issue — 1975

BC-52b

Face Design: Coat of Arms of Canada/—/Sir Robert Borden
Colour: Brown with multicoloured tint

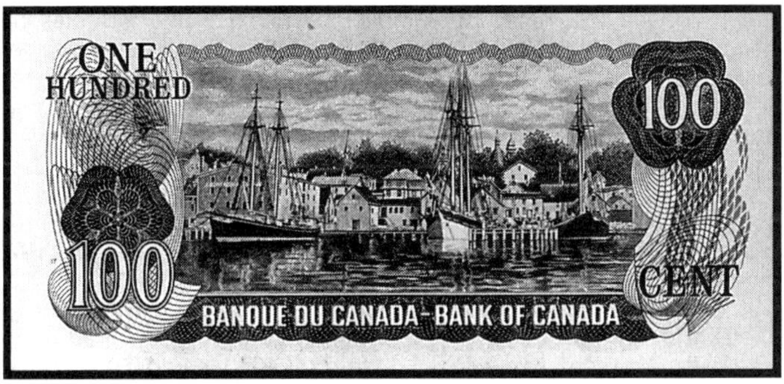

BC-52

Back Design: —/Lunenburg Harbour, Nova Scotia/—
Colour: Brown with multicoloured tint

Issue Date: Engraved: 1975
Printer: BABN Co.
Imprint: None

Signatures

Left: Engr.: R.W. Lawson
Engr.: J.W. Crow

Right: Engr.: G.K. Bouey
Engr.: G.K. Bouey

Official First Day of Issue: May 31, 1976

Cat.No.	Den.	Date	Variety	VG	F	VF	EF	AU	Unc
BC-52a	$100	1975	Lawson-Bouey; 2 letters	100.00	100.00	125.00	175.00	225.00	375.00
BC-52aA	$100	1975	Lawson-Bouey; *JA	150.00	275.00	400.00	600.00	900.00	1,200.00
BC-52aA	$100	1975	Lawson-Bouey; *JC	175.00	325.00	500.00	750.00	1,500.00	2,000.00
BC-52a-i	$100	1975	Lawson-Bouey; 3 letters	100.00	100.00	125.00	135.00	150.00	250.00
BC-52aA-i	$100	1975	Lawson-Bouey; AJX	300.00	450.00	700.00	1,100.00	1,600.00	2,300.00
BC-52b	$100	1975	Crow-Bouey; 3 letters	100.00	100.00	125.00	135.00	150.00	225.00
BC-52bA	$100	1975	Crow-Bouey; AJX	120.00	135.00	150.00	175.00	250.00	400.00

ISSUES OF 1979

The method of numbering the $5 and $20 notes was changed to a format which would be machine readable. The red and blue serial numbers were removed from the note faces, and replaced by black numbers printed on the backs. The BANK OF CANADA BANQUE DU CANADA inscription was removed from below the back vignette to provide a white background for the numbers. The previous $5 and $20 multicolour notes were not withdrawn but permitted to wear out in circulation.

Additional changes were made on the $20 note in response to the criticism that it was not sufficiently different from the $1 note to prevent confusion. The counters in the corners were clarified and strengthened, and the green tones of the face were reduced while the orange and pink tones were enhanced to increase the colour contrast between the $20 and the $1.

It was planned to convert all the notes eventually to the black serial number format. That plan was abandoned when events overtook the change and a new series was designed to keep pace in bank note printing technology.

Prefixes And Numbering

On the back format the black serial numbers consist of eleven digits, the first of which is characteristic of the denomination. The $5 notes have the denominational number 3 and the $20 notes begin with the denominational number 5. The next number indicates the printer, "0" or "2" denoting CBN and "6" BABN. Only the $20 notes have two printers. The next two digits indicate the series number and the last seven digits provide the number of the note within the series. The note numbers start at 0000000 and end at 9999999, so that each series consists of ten million notes, as in the past.

Signatures

Signatures of the following Bank of Canada officials occur on notes of the 1979 issues. In all cases the signatures are engraved on the face plates.

Senior Deputy Governor	*Term of Office*
R. William Lawson	March 1, 1973 to Feb. 29, 1984
John W. Crow	March 1, 1984 to Jan. 31, 1987
Gordon G. Thiessen	Oct. 27, 1987 to Jan. 31, 1994

Governor	*Term of Office*
Gerald K. Bouey	Feb. 1, 1973 to Jan. 31, 1987
John W. Crow	Feb. 1, 1987 to Jan. 31, 1994

Imprints

No imprints are seen on this issue. The second digit of the serial number is used to denote the printer: "0" or "2" for CBN and "6" for BABN. Only the $20 note was supplied by both printers.

Lithographed Backs

Some of the CBN $20 notes were printed from steel engraved back plates after the introduction of the lithographed back.

		Last Note With Engraved Back is	First Note With Lithographed Back is
$5		30461319998	30461320000
$5	Replacement	31003319999	Unknown
$20	CBN	50983239998	50891440000
$20	CBN Replacement	51004799999	51004800000
$20	BABN	56316799999	56316800000
$20	BABN Replacement	51601359999	51601360000

Replacement Notes

There are no asterisk notes in this issue. The replacement notes are designated by the second digit in the serial number.

The digit 1 following the first digit 3 of the $5 notes designates a replacement note. In the $20 denomination the replacement notes can be distinguished by "510" for the CBN company and "516" for the BABN company.

$5 Replacement note

BC-53aA

BC-53bA

$20 Replacement note

BC-54aA

BC-53bA

BC-54bA-i

Experimental Notes

Only experimental notes in the $5 issue are known. As in the past, they were released to test wearing properties of new papers or inks.

The digit 3 following the first digit 3 (denominational number) of the $5 note's serial number signifies an experimental note. Test or experimental notes are numbered by using "T" in the catalogue number.

$5 Experimental Note

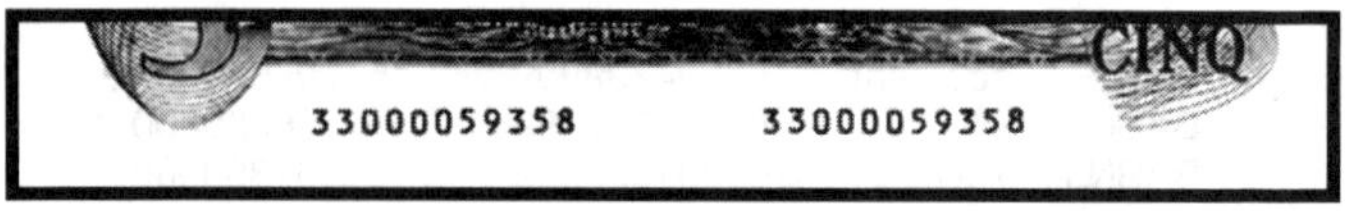

BC-53aT

Summary of Technical Details 1979

Cat.No.	Denom.	Variety	Printer	Series	Numbers	Qty.Printed
BC-53a	$5	Lawson-Bouey	CBN	"30"	30000000000-30461319998	461,319,999
BC-53aA	$5	Replacement Note	CBN	"31"	31000000000-31003319999	3,320,000
BC-53aT	$5	Test Note	CBN	"33"	33000000000-33000469863	500,000*
BC-53b	$5	Crow-Bouey	CBN	"30"	30461320000-30583019999	121,700,000
BC-53bA	$5	Replacement Note	CBN	"31"	31003320000-31004059999	740,000
BC-54a	$20	Lawson-Bouey	CBN	"50"	50000000000-50675999999	676,000,000
BC-54aA	$20	Replacement Note	CBN	"510"	51000000000-51003479999	3,480,000
BC-54b	$20	Crow-Bouey	CBN	"50"	50676000000-50999999999	324,000,000
BC-54b	$20	Crow-Bouey	CBN	"52"	52000000000-52053119999	53,120,000
BC-54bA	$20	Replacement Note	CBN	"510"	51003480000-51005560612*	2,280,000 (est.)
BC-54b-i	$20	Crow-Bouey	BABN	"56"	56000000000-56496399999	496,400,000
BC-54bA-i	$20	Replacement Note	BABN	"516"	51600000000-51601709669	1,800,000*
BC-54c	$20	Thiessen-Crow	CBN	"52"	52053120000-52662919999	609, 800.000
BC-54cA	$20	Replacement Note	CBN	"510"	51005760000-51009659999	3,900.000
BC-54c-i	$20	Thiessen-Crow	BABN	"56"	56496400000-56954399999	458,000,000
BC-54cA-i	$20	Replacement Note	BABN	"516"	51601800000-51605039999	3,240,000

Note: 1. BC-53a - $5 note number 30461319999 was damaged and thus destroyed.
2. Nearly one million (998,999) $5 "31" replacement notes were destroyed.

* Estimates

$5 Issue — 1979

BC-53a

Face Design: Coat of Arms of Canada/—/Sir Wilfrid Laurier
Colour: Blue with multicoloured tint

BC-53

Back Design: —/Salmon seiner, Johnston Strait, Vancouver Island/—
Colour: Blue with multicoloured tint

Issue Date: Engraved: 1979
Printer: CBN Co.
Imprint: None

Signatures

Left: Engr.: R.W. Lawson
Engr.: J.W. Crow

Right: Engr.: G.K. Bouey
Engr.: G.K. Bouey

Official First Day of Issue: October 1, 1979

Cat.No.	Den.	Date	Variety	VG	F	VF	EF	AU	Unc
BC-53a	$5	1979	Lawson-Bouey	5.00	5.00	6.00	9.00	20.00	35.00
BC-53aA	$5	1979	Lawson-Bouey "31"	15.00	30.00	80.00	150.00	250.00	400.00
BC-53aT	$5	1979	Lawson-Bouey "33"	1,000.	1,300.	2,000.	2,500.	3,000.	4,000.
BC-53b	$5	1979	Crow-Bouey	5.00	5.00	8.00	12.00	30.00	60.00
BC-53bA	$5	1979	Crow-Bouey "31"	50.00	80.00	175.00	400.00	600.00	1,000.00

$20 Issue — 1979

BC-54b-i

Face Design: Coat of Arms of Canada/—/Queen Elizabeth II
Colour: Green with orange and pink with multicoloured tint

BC-54

Back Design: —/Moraine lake, Alberta/—
Colour: Green with orange and pink with multicoloured tint

Issue Date: Engraved: 1979
Printer: CBN Co. and BABN Co.
Imprint: None

Signatures

Left: Engr.: R.W. Lawson
Engr.: J.W. Crow
Engr.: G.G. Thiessen

Right: Engr.: G.K. Bouey
Engr.: G.K. Bouey
Engr.: J.W. Crow

Official First Day of Issue: December 18, 1978

Cat.No.	Den.	Date	Variety	Printer	VG	F	VF	EF	AU	Unc
BC-54a	$20	1979	Lawson-Bouey	CBN	20.00	20.00	25.00	50.00	75.00	150.00
BC-54aA	$20	1979	Lawson-Bouey	CBN	50.00	100.00	300.00	500.00	850.00	1,500.00
BC-54b	$20	1979	Crow-Bouey	CBN	20.00	20.00	25.00	30.00	45.00	100.00
BC-54bA	$20	1979	Crow-Bouey	CBN	20.00	25.00	35.00	60.00	100.00	250.00
BC-54b-i	$20	1979	Crow-Bouey	BABN	20.00	20.00	25.00	30.00	40.00	80.00
BC-54bA-i	$20	1979	Crow-Bouey	BABN	20.00	25.00	35.00	60.00	110.00	275.00
BC-54c	$20	1979	Thiessen-Crow	CBN	20.00	20.00	25.00	30.00	40.00	60.00
BC-54cA	$20	1979	Thiessen-Crow	CBN	20.00	20.00	25.00	35.00	70.00	150.00
BC-54c-i	$20	1979	Thiessen-Crow	BABN	20.00	20.00	25.00	30.00	40.00	60.00
BC-54cA-i	$20	1979	Thiessen-Crow	BABN	20.00	20.00	25.00	35.00	60.00	125.00

SPECIMEN NOTES OF THE 1969-1979 MULTICOLOUR ISSUES

No specimen notes of this issue are known to have been available to collectors prior to the November 1999 Bank of Canada sale. These specimen notes have been overprinted with the word "SPECIMEN", in red, in the signature area and also vertically at the right, and again horizontally on the back. The $5 1972, $10 1971 and $20 1969 have been perforated diagonally with the word "SPECIMEN" three times.

There are no punch cancel holes in the signature area on these specimens. The specimen notes were generally described in the auction catalogue as AU. All have manuscript "set" numbers on the back.

Prefixes are AA, BA, CA, DA, EA, HA and JA (followed by seven zeroes) for the $1 to $100 of 1969-1975 respectively, while the $5 and $20 of 1979 have eleven zeroes with no prefix.

Cat. No.	Denom.	Date	Signatures	Quantity Sold Bank of Canada Sale	AU
BC-46aS	$1	1973	Lawson-Bouey	Specimen (635)	125.
BC-47aS	$2	1974	Lawson-Bouey	Specimen (635)	125.
BC-48aS	$5	1972	Bouey-Rasminsky	Specimen (640)	125.
BC-49aS	$10	1971	Beattie-Rasminsky	Specimen (635)	125.
BC-50aS	$20	1969	Beattie-Rasminsky	Specimen (640)	125.
BC-51aS	$50	1975	Lawson-Bouey	Specimen (633)	200.
BC-52aS	$100	1975	Lawson-Bouey	Specimen (625)	200.
BC-53aS	$5	1979	Lawson-Bouey	Specimen (632)	125.
BC-54aS	$20	1979	Lawson-Bouey	Specimen (620)	125.
Set of nine, $1 to $100				Specimen	1,275.

BIRDS OF CANADA

ISSUES OF 1986 TO 1991

On March 14, 1986 the Bank of Canada introduced a new series of banknotes. The new designs were launched that year with the issue of the $2 and $5 notes. No new design was prepared for the $1 note because of the Government of Canada's decision to introduce the one dollar coin for wide circulation in Canada during 1987. Distribution of the $1 note ended after June 1989. The $10 and $50 notes were released in 1989 and the $100 appeared in 1990. The $1000 followed in 1992 and the $20 in 1993.

A number of characteristics of the new banknotes are the same as those on the 1969-1975 issues. The notes are the same size and printed on the same paper. The dominant colour of each denomination remains unchanged. The portrait subjects on the front of each denomination are the same as in the 1969-1975 issues but the portraits are larger. A new portrait of Her Majesty Queen Elizabeth II was engraved. It first appears on the new $2 note and subsequently on the $20 and $1000 notes. New portraits of the four Prime Ministers who appear on the notes of the 1969-1975 issues — Sir John A. Macdonald, Sir Wilfrid Laurier, Sir Robert Borden and William Lyon Mackenzie King — have been engraved for the $10, $5, $100 and $50 denominations, respectively. The names of the Prime Ministers appear beside their portraits.

The designs on the back of each denomination of the new series are completely different. They feature birds found across Canada as the main focal point in a landscape and a stylized background sky depicting the word "Canada". The $2 note portrays the Robin; the $5 note, the Belted Kingfisher, the $10 note, the Osprey; the $20 note, the Common Loon, the $50 note, the Snowy Owl; and the $100 note, the Canada Goose. The $1000 note features the Pine Grosbeak. Each bird is identified by name.

Paper composition was initially 100% cotton for the "Birds" issue. In 1991 it was altered to 75% cotton with 25% kraft fibres. The planchettes glow under ultra violet light, as a security feature. Spexel Inc. manufactures the bank note paper in Canada.

For several years the Bank of Canada has been assessing methods of making denominations of banknotes distinguishable by the blind and the visually impaired. To assist the blind, the notes of this series are printed so that the denomination can be read by a small hand-held electronic device developed in consultation with the national offices of the Canadian National Institute for the Blind and the Canadian Council of the Blind. The electronic device "speaks" the denomination in either English or French. The new series has larger and more distinct counters which also help the visually impaired.

Prefixes And Numbering

The triple letter prefix, first introduced in 1981, forms part of the serial number for this issue. The first letter designates the printer, the second letter denotes the denomination, and the third indicates the series. The series letters may include all letters from "A" to "Z" excepting O, Q and X, the first two because of their resemblance to numerals and the last for its use to designate a replacement note. Series letter "I" began to be used, for the first time, on notes with the Bonin-Thiessen signatures. Each series is numbered from 0000000 to 9999999, with the zero note being removed and destroyed prior to issue. Thus any given denominational letter may accommodate twenty-two series, or 220,000,000 notes.

The series is back-numbered right and left in black similar to the 1979 issues. However, besides the triple prefix difference each denomination carries a barcode to the left of the serial number which can be read by banknote sorting and counting equipment.

Signatures

Signatures of the following Bank of Canada officials occur on notes of the 1986 issues. In all cases the signatures are engraved on the face plates.

The changeover from Crow-Bouey to the Thiessen-Crow signature combination on the 1986 issue $2 notes was unusually protracted. Previously, normal practise had been to terminate one signature combination at a precise point in the numbering of a particular series and begin the new signature combination immediately after that point. In the case of the $2 1986, both signature combinations appear on various notes of series AUG, AUH, AUJ, AUK, AUL, AUM, AUN and ARX, well mixed in terms of numbers.

It is understood that two presses were at work on $2 note production simultaneously, one equipped with plates bearing the engraved Crow-Bouey signatures and the other having plates engraved Thiessen-Crow. However, only one machine was used in applying the serial numbers to the otherwise finished notes. No effort was made to keep separate the notes produced from the two presses during numbering, so they were numbered sequentially from more or less randomly selected piles.

Senior Deputy Governor	*Term of Office*
John W. Crow	March 1, 1984 to February 1, 1987
Gordon G. Thiessen	October 27, 1987 to January 31, 1994
Bernard Bonin	May 13, 1994 to May 20, 1999
Malcolm Knight	July 5, 1999 to date

Governor	*Term of Office*
Gerald K. Bouey	February 1, 1973 to January 31, 1987
John W. Crow	February 1, 1987 To January 31, 1994
Gordon G. Thiessen	February 1, 1994 to January 31, 2001
David Hodge	February 1, 2001 to date.

Imprints

There are no imprints on these notes. The British American and Canadian Bank Note Companies have participated in the printing.

The first letter of the triple prefix letters indicate the printer: “A”, “B” and “C” “for BABN and “E”, “F” and “G” for CBN.

Plate Numbers

A yellow plate number was used on the backs of the $5 notes for the series ENA-ENZ and EOA-EOH. The plate number was then changed to blue. A similar change took place in the replacement (ENX) notes.

Clear back plate

Hidden Back Plate

The plate number on the $100 backs was originally somewhat obscured by waves. In series AJZ the waves were removed from a small rectangular window, making the back plate number more visible. A similar change appeared in the replacement (AJX) notes. $5 notes (BC-55c, Bonin-Thiessen, blue plate number) have been discovered with the back plate number shifted slightly upward, so that it is mostly obscured by grass. This may be the result of a shift, slightly out of register, of the blue coloured portion of the black printing. These notes are uncommon. The affected notes have been reported with prefixes GPF, GPG, GPH, GPL and GPW. The notes are not being accorded separate catalogue listing at this time, since the register shift is relatively minor. Sales have been reported at approximately $25 for uncirculated examples.

Replacement Notes

As in the triple prefix notes of the 1969-1975 issues, the identification of replacement notes is continued by the use of an "X" for the third letter. In the late 1990s the Bank of Canada opted to discontinue the use of identifiable replacement notes. It has been established that notes numbered 9,000,000 and higher have been inserted in new bundles of otherwise consecutively numbered notes, often from a different series, as replacement notes. However the remaining notes with serial numbers over 9,000,000 were issued as regular notes. Thus the goal of unidentifiable replacement notes appears to have been achieved. Recent issue bird series notes numbered in the last million of each series may or may not have been used as replacement notes.

$2 Replacement Note BC-55aA

$2 Replacement Note BC-55aA

Experimental Notes

"No experimental notes (test notes) are known to exist at publication time. Production trials exist but were not officially released. Collectors should be advised that ownership may be contested."

Anomalies Of The Birds Of Canada Issue

The Thiessen-Crow signature combination was intended to begin with $2 note AUK 1640000. However, notes with the Thiessen-Crow signatures have been discovered in series AUG to AUN. Those of series AUJ are very scarce, while series AUG and AUH are extremely rare with Thiessen-Crow signatures.

Checklist of Prefix Letters for Bird Issues

Cat.No.	Den.	Date	Variety	Denom.Letter	Series Letter
BC-55a	$2	1986	Crow-Bouey	AR	F G H J K L M N P R T U V W Y Z
BC-55a	$2	1986	Crow-Bouey	AU	A B C D E F G H J K L M N
BC-55aA	$2	1986	Crow-Bouey	AR	X
BC-55b	$2	1986	Thiessen-Crow	AU	G H J K L M N P R S T U V W Y Z
BC-55bA	$2	1986	Thiessen-Crow	AR	X
BC-55b	$2	1986	Thiessen-Crow	BB	A B C D E F G H J K L M N P R S T U V W Y Z
BC-55b	$2	1986	Thiessen-Crow	BG	A B C D E F G H J K L M N P R S T U V W Y Z
BC-55b-i	$2	1986	Thiessen-Crow	EB	A B C D E F G H J K L M N P R S T U V W Y Z
BC-55b	$2	1986	Thiessen-Crow	BR	A B C D E F G H J K L M N P R S T U V W Y Z
BC-55b	$2	1986	Thiessen-Crow	BU	A B C D E F G H J K L N P R S T U V W Y Z
BC-55b	$2	1986	Thiessen-Crow	CB	A B C D E F G H
BC-55b-i	$2	1986	Thiessen-Crow	EG	A B C D E F G H J K L M N P R
BC-55bA	$2	1986	Thiessen-Crow	BB	X
BC-55bA	$2	1986	Thiessen-Crow	BR	X
BC-55bA-i	$2	1986	Thiessen-Crow	EB	X
BC-55c	$2	1986	Bonin-Thiessen	CB	H I J K
BC-55c-i	$2	1986	Bonin-Thiessen	EG	R S T U
BC-55cA	$2	1986	Bonin-Thiessen	BR	X
BC-55cA-i	$2	1986	Bonin-Thieseen	EB	X
BC-56a	$5	1986	Crow-Bouey	EN	A B C D E F G H J K L M N P R S T U V W Y Z
BC-56a	$5	1986	Crow-Bouey (yellow plate)	EO	A B C D E F G H
BC-56aA	$5	1986	Crow-Bouey (yellow plate)	EN	X

Cat.No.	Den.	Date	Variety	Denom.Letter	Series Letter
BC-56a-i	$5	1986	Crow-Bouey (blue plate)	EO	H J K L M N P R S T U V W Y Z
BC-56a-i	$5	1986	Crow-Bouey (blue plate)	EP	A B C
BC-56a-i	$5	1986	Crow-Bouey (blue plate)	EP	W
BC-56aA-i	$5	1986	Crow-Bouey (blue plate)	EN	X
BC-56b	$5	1986	Thiessen-Crow	EP	C D E F G H J K L M N P R S T U V W Y Z
BC-56bA	$5	1986	Thiessen-Crow	EN	X
BC-56b	$5	1986	Thiessen-Crow	FN	A B C D E F G H J K L M N P R S T U V W Y Z
BC-56b	$5	1986	Thiessen-Crow	FO	A B C D E F G H J K L M N P R S T U V W Y Z
BC-56b	$5	1986	Thiessen-Crow	FP	A B C D E F G H J K L M N P R S T U V W Y Z
BC-56b	$5	1986	Thiessen-Crow	GN	A B C D E F G H J K L M N P R S T U V W Y
BC-56bA	$5	1986	Thiessen-Crow	FN	X
BC-56c	$5	1986	Bonin-Thiessen	GN	Y Z
BC-56c	$5	1986	Bonin-Thiessen (C)	GO	A B C E F G H I J K L M N P R S T U V W Y Z
BC-56c	$5	1986	Bonin-Thiessen (C)	GP	A B C D E F G H J K L M N P R S T U V W
BC-56cA	$5	1986	Bonin-Thiessen (C)	FN	X
BC-56c-i	$5	1986	Bonin-Thiessen (B)	AN	A B C D E F G H
BC-56cA-i	$5	1986	Bonin-Thiessen (B)	AN	X
BC-56d	$5	1986	Knight-Thiessen	AN	H I J K L M N P
BC-56e	$5	1986	Knight-Dodge	GP	W Y Z
BC-57a	$10	1989	Thiessen-Crow	AD	A B C D E F G H J K L M N P R S T U V W Y Z
BC-57a	$10	1989	Thiessen-Crow	AE	A B C D E F G H J K L M N P R S T U V W Y Z
BC-57a	$10	1989	Thiessen-Crow	AT	A B C D E F G H J K L M N P R S T U V W Y Z
BC-57a	$10	1989	Thiessen-Crow	BD	A B C D E F G H
BC-57aA	$10	1989	Thiessen-Crow	AD	X
BC-57aA	$10	1989	Thiessen-Crow	AT	X
BC-57b	$10	1989	Bonin-Thiessen	BD	H I J K L M N P R S T U V WY Z
BC-57b	$10	1989	Bonin-Thiessen	BE	A B C D E F
BC-57bA	$10	1989	Bonin-Thiessen	AT	X
BC-57c	$10	1989	Knight-Thiessen	BE	F G H
BC-58a	$20	1991	Thiessen-Crow (C)	EI No Serif I	A B C D E F G H J
BC-58aA	$20	1991	Thiessen-Crow (C)	EI No Serif I	X
BC-58a-ii	$20	1991	Thiessen-Crow (B)	AI No Serif I	ABCDEFGHJKLMNPRSTUVW
BC-58aA-ii	$20	1991	Thiessen-Crow (B)	AI No Serif I	X
BC-58a-i	$20	1991	Thiessen-Crow (C)	EI Serif I	J K L M N P R S T U V W Y Z
BC-58aA-i	$20	1991	Thiessen-Crow	EI Serif I	X
BC-58a-iii	$20	1991	Thiessen-Crow (B)	AI Serif I	W
BC-58aA-ii	$20	1991	Thiessen-Crow	AI Serif I	X
BC-58a	$20	1991	Thiessen-Crow (C)	ES	A B C D E F G H J
BC-58b	$20	1991	Bonin-Thiessen	ES	J K L M N P R S T U V W Y Z
BC-58b	$20	1991	Bonin-Thiessen	ES with back pl #	J K L M N P R S T U V W Y Z
BC-58b-ii	$20	1991	Bonin-Thiessen	ES no back pl #	Z
BC-58b	$20	1991	Bonin-Thiessen	EV with back pl #	A C D E F G H J K L M N P R S T U V
BC-58b-ii	$20	1991	Bonin-Thiessen	EV no back pl #	A B C D E H
BC-58b-i	$20	1991	Bonin-Thiessen	AI	W Y Z
BC-58b-i	$20	1991	Bonin-Thiessen	AS	ABCDEFGHIJKLMNPRTUVYZ
BC-58b-i	$20	1991	Bonin-Thiessen	AV	A B C D E F G H I J K L M N P R S T U V W Y Z
BC-58b-i	$20	1991	Bonin-Thiessem	AW	A B C

Note: (C) = CBN and (B) = BABN

Cat.No.	Den.	Date	Variety	Denom.Letter	Series Letter
BC-58bA-i	$20	1991	Bonin-Thiessen	AI	X
BC-58c	$20	1991	Knight-Thiessen	AW	C E F G H I J
BC-59a	$50	1988	Thiessen-Crow	EH	P R S T U V W Y Z
BC-59a	$50	1988	Thiessen-Crow	FH	A B C D E F G H J K L M \
BC-59aA	$50	1988	Thiessen-Crow	EH	X
BC-59b	$50	1988	Bonin-Thiessen	FH	M N P R S
BC-59c	$50	1988	Knight-Thiessen	FH	S T U V
BC-60a	$100	1988	Thiessen-Crow	Hidden BP# AJ	N P R S T U V W Y Z
BC-60aA	$100	1988	Thiessen-Crow	Hidden BP# AJ	X
BC-60a-i	$á-0	1988	Thiessen-Crow	Clear BP# AJ	Z
BC-60a-i	$100	1988	Thiessen-Crow	Clear BP# BJ	A B C D E F G H
BC-60Aa-i	$100	1988	Thiessen-Crow	Clear BP# AJ	X
BC-60b	$100	1988	Bonin-Thiessen	BJ	H I
BC-60c	$100	1988	Knight-Thiessen	BJ	I J K L M P R
BC-61a	$1000	1988	Thiessen-Crow	EK	A
BC-61aA	$1000	1988	Thiessen-Crow	EK	X
BC-61b	$1000	1988	Bonin-Thiessen	EK	A

Summary of Technical Details

Cat.No.	Denom.	Date	Variety	Prefixes	Numbers	Qty.Printed
BC-55a	$2	1986	Crow-Bouey	ARF-ARR	0000000-9999999	100,000,000
BC-55a	$2	1986	Crow-Bouey	ART-ARZ	0000000-9999999	60,000,000
BC-55a	$2	1986	Crow-Bouey	AUA-AUF	0000000-9999999	60,000,000
BC-55a	$2	1986	Crow-Bouey	AUG-AUN	Unknown	Unknown
BC-55aA	$2	1986	Replacement Note	ARX	0000000-1240485*	1,260,000 (est.)
BC-55aA	$2	1986	Replacement Note	ARX	1342147*-1399999	60,000 (est.)
BC-55b	$2	1986	Thiessen-Crow	AUG-AUN	Unknown	Unknown
BC-55b	$2	1986	Thiessen-Crow	AUP-AUZ	0000000-9999999	90,000,000
BC-55bA	$2	1986	Replacement Note	ARX	1279630-1339314*	80,000 (est.)
BC-55bA	$2	1986	Replacement Note	ARX	1400000-2319847*	920,000 (est.)
BC-55b	$2	1986	Thiessen-Crow	BBA-BBZ	0000000-9999999	220,000,000
BC-55b	$2	1986	Thiessen-Crow	BGA-BGZ	0000000-9999999	220,000,000
BC-55b-i	$2	1986	Thiessen-Crow	EBA-EBZ	0000000-9999999	220,000,000
BC-55b	$2	1986	Thiessen-Crow	BRA-BRZ	0000000-9999999	220,000,000
BC-55b	$2	1986	Thiessen-Crow	BUA-BUZ	0000000-9999999	210,000,000
BC-55b-i	$2	1986	Thiessen-Crow	EGA-EGP	0000000-9999999	140,000,000
BC-55b-i	$2	1986	Thiessen-Crow	EGR	0000000-1999999	2,000,000
BC-55b	$2	1986	Thiessen-Crow	CBA-CBG	0000000-9999999	70,000,000
BC-55b	$2	1986	Thiessen-Crow	CBH	0000000-6719999	6,720,000
BC-55bA	$2	1986	Thiessen-Crow	BBX	0000000-4796603*	Unknown
BC-55bA	$2	1986	Thiessen-Crow	BRX	0000000-3439999	3,440,000
BC-55bA-i	$2	1986	Thiessen-Crow	EBX	0000000-3839999	3,840,000
BC-55c	$2	1986	Bonin-Thiessen	CBH	6720000-9999999	3,280,000
BC-55c	$2	1986	Bonin-Thiessen	CBI-CBJ	0000000-9999999	20,000,000
BC-55c	$2	1986	Bonin Thiessen	CBK	0000000-9099999	9,100,000
BC-55c-i	$2	1986	Bonin-Thiessen	EGR	2000000-9999999	8,000,000
BC-55c-i	$2	1986	Bonin-Thiessen	EGS-EGT	0000000-9999999	20,000,000
BC-55c-i	$2	1986	Bonin-Thiessen	EGU	0000000-8159999	8,160,000
BC-55cA	$2	1986	Bonin-Thiessen	BRX	3440000-3579999	140,000
BC-55cA-i	$2	1986	Bonin-Thiessen	EBX	3840000-3999998	1,599,999
BC-56a	$5	1986	Crow-Bouey (yellow back plate #)	ENA-ENZ	0000000-9999999	220,000,000
BC-56a	$5	1986	Crow-Bouey (yellow back plate #)	EOA-EOG	0000000-9999999	70,000,000
BC-56a	$5	1986	Crow-Bouey (yellow back plate #)	EOH	0000000-2599999 (est.)	2,600,000
BC-56aA	$5	1986	Replacement Note (yellow back plate #)	ENX	0000000-2242643*	2,260,000 (est.)

Cat.No.	Denom.	Date	Variety	Prefixes	Numbers	Qty.Printed
BC-56a-i	$5	1986	Crow-Bouey (blue back plate #)	EOH	2600000-9999999	7,400,000 (est.)
BC-56a-i	$5	1986	Crow-Bouey (blue back plate #)	EOJ-EOZ	0000000-9999999	140,000,000
BC-56a-i	$5	1986	Crow-Bouey (blue back plate #)	EPA-EPB	0000000-9999999	20,000,000
BC-56a-i	$5	1986	Crow-Bouey (blue back plate #)	EPC	0000000-2399999	2,400,000
BC-56a-i	$5	1986	Crow-Bouey (blue back plate #)	EPW	9723137-9727125*	80,000 (est.)
BC-56aA-i	$5	1986	Replacement Note (blue back plate #)	ENX	2281348-3479999*	Unknown
BC-56b	$5	1986	Thiessen-Crow	EPC	2400000-9999999	7,600,000
BC-56b	$5	1986	Thiessen-Crow	EPD-EPV	0000000-9999999	190,000,000
BC-56b	$5	1986	Thiessen-Crow	EPW	0000000-9634097*	9,920,000 (est.)
BC-56b	$5	1986	Thiessen-Crow	EPW	9731488*-9999999	
BC-56b	$5	1986	Thiessen-Crow	EPY-EPZ	0000000-9999999	20,000,000
BC-56b	$5	1986	Thiessen-Crow	FOA-FOZ	0000000-9999999	220,000,000
BC-56b	$5	1986	Thiessen-Crow	FPA-FPZ	0000000-9999999	220,000,000
BC-56b	$5	1986	Thiessen-Crow	GNA-GNW	0000000-9999999	200,000,000
BC-56b	$5	1986	Thiessen-Crow	GNY	0000000-7759999	7,760,000
BC-56bA	$5	1986	Replacement Note	ENX	3486000-6259840*	2,800,000 (est.)
BC-56b	$5	1986	Thiessen-Crow	FNA-FNZ	0000000-9999999	220,000,000
BC-56bA	$5	1986	Replacement Note	FNX	0124475-8279999	8,280,000
BC-56c	$5	1986	Bonin-Thiessen	GNY	7600000-9999999	2,240,000
BC-56c	$5	1986	Bonin-Thiessen	GNZ	0000000-9999999	10,000,000
BC-56c	$5	1986	Bonin-Thiessen (C)	GOA-GOZ	0000000-9999999	220,000,000
BC-56c	$5	1986	Bonin-Thiessen (C)	GPA-GPV	0000000-9999999	In Issue
BC-56c	$5	1986	Bonin-Thiessen (C)	GPW	0000000-3559999	3,560,000
BC-56c-i	$5	1986	Bonin-Thiessen (B)	ANA - ANG	0000000-9999999	70,000,000
BC-56c-i	$5	1986	Bonin-Thiessen (B)	ANH	0000000-3519998	3,519,999
BC-56cA	$5	1986	Replacement Note (C)	FNX	8280000-8319999	40,000
BC-56cA-i	$5	1986	Replacement Note (B)	ANX	0000000-0199999	200,000
BC-56d	$5	1986	Knight-Thiessen (B)	ANH	3520000-9999999	6,480,000
BC-56d	$5	1986	Knight-Thiessen (B)	ANI - ANN	0000000-9999999	60,000,000
BC-56d	$5	1986	Knight-Thiessen (B)	ANP	0000000-4319999	4,320,000
BC-56e	$5	1986	Knight-Dodge (C)	GPW	3560000-9999999	6,440,000
BC-56e	$5	1986	Knight-Dodge (C)	GPY	0000000-9999999	In Issue
BC-57a	$10	1989	Thiessen-Crow	ADA-ADZ	0000000-9999999	220,000,000
BC-57a	$10	1989	Thiessen-Crow	AEA-AEZ	0000000-9999999	220,000,000
BC-57a	$10	1989	Thiessen-Crow	ATA-ATZ	0000000-9999999	220,000,000
BC-57a	$10	1989	Thiessen-Crow	BDA-BDG	0000000-9999999	70,000,000
BC-57a	$10	1988	Thiessen-Crow	BDH	0000000-0839999	840,000
BC-57aA	$10	1989	Replacement Note	ADX	0000000-5067254*	5,100,000 (est.)
BC-57aA	$10	1989	Replacement Note	ATX	0000000-2179999	2,180,000
BC-57b	$10	1989	Bonin-Theissen	BDH	0840000-9999999	9,160,000
BC-57b	$10	1989	Bonin-Theissen	BDI-BDZ	0000000-9999999	150,000,000
BC-57b	$10	1989	Bonin-Theissen	BEA-BEE	0000000-9999999	50,000,000
BC-57b	$10	1989	Bonin-Theissen	BEF	0000000-9599999	9,600,000
BC-57bA	$10	1989	Bonin-Theissen	ATX	2180000-2319999	140,000
BC-57c	$10	1989	Knight-Thiessen	BEF	9600000-9999999	400,000
BC-57c	$10	1989	Knight-Thiessen	BEG	0000000-9999999	10,000,000
BC-57c	$10	1989	Knight-Thiessen	BEH	0000000-6499999	6,500,000
BC-58a	$20	1991	Thiessen-Crow (C) (Letter I without serifs)	EIA-EIH	0000000-9999999	80,000,000
BC-58a	$20	1991	Thiessen-Crow (C) (Letter I without serifs)	EIJ	0000000-3999999	4,000,000

Note: * denotes high and low numbers seen

Cat.No.	Denom.	Date	Variety	Prefixes	Numbers	Qty.Printed
BC-58a-i	$20	1991	Thiesssen-Crow) (C) (Letter I with serifs)	EIJ	4000000-9999999	6,000,000
BC-58a-i	$20	1991	Thiessen-Crow (C)	EIK-EIZ	0000000-9999999	130,000,000
BC-58a	$20	1991	Thiessen-Crow (C)	ESA-ESH	0000000-9999999	80,000,000
BC-58a	$20	1991	Thiessen-Crow (C)	ESJ	0000000-4159999	4,160,000
BC-58aA	$20	1991	Thiessen-Crow (C) (Letter I without serifs)	EIX	0001326*-0999994	1,000,000 (est.)
BC-58aA-i	$20	1991	Thiessen-Crow (C) (Letter I with serifs)	EIX	1000225*-3599999	2,600,000 (est.)
BC-58a-ii	$20	1991	Thiessen-Crow (B) (Letter I without serifs)	AIA-AIV	0000000-9999999	190,000,000
BC-58a-ii	$20	1991	Thiessen-Crow (B) (Letter I without serifs)	AIW	0000000-3943945	4,000,00 (est.)
BC-58aA-ii	$20	1991	Thiessen-Crow (B) (Letter I without serifs)	AIX-	0000000-2039998	2,039,998
BC-58a-iii	$20	1991	Thiessen-Crow (B) (Letter I with serifs)	AIW-	4042436*-7599999	3,600,000 (est.)
BC-58b	$20	1991	Bonin-Thiessen (C)	ESJ	4160000-9999999	5,840,000
BC-58b	$20	1991	Bonin-Thiessen (C)	ESK-ESZ	0000000-9999999	130,000,000
BC-58b	$20	1991	Bonin-Thiessen	EVA-EVU	0000000-9999999	170,000,000
BC-58b	$20	1991	Bonin-Thiessen	EVV	0000000-3479999	3,480,000
BC-58b-i	$20	1991	Bonin-Thiessen (B)	AIW	7600000-9999999	2,400,000
BC-58b-i	$20	1991	Bonin-Thiessen (B)	AIY-AIZ	0000000-9999999	20,000,000
BC-58b-i	$20	1991	Bonin-Thiessen (B)	ASA-ASZ	0000000-9999999	220,000,000
BC-58b-i	$20	1991	Bonin-Thiessen (B)	AVA-AVZ	0000000-9999999	230,000,000
BC-58b-i	$20	1991	Bonin-Thiessen	AWA-AWB	0000000-9999999	20,000,000
BC-58b-i	$20	1991	Bonin-Thiessen	AWC	0000000-1999999	2,000,000
BC-58bA-i	$20	1991	Bonin-Thiessen (B)	AIX	2040000-3239999	1,200,000
BC-58c	$20	1991	Knight-Thiessen	AWC	2000000-9999999	8,000,000
BC-58c	$20	1991	Knight-Thiessen	AWD	0000000-9999999	In Issue
BC-59a	$50	1988	Thiessen-Crow	EHP-EHZ	0000000-9999999	90,000,000
BC-59a	$50	1988	Thiessen-Crow	FHA-FHL	0000000-9999999	110,000,000
BC-59a	$50	1988	Thiessen-Crow	FHM	0000000-2119999	2,120,000
BC-59aA	$50	1988	Thiessen-Crow	EHX	0881403-1431431*	800,000 (est.)**
BD-59aA	$50	1988	Thiessen-Crow	EHX	2542583*-4119999	1,700,000 (est)**
BC-59b	$50	1988	Bonin-Thiessen	FHM	2120000-9999999	7,880,000
BC-59b	$50	1988	Bonin-Thiessen	FHN-FHR	0000000-9999999	30,000,000
BC-59b	$50	1988	Bonin-Thiessen	FHS	0000000-6599999	6,600,000
BC-59c	$50	1988	Knight-Thiessen	FHS	6600000-9999999	3,400,000
BC-59c	$50	1988	Knight-Thiessen	FHT-FHV	0000000-9999999	In issue
BC-60a	$100	1988	Thiessen-Crow	Hidden BP# AJN-AJY	0000000-9999999	100,000,000
BC-60a	$100	1988	Thiessen-Crow	Hidden BP# AJZ	0000000-3172636*	Unknown
BC-60aA	$100	1988	Thiessen-Crow	Hidden BP# AJX	1282441-2432640*	2,800,000 (est.)
BC-60a-i	$100	1988	Thiessen-Crow	Clear BP# AJZ	6653865*-9999999	Unknown
BC-60a-i	$100	1988	Thiessen-Crow	Clear BP# BJA-BJG	0000000-9999999	70,000,000
BC-60a-i	$100	1988	Thiessen-Crow	Clear BP# BJH	0000000-1179999	1,180,000
BC-60aA-i	$100	1988	Thiessen-Crow	Clear BP# AJX	3165320*-3479999	700,000 (est.)
BC-60b	$100	1988	Bonin-Thiessen	BJH	1180000-9999999	8,820,000
BC-60b	$100	1988	Bonin-Thiessen	BJI	0000000-8939999	8,940,000
BC-60c	$100	1988	Knight-Thiessen	BJI	8940000-9999999	1,060,000
BC-60c	$100	1988	Knight-Thiessen	BJJ-BJR	0000000-9999999	In issue
BC-61a	$1000	1988	Thiessen-Crow	EKA	0000000-1879999	1,880,000
BC-61aA	$1000	1988	Thiessen-Crow	EKX	0000000-0339685	339,685
BC-61B	$1000	1988	Bonin-Thiessen	EKA	1880000-6039999	4,160,000

Note 1: *Some of the $20 1991 with prefixes ESZ, EVA, EVE (including, apparently, all with prefix EVB and EVH occur with no back plate number (Cat. No. 58b-ii). Number ranges are generally intermittent and incompletely defined, so thos with and without back plate numbers are combined in the listings on previous page. For the most current detailed information, see article by Dr. Lub Wojtiw in *The Canadian Paper Money Newsletter*, April 2001 issue, pages 15 to 17.

Note 2: ** Numbers outside the ranges given for BC-59aS may have been used for the 1975 $50 notes

Note 3: (C) = CBN and (B) = BABN

$2 Issue — 1986

BC-55a

Face Design: —/Queen Elizabeth II/Parliament Buildings
Colour: Dark Terra Cotta, pastel colours in a rainbow pattern

BC-55a

Back Design: —/Robin (Merle d'Amerique)/—
Colour: Dark Terra Cotta, pastel colours in a rainbow pattern

Issue Date: Engraved: 1986 **Official First Day of Issue:** September 2, 1986
Official Last Day of Issue: February 16, 1996
Printer: British American Bank Note Company;
Canadian Bank Note Company
Imprint: None
Signatures: **Left:** Engr.: J.W. Crow; Engr.: G.G. Thiessen; Engr.: B. Bonin — **Right:** Engr.: G.K. Bouey; Engr.: J.W. Crow; Engr.: G. G. Thiessen

Cat.No.	Den.	Date	Variety	VG	F	VF	EF	AU	Unc
BC-55a	$2	1986	Crow-Bouey (B)	2.00	2.00	2.00	2.00	6.00	14.00
BC-55a	$2	1986	Crow-Bouey (B); AUG	2.00	2.00	3.00	7.00	12.00	24.00
BC-55a	$2	1986	Crow-Bouey (B); AUH	2.00	2.00	3.00	7.00	12.00	24.00
BC-55a	$2	1986	Crow-Bouey (B); AUJ	2.00	2.00	2.50	6.50	11.00	22.00
BC-55a	$2	1986	Crow-Bouey (B); AUK	2.00	2.00	2.50	6.00	10.00	20.00
BC-55a	$2	1986	Crow-Bouey (B); AUL	2.00	2.00	2.00	5.50	9.00	18.00
BC-55a	$2	1986	Crow-Bouey (B); AUM	2.00	2.00	2.00	5.00	8.00	15.00
BC-55a	$2	1986	Crow-Bouey (B); AUN	2.00	2.00	2.00	3.00	6.00	14.00
BC-55aA	$2	1986	Crow-Bouey (B); ARX	4.00	6.00	8.00	10.00	25.00	60.00
BC-55b	$2	1986	Thiessen-Crow (B)	2.00	2.00	2.00	2.00	3.00	6.00
BC-55b	$2	1986	Thiessen-Crow (B); AUG	1,250.00	—	(one known)		—	—
BC-55b	$2	1986	Thiessen-Crow (B); AUH	1,000.00	1,100.00	(two known)		—	—
BC-55b	$2	1986	Thiessen-Crow (B); AUJ	250.00	300.00	350.00	400.00	500.00	1,000.00
BC-55b	$2	1986	Thiessen-Crow (B); AUK	2.00	2.00	2.50	6.00	10.00	20.00
BC-55b	$2	1986	Thiessen-Crow (B); AUL	2.00	2.00	2.00	5.00	8.00	15.00
BC-55b	$2	1986	Thiessen-Crow (B); AUM	2.00	2.00	2.00	3.00	6.00	12.00
BC-55b	$2	1986	Thiessen-Crow (B); AUN	2.00	2.00	2.00	3.00	6.00	12.00
BC-55bA	$2	1986	Thiessen-Crow (B); ARX	3.00	4.00	5.00	8.00	10.00	25.00
BC-55bA	$2	1986	Thiessen-Crow (B); BBX	3.00	4.00	5.00	8.00	10.00	20.00
BC-55bA	$2	1986	Thiessen-Crow (B); BRX	3.00	4.00	5.00	8.00	10.00	20.00
BC-55b-i	$2	1986	Thiessen-Crow (C)	2.00	2.00	2.00	2.00	3.00	6.00
BC-55bA-i	$2	1986	Thiessen-Crow (C); EBX	3.00	4.00	5.00	8.00	10.00	20.00
BC-55c	$2	1986	Bonin-Thiessen (B)	2.00	2.00	2.00	2.00	3.00	5.00
BC-55cA	$2	1986	Bonin-Thiessen (B); BRX	4.00	6.00	10.00	15.00	20.00	35.00
BC-55c-i	$2	1986	Bonin-Thiessen (C)	2.00	2.00	2.00	2.00	3.00	5.00
BC-55cA-i	$2	1986	Bonin-Thiessen (C); EBX	5.00	8.00	12.00	18.00	25.00	40.00

Two Dollar Bank Note Sheet

The two dollar uncut bank note sheets went on sale December 5th, 1990. The formats are five notes across and eight notes deep (76.2 x 55.88 cm) and four notes across and ten notes deep (60.96 x 69.85 cm). Issue price was $90.00, plus postage at $8.25 per parcel and taxes where applicable. The $2.00 sheet was withdrawn from sale on February 16th, 1996.

Summary of Technical Details

Printer	Sheet	Signature	Prefix	Quantity
BABN	5 X 8 Format	Thiessen-Crow	BBU	Unknown
BABN	5 x 8 Format	Thiessen-Crow	BBX	Unknown
CBN	4 x 10 Forrnat	Thiessen-Crow	EBA, EBB	Unknown
CBN	4 X 10 Format	Thiessen-Crow	EBX	Unknown
BABN	5 X 8 Format	Bonin-Thiessen	CBJ, CBK	Unknown
BABN	5 x 8 Format	Bonin-Thiessen	BRX	Unknown
CBN	4 X 10 Format	Bonin-Thiessen	EGT	Unknown
CBN	4 X 10 Format	Bonin-Thiessen	EBX	Unknown

Cat.No.	Denom.	Date	Signatures	Variety	AU
BC-55b	$2	1986	Thiessen-Crow	BABN Sheet Regular	175.00
BC-55bA	$2	1986	Thiessen-Crow	BABN Sheet Replacement (BBX)	600.00
BC-55b-i	$2	1986	Thiessen-Crow	CBN Sheet Regular	175.00
BC-55bA-i	$2	1986	Thiessen-Crow	CBN Sheet Replacement (EBX)	600.00
BC-55c	$2	1986	Bonin-Thiessen	BABN Sheet Regular	175.00
BC-55cA	$2	1986	Bonin-Thiessen	BABN Sheet Replacement (BRX)	2,500.00
BC-55c-i	$2	1986	Bonin-Thiessen	CBN Sheet Regular	175.00
BC-55cA-i	$2	1986	Bonin-Thiessen	CBN Sheet Replacement (EBX)	2,500.00

Note: These sheets generally show some minor signs of handling and are normally found in AU condition. Uncirculated perfect sheets may command a premium.

$5 Issue — 1986

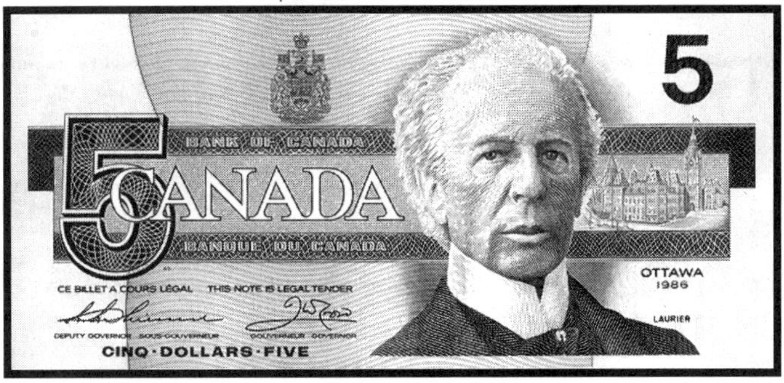

BC-56b

Face Design: —/Sir Wilfrid Laurier/Parliament Buildings
Colour: Dark blue, pastel colours in a rainbow pattern

BC-56b

Back Design: —/Belted Kingfisher (Martin-Pêcheur)/—
Colour: Dark blue, pastel colours in a rainbow pattern

Issue Date: Engraved: 1986 **Official First Day of Issue:** April 28, 1986
Printer: Canadian Bank Note Company and British American Bank Note Company
Imprint: None

Signatures

Left:		Right:	
	Engr.: J.W. Crow		Engr.: G.K. Bouey
	Engr.: G.G. Thiessen		Engr.: J.W. Crow
	Engr.: B. Bonin		Engr.: G.G. Thiessen
	Engr.: M.D. Knight		Engr.: G.G. Thiessen
	Engr.: M.D. Knight		Engr.: D.A. Dodge

Cat.No.	Den.	Date	Variety/Plate No./Prefix	VG	F	VF	EF	AU	Unc
BC-56a	$5	1986	Crow-Bouey, Yellow plate no.	5.	5.	5.	6.	10.	40.
BC-56aA	$5	1986	Crow-Bouey, Yellow plate no., ENX	10.	20.	35.	70.	110.	200.
BC-56a-i	$5	1986	Crow-Bouey, Blue plate no.	5.	5.	5.	6.	12.	35.
BC-56a-i	$5	1986	Crow-Bouey, Blue plate no., EPW	250.	400.	550.	600.	750.	1,200.
BC-56aA-i	$5	1986	Crow-Bouey, Blue plate no., ENX	20.	40.	75.	100.	160.	275.
BC-56b	$5	1986	Thiessen-Crow	5.	5.	5.	5.	5.	14.
BC-56bA	$5	1986	Thiessen-Crow, ENX	6.	6.50	7.	8.	12.	35.
BC-56bA	$5	1986	Thiessen-Crow, FNX	6.	6.50	7.	8.	10.	30.
BC-56c	$5	1986	Bonin-Thiessen (C)	5.	5.	5.	5.	6.	8.
BC-56cA	$5	1986	Bonin-Thiessen (C), FNX	30.	50.	75	150.	300.	600.
BC-56c-i	$5	1986	Bonin-Thiessen (B)	5.	5.	5.	5.	6.	8.
BC-56cA-i	$5	1986	Bonin-Thiessen (B), ANX	6.	8.	10.	20.	50.	120.
BC-56d	$5	1986	Knight-Thiessen (B)	—	—	—	—	—	6.
BC-56e	$5	1986	Knight-Dodge (C)	—	—	—	—	—	6.

$10 Issue of — 1989

BC-57a

Face Design: —/Sir John A. Macdonald/Parliament Buildings with Red Ensign flag
Colour: Purple, pastel colours in a rainbow pattern

BC-57a

Back Design: —/Osprey in flight (Balbuzard)/—
Colour: Purple, pastel colours in a rainbow pattern

Issue Date: Engraved 1989 **Official First Day of Issue:** June 27, 1989
Printer: British American Bank Note Company
Imprint: None

Signatures

Left:	Engr.: G.G. Thiessen	**Right:**	Engr.: J.W. Crow
	Engr.: B. Bonin		Engr.: G.G. Thiessen
	Engr.: M.D. Knight		Engr.: G.G. Thiessen

Cat.No.	Denom.	Date	Variety	Prefix	VF	EF	AU	Unc
BC-57a	$10	1989	Thiessen-Crow		10.00	10.00	15.00	25.00
BC-57a	$10	1989	Thiessen-Crow	BDH	50.00	150.00	250.00	350.00
BC-57aA	$10	1989	Thiessen-Crow	ADX	15.00	20.00	30.00	60.00
BC-57Aa	$10	1989	Thiessen-Crow	ATX	15.00	20.00	30.00	60.00
BC-57b	$10	1989	Bonin-Thiessen		10.00	10.00	10.00	15.00
BC-57bA	$10	1989	Bonin-Thiessen	ATX	15.00	30.00	85.00	175.00
BC-57c	$10	1989	Knight-Thiessen		10.00	10.00	15.00	20.00
BC-57c	$10	1989	Knight-Thiessen	BFE	12.00	20.00	30.00	50.00

TEN DOLLAR BANK NOTE SHEET

Some of the last $10 notes of the birds series were offered for sale to the public, beginning on 31 May 2001. Eleven thousand sheets were made available for sale, at the issue price $450 plus applicable taxes. The sheets were in the BABN format, five notes across and eight notes deep.

Collectors should be cautious about buying alleged "cutting errors" which may be fabricated by deliberately miscutting notes from a sheet. Sheets were issued with prefix BEH, with serial numbers reported to date being in the six millions.

Summary of Technical Details

Printer	Sheet	Signature	Prefix	Quantity
BABN	5X8 Format	Knight-Thiessen	BEH	Up to 11,000 sheets

Cat.No.	Denom.	Date	Variety	Prefix	AU
BC-57c	$10	1989	BABN sheet (40)	BEH	475.00

$20 Issue - 1991

BC-58a

Face Design: "20" on optical device, large "20" and Canada/ Queen Elizabeth II/Library of Parliament
Colour: Green, with other pastel colours

BC-58a-ii

Back Design: —/Common Loon (Huart a Collier)/—
Colour: Green with pastel colours in a rainbow pattern

Issue Date: Engraved: 1991 **Official First Day of Issue:** June 29, 1993
Printer: Canadian Bank Note Company and British American Bank Note Company
Imprint: None

Signatures:

Left: Engr.: G. G. Thiessen — **Right:** Engr.: J. W. Crow
Engr.: B. Bonin — Engr.: G.G. Thiessen
Engr.: M.D. Knight — Engr.: G.G. Thiessen

Varieties: Letter "I" in prefix printed with or without serifs

Cat.No.	Denom.	Date	Variety	VF	EF	AU	Unc
BC-58a	$20	1991	Thiessen-Crow (C), without serifs	20.00	20.00	25.00	45.00
BC-58aA	$20	1991	Thiessen-Crow (C), without serifs, EIX	20.00	20.00	50.00	70.00
BC-58a-i	$20	1991	Thiessen-Crow (C), with serifs	20.00	20.00	25.00	50.00
BC-58aA-i	$20	1991	Thiessen-Crow (C), with serifs, EIX	20.00	20.00	40.00	60.00
BC-58a-ii	$20	1991	Thiessen-Crow (B), without serifs	20.00	20.00	25.00	40.00
BC-58aA-ii	$20	1991	Thiessen-Crow (B), without serifs, AIX	22.00	25.00	60.00	90.00
BC-58a-iii	$20	1991	Thiessen-Crow (B), with serifs, AIW*	30.00	60.00	100.00	150.00
BC-58b	$20	1991	Bonin-Thiessen (C)	20.00	20.00	20.00	25.00
BC-58b	$20	1991	Bonin-Thiessen (C), ESZ, with back pl. #	20.00	20.00	25.00	40.00
BC-58b	$20	1991	Bonin-Thiessen (C), EVA, with back pl. #	20.00	20.00	25.00	50.00
BC-58b	$20	1991	Bonin-Thiessen (C), EVC, with back pl. #	20.00	20.00	22.00	35.00
BC-58b	$20	1991	Bonin-Thiessen (C), EVD, with back pl. #	20.00	20.00	22.00	35.00
BC-58b	$20	1991	Bonin-Thiessen (C), EVE, with back pl. #	20.00	20.00	22.00	35.00
BC-58b	$20	1991	Bonin-Thiessen (C), EVH, with back pl. #	20.00	20.00	22.00	35.00
BC-58b-i	$20	1991	Bonin-Thiessen (B)	20.00	20.00	20.00	25.00
BC-58b-ii	$20	1991	Bonin-Thiessen (C), ESZ, no back pl. #	20.00	20.00	22.00	50.00
BC-58b-ii	$20	1991	Bonin-Thiessen (C), EVA, no back pl. #	20.00	20.00	22.00	35.00
BC-58b-ii	$20	1991	Bonin-Thiessen (C), EVB, no back pl. #	20.00	20.00	22.00	35.00
BC-58b-ii	$20	1991	Bonin-Thiessen (C), EVC, no back pl. #	20.00	20.00	25.00	50.00
BC-58b-ii	$20	1991	Bonin-Thiessen (C), EVD, no back pl. #	22.00	23.00	30.00	50.00
BC-58b-ii	$20	1991	Bonin-Thiessen (C), EVE, no back pl. #	26.00	30.00	40.00	70.00
BC-58b-ii	$20	1991	Bonin-Thiessen (C), EVH. no back pl. #	50.00	60.00	100.00	150.00
BC-58bA-i	$20	1991	Bonin-Thiessen (B), AIX	23.00	24.00	50.00	70.00
BC-58c	$20	1991	Knight-Thiessen (B)	—	—	—	25.00

Note: *Prefix AIW, numbers 4000000 to 7599999 only.

$50 Issue - 1988

BC-59a

Face Design: "50" on optical device, large "50" and Canada/ William Lyon Mackenzie King/Parliament Building with Red Ensign flag
Colour: Red, pastel colours in a rainbow pattern

BC-59aA

Back Design: —/Snowy Owl (Harfang des Neiges)/—
Colour: Red, pastel colours in a rainbow pattern

Issue Date: Engraved: 1988 **Official First Day of Issue:** December 1, 1989
Printer: Canadian Bank Note Company
Imprint: None

Signatures

Left: Engr.: G. G.Thiessen, Engr.: B. Bonin
Right: Engr.: J. W. Crow, Engr.: G.G. Thiessen

Cat.No.	Denom.	Date	Variety	VF	EF	AU	Unc
BC-59a	$50	1988	Thiessen-Crow	50.00	50.00	55.00	75.00
BC-59aA	$50	1988	Thiessen-Crow EHX	50.00	55.00	100.00	150.00
BC-59b	$50	1988	Bonin-Thiessen	50.00	50.00	55.00	70.00
BC-59c	$50	1988	Knight-Thiessen	50.00	50.00	50.00	70.00

$100 Issue - 1988

BC-60a

Face Design: "100" on optical device, large "100" and Canada/ Sir Robert Borden/centre block of Parliament Buildings with Union Jack
Colour: Brown, pale beige

BC-60a

Back Design: —/Canada Goose (Bernache du Canada)/—
Colour: Brown, pale beige

Issue Date: Engraved: 1988 **Official First Day of Issue:** December 3, 1990
Printer: British American Bank Note Company
Imprint: None

Signatures

Left: Engr.: G.G. Thiessen; Engr.: B. Bonin
Right: Engr.: J.W. Crow; Engr.: G.G. Thiessen

Varieties: Back plate number hidden or clear

Cat.No.	Den.	Date	Variety	VF	EF	AU	Unc
BC-60a	$100	1988	Thiessen-Crow, Hidden BP#	100.00	100.00	120.00	190.00
BC-60aA	$100	1988	Thiessen-Crow, Hidden BP#, AJX	150.00	200.00	250.00	400.00
BC-60a-i	$100	1988	Thiessen-Crow, Clear BP#	100.00	100.00	120.00	150.00
BC-60aA-i	$100	1988	Thiessen-Crow, Clear BP#, AJX	110.00	125.00	175.00	250.00
BC-60b	$100	1988	Bonin-Thiessen	100.00	100.00	110.00	140.00
BC-60c	$100	1988	Knight-Thiessen	100.00	100.00	100.00	125.00

$1000 Issue - 1988

BC-61a

Face Design: "1000" on optical device, large "1000" and Canada/ Her Majesty Queen Elizabeth II/North side of centre block of the Parliament Buildings showing library of Parliament, the Canadian Maple Leaf flies above the Peace Tower

Microprint: Bank of Canada 1000 Banque du Canada

Colour: Reddish purple, with rose, yellow and olive tints

BC-61a

Back Design: —/Landscape with Pine Grosbeak (Gros-bec des pins)/—

Colour: Reddish purple, with rose, yellow and brown tints

Issue Date: Engraved: 1988 **Official First Day of Issue:** May 4, 1992
Final Day of Issue: May 11, 2000

Printer: Canadian Bank Note Company

Imprint: None

Signatures

Left: Engr.: G.G. Thiessen
Engr.: B. Bonin

Right: Engr.: J.W. Crow
Engr.: G.G. Thiessen

Cat.No.	Denom.	Date	Variety	VF	EF	AU	Unc
BC-61a	$1000	1988	Thiessen-Crow	1,000.00	1,000.00	1,100.00	1,200.00
BC-61aA	$1000	1988	Thiessen-Crow, EKX	1,000.00	1,100.00	1,500.00	1,800.00
BC-61b	$1000	1988	Bonin-Thiessen	1,000.00	1,000.00	1,025.00	1,100.00

CANADIAN JOURNEY SERIES

ISSUES OF 2001 TO DATE

This series, inaugurated with the Remembrance and Peacekeeping $10 released early in 2001, focusses on Canadian culture, history and achievement. The $5 is expected to follow late in 2001, with the higher denominations being introduced over the next few years while keeping abreast of anti-counterfeiting technology.

Note sizes and dominant colours of each denomination remain the same as for the birds issue. The individuals portrayed on the birds issue will remain on the new issue, although new enlarged portraits will be engraved.

Additional features support denomination identification by visually impaired persons. The denomination is indicated by raised dots, embossed at the upper right of the note face. The large numeral counter contrasts strongly against a white background, and an improved hand-held denomination reader is being developed for use with the new notes.

The new notes feature several state-of-the-art security elements. Under ultraviolet light, the Coat of Arms and denomination and bank name over the portrait glow blue, while white fibres glow red. Blue fibres visible under ordinary light do not glow, nor does the rest of the note.

The notes are printed on 100% cotton bank note paper.

Prefixes and Numbering

Triple letter prefixes and seven digit numbering constitute the serial numbers for this issue, following the pattern in use since 1981. The first letter indicates the printer, the second letter designates the denomination, and the third letter denotes the series. Each series spans the numbers 0000000 to 9999999, the zero note being removed and a replacement note substituted.

Signatures

The signatures of the senior deputy governor and the governor of the Bank of Canada are located at the lower right of the $10 peacekeeping note face. The signatures are lithographed, and are in the litho plate.

Senior Deputy Governor	*Term of Office*
Malcolm Knight	July 5, 1999 to date

Governor	*Term of Office*
Gordon G. Thiessen	February 1, 1994 to January 31, 2001
David Dodge	February 1, 2001 to date

Imprints

There are no imprints on these notes. The printer is indicated by the first prefix letter, letter "F" indicating CBN.

The back of the new $10 note indicates, at the bottom centre, the year in which the note was printed. At lower right is a Bank of Canada copyright notice.

Plate Numbers

Position numbers are located near the lower left on the face, below the orange panel, and at the centre right on the back, behind the veteran's back, in the pale blue rectangle.

Replacement Notes

No identifiable replacement notes have been printed for this issue. Some notes numbered over 9,000,000 have been discovered among consecutively numbered notes, often with distinctly different prefixes, indicating usage as replacement notes. However, it is not yet certain whether notes numbered over 9,000,000 may also be issued as regular notes as well. Uncirculated examples are sellling in the range of $15 to $18 at the time of writing.

Experimental Notes

No experimental notes are known for this issue at this time.

Checklist of Prefix Letters for Canadian Journey Issues

Cat. No.	Denom.	Date	Signatures	Denom. Letter	Series Letter
BC-63a	$10	2001	Knight-Thiessen	FD	T U V W Y Z

Summary of Technical Details

Cat. No.	Denom.	Date	Signatures	Prefixes	Numbers	Qty Printed
BC-63a	$10	2001	Knight-Thiessen	FDT-FDZ	0000000-9999999	In Issue

$10 Remembrance and Peace Keeping Issue 2001

BC-63a

Face Design: Sir John A. Macdonald / Library of Parliament, three maple leaves optical security device / Canadian flag and large 10 counter

Microtint: TEN 10 DIX, left of the portrait

Colour: Predominantly purple, with orange, yellow, magenta and green tints

BC-63a

Back Design: Poppies, "*In Flanders Fields*" / doves / modern peace keeping soldier / Vimy Memorial and two soldiers / two children and veteran
Colour: Predominantly purple, with yellow, red, pink and blue tints

Issue Date: Engraved ISSUE OF 2001 / EMISSION DE 2001 at lower right corner of face. The year in which the note was printed is shown at the bottom centre of the back (lithographed)
Official First Day of Issue: 17 January 2001
Printer: Canadian Bank Note Company
Imprint: None

Signatures

Left: Engr.: M. D. Knight **Right:** Engr.: G. G. Thiessen

Cat. No.	Denom.	Date	Variety	Unc
BC-63a	$10	2001	Knight-Thiessen	12.00

Lasting Impressions $10 Matched Sets

In 2001 the Bank of Canada offered sets of the last 1989 Birds of Canada series $10 and 2001 Canadian Journey series, with matching serial numbers. The notes were packaged in presentation folders, each containing an information booklet and an overview of the features of the notes. The sets were available at the Currency Museum, post offices and through participating dealers. Suggested retail price was $49.95 plus applicable taxes.

Fifty thousand sets were available for purchase. Serial numbers ranged from BEH 6,449,957 to BEH 6,499,998 and the notes were signed Knight - Thiessen. All were printed by Canadian Bank Note Co., even though the first letter "B" in the prefix normally denotes British American Bank Note Co.

Set	Signatures	Unc
Lasting Impressions Set	Knight - Thiessen	50.00

SPECIAL SERIAL NUMBERS

Serial numbers are the control numbers for the production, distribution and circulation of notes. They are printed on the notes in what may be termed the overprint stage by electromechanical counters which automatically cycle to the next number as each sheet enters the press.

Special serial numbers are grouped into six different categories: (1) Palindrome (radar) Notes, (2) Million Numbered Notes, (3) Ascending/Descending "Ladder" Numbered Notes, (4) Low Serial Numbered Notes, (5) Matching Numbered Notes, (6)Changeover serial numbers. Further subdivisions will occur within these main groups.

Values for Special Serial Numbered notes are formulated on uncirculated condition as this is the grade in which these notes are usually collected. It is naturally understood that some of the rarer combinations of numbers, if found on a lower grade, will have a substantial premium. To construct value tables that incorporate grades at this time is premature. The number of collectors in this specialized field is small but growing and it is hoped that this section will provide helpful information and possibly in future editions the value tables will expand as the market dictates. To obtain a grade value for individual notes in this section the following rule of thumb can be applied.

VALUE GUIDE

ALMOST UNC (AU): value equals 80% of the uncirculated premium.
EXTREMELY FINE (EF): value equals 60% of the uncirculated premium.
VERY FINE (VF): value equals 40% of the uncirculated premium.
FINE (F): value equals 25% of the uncirculated premium.
VERY GOOD (VG): value equals 15% of the uncirculated premium.

Prices are for the most common signatures. Please remember that this method will only yield market indications of value, with unforeseen supply and demand shifts altering the percentages dramatically either way.

PALINDROME OR "RADAR" NOTES

A Palindrome or Radar Note, as it is more commonly known, bears a serial number which will read the same from left to right as right to left. Palindrome means a word, verse or sentence which reads the same backward or forward and this meaning was transferred by paper money collectors to the numerals used in serial numbers. Radar is a radio detecting and ranging device. A transmitter sends out microwaves; a receiver detects the echo. If there were no interference then the echo received would simulate the beam sent out. Similarly when a number reading to the right and then "echoing" or reading back from right to left is the same, it would in fact mimic the meaning of the word radar or palindrome. The word "radar" incidentally also reads the same left to right as right to left, thus doubly describing the type of serial number carried by the note. In the 1969-1975 issues of the Bank of Canada when ten million consecutive notes are produced for a specific prefix, a maximum of ten thousand notes may be radars. The number of notes in a radar collection having one note for each prefix combination is the same as needed for a prefix collection, over three hundred for all the prefixes of the one dollar issue of 1973. However a radar collection would be much more difficult to assemble.

"SOLID NUMBERED " "RADAR" NOTES

A special type of radar note is the "Solid" Numbered Note where the serial number is made up of one digit, for example; the numbers 1111111, 2222222, etc. These are called "solid" numbers. For every ten million consecutive notes produced, a maximum of nine notes may have a "solid" number. These are the most desirable variety of "radar" notes.

1937 Issue	Type	$1	$2	$5	$10	$20	$50	$100
1937	Regular				Estimate, Fine $700.00			
1954	Devil's Face	900.00	900.00	1,000.00	1,000.00	1,000.00	1,100.00	1,200.00
1954	Modified	400.00	400.00	425.00	450.00	500.00	550.00	600.00
1967	$1 Confederation	600.00	—	—	—	—	—	—
1969-1975	Multicoloured Issues	325.00	350.00	375.00	400.00	400.00	500.00	600.00
1979-1989	11 digit numbers	—	—	1,000.00	—	1,000.00	—	—
1986-1991	Birds	—	350.00	350.00	350.00	400.00	500.00	600.00

Note: "Radar" notes of the 1937 issue are seldom offered.

* For circulated notes, please refer to the value guide on page 285.

TWO DIGIT NUMBERED "RADAR" NOTES

A Two Digit "Radar" Numbered Note is one where the serial number is made up of only two digits repeated throughout the serial number, for example; the numbers 1001001, 4244424 and 5552555 are two digit numbered notes.

Issue	Type	$1	$2	$5	$10	$20	$50	$100
1937	Regular	75.00	175.00	160.00	150.00	175.00	525.00	475.00
1954	Devil's Face	115.00	150.00	175.00	175.00	225.00	350.00	350.00
1954	Modified	25.00	25.00	75.00	75.00	125.00	225.00	275.00
1967	$1 Confederation	25.00	—	—	—	—	—	—
1969-1975	Multicoloured Issues	25.00	25.00	60.00	75.00	125.00	225.00	375.00
1979-1989	11 digit numbers	—	—	60.00	—	100.00	—	—
1986-1991	Birds	—	20.00	30.00	40.00	50.00	75.00	135.00

Note: For circulated notes, please refer to the value guide on page 285.

THREE AND FOUR DIGIT "RADAR" NOTES

Three and four digit "radar" notes are notes in which the serial number is comprised of 3 or 4 digits. These are the most commonly found "radar" notes.

3 Digit	4 Digit
1377731	1459541
4421244	6580856
2124212	0914190

Issue	Type	$1	$2	$5	$10	$20	$50	$100
1937	Regular	60.00	150.00	140.00	125.00	150.00	600.00	700.00
1954	Devil's Face	90.00	125.00	150.00	150.00	200.00	375.00	350.00
1954	Modified	15.00	15.00	50.00	60.00	90.00	200.00	250.00
1967	$1 Confederation	15.00	—	—	—	—	—	—
1969-1975	Multicolour Issues	10.00	18.00	45.00	50.00	105.00	250.00	250.00
1979-1989	11 Digit Numbers	—	—	60.00	—	100.00	—	—
1986-1991	Birds	—	10.00	12.00	20.00	35.00	70.00	125.00

Note: For circulated notes, please refer to the value guide on page 285.

ASCENDING/DESCENDING "LADDER" "RADAR" NUMBERED NOTES

Consecutive ascending and descending numbers will combine to form radar combinations which are almost in the same class of rarity as solid numbers.

In a ten million consecutive sequence of notes, a maximum of sixteen notes may be called consecutive Ascending/Descending or Descending/Ascending "Radar" Numbered Notes.

Ascending/Descending "Radar" Combinations		Descending/Ascending "Radar" Combinations	
0123210	1234321	0987890	9876789
2345432	3456543	8765678	7654567
4567654	5678765	6543456	5432345
6789876	7890987	4321234	3210123

Issue	Type	$1	$2	$5	$10	$20	$50	$100
1937	Regular	100.00	200.00	200.00	200.00	200.00	550.00	450.00
1954	Devil's Face	100.00	200.00	225.00	225.00	300.00	500.00	500.00
1954	Modified	100.00	125.00	150.00	200.00	250.00	400.00	400.00
1967	$1 Confederation	150.00	—	—	—	—	—	—
1969-1975	Multicoloured Issues	100.00	125.00	150.00	200.00	250.00	400.00	400.00
1979-1989	11 digit numbers	—	—	300.00	—	300.00	—	—
1986-1991	Birds	—	125.00	150.00	200.00	250.00	300.00	300.00

Note: For circulated notes, please refer to the value guide on page 285.

CONSECUTIVE ASCENDING OR DESCENDING "LADDER" NUMBERED NOTES

Ascending or Descending serial numbered notes are illustrated below; In a ten million consecutive sequence of notes, a maximum of ten notes will be found with consecutive ascending or descending serial numbers. these are the most desirable, but non-consecutive numbers are also collected.

Ascending		Descending	
0123456	1234567	6543210	7654321
2345678	3456789	8765432	9876543
4567890		0987654	

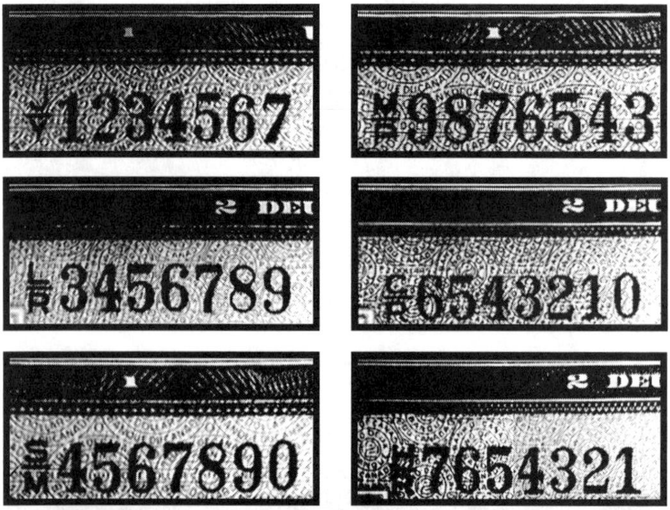

Issue	Type	$1	$2	$5	$10	$20	$50	$100
1937	Regular	200.00	250.00	250.00	250.00	250.00	550.00	450.00
1954	Devil's Face	200.00	250.00	275.00	275.00	300.00	500.00	500.00
1954	Modified	200.00	225.00	250.00	250.00	300.00	400.00	400.00
1967	$1 Confederation	250.00	—	—	—	—	—	—
1969-1975	Multicoloured Issues	200.00	225.00	250.00	275.00	300.00	400.00	400.00
1979-1989	11 digit numbers	—	—	300.00	—	300.00	—	—
1986-1991	Birds	—	225.00	250.00	275.00	300.00	300.00	300.00

Note: For circulated notes, please refer to the value guide on page 285.

MILLION NUMBERED NOTES

A Million Serial Number Note is one in which the serial number is all zeros preceded by any number from 1 to 10.

Before 1968, ten million numbered notes were printed by the Bank of Canada for the issues of 1935, 1937, 1954 and 1967. With these notes the last zero was printed on by hand as the numbering device could only print to 9999999

In the new issues with 11 digits (1979-1989), the first digit designating the denomination (3 for $5 notes, 5 for $20 notes) would not be included, such that a number like 30090000000 would be a ninety million numbered note.

Few collectors before 1954 are known to have collected this type of special sheet numbers and they are very scarce. Their values would vary widely if they were offered for sale and so will not be priced at this time.

The approximate number of notes issued with a ten million serial number is shown in the following table.

Issue	Denomination							
	$1	$2	$5	$10	$20	$50	$100	$1000
1935	4	0	0	0	0	0	0	0
1937	78	28	24	28	7	0	0	0
1954	125	53	49	39	21	1	1	0
1967	13	0	0	0	0	0	0	0

Source: Canadian Prefix Newsletter

Using the occurrence numbers of the above table and multiplying these by nine will approximate the number of million numbered notes produced for the same issues.

Million numbered notes are found at the bottom of a bundle of notes and since these bundles were wrapped with a paper band around them, many will be found in EF to AU condition because of some minor edge wrinkles or folds.

Issue	Type	$1	$2	$5	$10	$20	$50	$100
1937	Regular	400.00	400.00	400.00	400.00	400.00	500.00	600.00
1954	Devil's Face	350.00	400.00	400.00	400.00	450.00	600.00	700.00
1954	Modified	300.00	300.00	300.00	300.00	350.00	450.00	550.00
1967	$1 Confederation	400.00	—	—	—	—	—	—
1969-1975	Multicoloured Issues	250.00	275.00	300.00	325.00	350.00	400.00	600.00
1979-1989	11 digit numbers	—	—	800.00	—	800.00	—	—
1986-1991	Birds	—	275.00	300.00	325.00	350.00	375.00	450.00

Note: For circulated notes, please refer to the value guide on page 285.

TEN MILLION SERIAL NUMBER VALUES

Issue	Type	$1	$2	$5	$10	$20	$50	$100
1954	Devil's Face	1,500.00	1,700.00	1,700.00	1,700.00	2,000.00	2,000.00	2,000.00
1954	Modified	900.00	1,000.00	1,100.00	1,200.00	1,300.00	1,400.00	1,500.00
1967	$1 Confederation	1,500.00	—	—	—	—	—	—

Note: For circulated notes, please refer to the value guide on page 285.

LOW SERIAL NUMBERED NOTES

A bank note with a serial number less 25 may be classified as a Low Serial Numbered Note. Notes with matching numbers for different denominations were sometimes given as presentation sets. Notes in this category are generally AU to Uncirculated.

Generally a bank note with a serial number of less than 500 could be considered to have a low serial number. Serial numbers of less than 25 or in some cases less than 100 would be in higher demand, as would numbers less than 10. Some collectors try to obtain matching low numbers from different types and denominations of notes. Thus the scarcer the type and the lower the number, the higher the premium paid for the note. Notes with serial number 1 are eagerly sought after by some collectors. Most of these notes are in AU to UNC condition The value of these notes depends on the issue, the particular number and its condition and these would vary widely. Only a rough price range will be attempted.

Issue Type	$1	$2	$5	$10	$20	$25	$50	$100
1935 Comm								
English Text								
Serial # 1 Ser. A	1,050.	2,000.	3,500.	3,000.	16,000.	14,000.	14,000.	14,000.
Ser. B	1,300.							
Serial # 2 to 10 Ser. A	900.	1,900.	3,000.	2,500.	14,000.	12,000.	12,000.	12,000.
Ser. B	1,100.							
Serial # 11 to 25 Ser. A	800.	1,800.	2,500.	2,000.	12,000.	10,000.	10,000.	10,000.
Ser. B	1,000.							
Serial # 26 to 500 Ser. A	650.	1,500.	2,000.	1,800.	10,000.	8,000.	8,000.	8,000.
Ser. B	800.							
French Text								
Serial # 1	1,500.	5,000.	5,000.	5,000.	20,000.	20,000.	20,000.	20,000.
Serial # 2 to 10	1,100.	4,000.	4,000.	4,000.	18,000.	18,000.	18,000.	18,000.
Serial # 11 to 25	1,000.	3,500.	3,500.	3,500.	16,000.	16,000.	16,000.	16,000.
Serial # 26 to 500	900.	3,000.	3,000.	3,000.	14,000.	14,000.	14,000.	14,000.

Issue Type	$1	$2	$5	$10	$20	$50	$100
1954 Devil's Face							
Serial # 1	750.00	750.00	850.00	850.00	850.00	900.00	900.00
Serial # 2 to 10	160.00	200.00	225.00	225.00	275.00	400.00	400.00
Serial # 11 to 25	135.00	175.00	200.00	200.00	250.00	375.00	375.00
Serial # 26 to 1000	110.00	150.00	175.00	175.00	225.00	350.00	350.00
1954 Modified							
Serial # 1	400.00	400.00	400.00	400.00	450.00	600.00	700.00
Serial # 2 to 10	140.00	140.00	150.00	175.00	225.00	325.00	400.00
Serial # 11 to 25	60.00	70.00	90.00	110.00	170.00	275.00	350.00
Serial # 26 to 1000	35.00	40.00	65.00	80.00	120.00	225.00	300.00

Issue	Type	$1	$2	$5	$10	$20	$50	$100
1967 $1 Confederation								
	Serial # 1	600.00	—	—	—	—	—	—
	Serial # 2 to 10	200.00	—	—	—	—	—	—
	Serial # 11 to 25	100.00	—	—	—	—	—	—
	Serial # 26 to 1,000	50.00	—	—	—	—	—	—
1969-1975 Multicoloured Issues								
	Serial # 1	300.00	300.00	300.00	300.00	350.00	600.00	700.00
	Serial # 2 to 10	175.00	175.00	225.00	250.00	350.00	400.00	450.00
	Serial # 11 to 25	45.00	50.00	100.00	125.00	210.00	300.00	325.00
	Serial # 26 to 1,000	25.00	30.00	75.00	95.00	175.00	250.00	275.00
1979 11 digit numbers								
	Serial # 1	—	—	1,000.00	—	1,000.00	—	—
	Serial # 2 to 10	—	—	500.00	—	500.00	—	—
	Serial # 11 to 25	—	—	350.00	—	350.00	—	—
	Serial # 26 to 1,000	—	—	75.00	—	150.00	—	—
1986 - 1991 Birds								
	Serial # 1	—	350.00	350.00	350.00	350.00	500.00	650.00
	Serial # 2 to 10	—	60.00	75.00	100.00	125.00	200.00	300.00
	Serial # 11 to 25	—	20.00	30.00	35.00	70.00	150.00	250.00
	Serial # 26 to 500	—	15.00	25.00	30.00	60.00	125.00	200.00

Note: For circulated notes, please refer to the value guide on page 285.
Serial number "one" notes may command up to double the above premium.

MATCHING SERIAL NUMBERED SETS

This category consists of a set of notes of different denominations, usually of the same issue, having the same serial number. As with the Low Serial Numbered Notes, Matched Sets are usually low numbers collected at the Bank of Canada for presentation, or, formerly, obtained from the Bank of Canada for the Canadian Paper Money Society members. It is all but impossible to obtain a set of notes in denomination order that will have matching serial numbers from circulated notes.

Issue	No. of Notes	Denom.	AU-UNC
1954 Devil's Face	8	$1 to $1000	$9,000.00
	7	$1 to $100	$2,500.00
	6	$1 to $50	$1,700.00
	5	$1 to $20	$1,000.00
	4	$1 to $10	$ 700.00
1969 - 1975	7	$1 to $100	$1,000.00
Multicoloured	6	$1 to $50	$ 650.00
(2 letter prefix)	5	$1 to $20	$ 325.00
	4	$1 to $10	$ 200.00
1969-1975	5	$1 to $100	$ 650.00
Multicoloured (3 letter	4	$1 to $50	$ 400.00
prefix; no $5 or $20)	3	$1 to $10	$ 100.00
1979	2	$5, $20	$ 225.00
1969 - 1979	8 sets from Bank of Canada sale (1999) $5 (1972, 1979), $10 (pfx DA and EDA) $20 (1969 and 1979), $50, $100		$ 600.00
1986-1991	7 sets Bird Series	$2 to $1,000	$2,000.00
1986-1991	6 sets Bird Series	$2 to $100	$ 750.00

BIRTH YEAR SERIAL NUMBERED NOTES

Serial Numbers 1900 to 2001	UNC Prices						
	$1	$2	$5	$10	$20	$50	$100
1954	15.00	15.00	45.00	60.00	100.00	250.00	250.00
1967	10.00	—	—	—	—	—	—
1969-1975 Multicoloured Issues	10.00	15.00	45.00	50.00	100.00	300.00	350.00
1986-1991 Bird Series	—	15.00	20.00	25.00	35.00	75.00	125.00

CHANGEOVER NUMBERED NOTES

Changeover numbers are the numbers that occur at the end of one signature combination and at the beginning of the next signature combination when the same prefix letter combination is continued from the first type to the second type: Eg. BC-29a 7,200,000 to BC-29b 7,200,001. Although none of these exact numbers are known in private collections (most are in the Bank of Canada National Collection) the numbers coming as close as possible to these numbers are sought after by a few collectors. They are usually in circulated condition. The premium value for these numbers has not been determined as they have not been offered publicly.

Similarly high and low numbers of many of the asterisk or replacement notes are collected by a few as in most cases the actual number printed is at present unknown to collectors.

PAPER MONEY ERRORS

Paper money errors of Chartered and Private Bank Notes, Province and Dominion of Canada notes, and the 1935 and 1937 Bank of Canada notes are seldom encountered. The smaller quantities produced and the slower printing processes meant less chance of errors being produced and then escaping undetected. Also with fewer error note collectors those errors of the large-size notes that did reach circulation were more likely not saved.

The following listings of major categories of bank note errors have been produced to allow the collector to quickly and easily determine the value of most paper money errors based upon their appearance. The more unusual, startling or dramatic the appearance of the error the higher the value placed on it by collectors.

The production sequence for current Canadian paper money is back tint, face tint, face intaglio printing, overprinting and cutting. From 1956 to 1968 a sheet carried thirty-two note impressions, after 1968 the sheet size was increased to give 40 note impressions.

From 1935 to 1968 the serial numbers and signatures were added by the Bank of Canada in a final pass through a press, the overprinting stage. After 1968 only the serial numbers were added during the overprinting by the printing company. Since 1968 the signatures have been engraved on the face plates and printed during the face printing process by the bank note companies.

Valuations for error notes are listed with a price range covering EF to Unc condition. To the values listed must be added the face value of the note if over $5. As a general rule paper money errors are most avidly collected in the lower denominations, but a few collectors are willing to pay for errors in higher denomination notes. Contrary to expectation, a high denomination note or a rare note will often draw less premium as an error. Error notes are generally collected and found in uncirculated condition. Remember this is the area of the specialist and most will already have an example of a common error in their collection.

Replacement notes, (which have replaced errors found during the quality control process of the printers or at the Bank of Canada,) with errors will often carry a higher premium value

Some error notes, especially the more spectacular or multiple varieties, cannot be evaluated in a catalogue. Their value must be determined on an individual basis between buyer and seller.

These spectacular or multiple error notes very rarely find their way through the inspection process. With multiple errors the simple procedure of adding each individual type of error value together to obtain an overall value is insufficient. The multiple error note will move quickly into its own special category and its value must be determined on an individual basis. Likewise the value of large and spectacular errors will also be individually determined.

Some types of errors naturally lend themselves to fakery. The addition or removal of ink to simulate a genuine printing error can be accomplished. Colour changes from green to blue, brown or yellow can easily be produced by the application of bleach or alkali to a note. Asterisks and serial numbers can also be removed. Cutting errors can now be created from the $1 and $2 uncut sheets being sold by the Bank of Canada. Collectors should view notes from the newly released uncut sheets with suspicion if they surface as cutting errors.

FACE OR BACK PRINTING ERRORS

INCOMPLETE PRINTING

Any note which has had all or a portion of the face or back design left unprinted. An example is a note showing only the face or back design leaving the other completely missing, usually as a result of two sheets being fed through the press at the same time. In the case of the face design missing, the only printing might be the overprinted serial numbers and signatures on the notes prior to 1968. Incomplete printing can also result from insufficient ink. When a note displays weak, missing or irregular printing of the face or back design it may be caused by defects in the inking system or problems with the ink, or with other parts of the press which are used to apply ink to the plate.

Face or Back Printing Error	$1	$2	$5	$10	$20	$50	$100
Missing face or back printing up to 25%	75.00	75.00	100.00	100.00	125.00	150.00	150.00
Missing face or back printing from 25% to 50%	150.00	150.00	200.00	200.00	250.00	300.00	300.00
Missing back printing 50%	300.00	300.00	400.00	400.00	450.00	500.00	500.00
Missing face or back printing 100%	600.00	600.00	600.00	600.00	700.00	800.00	800.00
"Ghost" note (BC-63a, intaglio printing missing)	—	—	—	500.00	—	—	—

INK SMEARS

Occasionally a note may be found with various amounts of the printing ink in streaks or irregular patches on the face or back of the note. This is probably caused by incomplete wiping of the plate between rotations. They have been seen mostly on 1954 note issues.

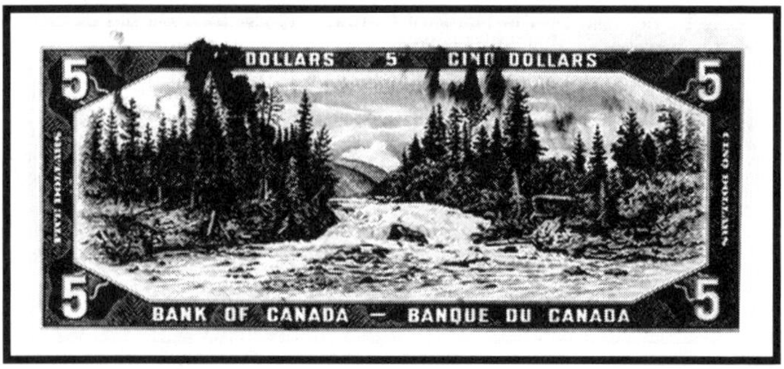

Printing Error	$1	$2	$5	$10	$20	$50	$100
Ink Smears	10.00	15.00	20.00	25.00	35.00	75.00	135.00

OFFSET PRINTING

The ink impression of all or part of the design, face or back, is transferred during printing to the face or back of a note resulting in a mirror image being offset to the opposite side of the note. An example of this process is the back design of the note being transferred to the face of the note. The value of an offset printing error depends upon the percentage of the design transferred, and the darkness and clarity of the transferred image.

The second type of offset error is that which is not caused by a transfer of ink from the press directly onto the note, but rather from an excess of ink, or insufficient drying of a sheet, such that the sheet below, after printing, receives an impression from the sheet above or vice versa. This error type is most often seen when the signature appears reversed in the normal position on the back of a note.

10 to 15% Offset

40% Offset

80% Offset

Offset Printing

Printing Error	$1	$2	$5	$10	$20	$50	$100
Offset, face or back, up to 25%	75.00	75.00	75.00	100.00	100.00	100.00	150.00
Offset, face or back, 25%-75%	200.00	200.00	200.00	250.00	250.00	250.00	300.00
Offset, face or back, 75%-100%	400.00	400.00	400.00	400.00	500.00	600.00	600.00

DOUBLE PRINTING

When a sheet is fed through the printing press twice. This error will show two complete images of the face or back design. Very rare.

PRINTING ON THE WRONG SIDE

Notes of the Birds Series exist in which the intaglio printing was applied on the back of an overturned sheet of notes instead of the face. The sheets were then turned over as usual for the final printing phase, resulting in the serial numbers being printed on the faces of the error notes. The verticle bars left of the serial numbers may appear on either side.

(Do not confuse with offset printing, which is much more commonly seen. Offset printing results in mirror-inverted images).

Printing Error	$2	$5
Intaglio printing on back, serial numbers on face	450.00	450.00

DOUBLE DENOMINATION NOTES

This error would be caused by a sheet of one denomination printed on one side being turned over and passed through a press printing a different denomination. This type of error has not been confirmed for a Canadian note.

OUT OF REGISTER PRINTING

A note that has the face or back printed out of the normal centered position due to faulty feeding of sheets through the press or by misalignment of the plates in the press. Usually either the face or the back of the note will be properly centered. The value of these will depend on the degree of misalignment and usually a misalignment of the face of a note is of more interest than on the back of the note. The larger the amount of the adjoining note printed, the higher the value.

Printing Error	$1	$2	$5	$10	$20	$50	$100
Double printing	150.00	150.00	150.00	150.00	250.00	250.00	250.00
Out of register	50.00	50.00	75.00	75.00	75.00	150.00	200.00
Out of register, with adjoining note	150.00	150.00	150.00	150.00	150.00	200.00	250.00

MISPLACED OPTICAL SECURITY DEVICE

Some $50 notes of the 1988 issue and $20 notes of the 1991 issue have been seen with the gold OSD dramatically misplaced. This probably happened when sheets misfed into the device applying the OSD.

The value of these error notes will depend on the degree of displacement of the OSD.

Printing Error	$20	$50	$100
Misplaced OSD	250.00	250.00	350.00
Missing OSD	300.00	300.00	400.00

SIGNATURE ERRORS

Signature errors will appear only on the 1967 and earlier issues. After the Confederation issue signatures were engraved onto the face plate thus being printed at the same time as the engraved face plate. For issues before 1967 the signatures were added (overprinted) by the Bank of Canada.

Misplaced Signatures

Misalignment of the sheet of notes being fed into the press results in signatures overprinted out of position. The error must be a major one; shifts of a few millimetres are insignificant.

Printing Error	$1	$2	$5	$10	$20	$50	$100
Normal position signatures printed on back	200.00	300.00	300.00	300.00	300.00	300.00	400.00
Signatures misaligned on face; up, down or sideways	200.00	300.00	300.00	300.00	300.00	300.00	400.00
Signatures misaligned on back; up, down or sideways	200.00	300.00	300.00	300.00	300.00	300.00	400.00

INVERTED SIGNATURES

The signatures are printed on the face or back of the note upside down. The sheet was fed into the overprinting press rotated 180 degrees from normal and in some cases also upside down to give an inverted back signature. These are also often out of alignment.

Printing Error	$1	$2	$5	$10	$20	$50	$100
Inverted signatures on the face	400.00	500.00	500.00	500.00	600.00	600.00	600.00
Inverted signatures on the back	500.00	600.00	600.00	600.00	700.00	700.00	700.00

OFFSET SIGNATURES

Printing Error	$1	$2	$5	$10	$20	$50	$100
Offset signatures on the back	150.00	200.00	200.00	200.00	250.00	300.00	350.00

NO SIGNATURES

Notes have completely missed the signature overprinting process.

Printing Error	$1	$2	$5	$10	$20	$50	$100
Signatures missing	400.00	500.00	500.00	500.00	500.00	600.00	700.00

OUT OF PLACE DUE TO FOLDING ERROR

A signature may be printed out of position, even on the back due to a sheet being folded before sheet numbers were printed.

Printing Error	$1	$2	$5	$10	$20	$50	$100
Signature out of place	250.00	250.00	250.00	250.00	300.00	300.00	400.00

SERIAL NUMBER ERRORS

MISMATCHED PREFIX LETTERS

This type of error is rarely found, but would result if the prefix lettering wheels became loose and rotated out of sequence to that printing the opposite side of the note. Usually the serial number is also mismatched.

MISMATCHED SERIAL NUMBERS

A note which carries two different serial numbers. Usually one digit is different, but occasionally 2 or more digits are different.

Printing Error	$1	$2	$5	$10	$20	$50	$100
Mismatched, one digit	300.00	300.00	300.00	300.00	300.00	300.00	400.00
Mismatched, two digits	400.00	400.00	400.00	400.00	400.00	400.00	500.00
Mismatched, three or more digits	500.00	500.00	500.00	500.00	500.00	500.00	600.00

PARTIAL DIGIT SERIAL NUMBER

A note which has one or more digits of the serial number split between two numbers. The numbering device did not rotate completely to the next number or became stuck partly rotated.

Printing Error	$1	$2	$5	$10	$20	$50	$100
Partial digit showing, one	25.00	25.00	25.00	40.00	50.00	70.00	120.00
Partial digit showing, two	50.00	50.00	50.00	60.00	70.00	80.00	140.00
Partial digit showing, three or more	75.00	100.00	100.00	120.00	140.00	160.00	180.00

MISMATCHED PREFIX LETTERS

A note with one or more of the prefix letters mismatched.

Printing Error	$1	$2	$5	$10	$20	$50	$100
One letter mismatched	600.00	400.00	600.00	600.00	600.00	600.00	600.00
Both or all letters mismatched	1,000.00	1,000.00	1,000.00	1,000.00	1,000.00	1,000.00	1,000.00

MISSING NUMBER

A note may have all (including the prefix letters) or one or more of the digits missing. Serial numbers can be removed and the collectors should be very cautious when assessing a note with this error.

Missing Serial Number, Three Digits

Missing Serial Number, Both Sides

Missing Sheet Number, Most of One Side

Printing Error	$1	$2	$5	$10	$20	$50	$100
Missing numbers, one digit	100.00	100.00	100.00	100.00	100.00	150.00	200.00
Missing numbers, two or more	125.00	150.00	150.00	150.00	150.00	200.00	250.00
Missing serial number, one side, left or right	300.00	300.00	300.00	300.00	300.00	300.00	300.00
Missing serial number, both sides (no serial numbers)	600.00	600.00	600.00	600.00	600.00	600.00	600.00

MISPLACED SERIAL NUMBER

The serial number may be overprinted out of register, inverted (printed upside down in the signature position), overprinted on the back or inverted on the back.

Printing Error	$1	$2	$5	$10	$20	$50	$100
Number out of register, up, down, sideways	150.00	150.00	150.00	150.00	200.00	250.00	300.00
Number on face instead of back	200.00	200.00	200.00	200.00	300.00	300.00	400.00
Number inverted on the face	300.00	300.00	300.00	300.00	300.00	300.00	400.00
Number on the back instead of face	200.00	200.00	200.00	200.00	300.00	300.00	400.00
Number inverted on the back	200.00	200.00	200.00	200.00	300.00	300.00	400.00

DUPLICATE SERIAL NUMBER

This type of error is very scarce and is caused by one or more digits, starting at the right of the serial number, in the numbering wheel becoming stuck and thus not rotating to the next number. This results in two or more notes having the same serial number. This type of error is seldom found, partly because it is not evident unless two or more notes are found together.

Printing Error	$1	$2	$5	$10	$20	$50	$100
Two notes with same serial numbers	600.00	700.00	800.00	900.00	1,000.00	1,200.00	1,500.00

MISPLACED ASTERISK

Printing Error	$1	$2	$5	$10	$20	$50	$100
Asterisk out of position	200.00	200.00	200.00	200.00	250.00	250.00	300.00
One asterisk missing	400.00	400.00	400.00	400.00	450.00	500.00	550.00
Asterisk on back	750.00	750.00	750.00	750.00	750.00	750.00	800.00

FOLDING AND CUTTING ERRORS

Folding and cutting errors will generally be found in "Uncirculated" condition.

SINGLE FOLDS

The paper sheet is either folded or creased before or during printing in such a manner that the resulting single note will show a white streak on the back or a white or partially white streak on the face of the note. Since the face of the note goes through the press twice, either the lithographed tint or the Intaglio printed design, or both may be missing in the folded area. Single vertical folds are commoner than multiple or horizontal folds.

Folding Error	$1	$2	$5	$10	$20	$50	$100
Single Fold, one	25.00	30.00	35.00	45.00	60.00	100.00	175.00
Single Fold, two or more	50.00	60.00	70.00	90.00	120.00	175.00	300.00

MULTIPLE FOLDS

The paper sheet is folded either before of after printing in such a manner that when the sheet is cut, an extra piece of the adjoining note or notes is attached. The attached piece or pieces may be blank or have printing from the face or back of the adjacent notes, depending on when the folding occurred. Folds occurring along the outside of the sheet will sometimes have alignment marks or colour bars appearing on the attached piece. Some double folds will result in three or more pieces of several notes being found together.

Folding Error	$1	$2	$5	$10	$20	$50	$100
Multiple Fold, small part attached	50.00	75.00	100.00	100.00	100.00	125.00	150.00
Multiple Fold, large part attached	125.00	150.00	175.00	175.00	175.00	200.00	250.00
Multiple Fold, more than two notes	500.00	600.00	700.00	700.00	700.00	900.00	1,000.00

Beware of alleged "cutting errors" which have been fabricated by deliberately miscutting notes from sheets of $1, $2 or $10 notes made available by the Bank of Canada.

CUT OUT OF REGISTER

A note cut with improper alignment of the sheet in the cutting press or the sheet being folded before cutting. The greater the misalignment the higher the value. Usually part of another note must show to result in a premium value. Sometimes the adjoining paper will show the "colour bar" either at the top or bottom of the note. The more "colour bar" showing the greater the value.

CUT OFF SIZE

Malfunctions in the cutting operation resulting in off size notes. Off size note errors will only apply to notes cut over the standard size, since any note could be made smaller after being issued.

Cutting Error	$1	$2	$5	$10	$20	$50	$100
Out of Register, up to 25%	75.00	100.00	100.00	100.00	125.00	150.00	200.00
Out of Register, 25% or more	125.00	150.00	150.00	150.00	200.00	250.00	300.00
Out of Register, with colour bar	350.00	400.00	400.00	400.00	450.00	500.00	550.00

REPLACEMENT NOTE ERRORS

Occasionally the same types of errors found on regularly issued notes can be found on replacement or asterisk notes. However, these will be mostly in the cutting or folding type of errors as most of the printing errors would be discovered when transferring a replacement sheet from its stack to the regular stack of notes. As a general rule, the value of these replacement errors would be 25% to 50% above the value of the same error on a regular issue note.

INVERTED DESIGN

The face printing of the note is inverted or upside down in relation to the back printing. Could be caused by the sheet being flipped over and rotated after one side had been printed. It has only been confirmed as an error on a Dominion of Canada 25¢ 1870 B fractional and 1954 modified portrait $1.

Printing Error	Value
25¢ fractional 1870 Issue - Inverted Back Design Face design and tint normal	$1,400.00
25¢ fractional 1870 Issue - Inverted Back Design Face and back tint normal; black face printing inverted	$2,300.00
$1 Bank of Canada 1954 Modified Issue - Inverted Back Design Face design and tint normal; Serial prefix N/L (BC-37a)	$1,750.00

APPLICATION FOR MEMBERSHIP / SUBSCRIPTION

Application for membership/subscription in ***THE CANADIAN PAPER MONEY SOCIETY*** may be made by any reputable party upon payment of the required dues.

Membership: ❑ Regular ❑ Life ❑ Reinstatement
(Please check one)

If reinstatement please indicate previous membership number. Membership in the Canadian Paper Money Society is subject to the by-laws of the Society. If my membership is accepted I agree to abide by the rules of the Canadian Paper Money Society.

❑ Mr. ❑ Mrs. ❑ Ms.

Name: ....

Street: ....

City: .... Province/State: ...... Postal Code/Zip:........................

Country: ....

Signature of Applicant: ....

Signature of guardian (if under 18 years of age): ....

Numismatic references, if any: ....

Terms of Membership: **Regular** – $25.00 **Life** – $375.00
(calendar year)

Dues:

Dues are shown in Canadian dollars to Canadian addresses and in U.S. dollars to all other addresses. Payment may be made by money order, bank draft or personal cheque. We regret we are unable to offer credit card services. Postage stamps are not acceptable. Currency (U.S. or Canadian only) is acceptable and should be sent by security registered mail only. Membership is not Goods and Services taxable. Please mail application and payment to:

THE CANADIAN PAPER MONEY SOCIETY
P. O. Box 562, Pickering, Ontario, L1V 2R7.

5
FIVE DOLLARS
5